PENGUIN BOOKS

THE SOMME BATTLEFIELDS

On a visit to France and Belgium in 1967 Martin Middlebrook was so impressed by the military cemeteries on the 1914–18 battlefields that he decided to write a book describing just one day in that war through the eyes of the ordinary men who took part. The book, *The First Day on the Somme*, was published by Allen Lane in 1971 and received international acclaim. Martin Middlebrook has since written other books that deal with important turning-points in the two world wars; these are *The Kaiser's Battle, Convoy, The Peenemünde Raid, The Battle of Hamburg, Battleship* (with Patrick Mahoney), *The Schweinfurt-Regensburg Mission, The Nuremburg Raid, The Bomber Command War Diaries* (with Chris Everitt), *The Berlin Raids, The Somme Battlefields* (with Mary Middlebrook) and *Arnhem 1944* (to be published in 1994). He has also written two books about the 1982 Falklands War, *Task Force: The Falklands War, 1982* and *The Fight for the 'Malvinas'*. Many of his books have been published in the United States and West Germany, and three of them in Japan, Yugoslavia and Poland.

Martin Middlebrook is a Fellow of the Royal Historical Society. Each summer he takes parties of visitors on conducted tours of the First World War battlefields.

Mary and Martin Middlebrook married in 1954 and have three grown-up daughters. While looking after their family and home, Mary Middlebrook has played an active part co-operating in her husband's literary and business activities. Her leisure interests are art and gardening.

MARTIN AND MARY MIDDLEBROOK

—————

THE SOMME BATTLEFIELDS

A COMPREHENSIVE GUIDE FROM CRÉCY TO THE TWO WORLD WARS

PENGUIN BOOKS

To Jane, Anne and Catherine – with our love

PENGUIN BOOKS

Published by the Penguin Group
Penguin Books Ltd, 27 Wrights Lane, London W8 5TZ, England
Penguin Books USA Inc., 375 Hudson Street, New York, New York 10014, USA
Penguin Books Australia Ltd, Ringwood, Victoria, Australia
Penguin Books Canada Ltd, 10 Alcorn Avenue, Toronto, Ontario, Canada M4V 3B2
Penguin Books (NZ) Ltd, 182–190 Wairau Road, Auckland 10, New Zealand

Penguin Books Ltd, Registered Offices: Harmondsworth, Middlesex, England

First published by Viking 1991
Published in Penguin Books 1994
1 3 5 7 9 10 8 6 4 2

Printed and bound in Great Britain by
Butler & Tanner Ltd, Frome and London

Contents

Illustrations   vii
Maps   xi
Introduction   1
Helpful Information   4

1 · Routes to the Somme   27
2 · The 1916 Area   48
3 · The 1918 Area   248
4 · Doullens   309
5 · Amiens   316
6 · The Western Somme   326

Appendix: Cemeteries, Graves and 'Lost' Bodies   351
Acknowledgements   359
Bibliography   361
Index   365

Illustrations

Photographs

All photographs are by Mary and Martin Middlebrook unless otherwise stated.

1 Battlefield grave of unknown British soldier at Thiepval in 1916. (*Imperial War Museum*)   6
2 Battlefield cemetery – one long grave in Luke Copse Cemetery.   10
3 Concentration cemetery – Adanac Cemetery.   13
4 Headstones in British cemeteries.   16–17
5 French and German graves.   20
6 American grave. (*American Battle Monuments Commission*)   21
7 Memorial on the Serre Road.   21
8 Memorial by survivors of the 34th Division, at La Boisselle.   23
9 Memorial to those who died in the Resistance, at Amiens.   24
10 The 1940 Defence of Calais Memorial.   26
11 Communal grave at Terlincthun British Cemetery.   35
12 Étaples Military Cemetery. (*Commonwealth War Graves Commission*)   38
13 V-1 bunker at Siracourt.   45
14 The Canadian Memorial on Vimy Ridge.   46
15 The grave of the first British soldier to die on the Somme front.   49
16 Soldiers' wartime cemetery names retained in the permanent cemeteries.   54
17 British Observation Post at Gommecourt.   63
18 Rossignol Wood Cemetery.   66
19 Luke Copse Cemetery, near Serre.   72–3
20 Cemetery signposts on the Serre Road.   75
21 Memorial in French cemetery.   78
22 The Caribou Memorial at the Newfoundland Park. (*Trevor Tasker*)   84–5
23 The 51st (Highland) Division Memorial.   85
24 Sucrerie Military Cemetery.   94
25 The River Ancre, near Hamel.   99
26 Lancashire Dump Cemetery in Aveluy Wood.   101

27 Aveluy during the retreat in April 1918. (*Imperial War Museum*)   104
28 The Ulster Tower.   110
29 The Thiepval Memorial at its inauguration in 1932. (*Commonwealth War Graves Commission*)   112
30 The Thiepval Memorial today. (*Ville d'Albert*)   114
31 A 'Dud Corner' near Grandcourt.   116
32 The Lochnagar Crater at La Boisselle. (*Département de la Somme*)   124
33 Monsieur Fouchat of Pozières.   130
34 July 1917 – Australian soldiers parade for the unveiling of a memorial to their 1st Division.   131
35 Graves in Pozières British Cemetery and the wall on which the Fifth Army missing of 1918 are commemorated.   133
36 The Triple Tambour mine craters.   138
37 No Man's Land at Fricourt, and the cemetery where the 10th West Yorks are buried.   140
38 Fricourt German Cemetery.   141
39 The entrance to the Devonshire Cemetery.   147
40 'The Devonshires held this trench; the Devonshires hold it still.'   148
41 The 38th (Welsh) Division Memorial looking out over Mametz Wood.   159
42 'Death Valley', with Mametz Wood on the left and Flatiron Copse Cemetery in the middle distance.   161
43 Flatiron Copse Cemetery; Mametz Wood in the background.   163
44 The New Zealand Memorial on a wall of Caterpillar Valley Cemetery.   166
45 Delville Wood with the South African Memorial and the new museum. (*Trevor Tasker*)   168
46 The view over Crucifix Corner to High Wood from near Bazentin-le-Grand.   170
47 The Canadian Memorial at Courcelette.   176
48 The memorial cross on the site of Maltzkorn Farm.   182
49 An Advanced Dressing Station on the Guillemont Road in 1916. (*Imperial War Museum*)   183
50 The Prime Minister's son's grave. (*Chris Everitt*)   184
51 The cross on the Dickens 'grave'.   186
52 The first Tank Corps grave.   189
53 The Guards Cemetery at Lesboeufs.   192
54 The cross on the memorial to Captain Cochin at Hardecourt.   200
55 Suzanne Communal Cemetery and the British extension.   210
56 The 58th (London) Division Memorial at Chipilly.   214
57 British graves from La Boisselle and Thiepval alongside the French cemetery at Cerisy.   215
58 The Basilica at Albert in March 1918. (*Bavarian State Archives*)   218

59 The Demarcation Stone at Albert. 221
60 Casualties at Dernancourt in September 1916. (*Imperial War Museum*) 225
61 Rows of graves at Dernancourt. 225
62 The 'three armies' crossroads at Hédauville. 235
63 Casualty Clearing Station. (*Imperial War Museum*) 242
64 Walking wounded at a Casualty Clearing Station. (*Imperial War Museum*) 243
65 Heilly Station Cemetery. 244
66 Pigeon Ravine Cemetery. 257
67 The 12th (Eastern) Division Memorial near Epehy. 258
68 The American Somme Cemetery at Bony with the Memorial Chapel. (*American Battle Monuments Commission*) 260
69 The 2nd Australian Division Memorial at Mont St Quentin. 268
70 The Somme Canal at Pithon. 271
71 Ham British Cemetery. 272
72 The Murat grave and memorial at Lihons. 281
73 The grave of Pilot Officer Mynarski, VC. 283
74 'In honor of an American boy...' 287
75 The 1st United States Division Memorial near Cantigny. 287
76 The Australian Memorial at Villers-Bretonneux Military Cemetery. 297
77 The French XXXI Corps Memorial near Moreuil. 301
78 Manitoba Cemetery. 305
79 The village war memorial at Proyart. 307
80 The March 1918 Conference Room in the Hôtel de Ville at Doullens. 309
81 Amiens memorials in the city centre and in the St Acheul Military Cemetery. 319
82 Plaque at Amiens Prison commemorating the RAF raid which breached the walls. 322
83 The unique French statue overlooking the graves in Vignacourt British Cemetery. 325
84 Second World War graves in Bourdon German Cemetery. 330
85 The Alpine Chasseurs Memorial near Liomer. 334
86 Crécy – the observation tower on the site of the windmill from which Edward III directed the English army in the 1346 battle. 343
87 The gateway of Noyelles-sur-Mer Chinese Cemetery. 347
88 A soldier in a Scottish battalion and a German soldier killed in March 1918. (*Bavarian State Archives*) 351
89 A post-war British search team. (*Commonwealth War Graves Commission*) 353
90 A War Graves Commission mason re-engraving a headstone. 358

Drawings

Drawings by Mary Middlebrook

1 View from Triangle Point   154–5
2 View from 'the Grandstand'   226–7

Maps

Maps by Reg Piggott from preliminaries by Mary Middlebrook.

The Somme Battlefields   xii–xiii
Routes to the Somme   28–9
The 1916 Area   56–7
The Gommecourt Salient   59
From Serre to the Ancre   71
Hamel to Aveluy   98
Thiepval   108
The Bapaume Road   119
The Péronne Road   136–7
The Horseshoe of Woods   157
The North   174
The Right Flank   181
The French Sector   199
The Somme Valley   206
Albert   220
The 1916 Rear Area   229
The 1918 Area   251
The Hindenburg Line to Péronne   254–5
The Somme Crossings   270
Roye   276
The Santerre   279
Montdidier   285
Villers-Bretonneux   290–1
Doullens   311
Amiens   317
The Western Somme   327
The 1940 River Line   329
The Deep South   333
Abbeville   338–9
Crécy   342
The Coast   346

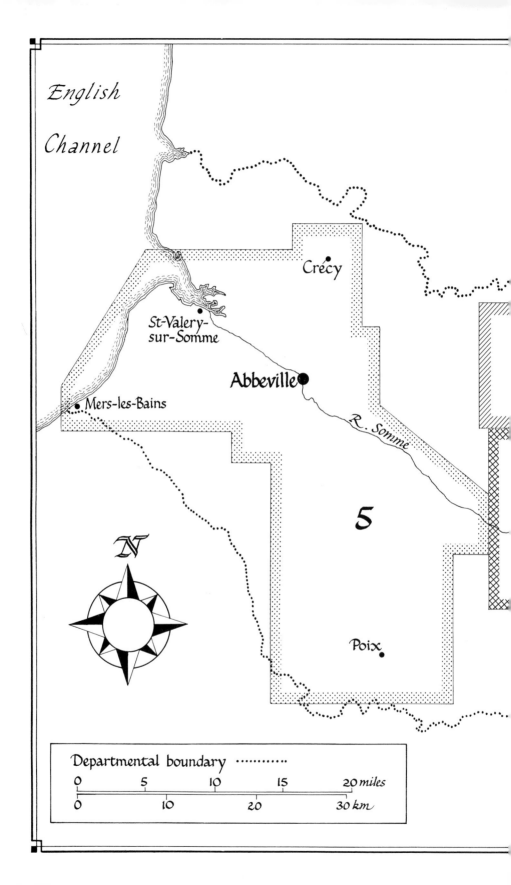

English Channel

Crécy

St-Valery-
sur-Somme

Abbeville

Mers-les-Bains

R. Somme

5

Poix

N

Departmental boundary ············

0   5   10   15   20 miles

0   10   20   30 km

THE SOMME BATTLEFIELDS

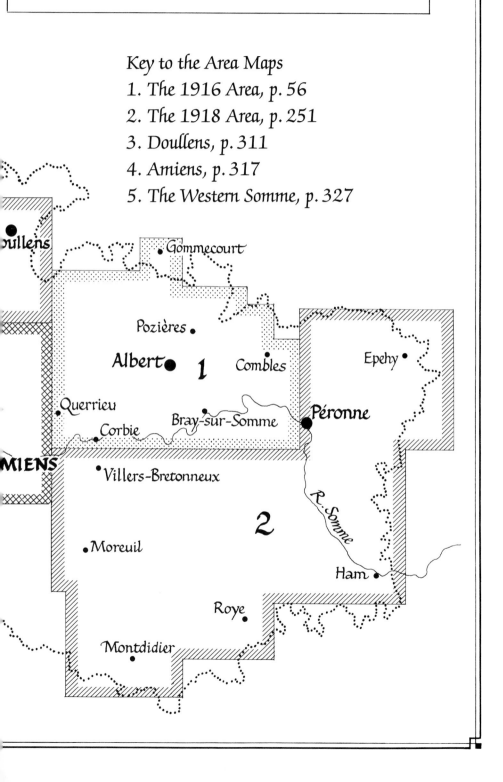

Key to the Area Maps

1. The 1916 Area, p. 56
2. The 1918 Area, p. 251
3. Doullens, p. 311
4. Amiens, p. 317
5. The Western Somme, p. 327

Doullens

Gommecourt

Pozières

Albert   1   Combles

Epehy

Querrieu

Corbie   Bray-sur-Somme   Péronne

AMIENS

Villers-Bretonneux

2

R. Somme

Moreuil

Ham

Roye

Montdidier

Introduction

This will be a very personal book and I will start with a personal explanation.

In 1967 a friend and I made our first visits to the First World War battlefields in France and Belgium. Although I lived through the Second World War as a schoolboy and remember it vividly, it was stories of 1914–18 that filled my childhood. My mother's sister had been present at the Battle of Mons – as English governess at a local château – and had then been under German supervision in Belgium for most of the war. Her brother was a platoon sergeant with the local Territorials, the Lincolns, who was wounded at Sanctuary Wood and died three days later at Poperinge. Another brother left home, enlisted in Kitchener's Army and was gassed and taken prisoner with the Gloucesters in the German offensive in March 1918; I think he threw his medals away after the war. The war ended just before my father was old enough to serve, but his boyhood friend was an observer in an RAF bomber and was shot down and killed five days before the Armistice. My friend had a similar background. His mother's fiancé was killed at Arras with the Manchester 'Pals' and has no known grave; his father was badly wounded with the East Yorks at Arras on Easter Monday 1917. We were thus both highly motivated for our visit to the battlefields. We believed that it might be our only opportunity and decided to cover as much of the Western Front as possible. We went to Verdun, the Somme, Arras and the Ypres Salient – all in less than a week, without guidebooks, and often frustrated because we did not know exactly where we should go.

It was a deeply moving experience. Although our relatives had been killed or maimed in the Ypres Salient and at Arras, it was the 1916 Somme battlefield, so peaceful but so crowded with cemeteries and memorials, that impressed me most. I decided that this tour was only a beginning. I needed to know more, more about the

Somme battlefields and more about the Army of 1916 whose survivors were still so numerous at that time. I decided that if I said I was going to write a book about the first day of the battle – 1 July 1916 – then I could study documents and the old soldiers would talk to me. They were recently retired men, mostly in their early seventies at that time, quite lucid and pleased to help. The book was published four years after that first visit. I called it *The First Day on the Somme.*

I hoped that the book would help to rekindle an interest in the battlefields. There had been pilgrimages between the wars but these had stopped in 1939. My friend and I met no other visitors on our travels and there seemed to be no organized tours. I added a simple 'Tour of the Somme Battlefield' at the end of the book so that future visitors would not be as frustrated as my friend and I had been. The book was modestly successful and I never returned to my earlier occupation of poultry farming but became a full-time writer of military history. I only wrote one more book about the First World War, *The Kaiser's Battle,* which described the great German attack of 21 March 1918, but it was the 1916 book which remained more popular. I never lost touch with the battlefields and I eventually started a little battlefield-touring organization. The challenge of showing parties of keen enthusiasts around the battlefields quickly expanded my knowledge.

I came to realize that the understandable concentration of interest on the 1916 Somme battlefield is somewhat of a distortion in pure military history terms. It is true that nothing can rival the 1916 fighting for intensity and tragedy, but there were other battles in the area we call 'the Somme' which were just as important historically, particularly two in 1918 and one in 1940. So I have decided to write this description of all the battles and battlefields in the Somme *département.* It has been both an opportunity to further my knowledge of the 1916 battlefield and a voyage of discovery into the 1918 areas and to those places where other wars were fought on the Somme.

This book appears under the joint names of my wife and myself. Anyone familiar with the life of an author will know that the production of a book involves far more than the actual writing of it. Mary has given me unfailing support during twenty years spent in producing twelve full-length books and several smaller works. She has read typescripts, checked proofs and helped with the dull work of indexing; she has been particularly good in redrawing my rough maps and diagrams for presentation to the publisher. All manner of items have been dealt with when I have been away from home. Mary has done much more for this book, accompanying me on three research tours, taking most of the photographs and producing the drawings and preliminary maps. It gives me great pleasure and pride to see her name joined with mine alongside the title of this book.

Helpful Information

The aim of this book is a simple one – to describe every place in the *département* of the Somme where some reminder of war can be seen, from a spot near Delville Wood where Julius Caesar is supposed to have addressed one of his legions, to the memorials of the Liberation in September 1944. There are two areas on the edge of the *département* which cause problems. Some villages such as Gommecourt, Serre, Martinpuich and Morval are just outside the Somme boundary, but the men who fought there would never forgive their omission from a description of the Somme battlefields. Similarly, the 'Somme American Cemetery' is actually just half a mile outside the Somme boundary. So the liberty is being taken of regarding such places as being 'on the Somme'. A separate part of the book will cover the places of interest on the routes across the Pas-de-Calais from the main Channel ports and from the Channel Tunnel to the Somme. The Calais–Boulogne area visits may also be of interest to those making only a day trip from England. Finally, the book is also written for the armchair tourist, with the text and the photographs hopefully enabling such people to be out on the battlefields in spirit.

The Somme *département* will be split into easily manageable sections in which every known place of military interest is shown on a map and a description of it given in the text. No itineraries are recommended; visitors will be able to select their particular areas of interest and plan their own routes.

For general navigation purposes, and also to take account of road additions and changes in future years, some French maps will be helpful. The Michelin 1:200,000 series (1 cm to 2 km) is freely available and is a sound stand-by; copies of these in the main battlefield areas overprinted with British cemeteries can be obtained from the Commonwealth War Graves Commission (at 2 Marlow Road, Maidenhead, Berks. SL6 7DX). The best maps for more detailed navigation are those of the French IGN (Institut Géographique National) Orange Series – 1:50,000 (2 cm to 1 km); these can currently be obtained in London at Stanfords, 12 Long Acre, WC2, or McCarta, 15 Highbury Place, London N5, or purchased locally in France.

No guidebook can remain completely accurate indefinitely; it will start to become out of date in small details as soon as it is published. Roads are widened or are closed; new ones are built – in particular, a major motorway being planned to cross the length of the Somme *département* as this book is being prepared will cause many changes. Museums close. Occasionally it is necessary to close a small cemetery and move the graves to a larger one. Memorials are damaged or removed, although new memorials are sometimes surprisingly added long after the events they commemorate.

The Somme and its Battles

The Somme is one of France's many rural *départements*. It is not an ancient title. When French local administration was reorganized in 1790, most of the old region of Picardy and a small part of Artois became the Somme *département*; the remainder of Picardy went to two other new *départements*, the Oise and the Aisne. (A *département* is administered by an elected council but with a Prefect appointed from Paris.) The new *département* took its name from the River Somme which flows from the eastern boundary right through to the English Channel. The name 'Picardy' is still kept alive, with the Somme, Oise and Aisne *départements* now combining their tourist promotion activities under that old region's name. The Somme *département* is eighty miles long at its widest part and has an average width of about thirty miles, giving it an area of 2,384 square miles and, with its population of about 550,000 people, making it roughly equivalent in size and population to any of the larger English counties.

War has visited the Somme frequently and violently. Modern war came when the Prussians invaded the area in 1870; the fiercest battle took place at a spot only a mile or so from the château from which the 1916 Battle of the Somme would be directed. The Germans came again in 1914 when the stalemate of trench warfare split France in two. Unfortunately for the Somme, the trench lines cut down the *département* from north to south, leaving the eastern

1 Battlefield grave of unknown British soldier at Thiepval in 1916.

quarter in German occupation and condemning that quiet country region to the misery and ravages of some of the most ferocious fighting in the world's history.

French troops manned the trenches on the Somme until well into 1915. There were some considerable battles and the huge death toll that accumulated on the Somme during the war was already well started when the expanding British Expeditionary Force took over the northern sectors of the Somme trenches in mid-1915. The junction with the French was on the River Somme and it was this that caused the area to be chosen for the major Allied offensive in France in 1916 which started on 1 July and lasted until the winter, with the Germans being pushed back only a few miles and remaining firmly entrenched in the Somme *département*. The Germans did leave the Somme in the spring of 1917 when they withdrew to the Hindenburg Line; but the war returned in 1918, with a huge German offensive in March which nearly reached Amiens and a decisive Allied counter-offensive in August which finally swept the Germans out of the Somme and on to their collapse further to the east in November.

Peace came. The Somme had been one of the most hard-fought-over areas of the Western Front. A third of the *département* was a devastated zone – 700 square miles where no building remained intact and most villages were merely heaps of brick rubble. The Somme had been a particularly tragic sector for the British.[1] The British Army had suffered more severely than any other. More than 200,000 British troops had died in the *département*, almost 30 per cent of British deaths on the whole of the Western Front. It was not just the numbers of British dead that made the Somme such an emotive battlefield, but the composition and character of the British units which fought here. The men who died or were crippled on the Somme in 1916 – the worst year – were mostly members of the volunteer citizen army which had rallied to Lord Kitchener's call soon after the outbreak of war and who came to the Somme from all over the British Empire with a spirit never to be seen again.

The Germans invaded again in 1940. This time it was the western part of the Somme which suffered. After Dunkirk, the French, with help from two British divisions, tried to hold the Germans by defending the bridges over the Somme between Amiens and Abbeville. The resulting battle was the fiercest of the 1940 campaign. After the French collapse, part of the French population refused to accept defeat and fought on in the secret war of the Resistance. That was a sad time for France, a time of torture, deportations, hostage-taking and execution, a time when outstanding courage ran alongside collaboration and treachery. This book will lead visitors to some emotive memorials where the Resistance fighters died. In 1944 came the Liberation. Fortunately, German resistance in France was virtually broken when British, Polish and American armoured units chased the Germans across the Somme in little more than twenty-four hours and with only a handful of casualties. Finally, one hopes, war departed from the Somme for good.

---

[1] The term 'British' is used in this book to cover soldiers from the United Kingdom, together with the dominions and the colonies of what was until 1931 the British Empire (thereafter the Commonwealth). 'English', 'Welsh', 'Scottish' and 'Irish' will all be used where relevant, but the term 'United Kingdom' will be employed when these require to be referred to collectively; it is hoped that the Southern Irish will not take exception to this; the period being described was before the formation of their independent state.

The British Cemeteries

The most unforgettable memory of the battlefields for most visitors is provided by the variety and individuality of the British cemeteries. Even before the end of the First World War it had been decided that the permanent British cemeteries on the battlefields would, in Winston Churchill's words, be 'an abiding and supreme memorial to the efforts and the glory of the British Army'.[2] The body which formulated early policy and then built and continued to care for British war cemeteries all over the world was the Imperial War Graves Commission, created in 1917 with representatives of the major imperial countries and financed by those countries in proportions based on the numbers of their graves. Churchill was an early Chairman of the Commission. The title was changed to 'Commonwealth War Graves Commission' in 1960. (Because of the confusion which may arise through the use of both 'Imperial' and 'Commonwealth' when referring to this body's work, the simple phrase 'War Graves Commission' will be used in this book.)

Work commenced even before the war ended, with the French and Belgian Governments granting free gifts of land and the Army Graves Service preparing cemeteries in the safer areas for eventual take-over by the War Graves Commission. A 'no repatriation' policy was quickly established which caused some resentment among families who had intended disinterring bodies and bringing these back home for burial, but the War Graves Commission felt that 'a higher ideal than that of private burial' would be found in the war cemeteries where 'those who fought and fell together, officers and men, lie together in their last resting place'.[3]

The massive work of constructing the cemeteries started as soon as the war ended. The Army Graves Service and the War Graves Commission jointly decided the number, size and location of the permanent cemeteries and the Army gathered in bodies from the

---

[2] *Hansard*, 4 May 1920; quoted in *The Unending Vigil* by Philip Longworth (London: Constable, 1967; Leo Cooper, 1985), p. 54.

[3] Longworth, *The Unending Vigil*, p. 42. The 'no repatriation' policy for British service personnel who died overseas was maintained for nearly fifty years; bodies could be moved – sometimes over long distances – to permanent cemeteries within a country, but they were not taken out of the country where the man or woman died. The policy endured until the Borneo confrontation in the early 1960s when the ban on repatriation was lifted because suitable permanent burial places could not be guaranteed.

more isolated cemeteries which were to be closed and searched the battlefields for isolated graves and lost bodies; the main battlefields on the Somme were searched at least six times. The War Graves Commission appointed architects to design each cemetery individually and hired local contractors to carry out the construction work. United Kingdom and Empire dead were treated equally, though some segregation of graves by the colour of a man's skin is to be found and officers are often buried separately from other ranks in the rear areas, but those distinctions were made by the Army in the original burials, not by the War Graves Commission.

One of the Somme cemeteries – at the Thiepval Memorial – was deliberately made 'Anglo-French' to commemorate the joint effort of the two armies in the 1916 battle, and two other cemeteries – at Cerisy on the River Somme and at Crucifix Corner near Villers-Bretonneux – have French and British plots side by side as a reminder of shared sacrifices in other battles. There were no other national distinctions in the British cemeteries until after 1945, when the Canadians, who served with such courage on the Western Front in both world wars, secured the privilege of having certain cemeteries which contained a high proportion of their men's graves designated as 'Canadian', having their Maple Leaf badge on the entrance and special Visitors' Books, and sometimes with the word 'Canadian' being incorporated into the cemetery name. There are six of these 'Canadian' cemeteries in the areas covered by this book. British cemeteries often contain a few German graves, usually prisoners of war who died of wounds and whose bodies have been allowed to remain undisturbed alongside those of the British soldiers. This is in contrast to the French and American attitude to German graves in their cemeteries. The French military cemeteries sometimes contain British or other Allied graves, but never German ones; the Americans are exclusively American. While Germany was divided, West Germany paid the full maintenance costs of the German graves in British cemeteries but the East Germans did not contribute.

The first two cemeteries on the Somme – at Forceville and Louvencourt – were completed by 1920 but the main work did not end until 1934 when Serre Road Cemetery No. 2 was completed. By that time, approximately 150,000 British dead had been buried in 242 military cemeteries in the Somme *département*. One cemetery on the Somme remained 'open'; this was the London Cemetery Extension at High Wood which was used to accommodate remains still being found on the battlefields. No less than 38,000 of these were discovered in France and Belgium between the end of the official British searches in September 1921 and the outbreak of the Second World War. That cemetery at High Wood was used until it became full some time in the 1950s. France and Belgium each have one cemetery for current 1914–18 finds and one for 1939–45 finds. The 'open' cemeteries in France are at Terlincthun near Boulogne for 1914–18 and St Charles-de-Percy in Normandy for 1939–45; the Belgian ones are Cement House Cemetery at Lange-marck for 1914–18 and the Canadian Cemetery at Adegem for 1939–45. About five British war dead from 1914–18 are still found in an average year in France and Belgium.

The British cemeteries can be split into at least five different types and visitors will gain more benefit from cemetery visits if they know of these differences. These are not official classifications and the descriptions which follow are my own interpretations. I will start at the front line and work towards the rear.

First comes the 'battlefield cemetery' where men are buried

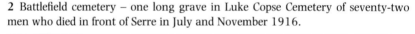

2 Battlefield cemetery – one long grave in Luke Copse Cemetery of seventy-two men who died in front of Serre in July and November 1916.

actually on the ground where they died in an attack. If the attack was successful, the burials probably took place within hours, usually by the men's own unit, sometimes in a large shell hole or a trench; sometimes the little cemetery thus created was reserved for men of one battalion. The proportion of bodies identifiable in these early burials was high. If the attack was unsuccessful, the bodies may not have been recovered for months or even years but the little cemeteries were still created, though with fewer bodies being identified and with units being more mixed. Battlefield cemeteries are easily identifiable; they are usually small, confined to a few dates of death, and are often in isolated locations away from a road. There were hundreds of such cemeteries on the battlefields at the end of the First World War but most had to be emptied due to the cost of permanent maintenance and the bodies were concentrated elsewhere. But we are lucky to have three areas on the Somme where battlefield cemeteries were allowed to remain – on the sector from Serre through Beaumont-Hamel down to the River Ancre, a small area between Mametz and Fricourt and the area to the south-east of Villers-Bretonneux where the Canadian Corps attacked in August 1918.

The second type of cemetery is to be found a few hundred yards to the rear of the front-line trenches and was established during the 'quiet' times of routine trench warfare. These cemeteries are usually located alongside a farm track or country lane or behind a front-line village. The men buried here were those who were killed during tours of trench duty and carried out by their friends for burial, or were wounded in the trenches and died at a forward Dressing Station. I call these 'comrades cemeteries', because it is so easy to visualize a group of soldiers burying one or two of their own comrades. Those comrades cemeteries that remain in their original form, together with the little battlefield cemeteries, are my favourites, being direct links with the routine life of danger of front-line soldiers and the times when they had to go 'over the top'.

Not far behind the comrades cemeteries are the 'communal cemeteries' where small plots of British graves are to be found in French civilian cemeteries. The word 'communal' is French; the cemeteries are the property of the local *commune* or parish. The burials here were often the earliest which took place on a sector, when it seemed the natural thing to bury the first casualties in the local civilian cemetery before military cemeteries were established. The main feature of communal cemeteries is the contrast between the neatly grassed War Graves Commission plots, with their rows of even headstones, and the civilian parts of the cemetery which usually have a gritted surface and a jumble of unkempt, rusty crosses. If space ran out, burials might be continued beyond the original cemetery boundary in what is now known as a 'communal cemetery extension'.

Further away from the fighting area are to be found the places where the Main Dressing Stations and Casualty Clearing Stations received wounded from the front. These medical units usually remained in the same place for several months and were able to bury their dead carefully in a field nearby. Further back still were the large base hospitals near the Channel ports which remained static for several years and built up huge cemeteries. The medical unit cemeteries are usually characterized by careful layout, usually by segregation of officers from other ranks (with more space for the officers), by a large mixture of units of the men buried and by almost total identification of the bodies. The main interest at such cemeteries is the wide range of regimental badges to be seen on the headstones and the surge in burials immediately after major battles, because the dead were usually buried in chronological order.

But, returning to the battlefield area, the War Graves Commission discovered that it had to provide new burial places for thousands of bodies because of the closure of small cemeteries and the discovery of scattered graves as the battlefield searches continued. The answer was the 'concentration cemetery', examples of which now dominate the most densely fought over battlefields such as the 1916 area of the Somme.

The 'pure' concentration cemeteries were made on large, new sites, always at a roadside for the easy access of future visitors. The graves were laid out neatly in small plots, with regular numbers of graves – usually ten – in each row. The evenly sized plots were laid out to create the image of a large army unit on parade, symbolic of soldiers still serving. Such cemeteries were usually given the simple title of their geographical location; Delville Wood and Warlencourt Cemeteries on the 1916 battlefield are good examples of the 'pure' concentration cemetery of relatively early post-war concentration. Most of the men buried in them came from the immediately sur-rounding battlefields. Often, however, the concentrations were made around or as an extension of original wartime cemeteries, sometimes

3 Concentration cemetery – 3,172 graves gathered in after the war to make Adanac Cemetery.

by filling in the gap between a cemetery in a field and the road. If the original cemetery was only a small one, then its graves might be almost lost to sight among the large numbers of surrounding headstones, but its identity was preserved by designating the original cemetery as Plot 1 and retaining the original soldiers' name for the cemetery. A good example of this on the 1916 battlefield is Caterpillar Valley Cemetery, where a small cemetery of twenty-five graves is now surrounded by more than 5,000 graves in thirty-one plots.

The concentration cemeteries may not be intimate, but they are certainly impressive, conveying as they do the heavy casualties in certain areas. The variety of regimental badges is of interest but there is often a high proportion of unidentified graves. No doubt Rudyard Kipling, a member of the War Graves Commission, whose son was killed and has no known grave and who could be buried in a concentration cemetery, had such places in mind when he coined the phrase 'the silent cities' for the war cemeteries.

The later stages of the post-war cemetery construction period on the 1916 battlefield ran into difficulties, and various expedients had to be used which resulted in the movement of bodies, sometimes over long distances, to their permanent burial places; several examples of this will be described later. A few determined relatives insisted that bodies should remain where they were first buried and they erected private memorials over such graves. The War Graves Commission persuaded most of the families to allow the bodies to be brought from these isolated places into the regular cemeteries in the 1950s, to ensure proper care, and only a very few of those battlefield graves now remain.

There was much discussion – and argument – as to the type of permanent marker the individual British graves should have. The decision was made to have not a cross but a standard sized headstone for every soldier, representing equality in death whatever a man's rank or religion. The erection of private crosses or memorials was banned; only a very few which had already been erected were allowed to remain. The result of the all-headstone policy for the visitor is twofold – a pleasing and regular appearance of the plots of graves, and space on the headstones on which far more information can be displayed than on the crosses, Stars of David or other forms of grave marker adopted by other nations.

Next of kin were informed that headstones would incorporate an engraved Christian cross unless the family asked for this to be omitted; the Jewish Star of David was the only other religious symbol to be allowed. The absence of a cross or a Jewish symbol on a headstone is thus the family's direct choice; the usual reason is atheism or agnosticism, although Unitarians, who believe that Jesus Christ was not the son of God but the foremost of the prophets, may also have decided against having a cross. Relatives were also allowed to choose a personal inscription not to exceed sixty-six letters, the space between two words counting as one letter. It was decided to charge for the inscriptions, it being felt that, by paying, families would have a more personal stake in the grave. Threepence half-penny ($3\frac{1}{2}$d) in old currency was charged, with a maximum charge of £1. There were some objections. The New Zealanders said they did not want personal inscriptions on their graves and refused to have them in both world wars. The Canadians would not allow their families to be charged; their Government paid. The charge was then made voluntary, but many poor families had already been deterred and that is one reason why many headstones do not bear an inscription. (The voluntary payment after the Second World War was limited to 7/6d, then raised to £1 again, but has now been allowed to lapse.)

So the headstones were made, for those on the Western Front mostly from Portland limestone, though some other types of stone are encountered in various cemeteries. On the face were engraved the soldier's name, regimental number (but not for officers), age (if supplied by next of kin), date of death, and the name and badge of his corps or regiment, as well as the cross, unless the family had requested otherwise. If the man had won the Victoria Cross, or later the rarer George Cross, a large engraving of that emblem replaced the standard cross. Any inscription the family might have chosen came at the foot of the headstone; many of these are very moving and some will be quoted in this book. Such was the format of the standard headstone of an identified soldier. If the burials were so close that there was insufficient space for each body to have its own headstone, then one headstone would contain the details for two or even three men; if two men, the cross had to be omitted; if three, the regimental badges also.

Large numbers of the dead could not be identified; but, unlike the French and the Germans, the British did not use mass graves for such bodies and every British soldier whose body was found has his own grave. For the completely unidentified the headstone has 'A SOLDIER OF THE GREAT WAR' or 'A SOLDIER OF THE 1939–45 WAR' above the cross and, below it, 'KNOWN UNTO GOD' – another phrase contributed by Rudyard Kipling. There were many partial identifications when a man's rank, or regiment, or date of death, or whether he was from one of the Empire countries, was known; in such cases the known details were inscribed on the headstone, but KNOWN UNTO GOD always remained.

The cemeteries which were completed during the following years remain virtually unchanged. All but the smallest cemeteries have a Cross of Sacrifice and a Stone of Remembrance. The stone Cross of Sacrifice has a sword attached to its face to symbolize both 'the military character of the cemetery and the religious affiliation of the majority of the dead'. There are four sizes of cross:

Type A1, $14\frac{1}{2}$ feet high, for cemeteries with 40–250 burials.
Type A, 20 feet high, for cemeteries with 251–2,000 burials.
Type B, 25 feet high, for cemeteries with over 2,000 burials.
Type C, 30 feet high, for special cases.

The only 'special case' cemeteries on the Somme are the Anglo-

4 Headstones in British cemeteries. A general, private soldier, unknown soldier, partially identified, Australian, Canadian, South African, New Zealander, Indian.

Victoria Cross, George Cross, naval battalion, Jewish, no cross (at family request), 'believed to be buried . . .', German prisoner of war, Chinese labourer – and another war.

French Cemetery at the Thiepval Memorial and Villers-Bretonneux Military Cemetery. The Stone of Remembrance is a large altar-shaped stone, mounted on three low steps, weighing twelve tons and originally costing £500 to produce and install. On its side are engraved the words 'THEIR NAME LIVETH FOR EVERMORE'. Over seventy years after the First World War, the War Graves Commission is in the process of adding stainless-steel historical notices with a map and descriptive text at every cemetery with more than forty graves.

Open spaces in the cemeteries are grassed and there are trees and bushes, with flower beds along the bases of the headstones. In most cases there are rose bushes in the flower beds, so that the shadow of an English rose falls across every grave at some time during the day. Every cemetery has a register – though it may not be available in the smaller cemeteries – and there is usually a book for visitors to record their names and make comments. The registers are a source of much useful information about both the cemetery and the men buried; the citations of those awarded the Victoria Cross, Albert Medal or George Cross are particularly interesting inclusions.

The British cemeteries are never locked and are open all through the year. A moonlight visit is quite an experience.

Other Cemeteries

Less space will be required to describe the cemeteries of other armies, for none has the intimacy or variety of the British ones. The French had the immense task after 1918 of clearing their battlefields and burying their dead, as well as reconstructing the towns, villages and roads in the huge devastated zone of their country. It is possible, also, that the French were more used to war on the continental scale and so, for various reasons, they put neither the money nor the emotional originality into the construction of their permanent cemeteries, which are all large ones of the concentration-cemetery type. There are only twenty-one of these 'National Cemeteries' in the Somme *département*, containing 64,757 graves from 1914–18 and 2,436 from 1940. The standard French soldier's grave was marked by a simple cross, economically made from a concrete aggregate on a metal framework. A small plate, difficult to read, gave only the briefest of details of the man buried. Those Frenchmen whose families did not want the Christian cross had a plain headstone, and the many Muslim soldiers of the colonial units were given a headstone with a curved, Moorish-style top. Most of the unidentified dead in the battlefield areas were buried in mass graves – *ossuaires* – at the rear of the cemeteries. A few British soldiers were sometimes buried in the French cemeteries and a few RAF bomber crews were added in the Second World War, the smart, light-coloured British headstones now looking strange among the grey French crosses. There are no German graves; they were the enemy and their bodies were sent elsewhere.

The French cemeteries may lack the variety of the British ones, and the standard of horticulture and maintenance is lower, but they are impressive in other ways. The French *tricolore* flag flies each day and the sheer numbers of graves remind the visitor of the huge French sacrifice in 1914–18. Most of the French cemeteries have display boards, on one side of which are maps of the local battlefield showing the main cemeteries and memorials in the area; on the other side are descriptions of the local battles, with maps and photographs (all of the text is in French). The French have also embarked upon the vast task of replacing their ageing concrete crosses and Muslim headstones with new, lighter-coloured and more durable ones made of a plastic and powdered marble compound. These give a more pleasing appearance to their cemeteries and the new labels are easier to read.

The Germans had even less opportunity to make attractive cemeteries after the First World War. Their own country was suffering economic depression and the French and Belgian peoples were not inclined to be generous with land or facilities. The concentration type of cemetery was again the solution, but this time with even fewer and larger cemeteries than the French ones. There are only thirteen First World War and one Second World War German cemeteries on the Somme. Large mass graves – *Kameradengräber* – contain most of the unidentified. For many years, the German cemeteries were simple burial grounds with gradually decaying wooden crosses, but in the last twenty years the German war graves organization[4] has replaced the wooden crosses with smart new metal or stone crosses and markers. The larger German cemeteries

[4] The Volksbund Deutsche Kriegsgräberforsorge, based at Kassel.

5 French Christian and Muslim grave markers of new replacement manufacture; German cross – two names on each side.

have also been given visitors centres, chapels, elaborate maps of the battlefields and new registers. The money for this work came from the West German Government and from private donations which are discreetly sought at the larger cemeteries. During the summer months, parties of young Germans can sometimes be found carrying out the annual maintenance work and some of the improvements. These young people stay in camps at nearby French villages and have gatherings with the local people in the evenings. The purpose of this activity is to show German youth something of the horror of war and to foster 'reconciliation over the graves' in the country which their armies twice invaded earlier in the century.

The Americans were latecomers to the First World War, but their men did fight on the Somme, firstly as 'learners' with the British and then in their own units. The first action by a complete American division in the First World War was on the Somme, although their main sectors of action in later months were elsewhere. The American soldiers who died on the Somme were buried with the French or British soldiers when they died, but their bodies were later collected up and either taken back to the United States[5] or concentrated in a new 'Somme American Cemetery'. This cemetery has the usual high-quality standard of American military cem-

[5] The United States was the only nation to allow large-scale repatriation of the bodies of war dead if families requested it; approximately 60 per cent of the First World War dead were returned home and 61 per cent from the Second World War.

6 American grave.

7 (*right*) Memorial – by the family of an infantry officer – on the Serre Road.

eteries – a marble cross or Star of David for each grave, a chapel, a tall flagpole and an American flag, detailed records, a visitors centre and resident custodian, and the most meticulous horticultural care. It is strictly American, with no other nationalities buried here. Opening hours are controlled. There are no Second World War American graves on the Somme; their dead, mostly airmen, were either taken home or moved to the Normandy American Cemetery which stands above Omaha Beach 100 miles away from the Somme.

Memorials

Perhaps the saddest casualties were those men whose bodies could not be identified or even be found. The War Graves Commission decided that every dead British soldier's name should be commemorated, either on his grave or on a memorial. Headstones were erected along the walls of British cemeteries for men 'Known to be buried' or 'Believed to be buried' in the cemetery. Small memorial blocks, again with headstones for each man, are also to be found for those who had been buried in a cemetery during the war but whose graves were later destroyed by shell fire or otherwise lost. These headstones are of the same type as those for ordinary burials, with family inscriptions if these have been requested; if not, the standard inscription 'THEIR GLORY SHALL NOT BE BLOTTED OUT' is engraved upon them. There are no bodies beneath any of these headstones; they are those men's memorials. For the much larger number of the British missing, however, large purpose-built 'Memorials to the Missing' were built on the principal British battlefield sectors. The American missing are also recorded on memorials, but these are always at one of their cemeteries. The French and Germans do not normally have such memorials.

There is a host of other memorials on the battlefields – national memorials, memorials to units of every size, memorials to individual soldiers killed. Their variety is almost limitless and they are an important aspect of battlefield touring. We found 150 on the Somme and there may be others not marked on maps that we did not know about. Two new ones were built while this book was being written. French memorials often contain strong anti-German sentiments and the Germans removed some of these when they came in 1940, but a new crop of memorials, with even more violent wording, appeared after the Liberation. The Germans were allowed nothing. The memorials erected by their units during the 1914–18 war – sometimes quite substantial ones – were all destroyed after the Armistice and no new German memorial of any kind was permitted by the French or Belgians to mark the invasion and devastation of their countries. The only German memorial I have seen in France is a small tablet recently attached to the porch of a French memorial chapel on the Serre Road.

An interesting type of memorial is the 'Demarcation Stone', a series of which were erected at roadsides by the French and Belgian Touring Clubs to mark the limits of the German advances in the spring of 1918. It was intended that each Demarcation Stone should be surmounted by a carved helmet of the type worn by whichever army held the Germans on that particular sector. The Belgians followed this rule but the French did not; all of the Demarcation Stones in France have French helmets, even on those sectors where British troops halted the German advance. More than 100 of these stones were erected; the money came from public donations and the name of the town or organization paying for each stone was

8 Memorial – by survivors of the 34th Division at La Boisselle.

carved into its base. Some were destroyed by the Germans after 1940 and others have been removed in road widening or after being damaged accidentally; only a few remain in France, rather more in Belgium.

Hints and Hazards

This part of the book will close with what it is hoped will be helpful advice and suggestions for a visit to the battlefields.

Do not try to do everything; do not hurry. It is better to see and absorb a part of the battlefields and go home having gained a true understanding of that part, rather than to try and cover everything. To cover the whole of the Somme would certainly require several visits. Keep your eyes open. There will be things to see not catalogued in this book – the lie of the land, a particular atmosphere only found at certain times of the day or the year, possibly a newly erected memorial. Get out on to the land whenever possible. Local farmers are well aware of the importance of the main battlefield areas to visitors and are remarkably tolerant, but do respect their rights and problems. Ask permission if you see the farmer; a friendly approach, an outstretched hand, and 'Bonjour, m'sieu' will rarely be rebuffed.

Learn a little French if you can, although sign language and a smile will take you nearly as far. If you can speak French, ask to look at the scrap-metal heap (*le tas de ferraille*) in his yard; you may find a rifle (*un fusil*) – rusty and with the wooden parts all gone, but still an interesting souvenir. He may give you, or sell for a few francs, the nose-cap of a shell (*une tête d'obus*).

Only walk on cleared land. Spring brings the best results; the winter frosts followed by rain on the autumn ploughed land will have revealed the white lines of trench diggings and expose souvenirs. If you are unexpectedly faced with a growing crop, walk along the rows or around the field boundary, or turn back; if you spoil a crop, you will lose the goodwill of the farmer for other visitors. Do not touch unexploded shells or hand grenades; most are safe but an occasional one will not be. There is a one-handed Frenchman at Pozières who collected one souvenir too many! Live rifle rounds are safe to handle but take the cordite out of the cartridges before returning through Customs. Finding souvenirs is a matter of luck; a field may be rich in discovery one year but seemingly barren the next. My two best finds in field walking were an old Lee-Enfield rifle found near Givenchy and a Queen Victoria shilling near Guillemont; I often look at the coin and think of it as a First World War soldier's basic pay for twenty-four hours of trench duty.

If you pass a small quarry, see if a trench or a dug-out is being

9 Memorial – to those who died in the Resistance, at Amiens.

gradually uncovered; I once found a lovely blue enamel German soldier's mug in a dug-out in a quarry near Puisieux. Talk to the War Graves Commission gardeners. They will appreciate 'Hello' or 'Bonjour' if nothing else; if you have a common language – many are British or partly so – they can often tell you interesting stories of local events or point out interesting graves. Take the time to walk around cemeteries, to pay homage to the dead and also to scan headstones for interesting items such as rare regimental badges, senior officers, unusual combinations of decorations or interesting personal inscriptions. This book will note many of the interesting graves to be seen in Somme cemeteries but visitors will find many more for themselves.

There are dangers, besides the obvious one of live ammunition. Roads change; maps become out of date. Nearly all shops and offices close from noon until 2.0 p.m. Never trust the weather; always travel prepared for rain or a cold wind arising unexpectedly. Try to avoid parking a car on the roadway, even on a quiet country road; it is technically illegal and you may be held responsible if an accident results. There are two further hazards which Mary and I found particularly harassing. The first was the French shooting season, which starts on the third Sunday in September and is pursued with great intensity over the next few weeks, particularly on Sundays. The shooting parties are almost fanatical. There will be little actual danger but the noise is continuous and the sportsmen will certainly expect you to keep out of their way; their shooting definitely takes priority over your battlefield touring. The worst hazard we have met, however, is from dogs. Keep clear of all dogs if you can. French dogs, particularly on farms, are trained to protect property. Mary and I have both been attacked at different times. My method of asking questions at a farm is to drive into the yard, sound the horn to gain attention if a dog is in evidence and the owner is not, and then speak through the open window of the car until I am assured that the dog is under control.

These few hazards can be overcome with sensible precautions. A carefully planned tour will prove a rewarding experience and the visitor will be able to take satisfaction and pride at having helped to keep alive the memory of the men of all nations who fought, suffered and died on those terrible battlefields. You will be making a pilgrimage following directly in the footsteps of the grieving relatives, the lonely fiancées and the groups of soldier survivors who

10 The 1940 Defence of Calais Memorial.

started to visit the battlefields in the early 1920s. We wish you 'bon voyage' even if your journey is only a journey of imagination from an armchair.

1·ROUTES TO THE SOMME

Most visitors to the Somme battlefields are British and most will commence their visits by crossing the English Channel. This part of the book is written to help such people by pointing out locations of interest to military enthusiasts along those routes. The Calais–Boulogne area is assumed to be the landing place for most visitors, but those using more northerly ports will still need to travel across this region. The fastest direct routes to the Somme are down the Paris motorway (*autoroute*) from Calais past Arras to Bapaume, or by the proposed new motorway from Boulogne to Abbeville and Amiens. The routes by ordinary roads to the western end of the Somme are simple ones down the coast but the cross-country roads to Amiens or the main battlefield areas in the east of the Somme are more complicated. If visitors can spare the time to go cross-country, however, they will be rewarded with a journey through quiet, gentle countryside, sometimes with scenes of genuine 'old France', as well as a selection of interesting wartime sites to visit. The major places of interest will be described here, but not at great length because this area – the Pas-de-Calais – is not the main subject of the book.

CALAIS

The first memorial might be seen before one even leaves a ferry coming into Calais harbour. The ferry terminals are in two groups separated by a jetty on which stands the modern Harbourmaster's office – the building with the sloping roof. If your ferry passes to the right of it a good view can be had of the *1940 Defence of Calais Memorial* ① which is near the building. It is a cross with a low wall

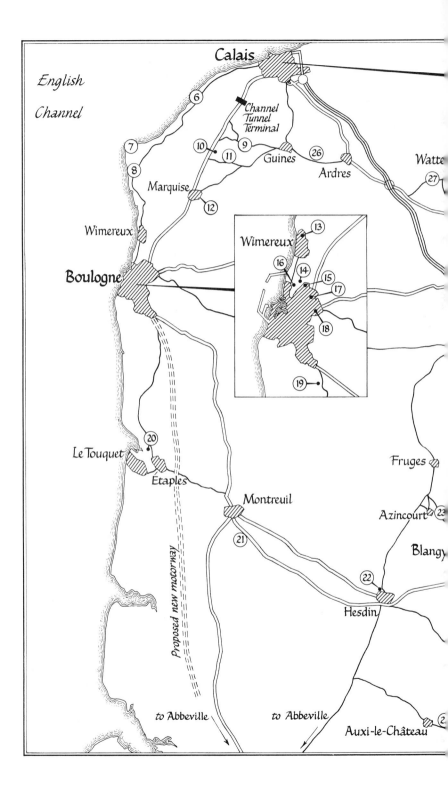

English
Channel

Calais

⑥

Channel
Tunnel
Terminal

⑦

⑩   ⑨

⑧   ⑪   ⑳

Marquise   Guines   Ardres   Watte

⑫   ⑯⑦

Wimereux

Boulogne

Wimereux   ⑬

⑯ ⑭ ⑮
          ⑦
          ⑰

⑱

⑲

Le Touquet   ⑳

Fruges

Etaples

Montreuil   Azincourt   ㉓

㉑   Blangy

㉒

Hesdin

Proposed new motorway

to Abbeville   to Abbeville

Auxi-le-Château   ②

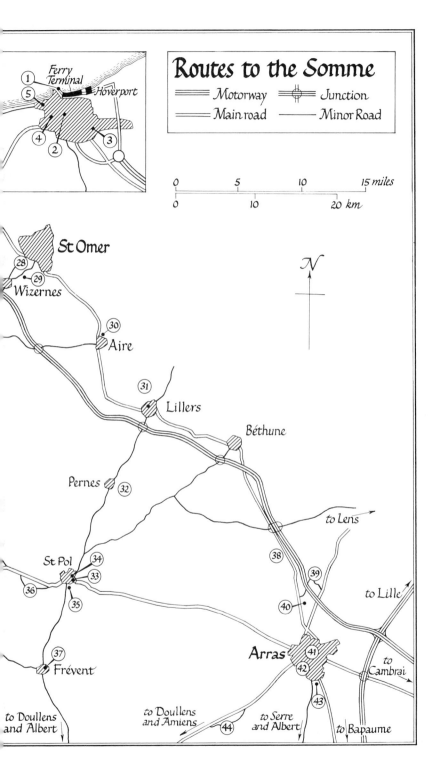

Routes to the Somme

Motorway · **Junction**
Main road — **Minor Road**

Ferry Terminal
Hoverport
1
5
4
2
3

0   5   10   15 miles
0   10   20 km

N

St Omer
28
29
Wizernes

30
Aire

31

Lillers

Béthune

Pernes
32

to Lens

St Pol
34
33
36
35

38

39

to Lille

40

37
Frévent

Arras
41
42
to Cambrai

43

to Doullens
and Albert

to Doullens
and Amiens

44

to Serre
and Albert

to Bapaume

on which are the regimental badges of the three battalions sent to hold Calais for as long as possible in May 1940 – the 2nd King's Royal Rifle Corps, the 1st Rifle Brigade and Queen Victoria's Rifles. The memorial is accessible by public road. Turn right immediately on leaving the fenced boundary of the port area at the docks exit and follow a road which runs between the car ferry assembly area and the railway station (the Gare Maritime). If in difficulty, ask the police at the docks exit for directions to 'the Green Jackets Memorial'.

In 1347, when the British under Edward III were besieging Calais, six leading citizens came out and offered their own lives if the starving population could be spared. The nobility of this gesture so impressed Edward III that he spared the six and allowed food to reach the town. A famous statue group by Rodin outside the *Town Hall* ② shows the six who offered their lives. In the park over the road is a Second World War museum in a wartime bunker.

There are three military cemeteries in Calais containing nearly 5,000 graves, nearly all from the First World War. Unfortunately they are away from the main roads taken by most travellers and do not attract many visitors. *Calais Southern Cemetery* ③ is a large civilian cemetery on the south side of the road to Marck, just across the canal which runs alongside the old road from the port. A War Graves Commission plot contains 720 British graves from the 1914–18 war and 225 from 1939–45. The First World War graves were mostly from the four army and three voluntary British Red Cross hospitals which were located at Calais. The Germans then used the pathways of that plot to bury British soldiers killed in the 1940 fighting together with a few airmen and seamen who died later in the war. Nearly a quarter of the 1940 graves are unidentified.

Calais Northern Cemetery ④ is actually on the west side of the town, just inside the ring road. It contains the graves of 1,056 Belgian soldiers, 1,048 Frenchmen and 365 German prisoners of war, all from the First World War. The Belgian plot is their largest in France. There are no British graves.

Les Barraques Military Cemetery ⑤ is right up against the sand dunes at Blériot-Plage, just out of sight to the ferries and hovercraft which pass only three-quarters of a mile away. The cemetery was started when the British plot in Calais Southern Cemetery became full in September 1917. There are 1,123 British graves, 236 of German prisoners of war, most of whom died in the influenza epidemic early in 1919, and 203 of Chinese Labour Corps men. The cemetery is closely associated with base units working at Calais. Sergeant A. G. Harman of the Royal Fusiliers, who died of heart failure on 19 August 1921, may have been the last British soldier to die in France in the closing-down period after the First World War. His grave is in the short Row 10A, just near the steps on the left-hand side of the cemetery. Close by are the graves of seven Second World War casualties, the crew of a Lysander of No. 26 Squadron, two King's Royal Rifle Corps men from May 1940 and three unidentified.

There are two roads from Calais to Boulogne, the coastal road and the more direct Route Nationale on which the Channel Tunnel terminal is situated. *Cap Blanc-Nez* ⑥ is the towering headland on which there is a large monument that is easily seen from the ferries. The monument is in memory of the British and French seamen of the Dover Patrol who protected the sea routes of the British Expeditionary Force between 1914 and 1918. It was destroyed by the Germans in the Second World War but rebuilt afterwards. In lower ground to the east of the headland was the Lindemann Battery which had the largest cross-Channel guns – 406 mm (16 inch) – installed by the Germans in the Second World War. The area in which the remains of the huge casements still stand may eventually be covered over by chalk dug from the Channel Tunnel. The church-yard of the nearby village of Escalles contains the solitary British grave of Marine A. J. Callow of No. 40 Commando whose body was washed ashore on this coast after the Dieppe Raid of August 1942. He is the closest to England of nearly three-quarters of a million British dead from the two world wars who are buried on the Continent.

To the east and south of the hamlet of Framzelle, close to Cap Gris-Nez, are the remains of another German cross-Channel gun position, the *Grosser Kurfürst Battery* ⑦. There were four 280 mm gun positions but they were heavily bombed and then partially demolished after the war. The remains have been abandoned to nature and have become little copses, but the shattered concrete gun casements are still visible. A mile and a half further south is the *Batterie Todt* ⑧ which had four 380 mm guns. This is the best preserved of the gun batteries on this coast and one of the casemates has been converted into a better-than-average museum.

*

There are three British Second World War cemetery groups on or near the Route Nationale from Calais to Boulogne but they are different in character and content.

First, on the eastern side of *Pihen-les-Guines* village there are two burial grounds close together ⑨ in which are 149 British graves, most of them of airmen shot down in this area.

Calais Canadian War Cemetery ⑩ is a large post-war concentration cemetery which stands on the crest of a hill, just back from the main road. Because more than four-fifths of the graves are Canadian, the cemetery was given its 'Canadian' subtitle and has the Maple Leaf emblem on the gateway. There are 603 army graves (525 of them Canadian), 117 air-force graves (69 Canadian), seven sailors and two completely unidentified; nineteen of the dead are Polish and six are Czechoslovak. Most of the casualties were from the September 1944 period when the First Canadian Army was fighting hard to take the Channel ports and the German gun batteries in this area. This is the largest British cemetery from the Second World War in either the Pas-de-Calais or the Somme.

There are some particularly interesting graves. In Row F of Plot 3 is the grave of Leading Aircraftwoman Margaret Campbell who was a WAAF nursing orderly in a casualty evacuation Dakota which strayed too close to the German garrison still holding out at Dunkirk in October 1944 and was shot down. There were no medical cases on board, but four crew members were killed. In the far left corner of the cemetery is the grave of Group Captain P. R. Barwell, DFC, Station Commander at Biggin Hill, who took part in a sweep over France in July 1942 and whose Spitfire was last seen falling back over the Channel; his body was washed ashore near Boulogne. Three rows further forward are the sad graves of two officer brothers, Majors Peter and Douglas Kennedy, from Galt, Ontario, killed within two days of each other in September 1944 while fighting with the Highland Light Infantry of Canada at Boulogne.

Mimoyecques V-3 Site ⑪ is reached by the next left turn after the Canadian cemetery. The V-3 was one of the 'revenge weapons' with which the Germans hoped to turn the tide of war in 1944–5. It was a set of huge, long-range guns in which successive charges along the 400-foot-long barrels would fire 6 inch shells as far as London, but it was so heavily bombed that it never came into use. Part of the extensive underground tunnel system built by forced labour has been reopened and is currently a museum, which is advertised locally as 'La Forteresse de Mimoyecques – Un Mémorial International'.

Marquise Communal Cemetery ⑫ is in the fork of two roads in the east of the town. There are 167 British graves, most of which were moved here in 1947 from the sand dunes at the Dunkirk evacuation beaches of 1940. It is unfortunate that a more suitable final resting place could not have been found nearer to Dunkirk than this plot, however neatly maintained, in the civilian cemetery of a scruffy town which has no other connection with British war dead.

BOULOGNE

Of the two main Channel ports Boulogne has the greater number and variety of military memorials and cemeteries. There are reminders of Napoleon's Grand Army which camped here in 1804. In 1914–18 the port was the main landing place for troops crossing from England as well as being a major medical centre which resulted in nearly 12,000 British soldiers who died being buried in five cemeteries in and around the town. The largest of these cemeteries – Boulogne Eastern, Wimereux and Terlincthun – were in the War Graves Commission's 'First Priority Programme' for permanent construction, and work on all three was completed by 1923. It was to these cemeteries that the first organized pilgrimages of ex-servicemen and relatives of the dead came and, because Folkestone–Boulogne was the most popular Channel crossing at that time, it was through Boulogne that most visitors to the battlefields came until 1939. Boulogne saw much action in the Second World War. The 2nd Irish Guards and the 2nd Welsh Guards were landed in May 1940 with orders to hold out for as long as possible; the port area was bombed many times when it was in German hands, and Canadian units had to fight particularly hard to capture the town in 1944.

Boulogne is actually closer to the Somme battlefields than Calais; there are some interesting cross-country routes and a new motorway being planned will run south from Boulogne and on to Abbeville, Amiens and the eastern parts of the Somme.

Wimereux Communal Cemetery ⑬ is the civilian cemetery in the northern part of this seaside town. It was used to bury men who died at local hospitals from October 1914 until the British plot became full in June 1918. The burials were very close together and it is hard to realize that there are nearly 3,000 war graves in this small enclosure. The headstones were laid flat, because of the instability of the sandy soil. But it is a very pleasant spot, on a south-facing slope, and is laid out as a series of terraces with plenty of flowers. The best-known grave in the cemetery is that of the Canadian doctor, Lieutenant-Colonel John McCrae. After the death of a close friend in May 1915, McCrae wrote the poem 'In Flanders Fields' describing the poppies growing among the crosses of the graves outside his Dressing Station at Essex Farm near Ypres:

> *In Flanders fields the poppies blow*
> *Between the crosses, row on row...*

McCrae died of pneumonia in January 1918. His grave is near the Cross of Sacrifice, level with a set of steps. He is also commemorated by a large plaque at the main cemetery entrance and by a memorial seat built into a wall of the British plot.

There are 2,847 First World War British graves, including six nurses, a German plot and a small Portuguese one, and then nineteen mixed 1940 casualties.

Terlincthun British Cemetery ⑭ is a cemetery in which the number of burials still grows. After the cramped British plots in the civilian cemeteries at Boulogne and Wimereux became full in June 1918, this new cemetery was opened in the countryside between the two towns. There were about 2,700 graves by the end of the war. Further burials followed in the winter of 1918–19 when an influenza epidemic raged and the cemetery then remained open for the burial of bodies found on the battlefields and the reburial of those whose graves had to be moved. This process still continues and there are now nearly 4,500 First World War graves together with 109 from the Second World War. It is an important and attractive cemetery, with spacious, well-laid-out plots and some fine cemetery architecture. A pleasing feature is that the soil is firm enough for the headstones to be in the normal, vertical position, unlike most of the Boulogne burials. The graves of those found on the battlefields in recent years are located just inside the main entrance on either

11 Terlincthun British Cemetery – the communal grave of fifty-one soldiers whose remains were found on the Somme in 1982.

side of the grass pathway. They are distinguishable by the visibly increasing newness of the headstones. There is one spectacular burial of the remains of forty-nine British and two German soldiers from 1916 found on the Somme at Ovillers in 1982 (the story of their discovery will be told later). These now have a communal grave with a unique large headstone just inside the entrance.

The Column of the Grande Armée ⑮ commemorates the assembly of Napoleon's army here in 1804, ready to invade England. The soldiers contributed money 'to honour Napoleon I's personality and works' and also to commemorate the first award ceremony of the Légion d'Honneur on 16 August 1804. The British victory at Trafalgar in 1805 caused the invasion plan to be abandoned and the statue of Napoleon on top of the column has his back sternly turned towards England. It is possible to ascend the tower at certain times. An interesting monument on the coast road ⑯ marks the spot where Napoleon's throne was during the first Légion d'Honneur award ceremony and there is a plan of where the regiments paraded in a large arc on the natural amphitheatre provided by the surrounding hills; those hillsides have still not been built on and the scene of 1804 can easily be visualized.

Meerut Military Cemetery ⑰ was on the outskirts of Boulogne until the growing suburb of St Martin surrounded it, but the cemetery is enclosed by a wall and is both spacious and peaceful. There are 281 Indian graves and a memorial to thirty-two more who were cremated according to the custom of their caste and religion. Twenty-six Egyptian Labour Corps men are also buried here, mostly victims of an air raid on their camp in September 1917.

Boulogne Eastern Cemetery ⑱ is a large civilian cemetery just east of the town centre and is actually in two parts divided by a public road, the Rue de Dringhem, which is quiet and available for parking. The British plots are in the southern of the two cemetery areas, starting just inside the gateway nearest the town centre. The burials started with a rush when seven men died in one bad day in October 1914. The ground available for British burials kept being extended as the war continued but eventually ran out in June 1918, by which time 5,578 casualties, including several nurses, were buried in long, narrow plots which run 240 yards on from the first burials, all with flat headstones in the sandy soil. There are also plots for French and for Portuguese soldiers. Space was found for 234 Second World War British graves in four small plots among the earlier burials; their headstones are in the vertical position.

The first Victoria Cross grave encountered in this book is that of Captain F. W. Campbell, a Canadian who was wounded at Givenchy in June 1915. His grave, with the Victoria Cross engraved upon the headstone, is in Plot 2, Row A, just opposite the Portuguese graves. Very close to him is buried Captain Hon. Julian Grenfell, DSO, of the 1st (Royal) Dragoons who died in May 1915 after being wounded at Ypres. Grenfell, a noted writer and poet, was the son of Lord Desborough. His younger brother, Second Lieutenant Hon. 'Billy' Grenfell of the 8th Rifle Brigade, was killed near Ypres two months later and has no known grave. The deaths of the two Grenfells are good examples of the heavy losses among the younger members of the British aristocratic and society families in the First World War and particularly of a small group of families known as 'the Souls' (see further comment on page 184).

One of the Second World War graves is of particular interest, that of Squadron Leader G. C. N. Close whose grave is in the front row of Plot 13 (on the right-hand side of the cemetery after the French graves). His headstone is engraved with the emblem of the George Cross, which replaced the Empire Gallantry Medal he won in 1937 when he tried to rescue the crew of a blazing aircraft at an airfield in Waziristan. Squadron Leader Close died when his Blenheim was shot down attacking shipping at Boulogne in May 1941. The George Cross emblem on a war grave is extremely rare; this is the only one I have seen.

St Étienne-au-Mont Communal Cemetery ⑲ is on the main road from Boulogne to Étaples just south of Pont-de-Briques. A plot at the rear of the cemetery contains the graves of 163 Chinese and five South African labourers who died at a Native Labour General Hospital in 1917–19. There is also a substantial memorial 'to the memory of Chinese labourers who died in service in France during the Great War'.

For those visitors who land at Boulogne or come down one of the coast roads from Calais, a favourable onward route to the Somme would be to continue further south before turning inland. This would allow them to visit two places which were of importance to the British Expeditionary Force in the First World War – Étaples, which became the main British reinforcement base and hospital area, and Montreuil, where General Headquarters were situated for most of the war.

Étaples Military Cemetery ⑳ has 10,776 British and 656 German graves from the First World War and 122 British graves from 1939–45. It is the largest British cemetery in France and has an impressive effect upon the visitor. The plots were carefully arranged so that there is no crowding and plenty of pathways. Officers have their own plots in single graves; British other ranks were usually buried in pairs; the Germans have two plots but some of their officers are buried with the British officers; Chinese and 'coloured' troops have small plots on the edges of the cemetery. There is just one Victoria Cross grave, that of Major D. Reynolds which is in the long officers' row just below and to the right of the steps down from the entrance. Reynolds won an early VC at the Battle of Le Cateau in August 1914, saving a howitzer from capture by the Germans. He died here after being gassed at Ypres in February 1916.

Turning inland, one comes to the pretty town of Montreuil with its ramparts (around which are lovely walks giving superb views, for those with a head for heights), old buildings (including a preserved artisans' quarter) and several hotels (including the château which is one of only two four-star hotels in the Pas-de-Calais). General Headquarters of the British Expeditionary Force moved here from St Omer in March 1916 to be more centrally located behind the growing length of British-held front. The French army barracks in the town, together with several public buildings, were taken over, and GHQ operated from here for the remainder of the war. Field Marshal Sir Douglas Haig was the Commander-in-Chief throughout this period and a fine statue of him on his horse 'Miss Ypres' stands on the edge of the market-place.

Haig chose as his private residence a modest country house, the *Château de Beaurepaire* ㉑, which is on the south side of the road from Montreuil to Hesdin. It is a road which has been upgraded to provide a good, fast route inland from Montreuil. The château is marked on maps as 'St Nicolas'. A small plaque at the gateway states that Sir Douglas Haig resided here from February 1916 to April 1919. The château is privately owned. The family received us hospitably but politely stated that they do not wish their home to become a tourist attraction and expressed the desire that their privacy should be respected. Haig apparently laid down two requirements for his choice of a residence: that it should be surrounded by

12 Part of Étaples Military Cemetery, the largest British cemetery in France.

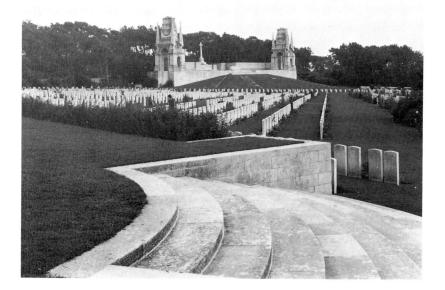

a wall and that it should have central heating, which was rare in those days.

Hesdin (pronounced 'Ay-da') is a lovely town, bypassed by main roads to leave a quiet old square with good restaurants and one or two hotels. *Huby-St Leu British Cemetery* ㉒ is a particularly attractive little cemetery set back from the road to Fruges. Nearly all of the fifty-two graves are from the last months of the First World War. Twenty-seven of them are of airmen who crashed or were shot down flying from local airfields. My eye was caught by the family inscription on the headstone of one pilot, Lieutenant C. N. Barker: *Living, he made it goodlier to live; dying, he will make it easier to die.*

The ground on which the famous *Battle of Agincourt* ㉓ was fought on 25 October 1415 is still accessible, open farmland. Henry V's army, having marched through Normandy and Picardy, was attempting to reach Calais when its way was blocked by the larger French army. The battle is well described at a monument and display table at the crossroads south of the battlefield; full credit is given to the English for their victory. The village of Azincourt (the French name for Agincourt) has a small museum which can be opened by asking at the Mairie or at a local café. An unusual, and very sad, link with the battle can be found in a memorial on the edge of the woods facing the entrance to the Château de Tramecourt which is to the east of the battlefield. The noble family de Chabot-Tramecourt still owns part of the ground on which the 1415 battle was fought and had a father and two sons killed in that battle. The memorial records how a second group of father and two sons died in German hands for being associated with the Resistance in the Second World War. The father died 'in captivity' on 14 July 1944 (Bastille Day), and the two sons died in Neuengamme concentration camp near Hamburg in 1945.

Fillièvres British Cemetery ㉔ has eighty-one First World War graves and nineteen of 1940 and 1944. There is a VC grave, that of Lieutenant E. F. Baxter of the 1/8th King's Liverpool, who won his Victoria Cross in April 1916 for cutting barbed wire in front of the German trenches on the Arras sector during two nights and then leading a raiding party on the third night; he was the only casualty of the raid and his body was recovered after the war from a German cemetery and buried here.

Wavans British Cemetery ㉕ also has a VC among its forty-three graves; the famous fighter pilot Major James McCudden, VC, DSO and Bar, MC and Bar, MM – the most decorated British pilot of the First World War – is buried here. After being credited with the destruction of fifty-seven German planes, he returned to England for a rest and to receive his VC at Buckingham Palace, and then flew back to France on 9 July 1918 in an SE5 to take command of No. 60 Squadron. Being unsure of his position, he landed at Noeux-lès-Auxi airfield (which was just up the lane from the cemetery). But his engine failed soon after taking off again and he crashed, possibly making the beginner's mistake of attempting to turn back to regain the airfield instead of continuing ahead and making a forced landing. Another 'ace' buried here was Flight Commander Robert Little, DSO and Bar, DSC and Bar, an Australian pilot in the Royal Naval Air Service with forty-seven victories to his credit. He was killed during the night of 27 May 1918 while flying a Sopwith Camel of No. 201 Squadron, probably shot down by the air gunner of the Gotha bomber he was attacking. The family inscription on Little's grave is: *From his ever loving wife and little son 'Blimp', also his loving father.* McCudden's is: *Fly on dear boy from this dark world of strife, on to the promised land, to Eternal Life.*

THE INLAND ROUTES

For visitors arriving at Calais or Dunkirk there is a variety of inland routes leading to the Somme battlefield area. There are interesting towns, some attractive countryside and, for those in a hurry, a fast motorway from the outskirts of Calais. One group of visitors should not take the motorway; those interested in the German V-weapons of the Second World War will find the main sites for those in this area.

The *Field of the Cloth of Gold* ㉖ is where Henry VIII of England and Francis I of France met in 1520, at a time when the major powers of Europe were realigning themselves. Each king tried to outrival the other in the splendour of his entourage and this gave the name to the meeting place. There is a simple memorial marker on the north side of the road between Ardres and Guines, about halfway between the two places. Those who are keen to see the exact location of this historical event may find the diversion worthwhile, but I was disappointed; the best part was the opportunity to drive the road between Calais and Guines, along the side of an old canal with its drawbridges, charming little canalside cottages and fishermen – a genuine piece of old France right on the doorstep of Calais.

The *Eperlecques V-2 Bunker* ㉗ is on the edge of the forest between Eperlecques and Watten; there are plenty of signposts to 'Eperlecques Blockhaus'. The first bunker planned here was to be a fully contained V-2 site with areas for the storage and assembly of rocket parts, a plant for the manufacture of the liquid oxygen propellant and silos for firing the rockets against England. But a raid by American B-17 Flying Fortresses in August 1943 completely ruined the bunker just when the concrete was setting. The Germans abandoned it and started a second, the one that can be seen now, though some remains of the first one are also visible. Further raids took place, both by the Americans and by the RAF, but the delay caused by that first American raid was never overcome and work on the second bunker was eventually abandoned without it being used.

It is a massive structure – a major feat of engineering, but a chilling, menacing place with numerous memorials to the thousands of forced labourers who suffered under the SS, who were in charge of the work. Approximately 2,000 of the workers were killed, mostly by the bombing. The bodies of some are still entombed in the concrete which they were pouring at the time of one raid; the other bodies were cremated and the remains scattered in the forest. The ground around the bunker is still heavily cratered and the damage on the edge of the bunker roof caused by one of No. 617 Squadron's 12,000 lb Tallboy bombs can be seen. The bunker is currently open from Easter to 11 November (afternoons only in April, May, October and November), but the commentary and displays are heavily biased towards the French workers and airmen.

St Omer was an important place in the First World War and GHQ of the British Expeditionary Force was located there in the early part of the war. But the only sign of the British involvement is at *Longuenesse Souvenir Cemetery* ㉘, just south of the town on the road to Fruges. The cemetery is in a V-shaped plot at a road junction and contains 3,096 British graves from the First World War and 445 from the Second World War, as well as French, Belgian, German and Chinese plots from the first war. It is an attractive and important cemetery, well worth a visit for the number and variety of its graves. The majority are from the second half of the First World War – 'died of wounds' at hospitals located at St Omer, although there are also some air-raid victims. There is some fine cemetery architecture and the longest continuous row of graves I have ever seen in the form of the British Plot 1 along the far wall, which is 150 yards long and has 174 graves. One of those graves is of Corporal C. R. Noble, 2nd Rifle Brigade, who won a VC at the Battle of Neuve Chapelle in March 1915.

The *Wizernes Bunker* ㉙ was another major V-2 rocket site. It is in a quarry and is reached by finding the railway crossing on the south side of Wizernes and then taking the lane to the east, in the direction of Blendecques, keeping to the road alongside the railway line. If in difficulty, ask for *la cupole* – 'the dome', which is the local name for the construction.

The main feature is a *one-million-ton* concrete dome which was built on top of a hill at the side of the quarry so that the tunnels excavated underneath would be bomb-proof. It was intended that V-2 rockets would be assembled in the tunnels, taken out on a railway and fired from the quarry; a rate of firing of fifty rockets a day was planned! The project survived four months of conventional bombing, but No. 617 Squadron finally dropped five Tallboy bombs so close to the face of the hill that the dome was undermined and the tunnel entrances were sealed off with hundreds of tons of stone. Once again, the Germans abandoned the site without it being used. The huge dome is still there and the railway entrance into the tunnels has been cleared. The quarry is disused and the entrance was locked on our visit, but a museum was due to open on the site in 1993.

If travellers to the Somme are using the St Omer–Béthune–Arras road, or are leaving the motorway at Lillers to take the road to St Pol, they will pass close to a number of cemeteries.

Aire Communal Cemetery ㉚ is on the northern edge of the attractive town of Aire-sur-la-Lys. There are 894 British graves of the First World War, many being casualties from a German offensive of April 1918. There are also twenty-one British graves from May 1940.

Lillers Communal Cemetery and Extension ㉛ is just north of the town centre, on the St Venant road. There are 965 British graves –

151 of them Indian, all of the First World War. There are two Victoria Cross graves – of Major D. Nelson, who won his VC as a sergeant in the famous action by 'L' Battery, Royal Horse Artillery, at Néry in 1914 but who died here in April 1918, and Corporal W. R. Cotter, 6th Buffs (the East Kents), who won his posthumous VC near Loos in March 1916.

Pernes British Cemetery ㉜ is west of the town, on the minor road to Sains. There are 1,076 graves from the First World War – mostly 'died of wounds' from the 1918 German offensives – and eighteen Second World War graves, from early September 1944 when this area was liberated by British troops.

St Pol (full name St Pol-sur-Ternoise) was an important forward base for the Allies during the First World War. *St Pol Communal Cemetery Extension* ㉝ is up a hill just north of the road to Arras. If in difficulty, ask for the 'Cimetière Militaire Thuillier'. The British plot forms almost an exact quarter of what is otherwise a French National Cemetery, the 226 British graves coming from March 1916 until the cemetery became full two years later. There is a pleasing sense of Allied partnership, with the French flag in the centre of the cemetery and the Cross of Sacrifice standing above the British graves. Further up the hill is the *St Pol War Cemetery* ㉞, which contains the graves of thirty-four British soldiers from 1940 and of twenty-five airmen, nearly all from Bomber Command, from later years.

St Pol British Cemetery ㉟, just by the road to Doullens, has 258 graves from the First World War and six from the Second World War. Among the first burials were sixteen Australian soldiers of the 58th (Victoria) Battalion who were killed by a long-range shell at St Pol Station on 27 March 1918, when their division was being transferred to the Somme to help stem the German offensive there. This cemetery has a link with the Unknown Soldier who was buried in Westminster Abbey in November 1920. The remains of four unidentified British servicemen were brought to St Pol from the battlefields of Ypres, Arras, the Somme and the Aisne and placed in the temporary chapel near this cemetery. The recovery parties then departed and an officer, who did not know which bodies had come from which battlefields, made a final random choice. What happened to the remaining three bodies is a little mystery. For many years it was assumed that they were buried in this cemetery, but that cannot be so; there are only two unidentified graves in the First

World War rows, one among the Australians killed at St Pol Station and one in another wartime row; there are none among the later burials in the cemetery. A more likely story has recently emerged – that, to maintain secrecy, the three bodies were taken by night to be buried in a shallow grave somewhere along the Bapaume Road on the Somme, so that they could be discovered by one of the routine search parties working in that area. This somewhat casual treatment of the bodies which came so close to being selected as the Unknown Soldier contrasts with the French process which took place at Verdun. One of eight bodies was chosen to be buried under the Arc de Triomphe in Paris; the other seven are buried in a specially honoured plot in a military cemetery.

The village of Siracourt contains another of those spectacular and ingenious V-weapons constructions. The *Siracourt Bunker* ㊱ was a huge bomb-proof store outside the central doorway of which a V-1 flying-bomb launching ramp pointed towards England. The site was bombed many times but it did come into operational use, although only at a reduced rate of firing, and it was soon overrun by the Allied advance from Normandy. It was the only one of the four massive V-weapon structures in the Pas-de-Calais which brought the Germans any return. The great bunker – 200 paces along the length of its roof and 50 paces wide – remains almost intact and is not commercialized. The entrance is at the northern end of the site. The only major damage caused by the bombing is where one of No. 617 Squadron's Tallboy bombs has ruptured and lifted a section at the edge of the roof. The village was completely destroyed by the bombing, but the inhabitants had all been evacuated earlier. Every building is of a post-war style more reminiscent of the rebuilt villages destroyed in Normandy than of those in this part of France.

On the north-eastern side of the town of Frévent is *St Hilaire Cemetery and Extension* ㊲, which has 515 British graves from the First World War and twelve from the Second World War. Most of the graves are of men who died of wounds and a large number are from the German offensives in 1918. The extension contains many pilots' graves, including that of Sergeant S. J. Mitchell of No. 2 Squadron, who died on 4 April 1918 after a crash; he had been awarded one of the first two Air Force Medals (the RAF had only been born four days earlier), but it has not been possible to find out

13 V-1 bunker at Siracourt, showing damage caused by a Tallboy bomb. Photographs taken from the ground do not show the huge scale of the construction; the section of roof in the background is 100 yards long and 12 feet thick.

how Mitchell won his medal. Another of the dead pilots was Captain S. W. Rosevear, a naval pilot of No. 201 Squadron, who crashed on a practice flight. Rosevear, a Canadian, was a successful pilot who had been credited with the destruction of twenty-three German planes.

Visitors choosing the Arras–Bapaume road for their final approach to the Somme pass through part of the Arras battlefield. The description of this is beyond the scope of this book but a list of the principal visits in this area may be helpful.

Notre Dame de Lorette French National Cemetery ㊳ has 20,000 graves in the cemetery and 20,000 unknown bodies in the ossuary; there is also a visitors centre and a museum. This place was the scene of a costly French offensive in May 1915.

Vimy Ridge Canadian Memorial ㊴ is where the Canadian Corps captured the prominent ridge on the first day of the Battle of Arras in April 1917. The memorial lists the names of 11,T84 Canadians who died in France and have no known grave. There is also a visitors centre and there are preserved trenches and tunnels, but the tunnels are not open during the winter.

14 The Canadian Memorial on Vimy Ridge, probably the most impressive war memorial on the Western Front.

Neuville St Vaast German Cemetery ㊵ contains the remains of no less than 44,833 German bodies in burial plots and mass graves.

The historic centre of Arras ㊶ is full of interest, including the extensive tunnels which were used during the First World War (guided tours start at the Hôtel de Ville). Arras has a good selection of hotels for those who cannot book rooms closer to the Somme battlefields.

Faubourg d'Amiens British Cemetery and Memorial ㊷ contains the graves of 2,647 British soldiers, most of whom died of wounds; there are also memorial walls to 35,928 men of the Third Army who died on the Arras front and have no known graves and a smaller memorial for British airmen with no known graves. The nearby *Mur des Fusilées* is an impressive memorial at the place where members of the Resistance were executed in the Second World War.

The modern Commonwealth War Graves Commission offices and workshops at Beaurains ㊸ make visitors welcome, particularly if they phone in advance; the current number is 21.230324.

Bailleulmont Communal Cemetery ㊹ contains the well-known grave of Private A. Ingham of the 18th Manchesters who was executed here in December 1916 for desertion. His family chose '*Shot at Dawn*' as part of their inscription on the headstone.

2 · THE 1916 AREA

The Germans came to this part of the Somme on 29 August 1914 when IV Reserve Corps of von Kluck's First Army, which had been in action against the British at Le Cateau three days earlier, swept through the area from the east, marching along the line Combles–Guillemont–Montauban–Mametz–Fricourt and reaching Albert; the few French troops present were brushed aside. The Germans went on to Amiens before turning south towards Paris. But they were diverted from that prize, held on the Marne, and fell back to the Somme where a stable line was established. Few of the trenches which the French and German soldiers dug on that line would change hands during the next year and a half. The French trenches became known as 'the old front line', a phrase which will often be used in the description of this area.

After their costly offensives in the first half of 1915, the French asked the growing British forces to take over part of their line. A new British army – the Third Army – was formed on 18 July and

Divisions	Sector	Date first units into trenches		
48th (S. Midland)	Foncquevillers to north of Serre	20 July	1/5th Gloucesters 1/8 Worcesters 1/4th Oxford and Bucks	
4th	Serre to Beaumont-Hamel	24 July	1st King's Own 2nd Essex	
51st (Highland)	Thiepval to La Boisselle	30 July	1/6th Seaforths 1/8th Argylls	
5th	Bécourt to R. Somme	2 August	1st Norfolks 1st Bedfords	

four divisions relieved the French on a seventeen-mile sector north of the River Somme. The table opposite shows how the take-over occurred from north to south. The first man to die was Private E. Whitlock of the 1/4th Oxford and Bucks Light Infantry; he was an Oxfordshire man, from Banbury, and was killed by an early-morning shell two days after his unit took over the French trenches. The first officer to die was another South Midland Territorial, Captain A. G. Rollaston of the 1/7th Worcesters, from Dudley, who died of wounds on 30 July.

The 18th (Eastern) Division also arrived, directly from England, to commence a remarkable connection with the Somme which would be unrivalled by any other British division. Its units sent small parties of men for 'trench instruction' with the 5th and 51st Divisions before taking over full responsibility for the Mametz–Fricourt section of the line on 22 August. Three of these early divisions – the 4th, 18th and 48th – would remain on the Somme for the next eleven months and would take part in the opening of the 1916 battle.

These first British troops on the Somme were delighted with the

15 The grave of Private Whitlock, the first British soldier to die on the Somme front.

conditions found there. This was a 'cushy' sector, where French and German soldiers had operated a 'live and let live' policy. There were deep, dry trenches with good dug-outs, unlike the waterlogged area of Flanders. There was no devastated zone, only green country-side right up to the trenches with near-intact villages immediately in the rear. French civilians were friendly. Unit histories and war diaries give some examples of life in the Somme trenches at this time. At Hébuterne the French handed over a milking cow in a field just behind the trenches and the 1/5th Gloucesters and the 1/4th Oxford and Bucks took it in turn to obtain fresh milk while they were holding the trenches – until the cow died from over-milking. The 18th Division found a plot of potatoes in No Man's Land which was raided regularly. Men swam in the River Somme right up to the front line and the 5th Division recorded that fishing was possible at Fargny Mill which was actually part of the front line.

But the quiet times and dry conditions did not last. The official British attitude to trench warfare was more vigorous; artillery fire, sniping, raiding and mining warfare underneath opposing trenches increased. Casualties mounted. The British units on the Somme suffered 7,708 casualties up to the end of 1915, a daily loss of forty-eight men, not a heavy rate by British standards but more than the French had suffered. The 18th Division records three incidents in December: a brigade commander hit by machine-gun fire while walking in the open behind the trenches; nineteen men killed and twenty-two wounded by a German mine exploding under the Tambour trenches at Fricourt; and nineteen men taken prisoner when a German raiding party surprised them in a dug-out. The 51st Division describes how an officer was killed while attempting to capture a German flag in No Man's Land and how Martinsart was bombed by a German aeroplane, a most surprising occurrence at that time. Then came winter and the Somme mud which was found to be of a particularly tenacious nature. Water was waist high in some of the 51st Division's trenches and the Germans could be heard splashing about in theirs. Twenty men of the 2nd King's Own Yorkshire Light Infantry died when a large dug-out near Carnoy collapsed.

The British Third Army ceased to be responsible for the Somme sector when General Sir Henry Rawlinson's newly formed Fourth Army Headquarters arrived in March 1916. New plans were now afoot for a major Allied offensive to be launched astride the River Somme later in the year and the British forces were reinforced in readiness for this. The four divisions which had taken over from the French in 1915 were increased to sixteen, with three more infantry divisions and three cavalry divisions in General Gough's Reserve Army which stood immediately in the rear, ready to exploit the hoped-for breakthrough. A further two divisions of the Third Army were to make a diversionary attack on the northern flank of the main British offensive and the French provided five divisions for their attack in the south; this made over half a million men ready to attack the Germans.

The battle opened at 7.30 a.m. on 1 July. The French did well but it was a disastrous day for the British. A faulty tactical plan drawn up by General Rawlinson and his staff left the attacking British infantry exposed in No Man's Land to German machine-gun teams who had survived the week-long preliminary bombardment in deep dug-outs of which the British should have been aware. The attacking units suffered 57,470 casualties that day – 21,392 killed, died of wounds or missing, 35,493 wounded and 585 prisoners of war. On only a quarter of the front attacked was there any advance. These are the worst casualties in the history of the British Army.[1] All hopes of a breakthrough faded, but the British and French persisted with what became a battle of attrition, hoping to wear down the Germans by colossal artillery bombardments followed by infantry attacks. The Germans resisted strongly, giving not a yard of ground willingly.

The Somme battle of 1916 passed into history as epitomizing a pitched battle of almost unimaginable intensity and it became, particularly for the British Empire, a haunting memory of the worst horrors of the First World War. The ceremonies at the Thiepval Memorial and on the old front line at a mine crater at La Boisselle still draw hundreds of people on 1 July each year. The battle lasted until mid-November. All but three of the sixty-four British Empire infantry divisions on the Western Front carried out attacks, some of them two or three times. The French, badly weakened at Verdun earlier in the year, used between twenty-five and thirty of their 100

[1] Martin Middlebrook's *The First Day on the Somme* (London: Allen Lane, 1971; Penguin, 1984) describes the battle of 1 July 1916 in detail.

divisions, the Germans ninety-five out of 121 on the Western Front. The exact number of casualties was never established, but the British suffered more than 400,000, the French about 200,000, the Germans 600,000 or more. The maximum British advance was less than seven miles, but the amount of ground gained was not the criterion for judging whether that determinedly sustained offensive was worthwhile. The question was, did the mainly British offensive weaken the German Army sufficiently to be worth the cost? That argument will never be settled.

The British and French troops spent a bleak winter manning makeshift trenches. The Germans were building a strong new line – the Hindenburg Line – fifteen miles to the east. They started falling back to this in March 1917, leaving the 1916 battlefield completely in Allied hands, an inhospitable area with a complete lack of habitation and its pre-war roads almost non-existent. The war returned to the Somme in March 1918 when the German spring offensive routed the British and French units at the junction of their armies and swept on for over thirty miles in just over two weeks. The whole of the 1916 battlefield fell in little more than one day and areas which had been safely in the rear in 1916 passed into German hands. The story of those critical battles of 1918 will be told in more detail later; suffice it to say that British troops fought and died again on the 1916 battlefield, but there are few permanent marks of the later battles other than small numbers of graves from that year in the 1916 cemeteries.

The Germans came again in 1940 when the 1st and 2nd Panzer Divisions of General Guderian's XIX Panzer Corps motored across the 1916 battlefield from the east on 20 May almost without opposition. The centre line of 1st Panzer's advance was along a road which many battlefield tourers take, the road from Péronne to Albert, past the First World War cemeteries at Maricourt, Mametz and Fricourt. 2nd Panzer followed the same route as had von Kluck's sweating infantry in August 1914, Combles–Guillemont–Montauban, before swinging round to the north of Albert. The only opposition was offered by a half-trained battalion of British Territorials which made a stand lasting less than an hour at Albert. The German tanks were in Amiens and Abbeville by nightfall, having covered forty miles in fourteen hours, one of the great advances of armoured warfare. Cemeteries at Albert and in the surrounding villages contain the graves of twenty-seven British soldiers and six airmen who died in those actions and a roadside memorial records the deaths of two French soldiers.

The next four years were spent under German occupation. Most of the War Graves Commission gardeners had been evacuated and the cemeteries were mostly left to nature. The Liberation which came after the Allied break-out from Normandy in 1944 was a swift, dramatic and joyous event for the French. On 31 August, the British Guards Armoured Division crossed some bridges over the Somme in the Corbie area which had been secured by French Resistance men who prevented the demolition of the bridges. This division was part of XXX Corps, commanded by the dashing Lieutenant-General Sir Brian Horrocks. German opposition was collapsing and Horrocks urged the Guards to press on towards Brussels as fast as they could. Armoured cars, tanks and lorried infantry raced north-westwards, passing north of Albert, past the First World War cemeteries on the Serre Road, on to Arras and were at Douai by nightfall, having advanced fifty miles and taken 2,000 German prisoners in a day's march that rivalled the German tank dash of May 1940. There is a crossroads north of Albert through which three armies moved in famous actions, that of Henry V on the way to Agincourt in 1415, Guderian's Panzers on their way to Abbeville in May 1940 and the Guards Armoured Division on that day in 1944. By coincidence, the only little engagement in this area during the Liberation was at Albert, just as it had been in May 1940. A small force sent to deal with the Germans at Albert met a commander there who was not yet ready to surrender; some casualties were suffered and Albert was not liberated until the following day, but the freeing of this whole area appears to have been achieved at the cost of only six British soldiers killed and some others wounded.

The 1916 battlefield is probably the most popular one in France for British visitors, who are drawn both by the memory of the battle and by the wealth of things to see. There are 165 cemeteries and seventy-four memorials on the actual 1916 battlefield and in the immediate rear of it. Most of these are British; there are only ten French and German cemeteries in the whole of the combined British and French parts of the 1916 battlefield. One aspect of the British cemeteries is remarkable. British cemeteries in many other parts of France often contain plots of German graves, but not on the 1916 battlefield where a policy seems to have been implemented to

16 Soldiers' wartime cemetery names retained in the permanent cemeteries.

remove all the German graves and leave the area as 'British' as possible.

It is a wonderfully quiet area, having reverted almost entirely to agriculture. The farms are large ones, so that the farmhouses are well separated, leaving extensive areas completely open, unlike the Ypres Salient where a small farmhouse is never far away. There are woods and streams; the countryside is not beautiful but it is pleasant. Only one main road crosses the area; the remaining roads have no traffic problems. The only motorway passes down the eastern extremity of the battlefield. The River Somme does not run through the British sector but is on the southern edge. It is the River Ancre, little more than a stream, which flows through the British battlefield. If the French had not fought on the other side of the Somme in 1916, the battle of that year would probably have been named after the Ancre. The natural centre for touring is the town of Albert from which all parts of the 1916 battlefield can be reached in less than half an hour.

The 1916 area will be described by splitting the area into thirteen geographical sections, each with a map. Every place where there is something for the visitor to see will be marked on the maps and described in the text together with the story of how the battle developed at each place. A few recommendations will be made, but visitors will mostly be left to make their own choices of where to go. The northern fringes of the 1916 fighting which are in the Pas-de-Calais will be included, but there is some overlap in the south between the French 1916 sector and the main 1918 fighting; whatever of 1916 is missed in that part will be described later in the book. The descriptions will start at the northern end of the old front line, at Foncquevillers, appropriately enough because it was to this sector that the first British troops came in 1915. The old front line from which the attack on the first day of the 1916 battle took place will then be followed down to the junction with the French, after which the area into which the battle spread in succeeding months will be covered and, finally, the areas behind the battlefield in the south and west will be described.

*

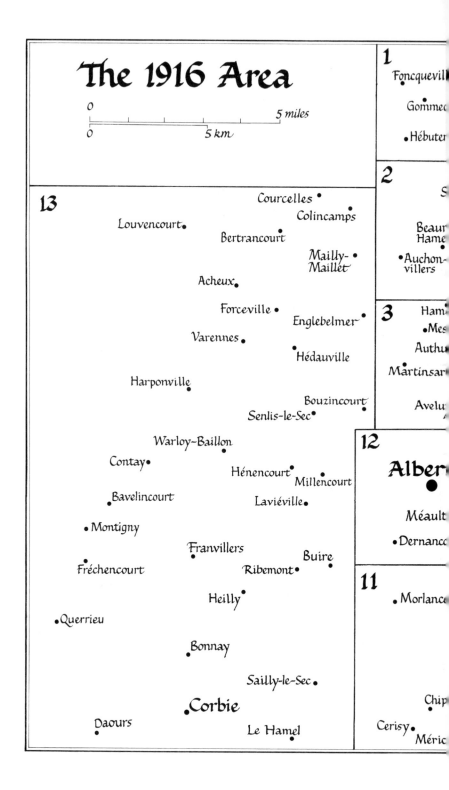

The 1916 Area

0   5 *miles*

0   5 *km*

1

Foncquevil

Gommec

• Hébuter

2

S

Beaur
Hame

• Auchon-
villers

3

Ham

• Mes

Authu

Martinsar

Avelu

13

Courcelles •

Colincamps

Louvencourt •

Bertrancourt

Mailly-
Maillet •

Acheux •

Forceville •

Englebelmer •

Varennes •

Hédauville

Harponville

Bouzincourt

Senlis-le-Sec •

Warloy–Baillon

Contay •

Hénencourt •

Millencourt

Bavelincourt

Laviéville •

• Montigny

Franvillers

Buire

Fréchencourt

Ribemont •

12

Alber

●

Méault

• Dernanc

11

• Morlance

Heilly

• Querrieu

Bonnay

Sailly-le-Sec •

Corbie

Daours

Le Hamel

Chip

Cerisy •

Méric

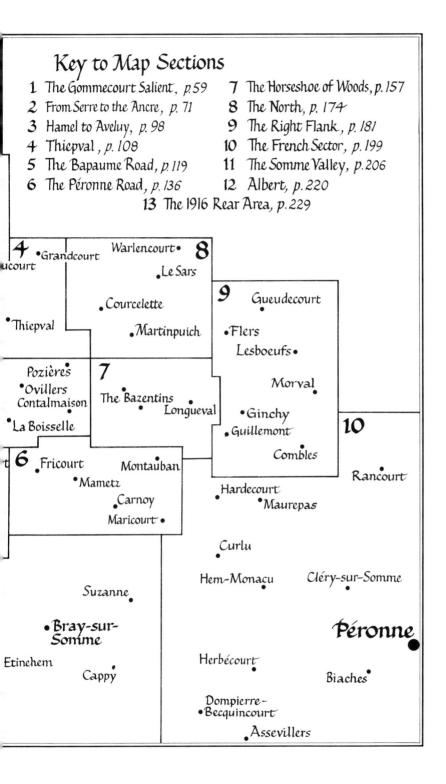

Key to Map Sections

1 The Gommecourt Salient, p.59
2 From Serre to the Ancre, p. 71
3 Hamel to Aveluy, p. 98
4 Thiepval, p.108
5 The Bapaume Road, p.119
6 The Péronne Road, p.136
7 The Horseshoe of Woods, p. 157
8 The North, p. 174
9 The Right Flank, p. 181
10 The French Sector, p.199
11 The Somme Valley, p.206
12 Albert, p.220
13 The 1916 Rear Area, p.229

4
•Grandcourt   Warlencourt• **8**
ucourt   .Le Sars

•Thiepval   .Courcelette   **9**   Gueudecourt
                .Martinpuich   •Flers
                                   Lesboeufs•

Pozières
•Ovillers   **7**   Morval
Contalmaison   The Bazentins •   •Ginchy
•La Boisselle   Longueval   .Guillemont   **10**
                                          Combles

t **6** •Fricourt   Montauban   Rancourt•
    •Mametz
      .Carnoy   Hardecourt
      Maricourt •   •Maurepas

                    Curlu
                     •

            Hem-Monacu   Cléry-sur-Somme
               •   •
    Suzanne
        •
•Bray-sur-
  Somme   **Péronne**
                                                  ●
Etinehem   Herbécourt
       Cappy   •   Biaches•

          Dompierre-
        •Becquincourt
            .Assevillers

THE GOMMECOURT SALIENT

A triangle of villages here formed a distinct sector of the 1916 front, Gommecourt with its château and park being in German hands and Foncquevillers and Hébuterne in British. The trench lines had been unchanged since October 1914. This was where the 48th (South Midland) Division were the first British troops to take over from the French on the Somme in July 1915, but this division had now moved a mile or so to the south, handing over to two further Territorial divisions – the 46th (North Midland) and 56th (London). The 46th Division held Foncquevillers and the trenches in front of that village and the 56th Division did the same at Hébuterne.

The German trenches jutted out in a prominent salient round the edge of Gommecourt Park and the trench at the point of the park was actually the most westerly post of all the Imperial German forces. Just behind the angle of trench there stood a prominent oak tree which the Germans called *die Kaisereiche* – the Kaiser's Oak. Because of the prominence of the salient, the German defences here, constructed and perfected over twenty undisturbed months, were very strong, with thick belts of barbed wire, several lines of inter-locking trenches, machine-gun posts and deep dug-outs, although this is a description which can be applied to many sectors of the German line on the Somme. At Gommecourt, the Germans also used the shape of the salient to construct an inner defence work called the Kern Redoubt around the south end of the village and part of the park. This all-round defence position would make it difficult for attacking troops who penetrated the outer defences to capture the village.

The British decided to attack at Gommecourt on the opening day of the 1916 battle, partly to cut off the awkward salient into their line but also to provide a major diversion at a point north of the main British attack front. This diversionary attack was controlled by the Third Army and preparations were to be made as obvious as possible to draw German attention away from the main attack by the Fourth Army. The salient was to be attacked not frontally but by each of the British divisions from a flank. The 56th Division had ingeniously dug a new front trench by night to reduce the width of No Man's Land to be covered; the week-long artillery preparation

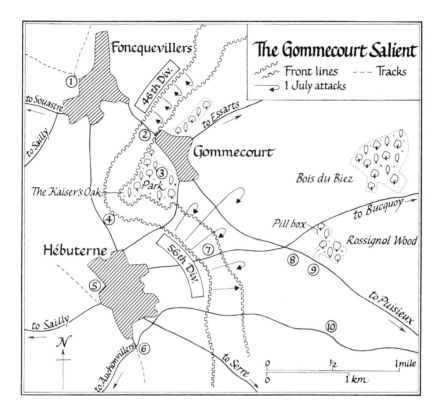

The Gommecourt Salient

Front lines   - - - Tracks
1 July attacks

Foncquevillers

46th Div.

to Souastre
to Sailly
to Essarts

Gommecourt

Bois du Biez

The Kaiser's Oak
Park

to Bucquoy

Pill box

Rossignol Wood

Hébuterne

56th Div.

to Puisieux

to Sailly

N

to Auchonvillers

to Serre

0   ½   1 mile
0   1 km

here was effective and much of the German barbed wire was destroyed. Three lines of trenches were captured and one small party even reached round to the back of Gommecourt. But the 46th Division's attack on the northern flank failed, with only a few men getting into the German trenches and quickly being wiped out there. The Germans concentrated their counter-attacks on the London troops, who were steadily forced back and eventually pushed out of the German trenches. The two divisions suffered 6,769 casualties, including 2,765 men killed and missing; nearly two-thirds of these casualties were in the 56th Division. The German casualties were 1,241, with 427 dead. The diversion had no effect upon the outcome of the main battle to the south. The commander of the 46th Division was sacked for failing to press his attack more strongly.

The Germans buried nearly 1,400 men who died in or near their trenches and the British buried others at Foncquevillers and

Hébuterne, but the bodies of the dead in No Man's Land had to remain in the open until February 1917 when the Germans withdrew. By chance, the 46th Division was back in this sector at that time and had the melancholy task of burying its own dead. Ten small battlefield cemeteries were made in the old No Man's Land. The Germans returned in 1918 when their March offensive reached the edge of Hébuterne but were halted there by the timely arrival and stout defence of the New Zealand Division which remained to hold the sector running south from Hébuterne for several months.

The graves in the battlefield cemeteries were brought together into two concentration cemeteries after the war, but the pattern of the permanent cemeteries neatly reflected the actions of the British units which fought here, with Foncquevillers and Hébuterne each having a comrades cemetery in the rear of the village and a concentration cemetery on the old No Man's Land where the 1 July 1916 attacks took place. The villages were rebuilt after the war and little has changed in this quiet area since the 1920s. It is a compact little sector, with its own unique story.

Foncquevillers

This village was the forward base of the 46th (North Midland) Division before and during the July 1916 fighting and was 'adopted' by the city of Derby in the post-war period when many British cities and towns made links with places where their men had suffered particularly heavy casualties.

Foncquevillers Military Cemetery ① is a quiet spot at the back of the village and just over half a mile from the old front-line trenches. It already contained the graves of 325 French soldiers when the British took over the cemetery in 1915 and the British continued to use the cemetery until 1917 when the Germans withdrew. The men killed in the British trenches or dying of wounds on 1 July 1916 were buried in one mass grave, in Plot 1, Row L, at the left rear of the cemetery. The French graves were removed after the war, leaving the empty area on the left near the lane. The British brought in seventy-four scattered graves but this did not spoil the 'comrades' character of the wartime cemetery. The 653 First World War graves were joined by those of five Canadian airmen killed when their Halifax bomber, of No. 427 Squadron, was shot down in June 1944 in a raid on a railway target at Arras; their graves are just inside the cemetery on the left.

In the third row back just inside the entrance on the right is the Victoria Cross headstone of Captain J. L. Green, Medical Officer of the 1/5th Sherwood Foresters, who was wounded on 1 July 1916 but still went up to the German barbed wire to rescue another wounded officer who had been caught while trying to cut a way through the entanglement. After pulling this officer into a nearby shell hole and dressing his wounds, Captain Green then dragged him back to the British trenches but was killed just before reaching safety. The officer he was helping died three days later.

Two rows in front of Captain Green's grave is that of Lieutenant-Colonel C. F. G. Humphries whose headstone records an impressive set of decorations – DSO, MC and Bar, and DCM – earned in a long and unusual war record. This New Zealander did not serve with his own country's units but, starting as a private, appears to have progressively served in the Army Service Corps, the Manchesters, the Highland Light Infantry, the Duke of Cornwall's Light Infantry, the Labour Corps (probably while recovering from wounds) and finally commanding the 1st Norfolks with whom he was killed in August 1918 when he was hit by shell fire in an attack on Achiet-le-Petit which is six miles away. His adjutant, Captain G. C. Tyler, was also killed and occupies the next grave.

Another grave worthy of mention is that of Private Thomas Palmer of the 1/4th Leicesters, who was killed in February 1917. He is buried in Row C of Plot 2, near the top right corner of the cemetery. One of his parents chose this moving inscription for his grave: *Will some kind hand in a foreign land place a flower on my son's grave.*

Gommecourt

On the road from Foncquevillers to Gommecourt is *Gommecourt Wood New Cemetery* ②. The 'New' in the title and the formal, regular layout of its plots in rows of ten graves illustrate the post-war concentration nature of the cemetery. But the contents and location are most appropriate to and in sympathy with what happened here. It is situated on a raised bank looking straight up the

No Man's Land where the 46th (North Midland) Division attacked on 1 July 1916 and a large proportion of the dead were from that division. A total of 739 men were buried here; the names of 464 of them could not be identified but badges and buttons of many of the bodies showed that they were from battalions in the division and their headstones have the badges of their regiments, mainly Notts and Derby (Sherwood Foresters) and North and South Staffords. In Plot 2, Row B, is buried Lieutenant-Colonel C. E. Boote, 1/5th North Staffords, one of the three battalion commanders killed on the battlefield; the other two may be among the unidentified graves. Set in the cemetery wall, close to the near right corner, is a metal memorial to the 46th Division's members 'who fell in front of Gommecourt 1st July 1916 and from that date to March 1917'.

This is an important and interesting cemetery, looking out as it does over the place where this Territorial division suffered so heavily in that forlorn attack on the first day of the battle. The row of electricity pylons on the left roughly coincides with the British front-line trench and the German trenches were a similar distance away on the right. The cemetery also contains the grave of Private E. Whitlock of the Oxford and Bucks Light Infantry who was the first man to die when British troops moved to the Somme in July 1915; his body was brought from its original burial place near Hébuterne and is now buried near the back of the cemetery on the right, in Plot 4, Row B. Also buried in the cemetery are fifty-six New Zealand soldiers who fought here in 1918.

Gommecourt village is small and quiet. It was adopted by Wolverhampton in the 1920s. There are no military cemeteries in the village; the German equivalents of comrades cemeteries were all removed after the war. The only memorial is the local one which shows that more civilians died locally when the village was the scene of fighting in 1914 than soldier sons were killed at the front in the next four years. The same memorial records the name of a later Mayor, a Second World War Resistance man betrayed to the Germans and executed at Arras. The remains of many of the trenches defending the village are still to be seen; access to these will require the ability to negotiate barbed-wire fences. The park is now more thickly covered in trees than it was in 1916. A deep section of trench of the *Kern Redoubt* ③ can clearly be seen inside its north-eastern corner and the front-line trench all round the western side of the park can be traced, with communication trenches running

17 British Observation Post overlooking Gommecourt Park.

back towards the village. The location of the point of the wood where the Kaiser's Oak once stood is not easy to establish; it is a case of not being able to see the wood for the trees when you stand there.

Hébuterne

In a grass field just off the road from Foncquevillers, among some bushes, can be found a well-constructed concrete *Observation Post* ④ or machine-gun post. It is close to the 'old front line' of 1915–16 but was actually constructed in the summer of 1918 by the 42nd Division's Royal Engineers as part of the 'Purple Line' of defences constructed in case the Germans attacked again after the spring offensive had been brought to a halt on the eastern side of Gommecourt Park. For twenty years I believed that this was one of the observation posts constructed here by the 48th Division after they took over the line from the French in 1915, only to be informed by an observation-post expert, Peter Oldham, of my error after the first edition of this book was published. Such are the hazards of attempting to describe places where more than one battle was fought.

Hébuterne is another quiet village; it was adopted by Evesham after the war because of its association with the Worcestershire battalions of the South Midland Division which came here in 1915. *Hébuterne Military Cemetery* ⑤ is reached by a tree-lined track and then a path between a farmyard and a pasture on the 'safe' side of the village. On my visit I noted its 'very peaceful setting'. It is a perfect example of a comrades cemetery. It was started by the South Midland units when they took over here from the French in 1915. Other divisions continued to use this cemetery, particularly the 56th (London) which suffered so heavily on the first day of the 1916 battle. There are 735 graves; no burials took place after the war so the contents of the cemetery are exactly as it was left by the soldiers in 1918.

The graves are in irregular rows or in scattered groups, because this was an orchard at the time and the dead were buried among the trees. A particularly sad row of graves is Row M of Plot 4, to the left of the Stone of Remembrance, where sixty-one dead of 1 July 1916 were buried so close together in a mass grave that there is only room for twenty-one shared headstones. I noted two sad personal inscriptions among them. Rifleman C. H. S. Ravenscroft's mother chose *One less at home, one more in Heaven,* and that on Gunner A. B. Parry's grave is *Among the rest 'my boy'.* Fifty-three New Zealand graves of 1918 were placed wherever gaps could be found among the earlier graves. One of the New Zealanders, Captain R. J. S. Seddon (Plot 1, Row F), was the son of a former New Zealand Prime Minister.

At the south end of the village is *Hébuterne Communal Cemetery* ⑥, where French units started burying their dead in October 1914 and the British used it in 1915 to bury three men of the Royal Warwicks before starting the larger cemetery in the orchard behind the village. A few more British burials took place later in the war, including a communal grave for seven artillerymen killed one night in October 1916 when their nearby telephone post was subjected to a sudden bombardment of shrapnel and gas shells. One French soldier, probably a local man, died on Armistice Day 1918. There are fifty-six British and fifty-four French soldiers' graves here.

When the Germans withdrew from this area in 1917, British troops collected the dead of the 56th (London) Division who had lain out on the battlefield since the previous July and buried them in four small cemeteries in the old No Man's Land. The second of these cemeteries, *Gommecourt British Cemetery No. 2* ⑦, originally had just four rows containing 101 graves. The present-day cemetery has the same name but contains 1,222 graves from the other local battlefield cemeteries and from areas to the east where fighting took place in 1917 and 1918. The result is a typical concentration cemetery built around the original wartime plot, but the cemetery is not too large and in a pleasant setting, and the graves are mostly of men who died close by. It is probable that a high proportion of the 681 'unknowns' were London men who died in No Man's Land on 1 July 1916. Two brothers, Riflemen H. E. and P. J. Bassett of the Queen Victoria's Rifles, are buried together in the middle of Plot 3, Row B, four rows inside the cemetery on the right. Unfortunately the ground of this part of the 1 July battlefield is of a rolling nature and cannot be as clearly viewed from one place as can the 46th Division's battlefield from the cemetery there.

Just to the east is an interesting little group of visits. The first of two small roadside cemeteries is *Rossignol Wood Cemetery* ⑧, which contains three distinct groups of graves reflecting the way fighting swept back and forth over this area during the war. The first graves are from an incident which took place in the early hours of 14 March 1917 when an attack was ordered here to hurry on the German retirement. The 1/5th and 1/6th North Staffords, from the same 46th Division which suffered heavily near here in July 1916, were rushed into a badly prepared attack on a wet night against a well-defended German position on the edge of Rossignol Wood. The attack failed and 133 men were killed or were missing. Thirty-four of them, including two company commanders and a company sergeant-major, were later buried in what are now the first two rows inside the cemetery. The Germans were back again in 1918 and seventy of their dead were buried on the left-hand side of the cemetery. Finally, seven New Zealanders from August 1918 were buried in the far right corner. This may be the only British war cemetery in which German graves outnumber British. If the cemetery had been inside the Somme boundary, which is just a mile away, the German graves would probably have been removed in

18 Rossignol Wood Cemetery – more German graves than British.

pursuance of the policy which seems to have been operated that British cemeteries in the area of the 1916 Somme battle would be cleared of German graves.

A few yards further on is *Owl Trench Cemetery* ⑨, where the dead of another forlorn attack on Rossignol Wood are buried. This attempt was at dawn on 27 February 1917 and was carried out by the 16th West Yorks (the 1st Bradford Pals). Their attack also failed. Two officers and 129 men were killed or were missing; both officers and forty-four of their men were buried in one mass grave; the bodies of seven unidentified King's Own Yorkshire Light Infantry men are in a shorter row.

Looking out over these cemeteries is Rossignol Wood, exactly as it was in those wartime years, dominating the low ground towards Hébuterne. The wood was a key point in the German defences which easily held off the attacks made on it in 1917. When the German advance was halted here in 1918, it again became part of their front line. It was in this area that Chaplain T. B. Hardy, VC, DSO, MC, won his Victoria Cross, the citation for which mentions four occasions when he fetched wounded men in from close to German positions. One of these, on 5 April 1918, was in Rossignol Wood when the 8th Lincolns made an attack but were driven back from the wood, leaving behind many wounded. Padre Hardy, helped by a sergeant, rescued one of the wounded men from a position very close to a German pillbox. He died of wounds later in the year at Rouen, the most decorated British army chaplain of the First World War. Just inside the south-west face of the wood, 120 paces from the road to Bucquoy, can be found the remains of a German pillbox, almost certainly the one where Padre Hardy rescued his wounded man.

On a parallel road to the south, between Hébuterne and Puisieux, is a *Demarcation Stone* ⑩ , one of the few surviving ones marking the limit of the German advance on the Somme in 1918. This one is out of position; the Germans were stopped by New Zealand and English troops three-quarters of a mile nearer to Hébuterne. The stone has also been damaged and it is not possible to read on the base the name of who sponsored it, but the French helmet on the top and the items of equipment around the sides are in good condition.

FROM SERRE TO THE ANCRE

The northern end of the main 1916 Somme battlefield is one of the most popular parts of the old Western Front. This section of the book will describe the battlefield there on a frontage of nearly four miles and the places immediately in the British rear. It is a large area but difficult to subdivide. There is a greater density of military cemeteries, memorials and other reminders of battle here than in any other part of the Somme, perhaps of the whole Western Front. And yet there were only two days of major action here in 1916, on 1 July and 13 November, the first and almost the last days of the battle of that year.

There was little exceptional about this area before July 1916. The French had made an attack on the northern part of it in June 1915 and pressed the Germans back a few hundred yards. The British took over soon afterwards and held the line without experiencing any major action for nearly a year. But then came a dense con-centrating of British troops and guns and preparation work for the opening of the 1916 battle. The solitary 4th Division which had held the whole of this sector on the British take-over in 1915 was still here, but joined now by the 29th, 31st and 48th Divisions. This was the area of Lieutenant-General Hunter-Weston's VIII Corps. Both he and his corps headquarters were new to the Western Front, having recently arrived after the evacuation at Gallipoli. The task of this corps was to capture the German front- and second-line trench systems and make a secure flank north of the River Ancre for the hoped-for breakthrough further south. Hunter-Weston's divisions needed to make an advance of more than two miles and capture the villages of Serre, Beaumont-Hamel and Beaucourt. Approximately 30,000 British infantry supported by more than 300 guns were available for the attack, outnumbering the Germans facing them by about four to one.

The attack on 1 July was a complete disaster all along this front. The overall Fourth Army plan was faulty, based as it was on the assumption that the week-long artillery bombardment would destroy the German barbed wire and deep dug-outs. The attacking infantry were ordered not to leave their trenches before Zero Hour and then to advance steadily in lines across No Man's Land, carrying heavy loads of reserve ammunition and trench stores. But the Germans survived the bombardment. Their machine-gunners and riflemen emerged from the dug-outs and caught the British infantry in the open spaces of No Man's Land. Ironically and tragically, the French had captured one of the deep dug-outs in their attack the previous year and this was now being used by British front-line troops who were well aware of the German dug-outs' ability to resist the heaviest of shelling. Much of the German barbed wire also survived the bombardment.

But Lieutenant-General Hunter-Weston made further errors which compounded the tragedy. On the front of the 31st Division facing Serre, Royal Engineer Tunnelling Companies, assisted by nearly 2,000 infantrymen, many of them North Country miners, had dug nine 'Russian Saps' out into No Man's Land almost up to the German barbed wire. These were shallow tunnels just below the surface of No Man's Land; attacking infantry could debouch from their exits close to the enemy trenches when the barrage lifted and catch the Germans still in their dug-outs. *Not one of these was used on the day of the attack.* The Royal Engineers had also tunnelled under a German strong-point near Beaumont-Hamel and were ready to detonate the explosive charge there. Corps commanders who had similar mines in sectors further south decided that their mines should be exploded two minutes before the infantry attacked; Hunter-Weston decided that his should be blown a full ten minutes in advance. This was successfully done but the timing of it alerted the German defenders over a wide area. The German artillery opened fire on the packed British trenches and the German infantry made ready to dash up their dug-out steps. The British were mowed down in No Man's Land all along this sector; only a few reached the German trenches and the attack quickly broke down. Only one small party of attackers was still in the German trenches at the end of the day and even that small gain was abandoned next morning. The total casualties of the attacking divisions were 14,468, made up of 5,415 men killed, 8,926 wounded and 127 becoming prisoners; German casualties were only one twelfth of those figures.

Operations were immediately halted and this became a quiet sector while the main battle raged to the south. There were some command changes. Lieutenant-General Hunter-Weston and his corps headquarters were moved away to the north; he went home on leave in October to fight and win a parliamentary by-election, but he returned to the front and continued in command of VIII Corps for the remainder of the war. The area passed out of General Rawlinson's Fourth Army control and came under General Gough's newly formed Fifth Army. Then, in the closing days of the Somme offensive, the second day of fighting here came on 13 November when four divisions attacked again where three had failed on 1 July. This operation was better handled than the earlier one but still only gained about half of its objectives. The north, opposite Serre, was again the scene of failure; the 51st (Highland) Division did well at Beaumont-Hamel, but only the 63rd (Royal Naval) Division in the south took all its objectives. The cost was again heavy. Nearly 12,000 men became casualties, making a total of 26,000 on this sector in little more than two days of fighting. About 9,000 British troops died here. Small-scale fighting flickered on for a few days and then the 1916 Battle of the Somme was over.

The Germans withdrew in early 1917 and British troops buried the dead on those parts of the battlefield untaken the previous

November. V Corps, which had handled the main part of the November 1916 attack successfully, made these battlefield cemeteries, giving them its own name, 'V Corps No. 1 Cemetery', and so on. The Germans came back in 1918 and actually captured most of the old British trench system here before being halted and pushed back again in August.

Many more men died further south than here, but this area had not been devastated and the neat little burial grounds made in November 1916 and the spring of 1917 still remained when the time came for permanent cemeteries to be constructed after the war. A fortunate decision was taken to leave as many as possible of the battlefield cemeteries in their original form. Most of the twenty-two small battlefield cemeteries thus remain. Only three were closed and emptied because of access difficulties. Two more, on the Serre Road, were enlarged in the need to find space for bodies from other areas. Only in a small area in the extreme south, near the River Ancre, were the wartime burials all concentrated into one place. Seventeen original cemeteries were thus left undisturbed and are a delight to the battlefield tourer because their contents reflect exactly what happened at those places. A large mine crater, two places where trenches remain and at least fourteen memorials of various kinds makes this one of the most rewarding areas of the battlefields to visit.

The Sheffield Park Area

The area north of the Serre Road neatly coincides with the attack sector of the 31st Division on 1 July 1916. At that time there were four small copses, named by the British soldiers Matthew, Mark, Luke and John. The ruins of a large farm – Touvent Farm – stood just behind the British trenches. The ground sloped upwards to the German trenches and the village of Serre. The British trenches here were not actually the 'old front line' dating from 1914. When the French made their attack here in June 1915, capturing the Touvent Farm area at heavy cost, the furthest limit of the French attack became the front line which the British took over soon afterwards. The 31st Division suffered 3,600 casualties on 1 July, nearly all in the eight battalions making the attack – 'Pals' from Accrington,

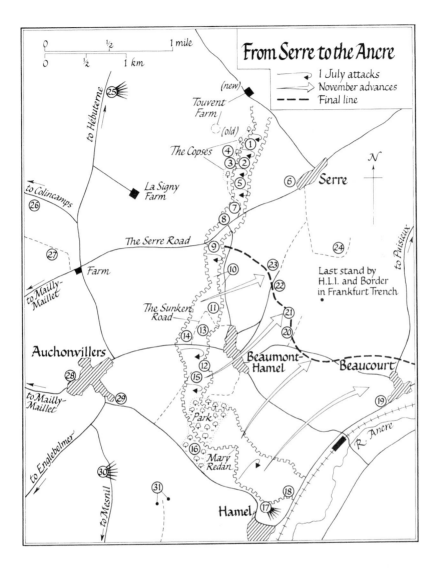

From Serre to the Ancre

↷ 1 July attacks
⇒ November advances
--- Final line

0 ½ 1 mile
0 ½ 1 km

to Hébuterne
(new)
Touvent Farm
(old)
The Copses ④ ① ③ ② ⑤
to Colincamps
㉖
La Signy Farm
⑥ Serre
N
⑦
⑧
The Serre Road
㉗
Farm
⑨
㉔
㉓
to Puisieux
⑩
㉒
Last stand by H.L.I. and Border in Frankfurt Trench
to Mailly-Maillet
The Sunken Road
⑪
⑬
⑭
㉑
⑳
Auchonvillers
⑫
⑮
Beaumont-Hamel
Beaucourt
㉘
to Mailly-Maillet
㉙
Park
⑲
R. Ancre
to Englebelmer
⑯
Mary Redan
㉚
to Mesnil
㉛
⑱
Hamel
⑰

Barnsley, Bradford, Durham and Leeds, and the Sheffield City Battalion, all fighting in their first battle.

Mark, Luke and John Copses have now been joined up to make

19 (*overleaf*) Luke Copse Cemetery in the No Man's Land near Serre where the attacks of 1 July and 13 November 1916 failed. The edge of the nearby wood marks the northern end of the main 1 July offensive.

one long piece of woodland; the trench out of which the 31st Division attacked on 1 July can be clearly seen all along its edge. To the north there is a mile-long gap in the attack front between the last trees of the old John Copse and the diversionary attack at Gommecourt. Matthew Copse has disappeared. A new Touvent Farm on a different site has replaced the old farm and a new road, the Chemin des Cimetières, was made into this area to allow access to the British cemeteries; this is the rough track we now use. Two small cemeteries at the northern end of the copses had to be removed because they were too distant from the road, leaving four of the original cemeteries in place. The trench, the cemeteries and the completely peaceful nature of the area probably make this the best of all places to examine the ground over which those failed attacks of 1 July and 13 November 1916 took place.

The most northerly of the No Man's Land cemeteries is *Luke Copse British Cemetery* ①, which contains one long grave of seventy-two men, but the staggering of the headstones allows each man to have his own. This is where the Sheffield City Battalion attacked on 1 July and fourteen of the identified bodies were of their men (the York and Lancaster headstones); it is probable that most of the unidentified are as well. Two Sheffield brothers are buried here, Lance-Corporal F. and Private W. W. Gunstone, but not in adjacent graves; their consecutive regimental numbers show that they enlisted together. (The Sheffield City Battalion lost two other sets of brothers on that day, Second Lieutenant C. H. and Private S. G. Wardill and Privates A. and R. H. Verner; they have no known graves and their names are on the Thiepval Memorial.) The remaining dead are from the 13 November attack with the 2nd Suffolks predominating.

The next cemetery is *Queen's Cemetery* ② with 311 graves in six rows. Fifty of the identified and many of the 'unknowns' are from the Accrington 'Pals' (East Lancashire headstones) which attacked here on 1 July. If the ground is clear, one should walk up the slope beyond the cemetery a distance similar to the length of the access path to it; the approximate position of the German front line is reached in this way and the same view over No Man's Land can be had as that of the German machine-gunners.

Level with Queen's Cemetery is the *Sheffield Memorial Park* ③, which is on a sloping site in the wood with the shallow remains of the front-line trench each side of the gateway and the mown grass

20 Cemetery signposts on the Serre
Road.

in the park revealing many deep shell holes. The memorial shelter
is a good place for a picnic. The park is actually about 100 yards
short of the Sheffield City Battalion's section of trench on 1 July; it
was the Accrington 'Pals' who attacked here. A small wooden plaque
nailed to a tree in the park is in memory of the Chorley Company
of the Accrington battalion. A stone cross just outside the park
commemorates Private A. E. Bull from Sheffield, whose body was
not found until several years after the war; he is now buried in Serre
Road Cemetery No. 2.

Just behind the park is *Railway Hollow Cemetery* ④, another cemetery made by V Corps in early 1917, but this time in the British
support line. Four simple rows contain 107 British soldiers, many
of them Accrington and Sheffield men, and two French soldiers from
1915. A light military railway which once ran through the nearby
valley gave the cemetery its name. The last cemetery in this area,
Serre Road Cemetery No. 3 ⑤, is in the old No Man's Land and
contains eighty-one graves, mostly from 1 July, mostly from the
Leeds and Bradford 'Pals' (West Yorkshire headstones).

The Serre Road and Redan Ridge

The busy road which cuts across the battlefield area and on to the village of Serre was known in 1916 as the Serre Road and is still known as such to British visitors. The small rise to the south of it was called Redan Ridge by the soldiers of 1916. This was the sector attacked by the 4th Division composed entirely of Regular battalions but reinforced for the day by two Birmingham Territorial battalions of the 48th Division. The attack was pressed home with great gallantry and some penetration of the German trenches took place. The fighting was particularly fierce in a position known as the Quadrilateral. But the German defence held and the men who reached the German trenches were killed, captured or pushed back to No Man's Land. A small party clung to the Quadrilateral but had to abandon it next morning. The division suffered 5,754 casualties, including a brigade commander and six battalion commanders killed and three more battalion commanders wounded. The attack was beaten off by a Württemberg regiment whose casualties were only 460.

The village of Serre is smaller now than it was in 1914. It is worth visiting to appreciate how its position on high ground gave the Germans such good artillery observation over the British lines. The village was adopted by Sheffield after the war and the *Sheffield City Battalion (12th York and Lancasters) Memorial* ⑥ now stands at the side of the road leading back to the cemeteries. The first of these to be encountered coming from the village is *Serre Road Cemetery No. 1* ⑦, which contains 2,412 graves, 1,728 of them unidentified; the proportion of unidentified, 71.6 per cent of the total, is one of the highest in Somme cemeteries. This is a very good example of a battlefield cemetery expanded by a post-war concentration of burials to link up with the road. A visit should start at the back of the cemetery, on the left. Rows G to A of Plot 1 should then be identified. Those seven rows were the original cemetery made by V Corps in May 1917. The 355 graves were mainly of men who died on 1 July 1916 near the junction of the 4th and 31st Divisions. There are many West Yorks and Durhams from the 31st Division, also King's Own Lancasters, Essex and Rifle Brigade from the 4th Division and Royal Warwicks, the Birmingham Territorials loaned from the 48th Division. In Row B is the grave of Sergeant M. H. Mossop, MM, whose family inscription actually says: *One of the original Leeds Pals.* In Row G lies Lieutenant M. W. Booth of the same battalion. Major Booth (the 'Major' was his Christian name) was a Yorkshire county cricketer – an all-rounder who twice played for England. He was killed by a shell on 1 July; his cricketing friend Roy Kilner was wounded nearby on the same day. It was to this cemetery that the annual pilgrimages of the Bradford 'Pals' and probably of the Leeds 'Pals' came until the advancing age of the survivors put a halt to those occasions.

More than 2,000 further graves were added to the cemetery after the war. Plot 1 was extended and Plot 2 added, with the new rows set at the same angle as the old ones; this was done to broaden the width of the permanent cemetery without disturbing the original graves. Then the main concentration plots were made on the lower level between there and the road. Most of the bodies brought in after the war came from other parts of the Somme battlefield.

There is one particularly sad headstone in Plot 4, Row C (on the right of the pathway, just before the Stone of Remembrance). The second grave contains two brothers, Lance-Corporal C. G. and Private P. J. Destrubé of the 22nd Royal Fusiliers. There were three brothers from this French-Canadian family in the battalion, described in an officer's diary as 'the most delightfully independent mad folk you ever saw ... always deserting when we were in England'.[3] One brother was wounded earlier in the war and returned to Canada. The others were then told that one of them had to become a lance-corporal; the one who *lost* the toss took the stripe! They were killed near Miraument in February 1917, their bodies being discovered in each other's arms. The family decided upon this inscription for the joint headstone: *Unis dans la mort comme ils l'étaient dans la vie* (United in death as they were in life); but the mason making the stone made a mistake, engraving *wie* instead of *vie*.

A few yards away is the *French National Cemetery* ⑧, which has an interesting background. When British teams were clearing the local battlefields after the war they found the bodies of about 150 French soldiers who were killed during the French attack in the Touvent Farm area in June 1915 and buried these in what are now

[3] *From Vimy Ridge to the Rhine: The Great War Letters of Christopher Stone* (Marlborough: Crowood, 1989), pp. 67 and 161.

21 Memorial in French cemetery to regiments which attacked in June 1915.

the last seven rows of this cemetery. As the battlefield clearance
process continued, the British found more French bodies over a
wider area and brought them to this cemetery, burying them
between the original plot and the road. It was not until 1933 that
the cemetery was handed over to the French with 817 graves. The
French then made the permanent cemetery and also added, at the
back of the first graves, a superb memorial to the men of the 233rd,
243rd and 327th Regiments who fell in the June 1915 battle; those
regiments came from the city of Lille which was under German
occupation at that time. The memorial quotes the words of a German
battalion commander who faced the French attack; translated they
read: 'You have undoubtedly sent against us élite troops. I went up
to the front-line trench of my battalion at the moment of the attack;
never have I seen troops who launched themselves into an attack
with more courage and spirit.'

Over the road from this cemetery is a small French memorial
chapel to the dead of that battle. I have never been inside because
it is always locked, but there is a large plaque at the entrance in
memory to a much-decorated French priest who was chaplain to
two of the regiments which fought in 1915; he was also a chaplain

in 1939–40. A much smaller memorial has been added more recently, a simple plaque with a German dedication which translates as: 'In lasting memory of our comrades who died at Serre. BRIR 1.' The 'BRIR 1' is probably the pre-unification Bundesrepublik Infantry Regiment No. 1 or Bundeswehr Reserve Infantry Regiment No. 1. This is the only German memorial I know of in the whole *département* of the Somme.

The remaining cemetery on this road – though by no means the least – is *Serre Road No. 2* ⑨, the largest cemetery on the Somme, a magnificent sight with an open front and forty-one plots of graves rising up the slope of the Redan Ridge. This is mainly a concentration cemetery, one so large that the original graves of 1 July and 13 November 1916 around which it was built can hardly be seen from the road; they are in rows set at an angle just behind the Stone of Remembrance. The 489 graves there were the original Serre Road No. 2 Cemetery, made by V Corps in 1917 from bodies found in the immediate area. The huge concentration process came in two stages. The cemetery was enlarged in 1922, probably at the same time as Serre Road No. 1 and in the same manner by squaring off the original plot and then filling in the space to the road. Then, in the final years of cemetery construction on the Somme ending as late as 1934, the cemetery was doubled in size again with the addition of twenty-eight more plots behind and on either side of the earlier burials.

There are now 7,139 graves, 4,944 of them unidentified. It is best regarded as a cemetery representing the whole of the 1916 Battle of the Somme because the men buried here came from nearly every part of the battlefield. It is very much a cemetery of ordinary infantry soldiers – no VCs, few senior officers, few artillery, just rows and rows of infantrymen from every regiment which fought in 1916, including all the Empire countries.

On the roadside to the left of the cemetery stands a memorial cross to 'Lieutenant Val Braithwaite' of the 1st Somerset Light Infantry, shown as being killed near here on 1 July 1916. The plinth of the cross has this lovely inscription: *God buried him and no man knoweth his sepulchre.* This officer was actually Second Lieutenant V. A. Braithwaite and the date of his death in official records is 2 July. His father was a general who commanded a division in 1917–18 and then a corps at the end of 1918. The German position known as the Quadrilateral, which was the scene of such fierce fighting, was in the field directly behind this memorial.

There is an interesting story from the Second World War connected with the cemetery. Mr Ben Leach, the cemetery's English gardener, was left behind when other War Graves Commission employees were evacuated on the approach of the Germans in 1940. Because the cemetery contained two German graves at that time, the Germans later gave Mr Leach a bicycle to continue travelling from his home at Beaumont-Hamel to look after the cemetery. Mr Leach later became a member of the organization for helping shot-down Allied airmen to evade capture. He used the tool-shed at the back of the cemetery to hide the airmen and the German army bicycle to travel to Arras on Sundays where a contact who worked in the *Kommandantur* obtained false papers for the airmen. Mr Leach and his eldest son helped thirty-two airmen during the war and received British and American decorations afterwards.

The Serre Road was the scene of a dramatic event on 1 September 1944 when the British Guards Armoured Division made its famous advance from the River Somme to Douai, a run of fifty miles in one day. The Serre Road was the main axis of the division's 600 tanks and the lorried infantry units on that day.

The Redan Ridge, south of the Serre Road, is one of the less well known parts of the battlefield; the Sheffield Park and Serre Road areas north of it and Beaumont-Hamel to the south usually attract more attention. The opposing front lines crossed the ridge in 1916, with the Germans being on the higher ground. The attack, by battalions of the 4th Division, failed here on 1 July, but the 2nd Division captured the German trenches on 13 November and this area marks the start of the ground gained from the Germans during 1916, the advance being of only a mile here but increasing steadily the further south one goes.

V Corps made two battlefield cemeteries on top of the ridge, *Redan Ridge Cemeteries No. 1 and No. 3* ⑩. No. 1, with 154 graves, is in the old No Man's Land and has the usual 1 July and 13 November mixture of graves for this area, but No. 3 is just inside the old German lines and the sixty-seven graves are nearly all of 13 November. A third cemetery, *Redan Ridge Cemetery No. 2* ⑪, is on the southern side of the ridge. It is a triangular shaped cemetery in the old No Man's Land with 279 close-packed graves from July and November 1916 again.

Beaumont-Hamel

Beaumont-Hamel is another of those names of tragic memory. This part of the German line was attacked by the 29th Division on 1 July 1916. This was a Regular division which had served throughout the Gallipoli campaign, but this was its first Western Front operation. The attack was unsuccessful and the division suffered 5,115 casualties, the third highest divisional casualties of the day. The opposing Germans, Württembergers again, suffered only 292 casualties. By contrast, the 51st (Highland) Division took most of its objectives when it attacked here in November at the more modest cost of 2,200 casualties.

Beaumont-Hamel village nestles in a hollow behind the old front line. It was adopted by Winchester after the war, probably because the 1st Hampshires of the 4th Division attacked just north of the village on 1 July with every one of their officers and 560 other ranks becoming casualties. In the village church is a small window panel showing the face of the Virgin Mary, taken home by a German soldier early in the war and recently returned by him or his family. The flagpole in the centre of the village was presented by the veterans of the 51st (Highland) Division.

The lane towards Auchonvillers crosses an interesting section of the old opposing trenches. A large mine of 40,600 lb (over 18 tons) was exploded under a German position known as the *Hawthorn Ridge Redoubt* ⑫. This was the mine exploded ten minutes before Zero Hour on 1 July which warned the Germans of the coming attack. The explosion was filmed by an army cameraman and the mushrooming eruption is frequently shown on television. The local German defenders were blown to oblivion and British soldiers rushed across to the crater, but the Germans reacted quickly and manned their side of the huge white hole in the chalk. That small British foothold on the edge of the crater was the only success on the 29th Division's front and even that was abandoned later in the day. The tunnel to the crater was used again for the 13 November attack and 30,000 lb (over 13 tons) of explosive was fired under the German trenches and helped the 51st Division advance. The crater still remains but unfortunately it is filled with bushes and small trees. It is possible to climb down into it and only then can the two linked craters be seen. If there were no bushes they would appear from the air to be in the shape of a figure eight.

On the northern side of the lane is *Beaumont-Hamel British Cemetery* ⑬, another of the lovely little battlefield cemeteries in this area. It is in the No Man's Land over which the 1st Lancashire Fusiliers attacked on 1 July and many of their men are buried here. The cemetery is long and narrow, with two simple rows of graves. It was made soon after the November 1916 success and only a few further burials were added later to make a total of 176 graves, nearly half of them unidentified.

Nearby, at the entrance to the 'Sunken Road', is the tall *8th Argyll and Sutherland Highlanders Memorial* ⑭ at the place where this unit attacked so successfully in November 1916. It is the battalion's main 1914–18 memorial on the Western Front and may be the largest British battalion memorial in France and Belgium. The Sunken Road was halfway across No Man's Land in July 1916 but it was the front line for the Argylls' attack in November; the entrances to some of their dug-outs can be seen in the bank of the road.

Moving south along the old No Man's Land one comes to *Hawthorn Ridge Cemetery No. 1* ⑮, reached either on foot across the fields from the crater or by road via Auchonvillers village and a well-signposted farm track to the cemetery. (The Auchonvillers cemeteries will be described later.) V Corps made the cemetery in 1917. One and a half rows of graves from 1 July and 13 November 1916 were made and a few 1918 graves were later added near the gateway. There are 153 burials in the cemetery, a number hard to believe at first sight, but most of the headstones have two names.

I am particularly fond of this cemetery because its position on the open ridge enables the surrounding battle area to be seen clearly. I usually walk to it, either from the crater to the north or by leaving the Newfoundland Park through the back gate, turning sharp left and crossing the fields of the old No Man's Land. I call it the 'public schoolboys' cemetery' because forty-two of the men buried here were from the 16th Middlesex, a New Army battalion raised by former public schoolboys. There are some typical members of the battalion in the back row: Second Lieutenant E. R. Heaton, a clergyman's son; Lieutenant H. D. Goodwin, son of a famous watercolour artist; Corporal H. N. Hosking, a musician; Private P. R. De Silva, who came from Ceylon to enlist; and Private S. Ellis, who came from Toronto.

*

Just south of here is the *Newfoundland Memorial Park* ⑯ , probably the most interesting place on the whole Western Front and, with the possible exception of the Menin Gate at Ypres, receiving the most visitors. It is a large expanse of ground containing the complete trench systems of the July–November 1916 period, three cemeteries and three memorials. It was bought by Newfoundland after the war to provide a memorial for its volunteer battalion which suffered so heavily in a forlorn attack launched more than an hour after Zero Hour on 1 July and after the initial attack had completely broken down in No Man's Land. With no other supporting infantry and with scarcely any artillery bombardment, the Newfoundlanders were a target for every German machine-gun on the sector and were mown down. It is unlikely that a single German soldier was killed by this stupidly originated venture. The Newfoundland casualty figures – 684 or 710 men killed and wounded (accounts differ) – were rivalled by only one other unit that day. The park is an important place; plenty of time should be allowed to obtain the full benefit from it.

May I suggest the following route for a walking tour. Enter the park, passing the *29th Division Memorial*, and then go on to the *Newfoundland Caribou and Memorial to the Missing* on which are listed the 586 men of the Newfoundland Regiment and the 288 Newfoundland sailors who died in the First World War and had no known graves. (The register for the memorial can be seen at the Superintendent's house – when he is in residence.) Then come back a little, cross the path and climb up to a mound behind the Newfoundland Trench. To appreciate the wartime situation, the visitor should now do two things. First, try to ignore the trees; the battlefield was open in 1916. Second, ignore the park's boundaries; the line of the Newfoundlanders' intended advance was half right from that point, not down the centre line of the park.

The Newfoundlanders were forced to move forward in the open from this support line because the communication trenches ahead of them were blocked by the dead and wounded of the earlier attack. They immediately came under fire; most of the casualties occurred in the ground immediately in front of you – on the ground up to the British front line, in the gaps in the British barbed wire through which they had to bunch to reach No Man's Land, and then in the first few yards of No Man's Land itself. You can now walk forward, crossing the British forward trench – that historic 'old front line'

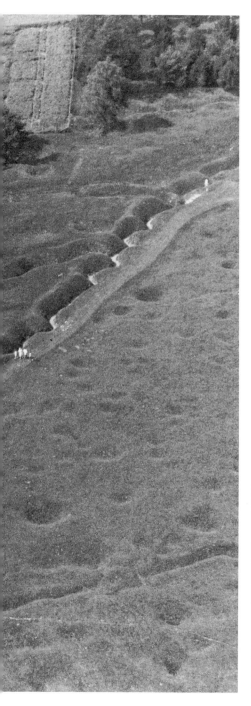

22 The Caribou Memorial among the preserved trenches of the Newfoundland Park.

23 The 51st (Highland) Division Memorial.

which ran from the North Sea to Switzerland – and out into No Man's Land to a small preserved tree rather dramatically called the 'Tree of Death'. The Newfoundland story effectively stops here because few men were able to advance much further than this point.

Continuing across the park, a more ragged trench will be encountered which is unmarked by the Canadian park owners, probably because it played no part in the Newfoundland story. Visitors are often confused by this and believe they have reached the German front line, but that is not so. When the November 1916 attack was being prepared, a new British advance trench was made in No Man's Land to reduce the amount of ground attacking troops had to cross. This was probably done by firing heavy shells in a line across No Man's Land, with pioneers then going out at night to link up the resulting shell holes into a continuous line and joining the resulting trench back to the original front line. The units attacking on 13 November – 1/7th Gordon Highlanders on the right of the park and 1/6th Black Watch on the left – moved off from those trenches in semi-darkness at 5.45 a.m. and carried out a successful attack.

Another lovely battlefield cemetery is to be found on the right-hand side of the park. This is 'Y' Ravine Cemetery, made by V Corps in 1917 and containing the bodies of 366 men. The cemetery appears to contain six rows of graves, but the two outer rows of headstones are memorials to men known or believed to be buried here. Thirty-eight of the graves belong to Newfoundlanders and some of the others are from the 63rd (Royal Naval) Division which was attacking immediately south of here in November 1916.

A few yards further on is the old German front line which always gives the impression of being strongly constructed, as German trenches usually were compared to British ones. It is deep, with well-pronounced bays and small saps out to the front, and it has a good, high 'reredos' of earth behind the trench so that German soldiers manning the firestep would not have their heads silhouetted against the skyline and would be protected from the effects of shells falling behind the trench.

Next comes the 51st (Highland) Division Memorial, standing on the German front line which the division captured on 13 November 1916, the magnificent statue of a kilted soldier on top facing the German rear. That Highlander is jokingly called the 'Duke of Edinburgh' by some of the local French people. The Germans had designs on the bronze statue when they were here in the Second World War and engaged a French contractor to remove it. Scaffolding was erected in readiness, but local talk says that a message sent to England, warning of the danger to the Highlander, resulted in Allied fighters frequently 'buzzing' the site. Whatever the reason, the contractor changed his mind and took down the scaffolding, and the statue remained. The Germans did, however, remove two field guns which once stood in the little grass plots on either side of the memorial.

Close by is a unique cemetery containing forty-six Highlanders killed in the November attack. They were buried soon after the battle in a large shell hole and the War Graves Commission imaginatively made this into a circular cemetery with the headstones set into the base of the Cross of Sacrifice. It was called *Hunter's Cemetery*, perhaps after the company commander whose men buried the dead.

Finally comes *Hawthorn Ridge Cemetery No. 2* in the far left corner of the park. It is another of my favourites, an open-fronted site approached through an avenue of trees, basically consisting of two very closely packed rows of graves of men who died near here on the first day of the 1916 battle, not in November. There are 214 graves from units of the 29th Division – 2nd Royal Fusiliers, 1st Border, 16th Middlesex, 1st Royal Dublin Fusiliers, Newfoundlanders. In the back row lies Second Lieutenant A. W. Fraser, DSO, 1st Border. This subaltern was thirty-nine years old and known as 'old Fraser' by his fellow officers. His company commander was ordered to remain behind for the 1 July 1916 attack, so that the battalion could have at least one surviving captain, and Fraser led the company into action. He was last seen at the German wire, encouraging his men forward. The resulting DSO for a junior officer was an unusual award, indicating a level of courage only just below that required for a VC.

A small row of nine graves was added after the war; four of these were Newfoundlanders from other parts of the battlefield, a sympathetic touch on someone's part to bring them to the Newfoundland Park for burial.

Hamel village was almost on the old British front line. Before dropping down into the village the visitor should pause at the side of the road nearly opposite the village cemetery at a place once known as

Suicide Corner ⑰ . A very good view is to be had from here over the valley of the River Ancre to the northern part of the 36th (Ulster) Division's attack on the Schwaben Redoubt area; the road seen running down the slope half a mile away was called Mill Road and was in the middle of No Man's Land before the Ulster attack.

The *Ancre British Cemetery* ⑱ marks a change in the nature of the battlefield. Here took place not two major attacks in 1916 but three, showing that we are gradually moving into a wider area of the battle. Two detached battalions of the Ulster Division failed in their attack here on 1 July. Five battalions of the 39th Division tried again on 3 September; some men entered the German trenches but were driven out again by concentrated artillery fire and counter-attacks and 1,850 casualties were suffered. But the third effort, on 13 November, was successful. The 63rd (Royal Naval) Division made up of eight naval battalions returned from Gallipoli and four army battalions, attacked from an advanced trench, part of which was actually on the left bank of the cemetery, and captured all its objectives by mid-morning the next day, including Beaucourt village a mile and a half away. The division's casualties – 3,500 men – were the heaviest divisional loss of the November attack.

The cemetery is in a beautiful setting. Hidden from the road by a high bank, it is set in a long, narrow valley that was once in the middle of No Man's Land. V Corps made a cemetery of 517 graves here in 1917; these can be seen in the unbroken rows of Plots 3 and 4 in the far left half of the cemetery. But seven small battlefield cemeteries near here were closed after the war to make a total of 2,497 graves, nearly all from the battalions making those three attacks in 1916. One of the graves is that of Captain E. S. Ayre of the Newfoundland Regiment, a member of a prominent St John's family which lost four officers killed on 1 July 1916; they were two sets of brothers, all cousins. Captain Ayre's grave is in Plot 2, Row E, a quarter of the way down the cemetery on the left. One of his cousins has no known grave; the other two Ayres will be mentioned later. But the cemetery is really the home of the memory of the Royal Naval Division whose bodies lie most thickly here. Among the officers are several of the already dead Rupert Brooke's literary friends who had a particularly strong bond which was shattered in the 13 November attack. One of them was Lieutenant Hon. Vere Harmsworth, son of Lord Rothermere, the newspaper proprietor; he is buried just inside the cemetery on the right in Plot 5, Row E.

A. P. Herbert recalls in his poem 'Beaucourt Revisited' crossing again the 'blood-red ribbon that once was No Man's Land ... and here the lads went over, and there was Harmsworth shot'. The cemetery stands right on, or very close to, that spot.

The old front-line areas of this important northern sector have now been described and it is time to look first at the ground held by the Germans into which the British troops advanced and then at the area behind the British lines.

At the south end of Beaucourt village is the fine *Royal Naval Division Memorial* ⑲ commemorating the battle of 13 and 14 November 1916. It is interesting to note that there is no reference to its being the 63rd Division in the Army's numbering.[4] Lieutenant-Colonel B. C. Freyberg, commander of the Hood Battalion and afterwards Governor-General of New Zealand, won a Victoria Cross in the fighting at Beaucourt and was badly wounded there.

A chain of four small cemeteries is situated on an open ridge north of Beaucourt and east of Beaumont-Hamel. There are no memorials and, on the face of it, there is little of importance here, but it is a place of significant historical interest for the diligent battlefield tourer because it was here that the 1916 Battle of the Somme ended.

The story centres around a German trench – Munich Trench, which was an objective of the 51st Division on 13 November, but the Highlanders were unable to capture it. On 15 November, the day after Beaucourt fell, General Gough asked permission of GHQ to continue the attack and attempt to capture the untaken objectives. 'All ranks were keen to attack again,' he said.[5] Haig reluctantly agreed. The attack, carried out on 18 November, was made on this sector by the 11th Border, 2nd King's Own Yorkshire Light Infantry and 16th and 17th Highland Light Infantry, all from the 32nd Division. The Official History describes how the attack took place at 6.10 a.m. 'in whirling sleet which afterwards changed to rain', the infantry 'groping their way forward as best they could through

---

[4] A second Royal Naval Division memorial has recently been made at Gavrelle, on the Arras front, where the division suffered heavy casualties making an attack in April 1917.

[5] Official History of the Great War, *Military Operations France and Belgium 1916*, Vol. II, p. 511; this and other volumes of the work will be referred to simply as the Official History in future references.

half-frozen mud that was soon to dissolve into chalky slime'.[6] The attack failed in front of Munich Trench with 1,387 men of the 97th Brigade killed or wounded.

But a group of 16th HLI men with a smaller number of 11th Border had got across Munich Trench and become isolated in the next German position, Frankfurt Trench. The party was 100 or more strong and they barricaded themselves into a section of captured trench and repelled German attempts to dislodge them. Two men of the Border escaped to the British lines three days later and a series of attempts was then made to reach the stranded party. The most serious of these was an attack by three companies of the 16th Lancashire Fusiliers (2nd Salford Pals) in the late afternoon of 23 November. This failed, with three officers and sixty-six men killed or missing and ninety-four men wounded. The stranded party, now much reduced by casualties, held out until the 25th, a week after the original attack, but then had to surrender. It was the last action of the 1916 battle.

The dead of those sad little actions lay out in the open all through the winter until the Germans withdrew in 1917. V Corps then made four little cemeteries on the ground where these actions took place. Those cemeteries are still there. It is possible to reach the vicinity by car; a walk along the line of them and back again is very rewarding, though some detours round field boundaries may be necessary when crops are growing. If one starts from the south (a northern start is equally feasible), the first cemetery is *New Munich Trench British Cemetery* ㉒, with 146 graves. This is the prettiest of the four cemeteries, with a different arrangement of graves, a flower bed and two trees. Ninety-three of the graves are 16th and 17th Highland Light Infantry (Glasgow Boys' Brigade and Glasgow Commercials), but the cemetery register is incorrect in stating that men of the 10/11th HLI are also buried here.

Next comes *Frankfurt Trench British Cemetery* ㉑, with 134 graves; the entrance gate is also inscribed 'V Corps Cemetery No. 11', a nice reminder of that formation's good work in clearing the battlefield and burying the dead in 1917. Again the Highland Light Infantry have the most casualties, though a few fellow Scots of the earlier attack by the 51st Division are also to be found here. In Row

---

[6] Official History 1916, p. 514.

B is buried Private John Charles Boon of the Machine Gun Corps. This is the first of three literary associations with this area. Private Boon was Henry Williamson's 'country cousin, Percy Pickering' in his *Chronicles of Ancient Sunlight* novels. In *The Golden Virgin*, Williamson has 'Percy Pickering' killed on the Somme on 15 September 1916, but Charley Boon actually died here on 16 November. They were not first cousins, though they were related. Superb views are to be had from this cemetery all the way south to the towers of Albert more than five miles away.

Across more fields is *Waggon Road Cemetery* ㉒, marked as 'V Corps Cemetery No. 10'; it has 195 graves. The largest number, forty-nine graves, are of the 11th Border from the 18 November attack, but in Row C is buried Lieutenant G. N. Higginson who led the abortive 16th Lancashire Fusiliers attempt on 23 November to rescue the party stranded in the German trenches. At least eleven of his men are also buried here.

The most northerly cemetery of this group is *Munich Trench British Cemetery* ㉓, 'V Corps No. 8', with 126 graves. An interesting view across to Serre village can be had from here. In the fields just west of this cemetery Lance-Sergeant H. H. Munro of the 22nd Royal Fusiliers was killed by a shell on 14 November 1916. This was 'Saki' the author, but he has no known grave. Another literary man who was somewhere near here was Second Lieutenant Wilfred Owen who joined the 2nd Manchesters in the line in January 1917. His experience in a packed and half-flooded dug-out under a heavy bombardment, when the man on duty halfway up the stairs was hit and blinded, led to his poem 'The Sentry'. In one of his letters Owen wrote: 'Tennyson, it seems, was always a great child; so would I have been, but for Beaumont-Hamel.'

There is one more cemetery in this area, *Ten Tree Alley Cemetery* ㉔, which needs to be reached from Serre, by turning south at a small wayside cross in the village, going down a narrow lane and then finding the cemetery in a field on the left. There are sixty-seven graves here representing three different actions. When the 32nd Division attacked Munich Trench on 18 November 1916, a few men penetrated even further into the German lines than the party trapped in Frankfurt Trench. The Official History describes how, with most of the officers killed, they 'struggled forward in small groups ... until their effort was spent. Isolated, exhausted, with little ammunition left, the survivors were overwhelmed.'[7] The 11th Border have the most graves with that date. The same division attacked here on 10 February 1917, capturing both Munich and Frankfurt Trenches; the 2nd King's Own Yorkshire Light Infantry graves represent that attack. The last graves to be found in this cemetery are of soldiers of the 62nd (West Riding) Division, a Second Line Territorial division newly arrived from England. Rifleman C. E. Ward from Leeds, in the left half of the front row, was killed on 15 February 1917, the first day units of that new division went into the line.

This is not on the regular 'tourist route' of cemeteries and only the most diligent of visitors come here. There is no access for buses, only a bumpy car ride or a long walk. There are just two rows of graves and the boundary wall has been built in a near-triangular shape to allow space for the Cross of Sacrifice. It is in a pretty setting in a gentle valley with small woods not far away and the little tree-lined lane which gave its name to a German trench is still nearby. None of the actions here were major ones and none of the casualties were celebrities, but Ten Tree Alley Cemetery, with its poignant original soldiers' name, its individual cemetery design and construction and its permanent maintainance, represents all that is unique and praiseworthy in the War Graves Commission policy of preserving small battlefield cemeteries.

It remains only to describe the British rear areas on this sector. On the road south of Hébuterne are the remains of another *Observation Post* ㉕ built by the 48th Division in 1915 or as part of the 1918 defence line. This one is in poor condition with its roof collapsed, but the field of view which the artillerymen had is unobscured, across the trench lines around Touvent Farm and as far as Puisieux, a mile and a half behind the German line.

Euston Road Cemetery ㉖ is on the lane along which so many men marched up to the trenches from Colincamps. It was a comrades cemetery, but the burials did not start when British troops came here in 1915 but after the 1 July 1916 attack when 139 men, nearly all of the 31st Division, were buried, men who were shelled in the British trenches, who died of wounds before being evacuated to the rear or whose bodies were recovered at night from the British side of No Man's Land. Their burials were well back from the road

---

[7] Official History 1916, Vol. II, p. 522.

in the continuous rows of Plot 1 which formed the original cemetery and it is at the front of this plot that any visit should start. The first two rows and part of the fourth are all 1 July graves, some of which have nice personal inscriptions. On the left-hand side of the first row is Private Willie Whitaker of the Bradford 'Pals': *A boy in years, a man in deeds.* In the fourth row is Second Lieutenant R. F. M. Dean who served in East Africa in 1914, was invalided home with malaria but rejoined to die on 1 July with the Machine Gun Corps: *The best of sons and he nobly did his duty to the last;* his headstone is that of his old regiment, the Royal Warwicks. There were two more further surges of wartime burials, the first after the 13 November 1916 attack and the second in 1918 when the New Zealanders fought off a German attack in front of Colincamps on 5 April, the day which marked the end of the German offensive here.

There were 501 graves at the end of the war. These were then linked to the road by a large concentration of graves from the surrounding area to make a total of 1,260 burials, 304 of them New Zealanders. Some fine mature trees now give the desired park-like appearance. Just inside at the entrance is a row of memorial headstones for men believed to be buried in the cemetery. I always go to see that of Sergeant Will Streets of the Sheffield City Battalion. Streets gave up the opportunity of going to a grammar school and became a miner, because of the need to support his younger brothers, but he wrote a book about coal-mining and several war poems. He was killed attempting to rescue one of his men from No Man's Land on 1 July; his two brothers – twins – were in the RAMC tending wounded men in the basilica at Albert on that day. I have always thought that Sergeant Streets represented the best qualities of the men who volunteered for Kitchener's New Army in 1914. His family inscription is from one of his poems: *I fell, but yielded not my English soul; that lives out here beneath the battle's roll.*

The *Sucrerie Military Cemetery* ㉗ is also on one of the routes from Colincamps to the line, close to where there was a small sugar-beet factory which gave the cemetery its name. The tree-lined track alongside the cemetery has hardly changed its appearance from the time that battalions tramped up and back to the line, usually for routine trench duty but also for the big attacks. The men who marched up at the end of June 1916 actually passed mass graves dug ready for their own dead.

The French had already buried 285 of their men before British

24 Sucrerie Military Cemetery and the track along which British troops marched up to the 1916 battle.

troops took over the line in 1915. (The French graves were removed after the war.) The 1st Royal Warwicks went into the line at 8.0 p.m. on 25 July 1915 and Privates W. E. Swainstone and W. Tarver were killed at 7.0 a.m. the next day, the first British deaths on this sector. They were buried in what is now Row A of Plot 3, near the Cross of Sacrifice. Sergeant D. Clint of the 2nd Seaforths died the following day but he was buried further down the track in what is now Row AA of Plot 1, to the right of what was the second entrance (now a tool shed). It is possible that each battalion had its rear headquarters at a different place along the track and all had their own little burial places, because further casualties from those battalions continued to be buried in those separate places, a good example of the 'comrades' aspect of the cemetery.

The burials continued steadily and it became one large cemetery. Row G of Plot 1 contains fifteen York and Lancasters of the Sheffield City Battalion killed in May 1916 when the Germans made a night raid on their trenches. Rows D and E contain many of the 1 July dead; that is probably where mass graves were prepared before the

battle. Among fifteen officers buried together in Row H are two of
the four battalion commanders of the 11th Brigade killed on 1 July –
Lieutenant-Colonels Hon. L. C. W. Palk, DSO, 1st Hampshires, the
son of a baron, and in the next grave J. A. Thicknesse of the 1st
Somersets, son of a bishop. (Thicknesse's own son, an artillery
brigadier, was killed in Holland in October 1944.) There were
further rushes of burials on two dates in 1918, in April when the
New Zealanders held the German attack and in August when the
42nd (East Lancs) Division pushed the Germans back; these graves
are mostly to the right of the entrance and in the long row at the
back of the cemetery. At the far right of the cemetery, next to
the Stone of Sacrifice, is buried Private A. McIntyre, a fifty-year-
old Cameron Highlander who had the bad luck to die on Christmas Day 1918 while serving with a Prisoner-of-War Company
clearing the battlefields. The permanent cemetery was constructed
after the war with 894 graves and a register was printed in
1929 with a plan of the cemetery and a list of names. In later
years, the War Graves Commission filled up many of the gaps
in the rows adding 210 more graves brought in from more distant places, but this did not alter the original character of the
cemetery.

The village of Auchonvillers – 'Ocean Villas' to the soldiers – was
only just behind the British line. Edmund Blunden, in *Undertones of
War*, describes how the French had fortified the whole village, how
the communication trenches started on the eastern edge of it and
how German shelling gradually destroyed most of the houses.
Auchonvillers Military Cemetery ㉘ was made on the safer side of
the village and remains a typical comrades cemetery, surrounded
by farm buildings and grass fields. It was built up steadily from the
back of what was then a small field by units taking their turn in the
front line as the months passed. The first week of July 1916 saw
ninety burials, mostly from 29th Division units. Men who fought
here again in 1918, including twenty-four New Zealanders, were
buried at the front of the wartime cemetery, but the very front row
was added after the war to make a total of 528 graves. Studying
the cemetery register I noticed several entries which reflect the
character of the army which fought on the Somme in 1916. Private
Cornish's brother Tom 'was very badly wounded at the same time
by the same shell' while serving with the 11th Royal Sussex, and
the next entry shows that Private Cornwell of the 24th Royal

Fusiliers was 'well-known in the Gospel Temperance Band at South-end'. A few pages further on Private Lovett 'left his coffee estate in India and returned to serve in the war' and to die on 1 July 1916 with the Public Schools Battalion at the age of forty-six.

On the south side of the village is *Auchonvillers Communal Cemetery* ㉙ in which there is just a single row of fifteen graves, thirteen of them being of men of the 1st Border killed on 6 April 1916 when a sudden German bombardment fell on a communication trench nearby. The headstones are of an unusual red sandstone known as Corsehill Stone, possibly used here because that stone is native to the western border region between England and Scotland where the Border Regiment recruited its men.

On the road to Mesnil is another *Observation Post* ㉚, stoutly and neatly built and still in good condition; the roof-supports are rail lines from the railway which ran nearby. The single observation slit gives a good view across the Ancre to the Schwaben Redoubt area. There would also have been a clear view up the Ancre valley, possibly all the way to Grandcourt, but bushes in the foreground and trees in the Newfoundland Park now conceal this.

Up a track north of Mesnil are to be found two more comrades cemeteries – *Mesnil Ridge and Knightsbridge Cemeteries* ㉛. They are situated in a fold in the ground about half a mile behind the front line, at a place where the communication trenches would start; the local trench was actually called Knightsbridge. The Doullens–Albert railway line once ran between the two cemeteries.

Mesnil Ridge Cemetery is the smaller and older of the two. The first graves were of the 1st Rifle Brigade, 4th Division, in August 1915. A long row of Irish graves at the back of the cemetery shows that the 36th (Ulster) Division manned the nearby trenches after its arrival in France in November 1915 up to the spring of 1916 when the 29th Division arrived from Gallipoli and was inserted into the line. A bad experience by the 2nd South Wales Borderers on 6 April 1916 is reflected by twenty-five graves on the left of the cemetery, the result of a German raid on the trenches at Mary Redan. There were few burials after the opening of the Battle of the Somme. There are ninety-five graves but, unusually, none of officers.

The much larger Knightsbridge Cemetery, with 548 graves, was started at the outbreak of the Battle of the Somme when units of the 29th Division buried their dead at the start of Rows G and H, many of them being Newfoundlanders and 1st Essex killed on 1

July. The 13th Cheshires added Row I when fifteen of their men were killed in an artillery bombardment of the trenches they were holding at the end of July. The main part of the cemetery, the long rows on the left, was started after the 39th Division's attack on 3 September 1916, followed by the 13 November attack, and then on to 1917 and 1918. A further 112 graves were added after the war (in the far right quarter of the cemetery), some from as far away as High Wood. One of those buried here was Second Lieutenant W. D. Ayre, in Row B, one of the four members of the Newfoundland family killed on 1 July 1916.

These two cemeteries are in a bare area of ground, of difficult access and away from the main routes around the battlefields. They receive few visitors, while the Newfoundland Park less than half a mile away across the fields is seen by thousands.

HAMEL TO AVELUY

This section of the book covers five villages, a large wood and a river valley which were all just behind the old front-line trenches in 1914–16. It was an area which gave considerable succour to French and then to British troops, an area where battalions had periods of rest between tours of trench duty and where artillery and forward medical units were located. It was where carrying parties would come back each evening from the line to meet their unit's 'transport' and collect rations and mail. It was where X Corps prepared for battle in June 1916, with the 36th (Ulster) Division attacking in the north, the 32nd Division in the south and the 49th (West Riding) Division in reserve. The Germans overran part of the area in 1918. What there is to see now is entirely British in character.

Hamel

Hamel was a front-line village. Three major attacks were mounted from here in 1916 before the German line was taken in November. Edmund Blunden, with the 11th Royal Sussex, describes the village in September: 'ruined houses with rafters sticking out, with half-sloughed plaster and dangling window frames, perched on a hillside, bleak and piteous that cloudy morning; half filled trenches crept

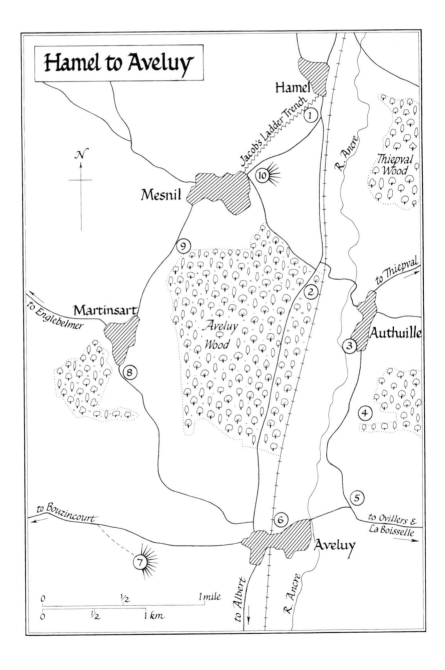

25 The River Ancre at the ruined mill near Hamel.

along below them by upheaved gardens, telling the story of wild bombardment'.[8] Blunden then goes on to describe the horror and confusion of his battalion's attack on 3 September when he was in charge of the dumps of battle stores in the village.

At the southern end of the village is *Hamel Military Cemetery* ①, described by Blunden as a 'soldiers' cemetery open all hours'; his main dump of stores was just across the road. It is a simple, attractive cemetery with 487 graves at the foot of a little slope. The very first burials are interesting. Privates F. Eames and W. Hawes of the 1st Hampshires both died on 31 July 1915 and are buried together in Row D; their regimental numbers are consecutive, showing that they enlisted together. The inscription on Private Eames's grave is *He laid down his life for his friend,* but the battalion War Diary gives no hint of how the two friends died, recording only 'a very quiet day in the trench'.[9] The three attacks made from here in 1916 are well represented, the dead including some senior officers from the Royal Naval Division – Lieutenant-Colonel F. J. Saunders, DSO, of

[8] Blunden, *Undertones of War* (London: Cobden-Sanderson, 1928; Four Square Books, 1962); p. 91.
[9] Public Record Office WO 95/1495.

the Anson Battalion (Plot 2, Row E), killed on the eve of the 13 November attack when his unit was shelled while moving up; Lieutenant-Colonel N. O. Burg of the Nelson Battalion (Plot 2, Row D), killed in the actual attack; and Surgeon G. A. Walker and Chaplain E. W. Trevor (in adjacent graves also in Row D) who may have been killed when a Forward Dressing Station was shelled on 14 November. Another Royal Naval Division CO was killed in February 1917, Lieutenant-Colonel E. C. P. Boyle, DSO, 1st Honourable Artillery Company, buried in Plot 1, Row E. By contrast to these officers, two soldiers of the Labour Corps died in April 1919, presumably by an explosion while clearing the battlefields, and were buried in the far left corner of the cemetery. Forty-eight bodies were brought in from the surrounding battlefields after the war, but it is difficult to see where they were buried and the wartime character of the cemetery was not spoiled.

Aveluy Wood

This is the largest wood on or near the 1916 battlefield. The whole of the West Riding Division and three battalions of the Ulster Division sheltered in it on 1 July 1916, waiting to be called forward to join in the attack on Thiepval. The remains of their assembly trenches can be seen in many parts of the wood. The author Henry Williamson was here; he was a Machine Gun Corps subaltern in the West Riding Division. The Germans captured most of the wood in 1918 and the front lines ran through it until August when the Germans were pushed out by the 38th (Welsh) Division.

There is a charming little cemetery in a clearing near the wood's northern end, *Aveluy Wood (Lancashire Dump) Cemetery* ②; it is another of my favourites. It was a place where men from the front-line trenches would come to bring their casualties and collect supplies; Lancashire Dump was its wartime name. The first burials are the scattered graves now seen in the lower left part of the cemetery; some graves here may have been destroyed by shell fire. More graves, in orderly rows, were added in 1917 and again after the 1918 fighting, but most of the graves at the bottom right of the cemetery and all of those by the road were brought in after the war. The cemetery is thus an interesting combination of comrades graves

26 Lancashire Dump Cemetery in Aveluy Wood, with a mixture of 'comrades', battlefield and concentration graves.

from the 1916–17 period, battlefield burials of 1918 and then post-war concentrations.

Authuille

This village lies close to the Ancre. The valley of this little river is always attractive with its trees and meadows; the water often runs in two or three channels, and large ponds where peat was once cut make this a favourite angling area. A café at the north end of the village, alongside one of the streams, is a haunt both of fishermen and of battlefield visitors. The village was adopted by the London borough of Leyton after the war.

Authuille Military Cemetery ③, with 472 graves, is a pretty spot with its rows of graves on a steep, curving slope running down to the Ancre and flanked by meadows and trees. It is not visible from the roads through the village, so it is not well known. Just to the left of the cemetery once stood the bridge on the Black Horse Road, a major access route from Aveluy Wood to the front line.

The cemetery is perfectly 'comrades' in character, with little groups of battalion graves in the rows. The earliest burials are at the bottom of the slope, although some Indian cavalrymen who held trenches near here in the autumn of 1915 have their own small plot higher up. One interesting group at the bottom of the slope is the communal grave of twelve men of the 1st Dorsets and a separate grave nearby of their officer, Second Lieutenant V. T. Bayly, all killed in May 1916 when the Germans heavily bombarded and then attacked their trenches near Thiepval with a raiding party. Another interesting group, in Row J near the entrance, contains the graves of some South African heavy artillerymen whose battery was located near here in 1916. Because the tracks to the front line fan out from Authuille, all three divisions of X Corps used the cemetery while preparing for the 1916 battle and most of the graves are from that preparatory period.

Blighty Valley Cemetery ④ is located in a particularly pretty valley and is the largest and most important cemetery in this area. The long rows of Plot 1, in the centre of the cemetery, were the original burials made soon after the opening of the 1916 battle and used through that year to bury 212 men. After the war, the battlefield on the other side of the wood was cleared and a further 789 bodies were buried in concentration plots. The graves are nearly all of 1916, from the battlefield of the 8th Division which attacked on 1 July from the front line which was just three-quarters of a mile away behind the wood. It is particularly associated with the four battalions of the 70th Brigade – the 11th Sherwood Foresters, the 8th King's Own Yorkshire Light Infantry and the 8th and 9th York and Lancasters. These were early volunteer units of Kitchener's New Army, formed mostly from mining communities. Their attack on 1 July with the 8th Division was a disaster. The brigade's objective was Mouquet Farm, over a mile in the German rear; the Sherwood Foresters were told that the attack would be a walk-over and that field kitchens would bring them lunch at Mouquet Farm! But only a few men even reached the German barbed wire and 1,987 men were killed or wounded, more than two-thirds of those involved. Two battalion commanders were among the dead; the other two were wounded. This experience was typical of the way in which untried New Army battalions suffered so heavily that day.

'So ends the Golden Age,' said the battalion history of the 9th York and Lancasters.

The ground where those battalions attacked was cleared after the war and the bodies brought to this cemetery. There are 532 unidentified graves but many of them have the badges of the regiments involved. The grave of one of the dead battalion commanders, Lieutenant-Colonel B. L. Maddison of the 8th York and Lancasters, is among the original burials, in Plot 1, Row B.

Crucifix Corner ⑤ was a place well known to British soldiers; units entered the communication trenches at this point to reach the front-line trenches facing Ovillers. It was a particularly busy place on 1 July 1916, with two battalions of reserves waiting in the fields nearby and dozens, perhaps hundreds, of wounded men lying on stretchers around the cross waiting for ambulances to evacuate them. The original crucifix was destroyed in 1918 but replaced by one of similar design after the war; it commemorates the dead members of some local families.

Aveluy

The road from Crucifix Corner to Aveluy (pronounced 'Avel-wee') crosses the River Ancre over two bridges. Alongside one of these are the remains of a makeshift bridge obviously made by British troops either during or soon after the war. The foundations are of concrete-filled 'elephant' shelter cupola sheeting and the bridge itself is of railway lines.

At the north end of the village is *Aveluy Communal Cemetery Extension* ⑥. This is on a steeply sloping site between the last of the village houses and the civilian cemetery, and it looks out over a valley towards Aveluy Wood. The first British burials in August 1915 are at the bottom right of the cemetery. The burials then spread up the slope and away from the road, with a thickening of dates in Row F at the opening of the 1916 battle. Two Casualty Clearing Stations moved to the village briefly in March 1917 and forty-nine men who died there are buried close together in Row N, to the right of the Cross of Sacrifice; forty of these were Australians who were wounded while following rearguards during the German retreat. Two Royal Engineer officers also involved with the German withdrawal are buried near the cemetery entrance. Lieutenant-

27 Aveluy during the retreat in April 1918; many of the tired infantry are the 'boy recruits' of that period.

Colonel H. M. Henderson, the senior RE officer of the 18th (Eastern) Division, and Major A. A. Chase, DSO, the commander of the 8th Royal Sussex, the Division's pioneer battalion, were inspecting a road at Grandcourt which was being improved to follow up the German retreat when they were hit by a shell. Chase was killed outright and Henderson died the next day at Aveluy. They were both buried here with full military honours. The German advance passed over the cemetery in April 1918 and the front line was only a few hundred yards away all through that summer but there were only two 1918 burials. The cemetery then contained 613 graves and was not added to after the war.

In fields just off the Aveluy–Bouzincourt road is *Bouzincourt Ridge Cemetery* ⑦. The German advance was halted on the ridge in 1918 by the 12th (Eastern) and 38th (Welsh) Divisions. The 38th Division was also responsible for pushing the Germans back here in August so there is a strong Welsh association with the cemetery. An original small cemetery was made in September 1918, when seven neat and regular rows of twenty-eight graves each were made; these are now Plot 1 in the far left of the cemetery. Further graves were added from nearby after the war to make a total of 708, some of 1916 but more of 1918. There is one VC grave, that of Lieutenant-Colonel J. S. Collings-Wells of the 4th Bedfords. On 27 March 1918 his battalion, tired and depleted after a long fighting retreat, was ordered to counter-attack just south of where the cemetery is now. Collings-Wells led the attack personally and kept going even though twice wounded until, as the citation for the VC says, 'He was killed at the moment of gaining the objective.' His grave is in the third row behind the Stone of Remembrance.

The track to the cemetery is rough and may not be passable by car in bad weather. It is a lonely situation and this is not a popular area, but there are strong links with the 1918 fighting and some fine views, to Martinsart village, Aveluy Wood, the Thiepval Memorial and Authuille Wood, then round to the Usna and Tara Hills near the Bapaume Road, and then south to Albert.

Martinsart and Mesnil

Martinsart is in a pretty valley location behind Aveluy Wood, with its own smaller wood adjoining on the west. Edmund Blunden describes Martinsart Wood in September 1916 'with its volcanic howitzers, its mud, its confusion of hutments and tents and bivouacs, and yet its sylvan genius lingering in one or two steep thorny thickets'.[10] *Martinsart British Cemetery* ⑧ is particularly attractive, situated on the edge of the village and surrounded by working farms and grass fields with the wood nearby. The cemetery hedge loops neatly round an old metal crucifix that stood here before the British came. The 482 headstones on the graves are of the red Corsehill type and contrast well with the green lawns, although the white of the Cross of Sacrifice looks strange. The burials started dramatically when a platoon of the 13th Royal Irish Rifles (County Down Volunteers) was hit by a heavy German shell while parading in the village on 28 June 1916, ready to go into the trenches for the attack on Thiepval. Seventeen men were killed, including the RSM and a CSM; they were buried in one long grave which is now just inside

[10] Blunden, *Undertones of War*, p. 117.

the cemetery on the left. The body of Colonel H. C. Bernard, commander of the 10th Royal Irish Rifles (South Belfast Volunteers), was buried further along in the same row after he was killed on 1 July. Another 1916 death was Lieutenant-Commander F. S. Kelly, DSC, who had been one of the pall-bearers at Rupert Brooke's funeral; he was killed with the Hood Battalion on 13 November and is buried about halfway along the right-hand row of graves. There were 136 graves at the end of the war and a further 346 were brought in from the surrounding area later.

The road from Martinsart to Mesnil was a main artery into the battle area in 1915 and 1916, being well concealed from German observation by Aveluy Wood. Mesnil (shown on French maps as Mesnil-Martinsart) was only a mile from the trenches and was often heavily shelled. Blunden was here too and describes a journey one night with transport limbers past the church, 'a cracked and toppling obelisk', with great craters in the road, and how his flesh 'crept at the delay in such a deadly place' when one of the limbers fell into a crater and had to be unloaded.[11] *Mesnil Communal Cemetery Extension* ⑨ is to the south of the village and has a similar history to the cemetery at Martinsart, starting in July 1916, being used again in 1918 and then being added to after the war to make a total of 333 burials. Both cemeteries have strong links with the Royal Naval Division which attacked from here in 1916 and halted the German advance in 1918. It is another pretty cemetery, this time with white headstones.

The ground just east of Mesnil gives good views over the Ancre valley. A trench known as 'Brock's Benefit' ⑩, after the commander of the Ulster Division's artillery, was much used by artillery observers in 1916. The road from the village down into Hamel was under German observation and could only be used at night, so a long communication trench, named Jacob's Ladder, was dug in the field alongside, starting at Mesnil and running all the way down the hill to Hamel, passing just behind the military cemetery there.

A story is told locally about an incident in the Second World War. In 1944 an RAF bomber crash-landed in a grass field near Mesnil water tower. Two Canadian crewmen were still aboard and hid until two Germans arrived on a motor cycle to guard the bomber.

[11] Blunden, *Undertones of War*, p. 96.

The Canadians stole the motor cycle and one returned after the war to tell the villagers how they drove nearly to St Quentin before their petrol ran out and that they evaded capture and reached England.

THIEPVAL

In 1916 the village of Thiepval, with its large château, stood on a ridge just within German lines. To the north was the Schwaben Redoubt, which was a triangle of interlocking trenches standing behind the German front line, and to the south were the defences on the spur called the Leipzig Salient. The whole sector was attacked frontally on 1 July 1916, by the 36th (Ulster) Division in the north and by the 32nd Division against Thiepval village and the south. The attacking battalions were nearly all New Army troops fighting their first major action. The Ulster Division achieved a dramatic initial success, but the 32nd Division failed except for a small foothold gained in the Leipzig Salient. As there was also complete failure to the north, across the Ancre, the Germans were able to concentrate their artillery and their infantry reserves against the Ulster lodgement, which was pushed back to the former German front line. Further progress was slow and painful. The 49th (West Riding) Division took over from the Ulsters near the Schwaben Redoubt but made little progress despite their efforts over several weeks. It was not until late September that the village fell to the 18th (Eastern) Division. Actions further in the German rear, near Grandcourt and around Mouquet Farm, will best be described later in the section. Suffice it to say that the whole area was a grim one for the British whose efforts produced an advance of only just over one mile in the north and of two miles in the south between 1 July and mid-November.

The place where most of the Ulster Division fought on 1 July is one of the few where a divisional attack area can be seen almost in its entirety from one spot. The *Ulster Memorial Tower* ① was built on the old German front line which was captured on 1 July; it is a replica of Helen's Tower at Clandeboyne near Belfast. Sometimes a custodian is in residence but, if not, the key can be obtained from a local person whose name and address should be displayed. The tower has a memorial room downstairs, and the viewing platform

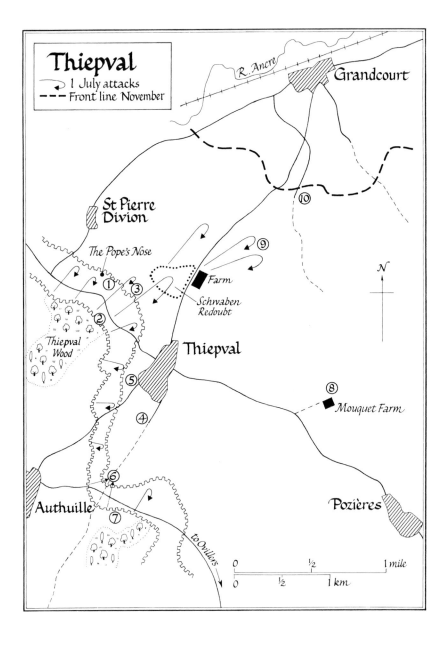

at the top is where the Ulster battlefield can be seen to advantage. Ten battalions attacked from Thiepval Wood. The leading troops made good use of the sunken road in No Man's Land and rushed the German trenches at Zero Hour. They swept over the Schwaben Redoubt and on, deep into the German rear, but on a diminishing frontage. The factor which caused the attack to run out of steam was the way the Germans blocked further passage across the old No Man's Land by an artillery bombardment all day and also by sweeping it with machine-gun fire from untaken positions to the north and south. The peaceful road which now runs below the tower towards Thiepval was a place of carnage that day. The Official History says that it was 'subsequently known as Bloody Road, owing to the mass of dead heaped up on it at the end of the day'.[12] The groups of Ulstermen in the German trenches fought on but were uncoordinated and unsupported. By the end of the day they had been pushed back to a small holding of German trench running from the present position of the tower for about 600 yards south towards Thiepval; the two nearby cemeteries are about level with the halfway point of that holding. The Schwaben Redoubt was lost. The Ulster Division suffered nearly 5,000 casualties and won four VCs.

There are often misapprehensions about the layout of the ground here. The impression is sometimes gained that the tower stands at the centre of the Ulster advance and that the Schwaben Redoubt was located behind the tower. The tower is actually on the extreme northern edge of the advance that day. A small German post made of concrete and steel rails, which may have been a machine-gun post, can be found in the field a few yards north of the tower. That position, known as the Pope's Nose, was in German hands until September. The nearest point of the Schwaben Redoubt was a quarter of a mile away in the direction of the large farm north of Thiepval village – as far as Mill Road Cemetery and then as far on again.

The *Connaught Cemetery* ② is the first cemetery on the old front line south of the Ancre and reflects the changing nature of the battlefield, with the dates on the headstones no longer being restricted to just one or two days of fighting. The original cemetery, of 228 graves, was made next to the road in the autumn of 1916; it consisted of the bodies of men killed here or close by on 1 July –

[12] Official History 1916, Vol. I, p. 417.

28 The Ulster Tower.

Ulstermen, Salford Pals of the 15th Lancashire Fusiliers who attacked next to the Ulsters on that day and West Riding Territorials who tried to support the Ulsters on 1 July and who remained in this area for several weeks. The cemetery was enlarged after the war with further plots being added on either side and at the back near the wood and there are now 1,278 graves of which almost exactly half are 'unknowns'. One grave which catches the eye is that of Company Sergeant-Major E. E. Iredale of the 1/5th West Yorks in Plot 2, Row J. The headstone shows that he reached that rank at the age of only nineteen and that he won the DCM and MM. The DCM, however, was wrongly added to the headstone; Iredale never won that decoration, but he must still have been a brave and resourceful young man.

The wood behind the cemetery was known as Thiepval Wood to the troops, although it is Authuille Wood to the French. The old front line from which the Ulster battalions attacked was at the edge of the wood and traces of the trench can still be seen. A mass of shell craters can be seen in the wood – as in all woods on the 1916 battlefield.

Up a long pathway on the other side of the road is *Mill Road Cemetery* ③. The original cemetery, made here in 1917 after the German retirement, is easy to spot because the ground in which the bodies were buried was over old German trenches and dug-outs and proved to be so unstable that the headstones had to be laid flat when the cemetery was made permanent. The concentration plots made after the war are on firmer ground and have normal headstones. The total number of graves is 1,304 – the largest number at Thiepval – and the unidentified are 815, more than 60 per cent. The graves are local ones, from the various divisions which fought at Thiepval – 32nd and 36th (Ulster) on 1 July, 49th (West Riding), 18th (Eastern) and 39th later. It was the 39th Division which completed the capture of the Schwaben Redoubt in mid-October, fifteen weeks after the Ulstermen occupied it temporarily on 1 July. A Tank Corps headstone – unusual in this area – is to be found in the second row on the left of the Cross of Sacrifice where Lieutenant H. W. Hitchcock is buried. He was killed on 13 November 1916. The main part of the Schwaben Redoubt was about 230 yards beyond the cemetery; there is no trace of it now except for the white chalk of trench diggings and shell holes seen when the land is bare.

The village of Thiepval was much larger before 1914 than it is now. It was nearly abandoned after the war. The original register at Mill Road Cemetery, published in 1927, stated that 'The village of Thiepval was destroyed and the former territory of the commune has now been distributed among the neighbouring communes'; a later register changed that to: 'The existence of the commune, after a long period of uncertainty, was preserved.'

The village was attacked directly from the west by the 15th and 16th Lancashire Fusiliers (1st and 2nd Salford Pals) on 1 July, but their attack failed. If one stands by Thiepval church and looks towards the Ulster Tower, one can easily imagine the field of fire over the Ulster Division area covered by the German machine-gunners in the village. The 18th Division's successful attack in September was from the south, along the line of the German trenches.

Just south of the village stands the impressive *Thiepval Memorial* ④, a massive multi-arched structure recording the names of the 73,357 missing of the Somme between the arrival of British units in 1915 and the retirement of the Germans in 1917; but the vast majority are of the July to November 1916 battle.

The site of Thiepval was chosen because it was on an open ridge with a suitable historical background and the memorial would be seen from all sides; it often appears on the skyline from various parts of the battlefield. It was designed by Sir Edwin Lutyens, one of the War Graves Commission's three principal architects. It stands 45 metres high, five metres less than the Arc de Triomphe in Paris. Part of the site for the memorial and the surrounding park was once the grounds in which the pre-1914 château stood. Several British soldiers' cemeteries had to be cleared from the park and from its surroundings before the work could be carried out and this probably explains why groups of graves from Thiepval are often found in cemeteries many miles away. The building work was carried out from 1929 to 1931 and the memorial was officially inaugurated by the Prince of Wales in 1932. It is the largest of the British Memorials to the Missing, with more names than any other, and was the last to be completed. It does not include all the missing of the Somme for 1915–17; the Australians, Canadians, New Zealanders, New-foundlanders and Indians are all commemorated on other memorials. All the names at Thiepval are from United Kingdom units except for 858 South Africans and one man of the West India

29 The Thiepval Memorial at its inauguration in 1932.

Regiment. It is not a Fourth Army memorial; the Third Army men who arrived in 1915 and those who fought at Gommecourt on 1 July 1916 are included. Seven Victoria Cross men are named on the panels. The register includes an interesting breakdown of regiments; the most heavily represented are: London Regiment (Territorials) 4,348 names, Northumberland Fusiliers 2,931, Royal Fusiliers (City of London) 2,502, King's Liverpool 2,166, Manchesters 1,877 and Royal Warwicks 1,803. As the years passed, the bodies of a few of the missing men were found – 280 at the time of writing – and those men now have normal war graves as well as names on the memorial.

When the memorial was nearing completion, it was decided that an Anglo-French Cemetery should be made in front of it to symbolize the joint efforts of the two armies during the First World War. Each country provided the remains of 300 of its soldiers. Facing the memorial, the French plot is on the right and the British on the left, just as they faced the Germans in 1916. The cemetery is approximately astride the old German front line which was attacked by the 16th Northumberland Fusiliers (the Newcastle Commercials) on 1 July 1916. German soldiers, Württembergers who had held the Thiepval sector since 1914, stood on their parapet that day, taunting the Newcastle men pinned down in No Man's Land and shooting any who moved. The 300 British remains for the joint cemetery were chosen from those still being found in 1931 and 1932. Some came from outside the Somme area but most were of the 1916 battle. Only sixty-one could be identified and only Rifleman James Ritchie, 14th Royal Irish Rifles (Belfast Young Citizens Volunteers), who was killed on 1 July 1916, definitely came from the Thiepval area, so the cemetery represents all of the British parts of the Somme battlefield.

The Battle of the Somme is still commemorated every year on 1 July by a mid-morning ceremony at the Thiepval Memorial with hundreds of people attending.

The *18th (Eastern) Division Memorial* ⑤ is more or less on the site of the pre-1914 château. This division has two memorials on the Somme; this one lists the original units in the division when it left England in 1915 and which fought on the Somme in 1916. Further south is the site of the *Leipzig Redoubt* ⑥, which formed a corner in the old German front line. The Official History describes this as 'a

30 The Thiepval Memorial today.

huge strongpoint, with numerous machine-guns, completely commanding No Man's Land to the south and west' and 'later, when it
became one large shell hole, it was renamed *Granatloch* (shell
hole)'.[13] This position was captured by the 17th Highland Light
Infantry (Glasgow Commercials) on 1 July; it was the 32nd Division's only success that day. The remainder of the Salient was not
captured until 24 August when it was taken by the 3rd Worcesters
and 1st Wiltshires of the 25th Division. That 'one large shell hole'
of the redoubt remains, filled with small trees and bushes now. A
pleasant walk further up the track here (the pre-1914 road to
Thiepval) comes out at the Thiepval Memorial.

The *Lonsdale Cemetery* ⑦ is in a field and is reached by a long
path. The main attack here on 1 July was made by the 11th Border,
also known as the 'Lonsdales' after Lord Lonsdale who helped to
raise this New Army battalion in the old counties of Cumberland
and Westmorland in 1914. The battalion did not attack directly

---

[13] Official History 1916, Vol. I, p. 396.

from the British front-line trench but left the shelter of the nearby wood half an hour after Zero Hour as a follow-up unit. They suffered heavy casualties as soon as they emerged from the shelter of the trees. A small cemetery of ninety-six graves was made there in 1917; this is now Plot 1 just inside the gate. A large concentration took place after the war to make the present cemetery of 1,519 graves, more than half of them 'unknowns'. Among the graves is that of Sergeant J. Y. Turnbull of the Glasgow Commercials who won a Victoria Cross in the Leipzig Redoubt on 1 July, the day he was killed. His grave is in Plot 4, Row G.

To the east of this area are three isolated places of interest. Near the Thiepval–Pozières road stands the large *Mouquet Farm* ⑧, 'Mucky Farm' to the British soldiers. The farm buildings and surrounding trenches formed part of the German main second line of defence. It was hoped to take this on 1 July, but no British soldier came anywhere near it that day unless as a prisoner of the Germans. The Australians reached the farm in August, attacking south from Pozières, but the battered ruins were not finally captured until 26 September when sixty-six Germans emerged from the cellars and surrendered to a mixed party of 11th Manchesters, 5th Dorsets and 6th East Yorks – all of the 11th Division – and a tank crew who brought along the machine-guns from their disabled tank. The farm was rebuilt after the war but on a slightly different site; the old farm was on the left of the approach track. The owner is friendly but speaks no English. Until recently he was very proud to receive an invitation from Australian veterans to join them in Pozières for their annual pilgrimage.

A mile to the north, and needing to be reached via Thiepval, are two small but very interesting cemeteries. *Grandcourt Road Cemetery* ⑨ comes first into the 1916 story. It is in a remote location in fields and is best reached from what the soldiers called Stump Road. The cemetery was made in 1917 from bodies found nearby, four rows with 391 graves. The visitor will notice that the ground rises slightly behind the cemetery. On the crest of that rise was the German position known as Stuff Redoubt, part of their main second line; it was taken by the 10th Cheshires, 25th Division, on 9 October 1916 and some of the graves are from that battalion.

But the Cheshires were not the first British troops to reach this area, for it was to here that the leading elements of the brave Ulster

31 A 'Dud Corner' near Grandcourt.

Division reached on 1 July when men from several battalions came up to the German second line, nearly a mile inside the German defences. But no reinforcements reached these weak parties and most were pushed back. There are four Ulster graves in the cemetery; all are from the 8th Royal Irish Rifles (East Belfast Volunteers); all of the headstones show '2nd July 1916'. These men may have still been fighting on 2 July or they may have been wounded prisoners who died that day. Whatever happened, those graves are a tribute to the advance of the Ulster Division. There may be more Ulstermen in some of the 108 unidentified graves. This important story should not detract from the main contents of the cemetery, because the majority of graves are of men of the 19th (Western) Division which tried to push forward here on 18 and 19 November 1916, in snow showers and bitter weather, the last gasp of the 1916 battle on this sector.

Not far away is *Stump Road Cemetery* ⑩, which has a different story. This is another battlefield cemetery made in March 1917 after the German retirement. There are 263 graves in three simple rows. The cemetery was actually made by the 7th Buffs – the East Kents – part of the 18th (Eastern) Division which fought here in late 1916 and was still here when the Germans retired in 1917. Most of the graves are from that division.

This gives me the opportunity to pay tribute to what I think was the most successful division to fight on the Somme in 1916. The 18th Division was an early New Army formation which was fortunate in obtaining some young Regular regimental and staff officers when it was formed and to have an exceptionally gifted commander in Major-General Ivor Maxse. The division was completely successful in its first attack on 1 July and again in the middle of July (these actions will be described later) before leaving the Somme for a quieter sector to absorb replacements for its 6,000 casualties. It returned to the Somme in September, capturing Thiepval where other divisions had failed, and remaining in this area until the end of the battle, making several more advances, never failing, and sustaining a further 5,271 casualties, of which the graves in this cemetery form a small part. The division was still here on 23 February 1917 and one of its members, Lieutenant F. L. Lucas, is credited with being the first to discover that the Germans had started their retirement when he led a patrol of the 7th Royal West Kents to the German front-line trench at a point about half a mile west of this cemetery. The 18th Division returned to the Somme to take part in the 1918 battles with equal success.

Just north of here is the village of Grandcourt which has no military cemeteries or memorials. It was just beyond the furthest advance by British troops in November 1916. A story can be told, however, about the Second World War. One night in July 1943, Resistance men removed a rail from the south-bound track of the main railway line just east of Grandcourt and the locomotive and several wagons on a German troop train were derailed. A north-bound goods train then hit the derailed train, telescoping the first three wagons. At least 152 German soldiers were killed and many more were injured. It is believed that the Germans took away three men from Grandcourt as a punishment and that only two of them returned after the war.

*

THE BAPAUME ROAD

It can be said that we have now come to the main 1916 battlefield, where action was more or less continuous from 1 July as the Germans were pushed back from the old front line. That slow and costly process was not in the original plan of course. The main road from Albert to Bapaume was intended to be the main axis of a rapid British advance – a breakthrough if possible – after the German front-line defences had been taken. The 8th and 34th Divisions were intended to advance two and a half miles on the first day. Just behind Albert three cavalry divisions and some reserve infantry divisions stood ready to exploit this success and push through to Bapaume as their objective. If that plan had succeeded, it would have been a success of historical magnitude, comparable to von Kluck's march across the Somme in 1914 and to the armoured advances of 1940 and 1944.

It did not happen that way. The units attacking here suffered the same fate on 1 July as those further north. Despite the help of two large mines exploded at La Boisselle, the attacks were repulsed nearly everywhere with crushing casualties. Approximately 18,500 infantrymen went into the attack here; more than 11,000 were dead or wounded by the end of the day. Of twenty-four battalion commanders, nine were killed, five were wounded and one later committed suicide; a brigade commander was also wounded. The 34th Division's casualties – 6,380 men – were the heaviest divisional casualties of that day. A small area around one of the mine craters and another on the extreme right flank were the only footholds gained in the German lines.

But there were British successes further along the line to the south and east and it was from there that the future progress of the British offensive would be made. The centre of gravity of the 1916 battle moved to that new area and the nature of the battle changed from one of swift exploitation to that of dogged attrition. Those major changes occurred almost overnight. The result was that the Bapaume Road area became the left flank of the main advance, the villages and German trenches here needing to be cleared as the main offensive on the right moved forward. The Germans defended

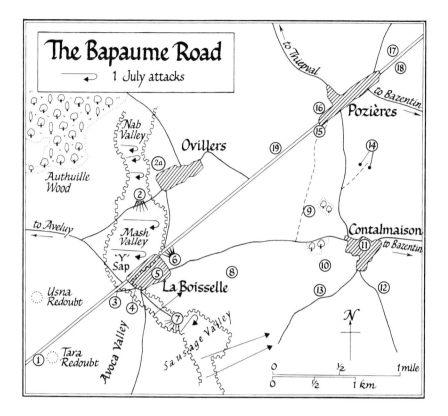

The Bapaume Road
1 July attacks

tenaciously and the British casualties were as heavy here as on any
other part of the 1916 battlefield.

The old Roman road climbs out of Albert to reach *Bapaume Post
Military Cemetery* ① just before the crest of a hill. The cemetery
was started after the 1 July battle and used until January 1917, by
which time 152 men were buried in Rows B to G of Plot 1. Two of
those early burials were of Lieutenant-Colonels W. Lyle and C. C. A.
Sillery of the Tyneside Scottish Brigade in which all four battalion
commanders were killed. The two COs are buried together in Row
G. A further 257 graves were added after the war. Many of the
graves are of 34th Division men killed on 1 July and of Canadians
and Australians who were fighting further up the road later in the
battle. This cemetery and Peake Wood Cemetery near Contalmaison
were the first cemeteries in the main Somme battle area to be

permanently constructed after the war. The work was completed and the cemetery register published in 1924.

Either side of the main road near here were the Tara and Usna Redoubts, situated on the ridge from which the Tyneside Irish Brigade attacked with such disastrous results on 1 July. The slopes down which they advanced were as bare that morning as they are now, exposing the Tynesiders to the fire of the German machine-gunners.[14]

Ovillers

The German trenches on this sector were on two spurs of high ground separated by wide valleys which became No Man's Land. The village of Ovillers is situated on one of the spurs, with Nab Valley to the north and the more pronounced Mash Valley to the south. It was in Nab Valley that the New Army battalions of the 70th Brigade suffered so heavily on 1 July (as described under *Blighty Valley Cemetery* on page 102) and it was against the intervening spur and in Mash Valley that the remainder of the 8th Division broke itself. The village was then attacked by the 12th (Eastern) Division on 2 July, but this attack also failed. The German Guard Fusilier Regiment was now defending the village and it held out until 15 July when troops of the 25th and 48th (South Midland) Divisions finally took the ruins, not by frontal attack but from the direction of the main road.

The impressive *Ovillers Military Cemetery* ② stands on the slope of the Ovillers spur, in the old No Man's Land. It is easily the largest cemetery in this area, having 3,436 British and 120 French graves. The original cemetery can be seen in the long, continuous rows of Plot 1 on the right-hand side of the cemetery. The register states that the first burials took place near a Dressing Station *before* the capture of Ovillers, but the earliest graves in Plot 1 appear to be from August 1916. The remainder of the cemetery is a vast post-war concentration, but the graves are mostly local from the fighting in this area, including many from La Boisselle where there are no military cemeteries. At least 2,477 of the graves are unidentified;

---

[14] The 103rd (Tyneside Irish) Brigade suffered 2,139 casualties, nearly three-quarters of their strength, attacking from the Tara–Usna Line; their story is told in *The First Day on the Somme*, pp. 139–42 and 167–8.

at 72.1 per cent of the total, this is the second highest proportion on the Somme, a testimony to the ferocity of the fighting near here. The plot of French graves on the far left side of the cemetery is from the Breton regiments which held a front line on the higher ground near Ovillers village before being driven back in 1915. One of the British graves is that of Captain John Lauder, son of the well-known singer Sir Harry Lauder. Captain Lauder was killed with the 1/8th Argylls on 28 December 1916, much further up the road towards Bapaume. His grave is in Plot 1, Row A (three graves to the right of the first bush). It is said that his father wrote the song 'Keep Right on to the End of the Road' after hearing of his death.

The front of the cemetery gives a fine view over the local battle-field. The wide Mash Valley below is where the 2nd Middlesex had to attack on 1 July, exposed to machine-gun fire from the head of the valley and from the high ground on both sides. The battalion com-mander, Lieutenant-Colonel E. T. F. Sandys, had earlier protested at the way the German defences had not been destroyed by the bombardment. He was so distressed at what had happened that he committed suicide by shooting himself in a room at a London hotel.

The German line ran along the edge of the main road on the far side of the valley. A large mine was blown under the position known as 'Y' Sap on 1 July, but the Germans suspected the presence of the mine and evacuated the position before the explosion. The crater was filled in by the local farmer in the 1970s; the shape of it can still be seen sometimes when the field is not covered by a crop.

Up a track to a position on the north-west edge of Ovillers is a memorial (2a) to the French 19th Infantry Regiment from Brittany which attempted to defend the crest of a ridge here in December 1914. The tall cross on a large plinth was paid for by the farmers of the *département* of Finistère.

In a field between the military cemetery and Ovillers, a local man found the remains of bodies in what was probably the old German front-line trench. This was in November 1982. The story, as told to me by a War Graves Commission gardener, was that the exhu-mation team recovered the remains of forty-nine British and two German bodies before work stopped for Christmas. When they returned, the farmer had ploughed up the site, anxious not to have *his* work further delayed. Another source says that the bodies were found during the demolition of some farm buildings. These were the bodies buried in a mass grave at Terlincthun British Cemetery near

Boulogne (see page 35). That grave has a special headstone showing the badges of five regiments to which it was known some of the dead belonged – the Royal Fusiliers, the West Yorks, the Royal Sussex, the Essex and the Royal Berks; battalions of those regiments were in the 8th and 12th Divisions which attacked Ovillers frontally during 1 and 2 July 1916. An Iron Cross represents the two Germans.

La Boisselle

This village is larger now than it was in 1914. There were no houses on the main road or near the road junction from Albert at that time. The line of the German forward trench, which was a few yards outside the village, is now covered by housing. The opposing trenches were very close at this point, the Germans determined to retain the high ground of the spur, the French and then the British equally determined not to give ground. It was a dangerous sector, even in quiet times. The village was not attacked frontally on 1 July. The Tyneside Scottish Brigade attacked on either side, hoping to surround the village from the rear, but this did not happen. It required another New Army division – the 19th (Western) – to fight its way doggedly through the village, a task which occupied the next four days. The one-eyed, one-armed Lieutenant-Colonel Carton de Wiart of the 8th Gloucesters won a VC at the head of his men in that fighting.

The village has many reminders of the battle. The beautifully designed *Tyneside Scottish and Irish Memorial Seat* ③ stands in the angle of the junction of the road from Albert. The opposing front line trenches were very close here in 1915 and early 1916. The French and British front line was at the other end of the small triangle of roads here; the German front line was where the first houses of the village now stand. The ground to the right and slightly forward of this is now a field of overlapping mine craters where both sides tried to edge their front lines forward a few yards in 1915–16 by the constant blowing of small mines. British soldiers called this the *Glory Hole* ④.

The village contains memorials of the two divisions which fought here. In front of the church is a modest stone cross for the *19th Division Memorial* ⑤ at the top of which is engraved the Butterfly divisional emblem. At the far end of the village, up a path near the water tower, is the much larger *34th Division Memorial* ⑥ with a bronze female figure of Victory on the top and the division's units listed around the base; the division's Chequerboard emblem is also shown – it has no particular significance. It is a handsome monument and there is an excellent view across Mash Valley to the cemetery near Ovillers where many of the division's dead are buried.[15]

Along a lane out of the village marked 'Trou de mine' is the *Lochnagar Crater* ⑦ formed when 60,000 lb (26.8 tons) of ammanol were exploded under the front of a German position known as the Schwaben Höhe two minutes before Zero Hour on 1 July. The name comes from a British communication trench, Lochnagar Street, almost certainly so named by the 51st (Highland) Division which was the first British unit to man these trenches in 1915. The explosive was actually placed in two chambers, resulting in most of the debris being blown away from the crater to form an unusually wide 'lip' and leaving a particularly clean and open hole. The attacking British infantry suffered some casualties from the shock of the huge explosion and falling debris but their advance was initially successful. The battalions involved were the 2nd and 3rd Tyneside Scottish on the La Boisselle side of the crater and the 10th Lincolns (Grimsby 'Chums') and the 11th Suffolks (from Cambridge) to the south, all belonging to the 34th Division. But no further advance took place and the gleaming white chalk crater soon became a refuge for men of many units. The tunnel for the mine was reopened later in the day and the first troops of the 19th Division, two companies of the 9th Cheshires, came into the new line through the tunnel.

The crater and lip remain unchanged except for a very light covering of grass and a few small bushes. It is the largest mine crater in area on the Western Front, though some of those blown on the Messines Ridge in Belgium in 1917 contained more explosive. The lip gives good views of the July 1916 battlefield, with La Boisselle

[15] The 34th Division War Memorials Book in Newcastle Central Library reveals interesting details of how such memorials were financed and built. The land for this memorial at La Boisselle was given free by the local lady owner, but a similar plot in Belgium cost £25. The combined cost of building the two memorials, which were unveiled in 1923, was about £2,450, £1,400 of which came from divisional funds remaining at the end of the war, the remainder from donations. The bronze figure on the La Boisselle memorial was made at Brussels.

32 The Lochnagar Crater at La Boisselle taken in late winter when the trench lines and other marks of battle can be best seen. The white spots are patches of snow in shell holes.

village where German machine-gunners were in such commanding positions and, in the direction of the Tara–Usna Line, the exposed slopes down which the Tyneside Irish tried to advance that morning. The valley between the crater and the main road was Avoca Valley. The longer but less distinct valley to the south-east was Sausage Valley. An Englishman, Richard Dunning, purchased the crater in the late 1970s after the 'Y' Sap crater had been filled in. A gathering of battlefield pilgrims always attends the simple ceremony which Mr Dunning arranges at the crater on 1 July each year at 7.30 a.m., the Zero Hour on 1 July 1916.

I was once told the story that the bodies of hundreds of British soldiers were rolled down into the crater after the battle, with army chaplains intoning the burial service all day, and some people still believe that British soldiers are buried there. But that is definitely not so; the British bodies were later removed and the crater is only a war grave for the Germans blown up in the mine explosion or crushed to death in nearby dug-outs. Unfortunately there is no British cemetery near the crater nor at La Boisselle village, although this is such an important and accessible part of the July 1916 battlefield. La Boisselle was systematically cleared of bodies after the war. Some of the dead who fell here were buried in Ovillers Military Cemetery or in Gordon Dump Cemetery (soon to be described), but it will be shown in later sections of the book that other groups of bodies from this area were moved considerable distances. It is a pity this happened, because a sector of the old front line nearly two miles long between Ovillers and Fricourt contains not a single British grave.

Half a mile away across the fields, in what was once the German rear, is *Gordon Dump Cemetery* ⑧, which has 1,641 graves, 1,052 of which are unidentified by name though often they are identified by regiment. A lane once ran from La Boisselle to Contalmaison, passing the south-eastern side of the cemetery. This is mostly a concentration cemetery and it was laid out after the war with a frontage on that lane and with its entrance in the middle of the wall by the lane. The plots of graves then spread out from that point in a fan-like manner up the slope, with the Cross of Sacrifice on a platform at the top. Unfortunately that lane fell into disuse and disappeared, so a new entrance to the cemetery had to be made at the other end of the cemetery. The view on entering the cemetery is now completely different to that intended by the architect, but the permanent headstones, when installed, were faced towards the new entrance. The visitor should walk down to the old entrance and look back to see the cemetery at its best; the register shows the old plan.

The first graves here were made on the battlefield in July 1916; they are in the two continuous rows just inside the present gateway. The post-war concentration process was a local one and reflects the local fighting. There are many graves from the 34th Division from around the Lochnagar Crater and from the 21st Division which captured its objectives between the crater and Fricourt. Later graves come from the Canadian and Australian units which fought at Pozières and Courcelette. It is an interesting cemetery. There is one VC grave, that of Second Lieutenant D. S. Bell of the 9th Green Howards (known as The Yorkshire Regiment in 1916). He won his VC on 5 July but was killed on the 10th. His grave is in Plot 4, Row A, just inside the present entrance; there are three Military Medal graves alongside his – a little group of heroism. The Green Howards have a close connection with this part of the battlefield. Their men won two more VCs near here and there are two memorials, one to a battalion and one to an individual officer.

Contalmaison

This village stood more than a mile back from the old German line and was the headquarters of the German units holding a large sector. It was the objective of the Tyneside Irish Brigade on 1 July, but the few men who reached it were captured or killed in front of the village defences. It was subsequently attacked several times by the 23rd Division and finally fell to the 8th and 9th Green Howards on the evening of 10 July.

A well-preserved, if slightly difficult to find *Bunker* ⑨ is situated about 400 yards up a track from the road to La Boisselle. It is in a bushy bank on the right-hand side of the track and was probably built by British troops after the Germans were pushed back, because its entrance faces the British rear. It would have been used as a brigade or battalion HQ, or as a Dressing Station. Some brickwork in the base of the walls shows that it might have been made of material from a local farm building.

In a field to the west of the village is the small personal memorial ⑩ to Captain Francis Dodgson, a company commander of the 8th Green Howards who was killed at that spot in the successful attack on 10 July. The little stone, only two feet high, is the smallest battlefield memorial I have seen. It is on the village side of a small field track which can be found south of Bailiff Wood. Captain Dodgson is buried in Serre Road Cemetery No. 2, nearly six miles away.

Contalmaison once had a château which housed the German HQ before the fall of the village and the cellars of which were later used by the British as a Dressing Station. *Contalmaison Château Cemetery* ⑪ was started in the château grounds and was used all through the summer of 1916 and again, briefly, in August 1918. A further forty-seven graves were added after the war to make a total of 289 graves but the cemetery retains its 'battlefield' character, its long use in 1916 being reflected in the great variety of regimental badges on the headstones. There is one VC grave, that of Private W. H. Short of the 8th Green Howards. He won his VC for an action well north of here on 6 August in which he was mortally wounded, and it was quite by chance that he was brought back to Contalmaison, the scene of his battalion's earlier success. His grave is in Plot 2, Row B. The cemetery is pleasantly situated; it is close to the village centre but surrounded by small grass fields and mature trees which once formed the park of the now disappeared château.

To the south of the village is the civilian cemetery, at the bottom of which is the *12th Manchesters Memorial* ⑫. A German trench which ran along the southern boundary of the cemetery was attacked by the Manchesters on 7 July 1916. It was the battalion's first major action of the war. There was confusion over the timing of the artillery support and heavy casualties were suffered from German machine-gun fire. The memorial is a tall, stone one of good quality and is this battalion's only memorial on the Western Front, commemorating its 1,039 members who died in the war, almost the exact equivalent of the number of men who sailed from England with the original battalion in July 1915. It is a pity that the memorial is in such a remote place and only seen by those who specifically seek it out.

South of the village, on the Fricourt road, is *Peake Wood Cemetery* ⑬, a small cemetery with just 101 graves on a hillside across the road from the small copse which the soldiers called Peake Wood. There are just three and a half rows of graves starting in mid-July 1916. Thirty-eight of the dead were artillerymen, a reminder that artillery units suffered steady casualties in the battle, often being kept in action for long periods. There are no unidentified graves. It is a pretty cemetery, a good example of the small country-lane cemeteries of the Somme. It was one of the very first cemeteries on the 1916 battlefield to be permanently constructed after the war. It might not have survived if its turn had come later, but would probably have been cleared and its graves moved to one of the concentration cemeteries.

Two more small battlefield cemeteries survived north of the village – the *2nd Canadian and Sunken Road Cemeteries* ⑭, which are up a rough track. The Canadian cemetery is unique in being the only one containing graves from one battalion to remain on the main 1916 battlefield, that is, away from the 'old front-line' areas. The 2nd (Eastern Ontario) Battalion used the cemetery from its arrival on the Somme on 1 September 1916 through to 13 October, burying forty-four of its men. These were all given well-spaced individual graves and all were identified. The location, in a little dip, may well have been the battalion rear HQ during the Canadian attacks in the Courcelette area. The cemetery gate has a Maple Leaf plaque showing that the War Graves Commission has classified it as specially Canadian. Just 100 paces away is the Sunken Road

Cemetery with 214 graves – 148 Canadians of various units, sixty-one Australians and just five British artillerymen. This is another undisturbed battlefield cemetery. Only the British would preserve two such small cemeteries so close together in such an isolated area.

Pozières

The location of this large village was important for two reasons – its situation on the Bapaume Road and its dominance on the crest of the extensive high ground known as the Pozières Ridge. It was, most unrealistically, the final objective of the 8th Division on 1 July, but the attack did not progress a yard beyond the German barbed wire at Ovillers and Mash Valley a mile and a half away. Pozières was eventually taken by the 1st Australian Division on 25 July after the most intense fighting. The Australian attack was from the south, because this was now the flank of the main battle area. The 2nd Australian Division then took over and slowly and painfully pressed the Germans back still further to complete the capture of the actual crest on 5 August. These two divisions, together with the 4th Australian Division which later fought in the Mouquet Farm area, suffered casualties of 701 officers and 22,592 men during consistently heavy fighting; this was approximately 60 per cent of the strength of the Australian infantry going into action. Five Australians won VCs here. All of this resulted in a particularly strong bond between Australia and Pozières which still exists. A container of soil was taken from here to the Australian National War Memorial at Canberra. Approximately 8,000 Australians died in and near Pozières.

There are two memorials at the south end of the village. By the side of the main road is the small *King's Royal Rifle Corps Memorial* ⑮, which is dedicated to its thirteen battalions which fought on the Somme. None of these was particularly involved at Pozières and the memorial was probably placed here simply because of the village's position on a main road. A little back from the road, on the other side, stands the handsome and impressive *1st Australian Division Memorial* ⑯. Just over the road from the memorial is an overgrown hump of ground under which are the remains of a village house in which the Germans built a concrete fortification known to the Australians as Fort Gibraltar and which was the centre of resistance in this part of the village. Its underground chamber was partially opened up in 1986, but work ceased because of fears that the roof would collapse.

There are two more memorials at the other end of the village. A mound on the north side of the road is all that remains of *Pozières Windmill* ⑰. The ground there, just over 160 metres above sea level, is the highest point not only of the Pozières Ridge but of the entire 1916 battlefield. The grass-covered ruins were left undisturbed and are now an Australian memorial. A stone tablet states that this spot was the centre of the struggle in this area and was captured by Australian troops 'who fell more thickly on this ridge than on any other battlefield of the war' – even more thickly than at Gallipoli, one assumes.

On the other side of the road is the *Tank Memorial* ⑱. (The road is very busy; take care when crossing it.) The story of the tanks, first used on the Somme in 1916, will be told later. The main tank action was further to the east, but three tanks of what was then 'C' Company, Heavy Branch Machine Gun Corps, set off from this point on 15 September, the first day tanks were used in war. (This unit later became the 3rd Tank Battalion and is now the 3rd Royal Tank Regiment.) The three tanks setting off from here were supporting infantry of the 2nd Canadian Division and advanced along the road to reach and help capture the old sugar factory and nearby trenches (see map on page 174). It is sometimes said that this was the starting-point for the more famous tank advance on Flers village, but that is not correct.

The Tank Corps chose this spot after the war for its main 1916–18 memorial. Some lovely scale models of four types of British tank have survived the intervening period with no more than a bullet hole through one of them. The high ground here gives some marvellous views over the surrounding area and it is easy to understand why the Germans defended it so vigorously.

The village has several inhabitants who are well known to battlefield tourers. Josianne keeps the local café, which is a popular rendezvous and contains a little museum assembled by her husband, Pierre, who is a diligent collector of souvenirs; his stump of a right arm is a warning of what happens when something goes wrong when handling live ammunition. Another couple, Yves and Christianne Fouchat (pronounced 'Foo-ka'), have one of the finest private collections of souvenirs I have ever seen, in their little home

33 The private collector – Monsieur Fouchat of Pozières.

near the church. A polite request to see this is usually granted. They insist that the souvenirs are a 'collection' not a museum, and donations towards its upkeep or for their trouble are firmly declined; they say that the satisfaction of keeping alive the memory of the British soldiers who fought here is sufficient recompense.

Outside the village, on the main road back to Albert, is the *Pozières British Cemetery and Memorial* ⑲, with its imposing gateway and cemetery architecture. The cemetery started as a simple battlefield one in 1916; this is now Plot 2 with its continuous rows inside on the right. The Germans buried fifty-seven of their soldiers here in 1918, but their graves were removed after the war to leave just 270 British wartime graves.

Two things happened after the war to alter the scene completely. This open site near the main road was an ideal place for a con-centration cemetery and nearly 2,500 new graves were collected from the surrounding area to make a new total of 2,733. Almost exactly half of these are 'unknowns', but it is known that 690 Australians and 218 Canadians are among the dead. One Australian VC is buried here (although he had English parents); this is Sergeant C. C. Castleton of the Australian Machine Gun Corps who was killed

34 July 1917 – Australian soldiers parade in the mud for the unveiling of a memorial to their 1st Division which fought here a year earlier. The memorial no longer exists, but the graves now form Rows D, E, etc., of Plot 2 in Pozières British Cemetery.

in July 1916 while bringing wounded men in from No Man's Land. His grave is in Plot 4, Row L, on the right-hand side of the cemetery. There are also two brothers, Privates J. W. and R. Christy who were killed on the same day in January 1917. They are now buried together at the left-hand end of Row G of Plot 2. The two brothers were in the 1st King's Liverpool but were actually Manchester men; their regimental numbers were only separated by one figure, so a third brother may have enlisted at the same time.

The history of the *Pozières Memorial*, which was then made by adding panels of names to the walls of the cemetery, is an interesting one. This is the memorial to the Fifth Army's missing during the German offensive in 1918 which pushed the Fifth and Third Armies back for thirty miles in sixteen days. It was originally intended that each army would have a memorial to its missing of that campaign, the Fifth Army's at St Quentin and the Third's at Pozières. But French protests at the amount of ground being required for British memorials led to that plan being abandoned. The Third Army's missing were added to memorial walls at an Arras cemetery and the Fifth Army's were put on similar walls here at Pozières. The ironic, and historically important, fact is that this decision did not take into account that Pozières was in the Third Army area during the retreat; the Fifth Army was fighting south of the River Somme and its nearest sector was seven miles away from Pozières. Perhaps there was no cemetery south of the river large enough to accommodate the walls, or perhaps the decision was arrived at without anyone realizing that Pozières was not the correct place for the memorial.

There are 14,644 names of missing men. As at Thiepval there are only United Kingdom men and South Africans, 320 of the latter. Most of the names – 12,741 – are from the sixteen days of the main retreat, from 21 March to 5 April 1918; the remaining names are from the quieter period when a line was stabilized until 7 August, the eve of the Allied counter-offensive. The names, being on continuous walls, are much easier to read than those at Thiepval and the different parts of the army easier to find, starting – as all Memorials to the Missing do – on the left with Royal Navy units (the senior service), then Commands and Staff, then the various corps, then cavalry, artillery and engineers, finally reaching the great mass of infantry, the Guards first followed always by the Royal Scots, the senior of the line regiments.[16] The heaviest losing regiments on the Pozières Memorial are the Rifle Brigade with 657 names, the Durham Light Infantry with 620, the Machine Gun Corps with 570 and the Manchesters with 494. There is one brigade commander's name on the memorial – Brigadier-General G. N. B. Forster, killed on 4 April 1918 when his brigade of the 14th (Light) Division was in action near Villers-Bretonneux.

---

[16] This seniority of regiments lies behind the expression, 'Steady the Buffs', the original of which was:

Steady the Buffs,
Halt the Queen's
Let the Royals go by.

The Royal Scots (the Lothians) were the First of Foot; the Queen's (the Royal West Surreys) were the Second; and the Buffs (the East Kents) were the Third.

35 Graves in Pozières British Cemetery and the wall on which the Fifth Army missing of 1918 are commemorated.

THE PÉRONNE ROAD

This section will cover the right wing of the British attack on the first day of the 1916 battle when four divisions and part of a fifth attacked a five-mile-long section of the German trenches and were successful nearly everywhere. The advances made were the only substantial and permanent British gains of that day. They were not made cheaply; British casualties numbered 14,947. But the Germans suffered heavily, losing about 5,500 men and their laboriously prepared front-line defences. This sector then became the basis for the continuing British attacks in the following weeks, somewhat unexpectedly it should be said, because the British generals had only viewed this area as the right flank of the main advance before the failure astride the Bapaume Road moved the centre of gravity of the battle to this area.

I always feel that I have come to a completely new part of the battlefield when I visit this area. It may be because one takes a fresh road out of Albert, but the main reason is that the opening attack turned out to be one of success instead of repetitive, costly failure. There is much to see; in particular this was an area where some of the small battlefield cemeteries were retained after the war. Because the British were moving forward, the dead were quickly collected and buried, often by men of their own battalion, and it is some of those little exclusive burial grounds made immediately after the battle that survived.

This area was the scene of other famous military actions. It is believed that Henry V and his army marched up the road from Péronne on their way to Agincourt in 1415 and one of Guderian's Panzer divisions certainly took the same route in May 1940.

Fricourt

Fricourt was the only place on this sector where the British failed on 1 July. It was not in the plan for Fricourt to be attacked frontally that morning; it was hoped that advances on either side of the village would encircle it and lead to its fall later. The pretty *Fricourt British Cemetery* (*Bray Road*) ① is right in the middle of the old No

Man's Land where 'A' Company of the 7th Green Howards was facing the village, with orders not to move. But the company attacked, for reasons which were never explained, and 108 of its 140 men became casualties. Eighty-nine men of the Green Howards died in this and in later actions that day and were buried in a large shell hole which is now the centre of the cemetery. The headstones are arranged in symbolic rows and are not directly above individual graves. Further burials took place later and there are now 132 graves. The Green Howards later erected a timber memorial listing the names of their dead. This was a common practice, but its replacement by the present granite memorial actually inside the cemetery was a rare concession, against normal War Graves Commission procedure; it is the only such memorial I have seen in a British cemetery.

The people of Fricourt chose to remember an officer of another battalion, Major R. G. Raper of the 8th South Staffords. Major Raper was a solicitor from Battle, Sussex, and a former Territorial officer. His diary entries written before the attack forecast that 'it may be the greatest battle the world has ever known' and he showed anxiety about his own task, the leading of bombing parties to clear the village and the nearby wood on the second day of the battle. The village fell easily that next morning and the battalion took more than 100 German prisoners, but stronger opposition was met in the wood and Major Raper was killed. His body was carried back and buried in a solitary grave just over the road from where the Green Howards were buried in their shell hole. His family made a private grave there after the war. The people of Fricourt saw Major Raper as the liberator of their village and named a road after him (and another after the town of Ipswich which adopted Fricourt). The Raper family also gave a sum of money to help rebuild the church. It was not until 1965 that the family allowed the War Graves Commission to exhume Major Raper's body and bury it in its present position in the back row of the cemetery.

The long rue Major Raper runs from the village war memorial to *Fricourt Church* ②; the key can probably be obtained at the nearby café if the church is locked. A plaque inside states that the Stations of the Cross are in memory of Major Raper. Also in the church is the 17th (Northern) Division's 1914–18 memorial commemorating the 494 officers and 8,421 other ranks of the division who died in France and Belgium, a figure which represents well over the original

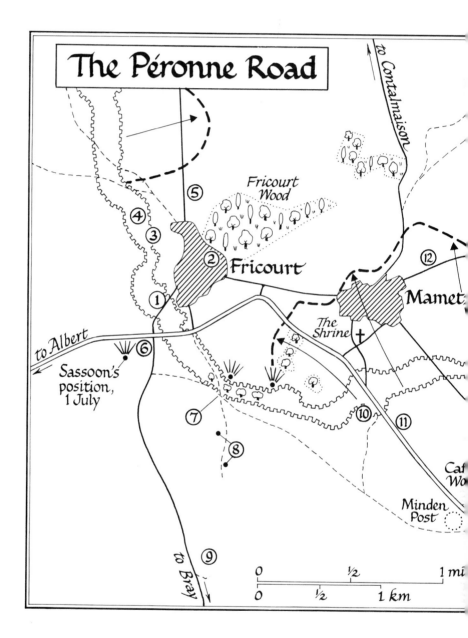

The Péronne Road

to Contalmaison

Fricourt
Wood

⑤

④

③

② Fricourt

⑫

Mamet

The
Shrine †

①

to Albert

⑥

Sassoon's
position,
1 July

⑦

⑧

⑩

⑪

Caf
Wo

Minden
Post

to Bray

⑨

0		½		1 mi

0		½		1 km

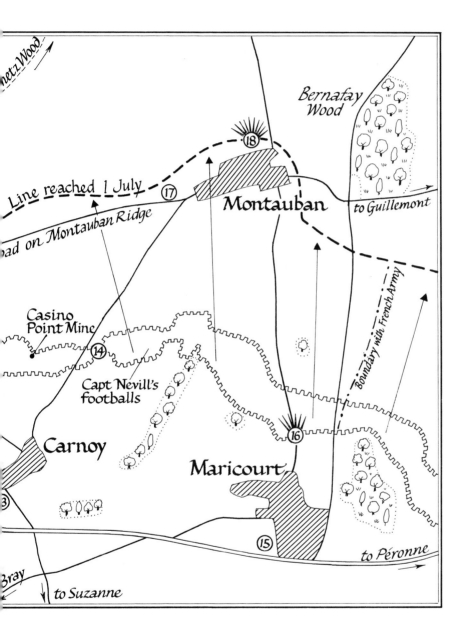

Bernafay Wood

Line reached 1 July

⑰

⑱ Montauban

to Guillemont

ad on Montauban Ridge

etz Wood

Boundary with French Army

Casino
Point Mine

⑭

Capt Nevill's
footballs

Carnoy

Maricourt

⑯

3

⑮

to Péronne

Bray

to Suzanne

36 The Triple Tambour mine craters.

number of infantry officers in the division and about 70 per cent of the original other ranks. Ironically, the parishioners placed a statue of St Joan of Arc directly above the memorial; she was burned for witchcraft by English soldiers at Rouen in 1431. Also in the church is a private memorial to a French soldier of the 156th Infantry Regiment who fell at Fricourt in October 1914.

A track on the other side of the village leads to the scene of the worst tragedy of the 1916 battle. The visitor should find the enclosure in which the craters of the *Tambour Mines* ③ are still to be found. This was the German-held sector facing the 21st Division, which had a brigade of the 17th Division temporarily attached. The Tambour area (named by the French from their word for drum) was a difficult one. The opposing trenches were very close and many small mines had been exploded there. In addition, the trench line had a pronounced 'kink' which led to the German trench being able to fire in enfilade into the right flank of the 21st Division's advance. The division gave the task of attacking on that flank to the 10th West Yorks, from the attached brigade of the 17th Division. This was a New Army battalion which had not carried out an attack before and this ground was unfamiliar. The Royal Engineers had prepared three medium-sized mines to explode just short of the German front line at the Tambour, partly to crush the German defenders but mainly to throw up a shield of chalk debris to cover the attack of the West Yorks from German fire from Fricourt village. A look around the area will show the tactical position; the nearby cemetery is in the old No Man's Land over which the West Yorks attacked.

Several things went wrong. The shelling of Fricourt village had not been effective. Only two of the three mines exploded; later inspection showed that the third charge had become damp. The leading platoons were quickly over No Man's Land and into the German trenches but the remainder of the battalion was caught by just two German machine-guns, one firing from the Tambour and one from the village, the debris from the mines not being high enough to obscure its aim. The gun by the Tambour was spotted and reported to the artillery, but liaison was bad and two hours passed before it was shelled. The ground of No Man's Land rises slightly from the Tambour and not only were the West Yorks cut down by those machine-guns but the survivors were exposed on the slope for the remainder of the day. The battalion casualties were 396 killed and 314 wounded. The proportion of dead – nearly 56 per cent – was extraordinarily high; the usual proportion was one-third killed and two-thirds wounded. A second attack, attempted in the afternoon by the 7th East Yorks, was stopped as soon as it left the British trench. The casualties of the West Yorks were the heaviest battalion loss of 1 July. The CO, the Second-in-Command, the Adjut-ant, two Company Commanders, six Platoon Commanders and two CSMs were among the dead. Only one officer, himself wounded, and twenty men of the 10th West Yorks remained at the end of the day.[17] The Tambour mine craters are still there. The line of the German trench can clearly be seen running from the northernmost crater to the enclosure boundary; the German machine-gun which caused so many casualties was in or very close to that trench.

The survivors of the 10th West Yorks made the nearby *Fricourt New Cemetery* ④ soon afterwards. The neat rows of headstones

[17] The officer was Lieutenant Philip Howe who had been in the leading wave which reached the German trenches. I was fortunate enough to receive his help when I wrote *The First Day on the Somme* and his story is told at several places in that book.

37 No Man's Land at Fricourt where the 10th West Yorks suffered the heaviest casualties of 1 July and the cemetery where many of their dead are buried.

conceal the fact that the cemetery is a number of mass graves containing the bodies of 159 men of the 10th West Yorks and thirty-eight of the 7th East Yorks, together with a few individual graves from later in 1916. The West Yorks' CO, Lieutenant-Colonel A. Dickson, is buried there, with the headstone of his old regiment, the South Lancs; also young Captain J. W. Shann, the Adjutant. I looked for the headstone of Major J. L. Knott, DSO, the Second-in-Command, but could not find it. I supposed that his body had been lost but found that it had been taken after the war to be buried in Ypres Reservoir Cemetery in Belgium, next to his brother, an officer in the Northumberland Fusiliers who died in 1915. The family inscriptions on both graves read: *Devoted in life, in death not divided.*

The ground continues to rise beyond the cemetery, to the area where the main 21st Division attack took place that day. That area is one of those parts of the battlefield that can easily be overlooked. There are no villages, no roads, no cemeteries, no memorials – just open country, hardly a bush or a hedge. The 21st Division did not take all of its objectives on 1 July, but it captured the whole of the

38 Fricourt German Cemetery; one Jewish grave is visible.

German front-line system and gained sufficient ground to cause the Germans to evacuate Fricourt; the captured ground then formed a substantial flank in the attacks which developed in the next phase of the battle. The 21st Division suffered 4,256 casualties on 1 July; spare a thought for them before you leave this area.

Just north of the village is *Fricourt German Cemetery* ⑤, the only German cemetery on or near the British part of the 1916 battlefield. The Germans were given just this one site after the war to bury all their dead in this area. When I first visited this place in the late 1960s there were only wooden crosses which were starting to deteriorate, but these have now been replaced by permanent black metal crosses, most of which carry four names. A few headstones with the Star of David mark the graves of the Jewish soldiers. There are 17,026 Germans buried in the cemetery, 5,056 in the main cemetery plots and 11,970 in the mass graves at the back. A survey of dates on the crosses indicates that about 5,000 of the graves are from 1916 and a similar number from 1918, with smaller numbers from 1914 and 1915. It might be thought surprising that there are not more 1916 graves, but a general rule during the war was that the side which was advancing in a battle had both the opportunity and inclination to identify and bury its own dead, but usually disposed of enemy bodies with much less care. The bodies of many more German soldiers from 1916 still lie under the Somme fields.

The road junction at the south end of Fricourt ⑥ has some interesting features. One of the unsung British achievements of 1916 was the way that supply services were maintained over a network of minor country lanes and tracks, a situation made worse by the switch of the main effort away from the Bapaume Road. The little road in from Bray, to the south, which passed through Fricourt village became one of the principal arteries of the 1916 battle. A census was taken at the crossroads on 21 and 22 July which recorded the following traffic passing in just under twenty-four hours: 26,536 troops, 63 guns, 2,746 mechanical vehicles, 6,162 horse-drawn vehicles, 5,404 single horses and 1,043 men on pedal cycles. In a big jump forward in time, the civilian cemetery at the crossroads contains the three-man crew of a Blenheim aircraft of No. 59 Squadron which was shot down while carrying out a reconnaissance flight on 22 May 1940, two days after the 1st Panzer Division passed down this road. On the hill just behind the cemetery is the spot where Siegfried Sassoon spent all day on 1 July 1916. His company was providing carrying parties and he had no part to play in the battle. His diary records his observations of the action nearby. At Zero Hour it was 'Inferno-inferno-bang-smash' and, later in the morning, 'I am looking at a sunlight picture of Hell.' His vantage-point, as far as can be estimated, was close to a concrete electricity pylon which now stands in the field. Trees in the civilian cemetery now obscure Sassoon's view of the village, but to the left of the trees one can see the bushes and tumbled ground of the Tambour mines area, the ground around Fricourt New Cemetery where the 10th West Yorks suffered so heavily and then the long bare ridge where the 21st Division attacked that day.

Further up the track from the crossroads is the *Bois Français* ⑦, a most interesting place. It was a place of great importance before July 1916 for two reasons – it was at the corner of a distinct 'L' in the trench lines and, being on a prominent ridge, gave excellent observation both along the trench lines and into the rear, particularly into the rear areas held by the Germans. Both sides had fought for the crest in 1914 and 1915 when the French were here; the opponents eventually settled down with their forward trenches very close to each other but with neither side holding the actual crest. With trenches so close it was a natural place for mine warfare and the crest was soon covered with craters. The British 7th Division was holding the sector in the first half of 1916. Siegfried Sassoon and Robert Graves, serving together in the 1st Royal Welch Fusiliers, both described their time spent at the Bois Français at some length. It was a 'hot' sector. Graves describes how the battalion, having suffered no officer casualties for six months, suddenly had three killed in four days in March 1916 – all his close friends. Graves went home on leave, missed the July attack and returned to join another battalion later in that month. Sassoon describes how he won his Military Cross rescuing wounded men from the craters after a raid in May in which Corporal O'Brien, his companion on many patrols in No Man's Land, was killed. (He is buried in Citadel New Cemetery, Plot 3, Row F.) The German trenches here were not attacked on 1 July until 2.30 p.m., when two companies of the 20th Manchesters and bombers of the 1st Royal Welch Fusiliers captured the German front line but were able to make little further progress. The Germans withdrew from the sector that night.

The area is well worth a little tour on foot; may I suggest the following route. Go up the track from the village; the German front line was a few yards away in the field on your left. On nearing the trees, stop and get on to the highest piece of ground possible, turn and then observe the view that the Germans were fighting to deny to the French and British. From the far left can be seen in turn: the village of Méaulte and its aircraft factory (over 2 miles away); Sassoon's look-out point on 1 July; the town of Albert (3 miles); Bécourt Wood ($1\frac{1}{2}$ miles); Aveluy Wood (over 4 miles); the Tambour and the nearby cemetery and beyond it the ridge all along which the 21st Division attacked on 1 July; Fricourt village; the top of the Thiepval Memorial over the village ($4\frac{1}{2}$ miles); and then Fricourt Wood where Major Raper was killed. Now go to the top of the track, turn right (westwards) at the junction, walk 120 paces along the track and then into the wood to find the grave of a French soldier, H. Tomasin of the 26th Infantry Regiment, who was killed in 1915 and whose family made his permanent grave here after the war. The 'CL1900' on the cross means *Classe de 1900*, the year in which he was called to compulsory military service, so he would probably have been a reservist in his thirties when he was recalled in 1914. He was buried a few yards behind the old French front-line trench.

Return to the track junction and go straight across (eastwards) to come to the well-preserved and extensive crater field where Sassoon won his MC. The French and British front line, between the track and the craters, can be identified, but the German line is in the trees and not so easy to distinguish. Close to the track are some peculiar concrete lined pits; they were French anti-aircraft gun positions built in 1939–40 to protect the Méaulte aircraft factory. Now find your way to the north-east corner of the wood for another good viewpoint, this time along the southern leg of the L-shaped front lines. You are standing more or less on the German front line known as Kiel Trench. Again scanning from the left can be seen: Fricourt and Fricourt Wood; Mametz; Mametz Wood beyond the village; the two Bazentin Woods beyond that (3 miles away) and, over the top of the smaller Bazentin Wood, High Wood (nearly $4\frac{1}{2}$ miles); then comes Dantzig Alley Cemetery outside Mametz village and, beyond that, Longueval Ridge with Longueval village and Delville Wood at its far end (nearly $4\frac{1}{2}$ miles). Some small woods near to you conceal further views up the area of the old trench lines and to Montauban, but those places would have been visible in 1916.

There are two interesting comrades cemeteries on the reverse slope of the ridge – *Points 110 Old and New Military Cemeteries* ⑧, which were named after the 110 metre contour line on the military maps; they were both started by French troops and handed over to the British in 1915. The Old Cemetery was nearer the front line, close to where the communication trenches started. The very first British soldier to die on this entire sector, Private F. Footman of the 1st Duke of Cornwall's Light Infantry who died on 2 August 1915, is buried in the far right corner of the cemetery, but it is not an original grave; his body was brought in here well after the war. This cemetery was full by February 1916 so the British started using the New Cemetery again, burying sixty-four men, including Robert Graves's officer friends – Second Lieutenants David Thomas and David Pritchard and Captain Mervyn Richardson, all buried together in the second row. Nearly half of the graves are from the 20th, 21st and 24th Manchesters, including eleven of the 24th Manchesters in a group at the back of the cemetery, all killed in February 1916 when a shell scored a direct hit on their dug-out.

Further to the rear is the larger *Citadel New Military Cemetery* ⑨, with 378 graves. The area in which the cemetery stands had two quite different connections with the war. There were Dressing Stations and artillery batteries here before the opening of the 1916 battle. Most of the graves in the cemetery came from that period and were of men who died of wounds there. But, when the fighting moved on in the second half of 1916, there was no village in this area to provide accommodation for troops going up to the line or returning from it so a large encampment – Citadel Camp – was made and became an important staging-point into the 1916 battle area. Sydney Rogerson in his book *Twelve Days* describes the camp in November 1916 as 'a dreary collection of bell-tents pitched insecurely on the hillsides'. There were only about thirty further burials in the cemetery when the camp was here after July 1916; most of these were the twenty-one officers buried close together in Rows A and C of Plot 2, just to the left of the terraced entrance path. It appears that it was the custom in some units returning from the battle to carry the bodies of those of their dead officers which could be recovered back to the camp and bury them in this cemetery. Ten of the officers were from the Guards Division, two interesting ones of whom were Lieutenant-Colonel Hon. G. V. Baring of the 1st Coldstream Guards, who was also Member of Parliament for Winchester, and Captain A. K. S. Cuninghame of the 2nd Grenadier Guards who was the last surviving officer of the original battalion which went out to France in August 1914. Among the others was Brigadier-General L. M. Phillpotts, CMG, DSO, the artillery commander of the 24th Division.

Mametz

This German-held village fell in the afternoon of 1 July 1916 when it was taken by units of the 7th Division. There are two particularly interesting cemeteries south of the village where the opposing front lines ran across the Péronne Road.

The *Devonshire Cemetery* ⑩ is in a small wood, Mansel Copse, just off the main road.[18] The cemetery is associated with one of the

[18] Mansel Copse was probably named after Second Lieutenant S. L. M. Mansel-Carey of the 9th Devons who was mortally wounded here in February 1916; he is buried in Corbie Communal Cemetery.

best-known stories of the first day of the 1916 battle. At Zero Hour on 1 July, the 9th Devons attacked from a trench which ran across the hill on which the copse stands. One of the Devons' officers, Captain D. L. Martin, had earlier made a plasticine model of the area and had forecast that a German machine-gun position at The Shrine, the crucifix in the village cemetery, would cause them heavy casualties if it was not destroyed by the bombardment. (It is important to know that the attack was not across the main road, in the direction of Mametz, but alongside the road in the direction of the more distant Fricourt; the machine-gun would be firing into the right flank of the attack.)

It happened exactly as Captain Martin had predicted. The machine-gun post survived the bombardment and caused heavy casualties to the 9th Devons and the 8th Devons who followed, although all their objectives were eventually taken. The Devons came back later and buried their dead – 123 men of the 9th and thirty-eight of the 8th – in part of their old front-line trench. They put up that famous sign:

THE DEVONSHIRES HELD THIS TRENCH;
THE DEVONSHIRES HOLD IT STILL.

Among the dead were Captain Martin and also Lieutenant Noel Hodgson, one of the war poets. Hodgson had written this prophetic verse before the battle:

I, that on my familiar hill
Saw with uncomprehending eyes
A hundred of Thy sunsets spill
Their fresh and sanguine sacrifice,
Ere the sun swings his noonday sword
Must say goodbye to all of this!
By all delights that I shall miss,
Help me to die, O Lord.

The Devonshire Cemetery, up a pathway and set among the trees of the copse, is now one of the prettiest on the Somme. The old sign put up has long gone, but the wording is now preserved on a memorial stone standing outside the cemetery gate. The only

39 The entrance to the Devonshire Cemetery.

40 'The Devonshires held this trench; the Devonshires hold it still.'

addition to the original burials was the graves of two artillerymen who died a few weeks later. It is really just one long mass grave, but the permanent cemetery was made with groups of ten headstones to improve the appearance. Unfortunately, space ran out at the far end of the cemetery and Captain Martin's headstone is among a group with ten names on four headstones, with a further stone engraved only with a cross to be shared by all ten men. By climbing over the end wall of the cemetery it is possible to follow the line of the trench in the copse until it swings to the left at the end of the trees. From there one can see the ground to the left of the road where the Devons attacked and, on the right, the new cross in Mametz cemetery where the German machine-gun was.

Another battalion of the 7th Division buried its dead in the *Gordon Cemetery* ⑪. The 2nd Gordon Highlanders attacked alongside the Devons, but on the other side of the road. They collected ninety-three of their men and buried them in their old support trench and then buried six second lieutenants nearby. The headstones of the burials in the trench are beautifully arranged in semi-circles around the Cross of Sacrifice; the officers' graves are against a hedge. That cemetery was one of the first I visited when driving into this area from Péronne on my first visit to the Somme in 1967. I remember being impressed by two things – the repetition of the date '1st July 1916' on the headstones and the six subalterns' graves in a corner of the cemetery. I had been a second lieutenant during my National Service and could visualize the bodies of six young officers awaiting burial. That cemetery, together with so many other '1st July 1916' graves seen in other cemeteries, led to my first book, to a further writing career and now to this book.

The scene completely changes on the other side of Mametz. *Dantzig Alley British Cemetery* ⑫ is a mainly concentration cemetery of 2,037 graves. It stands at the place where the 2nd Queen's and the 22nd Manchesters captured Dantzig Alley trench on the other side of the road. It is a fine cemetery, well laid out, well positioned on the crest of Montauban Ridge and with good views from the back towards Mametz Wood and to the Longueval Ridge. The importance of those places will be described later. Many of the burials are the dead of the successful 1 July attack, not only of the 7th Division which fought here but of the 18th (Eastern) and 30th Divisions which captured their objectives around Montauban. The policy of retaining battlefield cemeteries did not extend to the area in which those divisions fought and their dead were brought here after the war; only the 183 graves of Plot 1, in the continuous rows near the road, are original burials.

Two memorials are incorporated into the walls of the cemetery. Just inside the entrance is a stone with inscriptions in English and Welsh for the Royal Welch Fusiliers killed on the Somme in 1916–18, and at the back of the cemetery is the 14th Royal Welch Fusiliers memorial seat. This battalion – recruited in Carnarvon and Anglesey – had its first, costly introduction to battle between here and Mametz Wood. There is a small point of interest for students of regimental badges on several King's Liverpool graves near the seat. The New Army ones – the Liverpool 'Pals' – have the crest of Lord Derby who helped raise the battalions in 1914; this 'Eagle and Child' is sometimes irreverently called the 'Bird and Brat' or the 'Bustard and Bastard'; the Regular King's battalions have a different badge.

*

Carnoy and Maricourt

There are two points of interest about the junction on the Péronne Road south of Carnoy. A deep hollow on the south side was Minden Post in 1916, a major gathering point for troops waiting to go into action. An army cameraman spent some time here on 1 July, filming lightly wounded British soldiers and a long file of German prisoners coming from the battle. The wood on the village side of the junction was one of several places where army maps spelt French names incorrectly. It is Caffet Wood but was called Caftet Wood during the war. Three companies of the 6th Northamptons assembled in the wood before moving up to the battle area on 1 July. Carnoy was adopted by Swansea after the war, probably as a link with 1918 actions.

In the village is *Carnoy Military Cemetery* ⑬ with 837 British graves, all in wartime continuous rows in an attractive oval-shaped site. It was used as a comrades cemetery from August 1915 until July 1916 and then by medical units until 1917. There are some interesting graves. Captain B. P. Ayre of the 8th Norfolks, the fourth member of that Newfoundland family to die on 1 July 1916, is buried in Row D. In Row E are the graves of seven officers of the 8th East Surreys also killed on 1 July, including Captain W. P. Nevill whose 'football' story is told below; his headstone has the badge of his parent regiment, the East Yorks. This cemetery was another of those used for the burial of senior officers, and in this case two staff officers, brought back from the 1916 battlefield; a wander round the cemetery with the register will identify them.

The road from the village to Montauban reaches the old front-line area at a small crest for which both sides had fought for control in 1915 and early 1916. Several small mines had been blown, leaving a crater field ⑭ which can still be seen. In the fields to the left, a 5,000 lb mine was exploded on 1 July 1916 under the German position known as Casino Point which was being attacked by the 6th Royal Berks, and it was across to the right that Captain Nevill of the 8th East Surreys encouraged his platoons in their attack by giving them footballs to kick across No Man's Land. Casino Point crater was still there a few years ago but has now been filled. In March 1917, a hutted camp stood near the road and an abandoned mine charge exploded spontaneously, killing two officers and ten men of the 12th King's Liverpool and an officer of the 5th Border;

eleven of these casualties were buried at Carnoy Military Cemetery (in Rows A, Y and Z), but the remains of two of the men were never found. More than fifty other men were injured.

In the spring of 1916 the village of Maricourt marked the extreme right wing, not only of the Fourth Army but of the whole BEF; the boundary with the French Sixth Army ran just to the east of the village. *Péronne Road Cemetery* ⑮ was started during the 1916 battle by British medical units and there were 175 graves by the end of the war; these are the continuous rows of Plot 1, to the right of the entrance. It was greatly increased by post-war concentrations and now has 1,324 graves, 366 of them unidentified. Most of the dead are of the 1916 battle, but 1918 is also represented, one from that year being the VC grave of Lieutenant-Colonel W. H. Anderson, 12th Highland Light Infantry, killed leading a counter-attack at Maricourt during a critical stage of the March 1918 fighting. His grave is in Plot 2, Row G, on the left side of the cemetery; the inscription, probably chosen by his wife is: *When my spirit enters to its rest, my lips shall say 'I too have known the best'.* The register of the Péronne Road Cemetery has a map which shows that there was another British cemetery near here after the war, the 'Maricourt British Cemetery' which was near the village crossroads, but the entire cemetery was emptied and the 260 graves are now to be found in a cemetery nine miles away at Cerisy-Gailly which will be described later.

Two roads lead northwards from Maricourt to the old front lines. The more easterly one was the boundary with the French in the attack on 1 July when the commander of the 17th King's Liverpool actually linked arms with the local French commander to ensure smooth co-operation. I prefer to take the western road, the direct one to Montauban, to reach a good vantage-point ⑯ on the old British front line, in order to view the ground over which the 30th Division advanced that morning to capture Montauban. This division was made up of four battalions of Liverpool 'Pals' and four of Manchester Pals – all in their first attack – and four Regular battalions. These units were helped considerably by French heavy guns firing over the boundary and destroying much of the German barbed wire and trench defences, but the 30th Division still performed very well, capturing over 500 Germans and several field guns and taking all its objectives. The little wood to the left of the viewpoint, Machine Gun Wood, was behind the British line; the more distant one on the right, German's Wood, was in German-held ground. The British units attacking astride the road here were King's Liverpool 'Pals' battalions.

The ruins of Montauban village were captured by 10.30 a.m. The village now stands quietly on the crest of a ridge. It was left to Maidstone, in Kent, to adopt Montauban after the war; the 7th Royal West Kents were fighting with the 18th Division just to the west. It was 1994 before some Liverpool people erected a memorial at the crossroads to the Liverpool and Manchester Pals who took this first village to be captured by British troops in the 1916 battle. There are no military cemeteries, even though more than 800 men of the 30th Division were killed; their graves were moved after the war. There is a small monument ⑰, at the side of the road to Mametz, but that honours the French Captain de Monclin and the men in his company of the 69th Infantry Regiment who fought here in September 1914.

It is worth going further along the road to Mametz to study the lie of the ground. This is the Montauban Ridge, captured along its entire length by the 18th Division in hard fighting on 1 July. These troops then consolidated their positions in a long German trench, Montauban Alley, which ran parallel with the road. If there are no crops, walk 220 paces to the north of the road and then see what a fine position the 18th Division took from the Germans that morning and from where later attacks could be mounted. It was expected that the Germans would counter-attack these lost positions, but only a few weak attempts were made at Montauban itself and these were easily repelled.

A visit to this area should end by returning to Montauban and finding *Triangle Point* ⑱, just outside the north end of the village where Montauban Alley trench crossed the road. This was the position reached by the 17th Manchesters (2nd Manchester Pals) in the late morning of 1 July. The Manchester men fired on German infantry fleeing across the wide valley in front and on artillerymen trying to save their guns. I regard Triangle Point as one of the most important places on the battlefield. It represents the culmination of the success of the British right wing on 1 July, a success that was completely unexpected by General Rawlinson whose diary shows that he had little confidence in the 30th Division, which he nearly replaced in the line before the battle. The unexpectedness of the success here is one reason why no immediate exploitation was attempted, even though cavalry were available. But Triangle Point is also important because of the view it gives over the ground which would be fought over in the next phase of the battle. It thus makes a distinct turning-point in any tour of the battlefields, and the next section of the book will start at the same place.

THE HORSESHOE OF WOODS

If one looks at a map of the British part of the 1916 battlefield as it was before July 1916, it can be seen that the major woods in the north – Thiepval, Aveluy and Authuille Woods – were all on the British side of the trench lines, but that nearly all the woods in the south were on the German side. If the Haig–Rawlinson plan for the first stage of the battle had been successful, this chance allocation of woods would not have been serious. But the failure in the north and centre and the success in the south resulted in the southern woods becoming a major factor. The British persisted with their attacks astride the main road at Ovillers and La Boisselle for a few days after 1 July, but little progress was made and it became obvious that future advances would have to be carried out on the more favourable sectors in the south where the Germans had lost their strong forward defences. But the Montauban Ridge, which would be the jumping-off point for further attacks, faces what I call 'a horseshoe of woods'. The small Fricourt Wood, on the extreme left, was no problem; it was captured at modest cost on the morning of 2 July. The other woods, however, were dense masses of mature trees in which the Germans could move troops and set up defensive positions free from artillery observation. Preliminary bombardments only smashed the trees up and made worse the natural barriers to observation and progress. The necessity to attack through the area of these woods was the legacy of the outcome of the 1 July operations, but attacks in the open spaces between them would have been almost suicidal; to clear the woods eventually entailed fighting of the most difficult and costly nature. *Triangle Point* ① is one of the few places where all the woods in that 'horse-shoe' can be seen. Looking at them from left to right their names read off as a roll call of doom – Mametz Wood, the Bazentin Woods,

High Wood, Delville Wood, Trônes Wood and Bernafay Wood. That is why I see Triangle Point as an important place – the peak of success on the first day and the threshold of the next phase of the battle.

It started quietly. After a few feeble counter-attacks, the Germans made no further attempt to recapture their lost positions. Their Battle of the Somme would be one of tenacious defence rather than of counter-offensive. Nor did they bother to occupy the long valley between Montauban Ridge and the next piece of high ground, Longueval Ridge. For nearly two weeks there was no contact between the opposing forces on a frontage more than a mile and a half long, a situation which would not be seen again that year. The British had two tasks to complete during that two-week period – to redeploy their forces, particularly the heavy artillery, and to clear the flanking woods of the 'horseshoe' before a major move could be made in the centre of it. So Mametz Wood on the left and Bernafay and Trônes Woods on the right were attacked during that period, though not all of Trônes Wood was cleared. It was a costly process and at least one division was so hurt that it would not be fit to take part in major operations again for more than a year.

Then the next 'big push' came on 14 July when five divisions carried out an attack using all the tactics which had been ignored on 1 July – deployment of infantry close to the German trenches during darkness, a hurricane bombardment of only five minutes' duration, an assault on the German trenches at first light. Many of the Germans were caught in their dug-outs and the attack was mainly successful. Troops in the centre even reached High Wood,

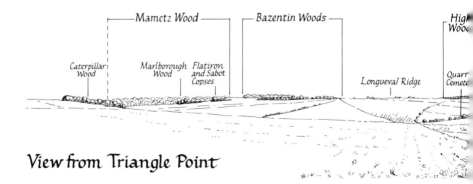

View from Triangle Point

more than a mile from their jumping-off point, but that furthest
gain was not held. The British casualties were about 10,000 men
killed and wounded, an acceptable price in return for the seizure of
the Longueval Ridge and the destruction of several German units.
Most of the successes were gained by New Army battalions which
had not been trusted to carry out this type of attack two weeks
earlier. But the Germans managed to retain their hold on two of the
larger woods, High Wood and Delville Wood, and there were no
more easy successes. Delville Wood took six weeks to secure and
High Wood was still holding out two months later. The British
offensive degenerated into a long slogging match during the next
two months, both at the woods and to the east towards Guillemont
and Ginchy where the French persuaded the British to spread their
frontage, moving the centre of gravity of the battle still further to
the right. The fighting during the next two months, in the heat of
high summer, with relentless, pounding artillery barrages, with
attacks by division after division either failing or capturing only a
few yards of pulverized ground, represent, I think, the true heart
and horror of the 1916 Battle of the Somme.

This section of the book will cover the waiting period after 1 July,
the clearance of the flanking woods, the 14 July attack and then
the attrition until mid-September. Not only was it a different battle
to the one described so far, but the nature of the battlefield will also
change. There will be no more 'old front line' and no more little
battlefield cemeteries. The mainly large concentration cemeteries in
this area are all that we have of burial grounds to cover those weeks,
but they serve their purpose well, reflecting the huge losses and the

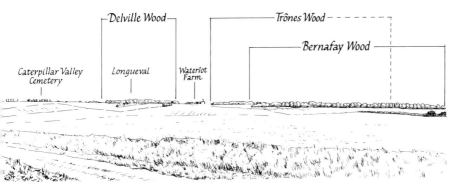

large number of units involved. Three of the four largest cemeteries on the Somme are in this area.

Just north of Triangle Point is *Quarry Cemetery* ②. The valley in which it stands was the main German artillery position before the Manchesters reached Montauban on 1 July and fired on the gun teams. The entrance to the cemetery used to be flanked by banks attractively covered with flowers and shrubs, but a local farmer bulldozed those away in the early 1980s to leave a less pleasing scene. But the interior of the cemetery is very pretty and peaceful. The burials started two days after the 14 July attack and the graves nearest the entrance, in Plots 5 and 6, were made in the following months when the quarry became a busy place, sheltering forward medical units. There were only 152 graves at the end of the war, but 583 more bodies were brought in from the surrounding area afterwards and buried in the centre and rear of the cemetery. Many of these were men of the 3rd and 9th (Scottish) Divisions which took part in the successful attack near here on 14 July, taking Longueval Ridge and the village which can both be seen one mile ahead. The presence of many artillery graves, particularly in Plot 4 in the centre of the cemetery, shows that British batteries also used the nearby valley. The cemetery register entry for one of the artillery graves mentions an unusual unit; Captain W. J. Ralphs, who is buried in Row B, is shown as the 'late OC of the Shanghai Light Horse'.

Bernafay and Trônes Woods

Trônes Wood was another of those places in this area where the army map makers either made a mistake or deliberately altered the name; the French name is Bois de Troncs. Both woods were level with the advance made by the 30th Division on the morning of 1 July but they were not an objective for that day. All that happened was that a British patrol investigated Bernafay Wood and found only a few Germans, who were taken prisoner. Both woods could probably have been seized that afternoon by resolute action but, because of the major British failure elsewhere and the difficulties of rapid co-operation with the French, nothing was done. Two battalions of the 9th (Scottish) Division were able to take Bernafay

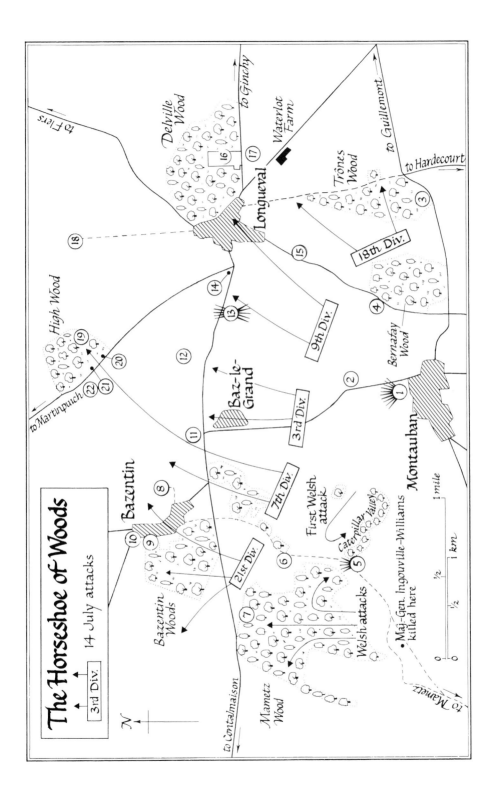

The Horseshoe of Woods

3rd Div.

14 July attacks

N

Bazentin

High Wood

to Martinpuich

to Flers

Delville Wood

to Ginchy

Waterlot Farm

Longueval

Trônes Wood

to Guillemont

to Hardecourt

18th Div.

Bernafay Wood

9th Div.

Baz-le-Grand

3rd Div.

7th Div.

21st Div.

Bazentin Woods

Mametz Wood

to Contalmaison

to Mametz

Welsh attacks

First Welsh attack

Caterpillar Valley

Maj.-Gen. Ingouville-Williams killed here

Montauban

0   ½   1 km

0   ½   1 mile

Wood two days later at a cost of only five casualties, but the Germans reinforced Trônes Wood and units of the 18th (Eastern) and 30th Divisions then had a tough time making progress in their attempts to take it. The Official History describes the conditions:

The wood itself presented an immense obstacle, for its undergrowth, which had not been cut for two years, formed dense thickets, and there was a chaotic tangle of trees and branches brought down by the bombardment. German communication trenches, and a few clearings through which ran light-railway tracks, formed the only easy lines of passage; it was all but impossible to keep direction without a compass bearing.[19]

It took from 8 until 14 July to take Trônes Wood, though action was not continuous throughout that time. The final capture was achieved by the 18th Division; the wood had cost about 4,000 British casualties.

Both woods remain exactly in their original shape. Shell holes are everywhere. The *18th (Eastern) Division Memorial* ③ is on the edge of Trônes Wood. By a coincidence, that division captured the wood again in August 1918 and both dates are mentioned on the memorial. The elegant, slender column has this enigmatic inscription on the base: 'The Greatest Thing in the World.'

The only cemetery in the vicinity is *Bernafay Wood British Cemetery* ④. It lies on the reverse slope of Montauban Ridge, so that the rows of graves have a pleasing terraced aspect. The continuous rows which are situated away from the road constitute the original cemetery of 284 graves; the remaining 638 graves are a post-war concentration of which more than half are 'unknowns'. The original graves are mostly identified, mostly being burials at a Dressing Station which was established here in the later stages of the 1916 battle and in the following winter. My eye was caught by the grave of Private G. S. Smith, a forty-six-year-old Australian infantryman who died of wounds here on Christmas Day 1916; the inscription on his headstone reads: *Too far away your grave to see but not too far for my memory.*

*

[19] Official History 1916, Vol. II, p. 39.

41 The 38th (Welsh)
Division Memorial
looking out over
Mametz Wood.

Mametz Wood

This larger wood was on the left flank of the open ground on which the next major attack was planned to take place on 14 July and this required the wood to be captured first. An opportunity to take it immediately after the 1 July attack was missed and the Germans soon put a battalion of the crack Lehr Regiment and other units into it. It was the usual dense Somme wood, a large central mass with several irregularly shaped spurs attached; it also contained several trenches well protected by barbed wire.

The story of Mametz Wood is the story of the 38th (Welsh) Division which was composed of the Welsh equivalent of 'Pals' battalions. The division was very much the creation of Lloyd George who had persuaded Kitchener to accept his nominations for many of the senior posts, including that of the divisional commander.[20] The capture of Mametz Wood was the division's first major task since arriving in France in December 1915. But the initial attack, a weak

---

[20]*Mametz: Lloyd George's 'Welsh Army' at the Battle of the Somme* by Colin Hughes (Gerrards Cross: Orion Press, 1979) provides a good description of the formation of the division and of its actions at Mametz Wood.

attempt from due east on 7 July, failed and the divisional commander was relieved two days later. A fresh effort, using the whole division and under more forceful command, then took place from the south-west at dawn on 10 July. It took the Welshmen two days of bitter fighting to clear the wood at a cost of nearly 4,000 casualties, including seven battalion commanders. The division was then withdrawn and took no further part in the 1916 battle. It had been a bloody, traumatic experience for this untried division and its eventual success made a valuable contribution to the ability of General Rawlinson to launch his next major operation.

There is no proper road to Mametz Wood, but a long track running from Mametz village to Bazentin provides access to some interesting places. Just south of the track from Mametz was where the most senior of six general officers to die on the Somme in 1916 was killed. This was Major-General E. C. Ingouville-Williams, CB, DSO ('Inky-Bill' to his troops). His 34th Division had suffered the heaviest divisional casualties of the day on 1 July, but he was considered to be one of the most able of the younger generals and, when two shattered brigades had to be withdrawn after that disaster, his divisional organization remained, with two fresh brigades being transferred from the 37th Division for further operations – an unusual arrangement. The reconstituted division went into action again on 19 and 20 July but was in reserve when Ingouville-Williams was killed by a shell on 22 July. The division's War Diary[21] says that he was reconnoitring ground with his ADC; Guy Chapman, an officer in one of the battalions temporarily serving in the 34th Division, records how his men 'hooted with derision' when the rumour spread that Ingouville-Williams had been killed while souvenir hunting.[22] A small memorial marking the place of his death no longer remains.

Further along the track is the *38th (Welsh) Division Memorial* ⑤, which was only erected in 1986, a belated tribute to the harsh Welsh experience here, but also evidence of the continuing fascination with the 1916 battlefield. A defiant dragon stands on the memorial facing Mametz Wood; the inscription in Welsh translates as: *Let us respect their endeavours. Let our memories live on.* A good view is available

[21] Public Record Office WO 95/2432.

[22] Guy Chapman, *A Passionate Prodigality* (Nicholson & Watson, 1933; London: Buchan & Enright, 1985), p. 106.

42 'Death Valley', a main route into the battle area, with Mametz Wood on the left and Flatiron Copse Cemetery in the middle distance.

from the bank behind the memorial, both of the wood and of the valley along which the track continues northwards to Bazentin. That track became one of the main supply and reinforcement arteries for the continuing battle and was used by thousands of British soldiers. The track up to this point followed the Willow Stream from Fricourt and became known to British soldiers as Happy Valley. It branched here; the part following the stream into Caterpillar Valley was still Happy Valley to the troops, but the one going north from here towards the battlefield became Death Valley.

Further up the track is *Flatiron Copse Cemetery* ⑥, so named from a small piece of woodland on the opposite side of the track. It is most attractively located, on a slope, with Mametz Wood behind. The headstones are not of the normal type of Portland stone but appear to be of a soft type of granite. Although their colour is grey rather than the normal white, they do not seem to suffer so much from the green staining which affects white headstones in wet seasons.

The line of the northern boundary wall was almost exactly the line on which the left battalions of the 7th Division – the 8th Devons and 2nd Border – deployed for their successful dawn attack against Bazentin on 14 July.

A Dressing Station was established here soon after that date and made the 373 graves in the continuous rows which now form Plot 1. The remainder of the cemetery is post-war concentrations from the surrounding battlefields and there are now 1,522 graves. There is one Victoria Cross grave, that of Corporal E. Dwyer, 1st East Surreys, one of four men who won the VC at Hill 60 near Ypres in April 1915; he was killed near Guillemont in September 1916. His grave is in Plot 3, Row J, in the right centre of the cemetery. The most remarkable feature of the cemetery, however, is the graves of three sets of brothers buried together. In one of the original rows, Plot 1, Row D, are Privates Ernest and Herbert Philby of the Middlesex Regiment. The register wrongly describes them as belonging to the 1/8th Middlesex Regiment. The brothers enlisted together at Ealing and served in the 1/8th before being transferred to the 1st Middlesex. The two Philbys died on 21 August 1916 when their battalion suffered twenty-three casualties through poison-gas shelling in Mametz Wood. The other two sets of brothers are both in the concentration part of the cemetery behind the Stone of Remembrance and were both casualties of the Welsh Division's fight for Mametz Wood in July. Lieutenants Arthur and Leonard Tregaskis of the 16th Welch (Cardiff City Battalion) are buried in Plot 6, Row G, and Corporal T. and Lance-Corporal H. Hardwidge are buried in Plot 8, Row F; they served in the 15th Welch (Carmarthenshire Battalion).

A new memorial stone ⑦ is to be found just inside the gateway in the northern end of Mametz Wood. It commemorates former Lance-Corporal Harry Fellows who served in the 12th Northumberland Fusiliers, 21st Division, from 1914 to 1917. He was a regular attender at ceremonies on the Somme right up to his death in 1987, reading war poems he had written and representing with great dignity the fading generation of First World War soldiers. His battalion relieved the exhausted Welshmen at this place in Mametz Wood on 12 July 1916 and suffered a heavy German bombardment, and it was from the edge of the wood that his battalion took part in the famous dawn attack on 14 July. The memorial quotes part of one of Harry's poems:

43 Flatiron Copse Cemetery with wartime graves at the front and concentration plots in the rear – Mametz Wood in the background.

Where once there was war,
Now peace reigns supreme,
And the birds sing again in Mametz Wood.

The Bazentins

The names of these two places can be confusing. The main village was called Bazentin-le-Petit by the British but is simply 'Bazentin' on French maps. Bazentin-le-Grand, despite its name, may have been a small village in 1914 but is now no more than the buildings of a large farm. Both villages and their respective woods were captured in the successful attack of 14 July and both villages were adopted by Ipswich after the war for reasons which are not obvious.

After the capture of Bazentin-le-Petit on 14 July, two men – an RSM of the Loyals (the North Lancs) and an officer of the Gloucesters – were buried in the civilian cemetery and their graves still remain there, an unusual occurrence in the middle of the 1916 battlefield. The *Bazentin-le-Petit Communal Cemetery Extension* ⑧, a pretty soldiers cemetery with 186 graves, was started alongside soon afterwards. Its main feature is the number of graves of the 1st Northamptons who were fighting between Bazentin and High Wood in August and used the cemetery to bury five officers and forty-two other ranks. The markers put over the graves of the officers all survived, but those of the other ranks did not and they are now commemorated by memorial headstones around the walls.

The *Bazentin-le-Petit Military Cemetery* ⑨, up a pathway in the main village, is more orderly. There were a few early burials, but the main use was from October 1916 until the following spring when a Dressing Station operated here. Most of the graves are identified and are in neat rows; fifty-five Australians are among the 181 dead. The gaps in the rows are the result of German graves being removed after the war.

At the north end of the village ⑩ is one of the nicest little memorials on the Somme, to 'Nine Brave Men' of No. 3 Section of the 82nd Field Company, Royal Engineers, which was building strong-points in front of the village throughout the night of 29 July 1916. The work was accomplished even though nearly every man in the section was killed or wounded. The Royal Engineers later took bricks from the ruined village and built a memorial naming the nine men who died. The names gradually wore away, but the Royal Engineers have recently renewed the inscriptions. (Sadly, only one of the nine men has a known grave – Sapper J. Higgins who died of wounds and is buried in Bécourt Military Cemetery – but Sapper C. D. Ellisson is known to be buried in Caterpillar Valley Cemetery, although the exact position of his grave is not known.)

The road from Bazentin to Longueval is full of interest. The first part is in a dip, but the road quickly rises to run along the Longueval Ridge, most of which was seized in the 14 July attack by the 3rd and 9th (Scottish) Divisions. At the road junction near Bazentin-le-Grand is *Crucifix Corner* ⑪, named after a metal wayside cross which still stands with the marks of shell fire on it, one of the very few original items on the 1916 battlefield to survive. The cross is only three-quarters of a mile from High Wood. The fields in the low ground nearby are where two cavalry regiments assembled before their charge near High Wood on 14 July. A little further on is *Thistle Dump Cemetery* ⑫, which is reached by a rough track. It is in a little valley on the forward slope of the ridge; its sheltered location was an obvious place for a Dressing Station and 133 men were buried here including many New Zealanders and Australians whose units served near here. A further fifty-six graves were added after the war; those of them which were identified show that this was a long-distance move, many being 1 July 1916 deaths from Thiepval and the Serre Road.

Next comes the hugely impressive *Caterpillar Valley Cemetery* ⑬, important for its size and interesting both for its location and its composition. It stands on the crest of Longueval Ridge and its rear wall is approximately on the main German trench position which was captured by the 12th Royal Scots and 9th Scottish Rifles (the Cameronians) on 14 July. A fine view from the back of the cemetery shows, from left to right, Waterlot Farm, Trônes and Bernafay Woods, Montauban village and the ridge to the right of the village which was captured on 1 July, and then Mametz Wood. The front of the cemetery has an equally good view of High Wood, with to the right of the wood, the scene of the cavalry charge on 14 July and, all across the front of the wood, the open approaches on which so many later attacks foundered. The cemetery, of 5,539 graves, is the second largest on the Somme and reflects the struggles of units which fought on from this position in the two months of bitter fighting after the 14 July success. More than two-thirds of the graves are unidentified. On first sight it appears to be a purely concentration cemetery, but there is an original plot in the near left corner of the cemetery containing just three short rows, each of eight headstones, which are set at an angle to the other rows of the cemetery. The main cemetery is almost entirely 1916 in content, but that original plot was made in August 1918 by the 38th (Welsh) Division which was advancing here at that time. The 1918 soldiers called it Caterpillar Valley Cemetery, a misleading choice because that valley is well over a mile away; 'Longueval Ridge Cemetery' would have been more appropriate, but the original name was retained when the main cemetery was made after the war.

The New Zealand Missing Memorial is on the left side wall of the cemetery. New Zealand decided that its missing soldiers should be commemorated on small memorials located near the actual battlefields on which they died and this one covers the New Zealand Division's actions to the north and north-east of this place in September and October 1916 when 1,560 men were killed. It is a reflection of the intensity of the fighting that 1,205 of the dead have

44 The New Zealand Memorial on a wall of Caterpillar Valley Cemetery.

no known grave and are named on this memorial. Nearly all died in the period 15 September to 2 October. The regiments with most names are the New Zealand Rifle Brigade with 341 names and the Otago Regiment with 245 names.

Longueval

This village stands at the eastern end of the ridge to which it gives its name. Most of the village was taken by the 9th (Scottish) Division on 14 July, but the northern part, together with Delville Wood and Waterlot Farm, all defied capture. The 5th Cameron Highlanders supported by some South African troops captured Waterlot Farm on the following day, but the village and the wood continued to be the scene of the most vicious fighting, with positions constantly changing hands and an inferno of shell fire falling on the troops of both sides. The wood was not completely secured for a further six weeks.

The *12th Gloucesters Memorial* ⑭ , at a road junction, was erected for this New Army battalion in the 5th Division which made a successful attack near here on 29 July. The original cross made in the 1920s had disappeared by 1945 and the present one was made in Bristol City Council's workshops and erected in 1986. The battalion was known as 'Bristol's Own'.

Longueval Road Cemetery ⑮ is an interesting place. Just outside the cemetery is a small shrine; local legend says that Julius Caesar addressed one of his legions there during the invasion of Gaul. The same spot, on 14 July 1916, was where the 8th Black Watch deployed in No Man's Land for its dawn assault on Longueval. A Dressing Station was established here in September 1916 and 171 men were buried, including a few in 1918; forty-nine more graves were concentrated after the war.

Delville Wood is now the property of South Africa. The South African Brigade, attached to the 9th (Scottish) Division, fought its first battle here. It went into action 3,153 men strong, captured most of the wood between 14 and 20 July, but emerged with only 778 men to answer roll call. Five other divisions – the 2nd, 3rd, 5th, 14th (Light) and 17th (Northern) – all fought in Longueval and Delville Wood in July 1916, but the South Africans deserve the credit for the main capture of it. This place was a fitting choice for the *South African National Memorial* ⑯ after the war and a beautiful park was laid out among the stumps of the devastated wood. The original memorial was unveiled in 1926 and commemorates the 10,000 South African dead of 1914–18; it is not a memorial to the missing and there are no names on it. A further stone memorial was placed in front of the original to commemorate the South African dead of 1939–45 and then, in 1986, the South African Government decided to build a national military memorial museum behind the 1914–18 monument and also a new visitors centre by the road. The latter is much appreciated by visitors and the new museum is handsomely built, but there was opposition to its erection by those who felt that this 1916 site was being exploited to improve South Africa's image in the 1980s. The trees in the wood have grown again and the rides have stone markers recording the names of streets of London, Edinburgh and Glasgow given by the 9th (Scottish) Division to those spots during the fighting. A single hornbeam is the only original tree left in the wood; it stands behind the left corner of the new museum.

On the other side of the road is *Delville Wood Cemetery* ⑰, the third largest cemetery on the Somme with 5,523 graves, including

45 Delville Wood with the South African memorial and the new museum.

those of three unidentified bodies found in the wood during the building of the new museum (in Plot 13, Row J, and identified by their smooth-faced new headstones). This is entirely a post-war concentration cemetery with no original burials; 3,593 – 65 per cent – of the graves are 'unknowns', but the register entries of the remainder show that nearly all are from late July and from August and September of 1916 and the cemetery represents the many units of the British Army which fought in this area. There are 152 South African graves from the brigade which fought so valiantly in the wood. There is one VC grave, that of Sergeant A. Gill, 1st King's Royal Rifle Corps, killed on 27 July 1916 while leading a platoon attack in the wood.

Across a field behind the cemetery is the sugar-beet factory which replaced the one known in 1916 as Waterlot Farm, though it was never a proper farm. The now derelict factory and workers' houses are an ugly blot on the 1916 battlefield and it would be a blessing if the buildings were to be demolished.

The *New Zealand Memorial* ⑱ commemorates the part played by the New Zealand Division in the 1916 battle. It is a fine, tall monument in a small enclosure on an otherwise open site. An inscription tells how 'The New Zealand Division, after gaining this position as their first objective, launched from it the successful attack on Flers, 15th September 1916.' Another inscription, FROM THE UTTERMOST ENDS OF THE EARTH, reflects the fact that New Zealand is exactly on the other side of the world from this part of Europe.

High Wood

This wood always seems particularly large, possibly because there is nothing nearby to draw the eye from it, or because it looms large in the memory of 1916. It is, in fact, one of the smallest of the horseshoe of woods. But it stands on the highest ground in this area; a point between it and the New Zealand Memorial reaches almost 160 metres in height, only a fraction below the site of Pozières Windmill which is the highest point of the 1916 battlefield. The French name is Bois des Forceaux – Raven Wood.

The swift capture of the Longueval Ridge on the morning of 14 July opened the way to the possible seizure of High Wood; it would have been an invaluable prize if it could have been taken that day. A brigade commander actually walked up the slope to the wood that morning and returned without being fired on; the wood was virtually empty. But nothing was attempted until the evening when two battalions of the 7th Division, the 2nd Queen's (the West Surreys) and the 1st South Staffords, moved forward in conjunction with two cavalry regiments, the 7th Dragoon Guards and the Deccan Horse. The infantry entered the wood but were not able to complete its occupation before darkness fell; the cavalry advanced on the right in the only serious cavalry action of 1916 but were soon stopped and pinned down by machine-gun fire. The Germans arrived in force and quickly recovered most of the wood and all subsequent attempts to capture it during the next two months failed with heavy casualties.[23] It is not surprising that no less than seven wooden unit memorials were erected at High Wood soon afterwards; there are four memorials and a large cemetery there now.

[23] The fighting is well described in *The Hell They Called High Wood* by Terry Norman (London: Kimber, 1984).

46 The view over Crucifix Corner to High Wood from near Bazentin-le-Grand. The cavalry attack of 14 July started from the low ground around Crucifix Corner and proceeded to the right of the wood. The photograph shows how the wood dominated the open ground over which many subsequent infantry attacks took place.

The wood is private property and entry is not encouraged, but it is possible to walk all around its edge. On the south-eastern face is the *Cameron Highlanders and Black Watch Memorial* ⑲; their 1st Battalions attacked at this point on 3 September 1916. Forty-five paces further on (going away from the road) is a double mine crater behind a screen of bushes; the fighting was so static that a tunnel was dug and two mines were blown under the German trench here in early September. The crater is unique in that it is the only one on the Somme to be filled with water.

There are three memorials along the roadside. The first to be erected was the large stone memorial ⑳ to the 47th (London) Division, the unit which finally completed the capture of High Wood in the great attack of 15 September (which will be described later); in a gesture to a wartime ally, the stone surround for the cross was brought from Verdun. One of the early timber memorials which failed to survive was to the 20th Royal Fusiliers, a 'public schoolboys' battalion' of the 33rd Division. In 1988 a tiny oak tree was planted a few yards from the London Division memorial to commemorate that battalion again; I hope it survives. Further along is a particularly interesting memorial ㉑, to the 1/9th Highland Light Infantry – the Glasgow Highlanders, another 33rd Division unit. It is an echo of an old Highland custom where each man coming to a battle added a stone to make a pile and each survivor removed a stone afterwards; the stones remaining represented the number of casualties. In 1972 a Glasgow man (Alex Aiken) and his wife fetched 192 stones from another High Wood near Culloden and built a cairn 5 feet, 7 inches high to commemorate the 192 Glasgow Highlanders killed here in 1916. The height represents the minimum height for recruitment to that battalion.

The *London Cemetery and Extension* ㉒ is another of the large, impressive cemeteries in this area. It has a complicated and unusual background, best described by cataloguing the different phases of its construction.

1 A small cemetery was made at the side of the road soon after the capture of the wood; many of the bodies were simply buried in a large shell hole. The total eventually buried was 101, mostly from the 47th (London) Division. It was called the London Cemetery and was made into a permanent cemetery after the war.

2 When the large Serre Road Cemetery No. 2 was completed in 1934, there still remained a considerable number of bodies to be reburied and an extension to the little London Cemetery commenced behind the brick shelter and the screen of bushes which now separate the original cemetery from the extension. Nearly 3,000 bodies were buried between 1934 and 1939 when the Second World War stopped this work. These bodies appear to have come from all parts of the 1916 battlefield and are to be found in the main parts of Plots 1 to 10, but not the two rows at the back of each plot.

3 The cemetery was used again after 1945. Bodies from the First World War were still being found and two further plots – 11 and 12 – were made behind the Cross of Sacrifice at the bottom of the cemetery. Much of Plot 13 was made for 165 Second World War casualties – 146 soldiers and nineteen airmen; most of the bodies came from the Amiens and Abbeville areas.

4 The very last burials are in the two rows at the back of each of the main plots in the main part of the cemetery, between the trees and near the boundary hedges. Entries in the cemetery register

for the few identified graves in those rows reveal that they came from many parts of the 1914–18 Western Front and the dates of death are from the first month of the war through to the last.

Approximately 890 First World War bodies were buried after 1945 to make a total of 3,769 1914–18 graves in the extension, the fourth largest on the Somme. The number of unidentified First World War graves in the extension is 3,112, which, at 82.6 per cent, is the highest proportion of unidentified in any major cemetery on the Somme and reflects the late finding of many of the bodies. The post-1945 burials in Plots 11 and 12 and in the rows near the side boundaries are 94 per cent unidentified. The last burials probably took place in the late 1950s and the new cemetery register for the combined London Cemetery and Extension was published in 1961, thirty-four years after the original register for the London Cemetery.

THE NORTH

The northern part of the main 1916 battlefield is a large area over which the last two months of the battle were fought. The southern edge of that area was the centre of the major attack of 15 September when ten divisions attacked at dawn on a frontage of eight miles, supported by thirty-seven of the first tanks ever to be used in war. It was the second largest set-piece attack of 1916 and more ground was captured that day than on any other single day of that year. Three cavalry divisions were waiting for the opportunity to come into action, but the Germans quickly established a new line and there was no opportunity for exploitation. Some historians think that Haig would have done well to close down the battle after that success. Since 1 July, the Germans had been dispossessed of their carefully prepared front-line defences, had been driven back five miles and had suffered serious casualties. The British had suffered too, but most of their divisions were still in good heart. It might have been a good time to stop, draw breath and resume the offensive in the following spring. But Haig had no intention of breaking off. He believed that several weeks of dry weather might still be available and that the Germans were suffering more heavily than the British. There followed two months of further attacks, with division after division being committed, some for the second or third time that year. The weather broke but still the attacks continued in the most miserable of conditions on the devastated battlefield. During the final two months of fighting, the average advance in this area from the line reached on 15 September was only 2,300 yards – just over a mile and a quarter.

Historically, this is as important an area as any other on the 1916 battlefield, but the main feature now is its emptiness. The Bapaume Road runs across it but, except for the villages on or alongside the road, there is nothing but open space. There are no woods. Over a large area to the north and east of Martinpuich there is not one memorial or one cemetery although the fighting was as heavy there as anywhere and the conditions for the troops more miserable than most. It is a feature of campaigns that the later stages are never as well commemorated as the early ones. Le Sars, Morval and Combles are not as well remembered as Beaumont-Hamel, La Boisselle or Fricourt. If you visit this section of the Somme battlefield, do not take the absence of cemeteries and memorials and the brevity of notes in this guide as evidence that the struggle here in late 1916 was not as bitter as in better-known parts of the battlefield.

Martinpuich

This village was probably a German headquarters at the opening of the 1916 battle. A double bunker ① which still remains at the south-eastern end of the village may have been a divisional battle headquarters. Martinpuich was captured on the morning of 15 September by the 15th (Scottish) Division supported by one tank. The bunker shows signs of shell fire on the side from which the Scots were attacking. The small *Martinpuich British Cemetery* ②, on the slope of a little hill, was not started until the end of the 1916 battle and its 115 graves are well spaced. Thirty-four of the men buried here were Australians and among a few 1918 casualties is an eighteen-year-old Scots pilot, Second Lieutenant W. R. Sellar, shot down while flying a DH9 of No. 98 Squadron; his grave is in Row A. The most interesting burials, however, pre-date the 1916 battle. At the far end of Row A are the graves of Second Lieutenant

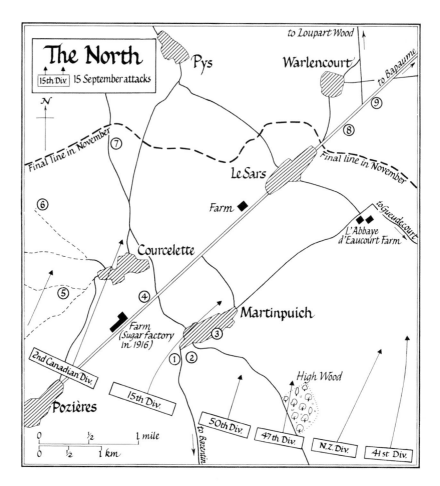

N. C. Blakeway and three men of the 1st Dorsets who died on 27 March 1916. The three men were killed and the officer fatally wounded making a night raid on the German trench at 'Y' Sap near La Boisselle; their bodies were brought back to Martinpuich by the Germans and buried in the civilian cemetery. Their graves were temporarily lost when this area was fought over but were discovered in recent years and transferred to the military cemetery. Five other British soldiers – one unidentified – are still buried in the civilian cemetery which is only a few yards away.

In the main street of the village, in front of the school, is the *47th*

(*London*) *Division Memorial Gateway* ③, and just behind it is a brick loggia, a gift from the division to the village. The placing of the memorial here was in connection with the division's successful attack at High Wood on 15 September 1916 and the gateway was unveiled on the same day in September 1925 as the division's memorial at High Wood. The local war memorial is in the same area to complete an interesting historical group in a tranquil, tree-shaded spot.

Courcelette

This village, on the other side of the Bapaume Road, and the battlefield to the north of the village belong to Canadian memory. The Canadian Corps took over the sector to the left of the Bapaume Road from the Australians early in September and remained there until the 1916 fighting ended. Courcelette and the nearby sugar factory were captured by the 2nd and 3rd Canadian Divisions with the help of six tanks in the 15 September attack; it was one of the best advances of that day. Further Canadian divisions then took it in turn to carry out later attacks until the end of the battle in mid-November. Their casualties were over 17,000 men during that period.

The *Canadian Memorial Park* ④ is by the main road, handsomely laid out in the style used for all Canadian national memorials on the Western Front, with a central granite block inscribed in English and French with a summary of the operations here in 1916. Unfortunately, the original trees outgrew themselves and had to be removed in the 1980s; their replacements will take many years to mature. The boundary of the Somme *département* runs along the road here; Courcelette and the park are in the Somme, but Martinpuich is not.

Courcelette British Cemetery ⑤ is in an attractive location on a hillside facing the village, with an open front and containing some fine oak trees. A German trench, the Fabeck Graben, ran along the nearby track in 1916 and was captured on 15 September by the Princess Patricia's Canadian Light Infantry. The original cemetery, of just seventy-four graves, was made at the end of the 1916 battle and now forms part of Plot 1, just inside the cemetery on the right. The other graves were made after the war by the concentration of

47 The Canadian Memorial at Courcelette.

bodies from the surrounding battlefield. There are 1,956 graves now, of which 1,177 are unidentified. The cemetery faithfully represents the divisions which fought in this area and includes at least 514 Australians who fought around Pozières and Mouquet Farm, which is just a mile away across the fields to the south-west, in July and August, 780 Canadians from September onwards and 657 United Kingdom troops. Just inside the entrance on the right is a memorial headstone to Lieutenant J. C. Newburn of the 18th (Western Ontario) Battalion, son of the Canadian Minister of Militia and Defence, killed on 15 September and believed to be buried in the cemetery. Further to the right, in Plot 2, Row A, is buried Private George Ritchie of the Royal Canadian Regiment, who died the following day aged only sixteen; his family inscription is: *For King and Country*.

In the fields north of Courcelette are two major cemeteries on the Canadian battlefield – *Regina Trench Cemetery* ⑥ and *Adanac Military Cemetery* ⑦. They are of similar character, both being largely concentration cemeteries from the local battlefields, both being 'Canadian' in that the visitors books are bilingual and Maple Leaf plaques are on the gateways. Both are in completely open ground, off the normal 'tourist route' and deserve more visits.

Regina Trench was the name given by the Canadians to a long German trench running east–west across this area. It was captured in a carefully prepared attack by Canadian and English divisions on the morning of 21 October. The line of the trench ran through the present location of the cemetery. The original burials made in the winter of 1916 – the graves in the close-packed last four rows of Plot 2, at the far end of the cemetery – are exactly where the old Regina Trench was. The remainder of the cemetery was concentrated after the war. Its layout gives every indication of having been planned to have its entrance at what is now the far end of the cemetery; the actual entrance, by the Cross of Sacrifice, was probably the result of a later decision. There are 2,265 graves; 1,077 are unidentified, but at least 563 Canadians are buried here. There is a group of four airmen's graves in Plot 9, Row A (near the Stone of Remembrance). First Lieutenant Ervin Shaw from South Carolina, an American pilot attached to the RAF, is buried here with his observer, Sergeant T. W. Smith; their Bristol Fighter of No. 48 Squadron was shot down, probably while ground-strafing near here in July 1918. Next to them are two other airmen, but they are unidentified.

Adanac Military Cemetery is larger, with 3,172 graves, 1,712 of them unidentified. There are at least 1,071 Canadian graves and the Maple Leaf badges on headstones are particularly numerous in the front plots. 'Adanac' is Canada written backwards. This is entirely a concentration cemetery with the exception of one grave, that of Private A. Edwards of the Machine Gun Corps who was killed when British troops recovered this ground in August 1918; his grave – now in Plot 4, Row D, on the left of the cemetery – was left undisturbed when the cemetery was constructed around it. There are superb views to be had of the surrounding ground. The concentration burials, particularly in the rear plots of the cemetery, appear to have been drawn from a wide area, with many bodies from United Kingdom units being brought in from the triangle bounded by Le Sars, Martinpuich and Flers, which is three miles away across the Bapaume Road and where there are no cemeteries. There are two VC graves. That of Sergeant S. Forsyth of the New Zealand Engineers is almost the first grave on the left inside the cemetery; his posthumous VC was awarded for the capture of

German machine-gun posts in an attack two miles away at Loupart Wood in August 1918. The other VC was Piper J. C. Richardson, a Scot who emigrated to Canada and fought with the 16th (Manitoba) Battalion. He piped that battalion 'over the top' on 9 October 1916 and rallied the attack when it was held up. He was escorting prisoners to the rear after the action when he decided to return and recover his bagpipes, despite the entreaties of his friends not to do so, and was not seen again until the battlefield was cleared. His grave is in Plot 3, Row F, on the right of the cemetery.

Le Sars and Warlencourt

Le Sars lies just inside the furthest limits of the British advance in 1916, just over five miles along the Bapaume Road from where the battle started at La Boisselle in July. Just beyond the village was a ridge which Haig wanted to capture before the fighting ended that autumn. At least four divisions – the 23rd and 47th (London) in mid-October, then the 48th (South Midland) and 50th (Northumbrian) – carried out attacks here, but the German defence always held. The weather had broken and those operations took place in the most appalling conditions of cold, rain and swampy mud, with exhausting approach marches across the battlefield even to reach British trenches which were always under German observation from the ridge, and with the prospect of a most difficult evacuation for the wounded and for those succumbing to sickness.[24]

The *Butte of Warlencourt* ⑧, an old burial mound, sits like a pimple on the ridge. It was the objective of many of the attacks and the scene of the most bitter of the fighting. British troops several times managed to gain a foothold but were always driven off and the Germans still held it when the fighting ended in November, a gleaming white dome swept bare by artillery fire of all earth and vegetation. Bushes and small trees cover the Butte now, but it is interesting to climb it and look down over the low ground between there and Le Sars village where the October and November attacks were mounted and where the British front line remained throughout

---

[24] For an excellent description of this fighting I commend *The Somme 1916* (London: Kimber, 1974), by Norman Gladden, a southerner drafted to a hard-bitten Northumberland Fusilier battalion taking part in these attacks.

the following winter. Several wooden memorials were erected on the crest but these have all gone now; one, made of ammunition boxes and timber beams in memory of three Durham Light Infantry Territorial battalions which attacked the Butte on 5 November, is now in Durham Cathedral. But the Western Front Association purchased the Butte in 1990 and has erected a new memorial on the crest, another example of the enduring interest in the battlefield.

A little further up the main road, just beyond the limit of the 1916 battlefield, is *Warlencourt British Cemetery* ⑨. This is an impressive and important cemetery containing the dead of the units which attacked the Butte and also those which fought in that large area of battlefield all the way back to Martinpuich, High Wood and Flers which has no other cemeteries. It is an excellent example of a concentration cemetery, carefully and attractively laid out, and with its impressive entrance on a main road for easy access by visitors. There are 3,450 graves, making it (with AIF Burial Ground) the fifth largest British cemetery on the Somme. It was made very soon after the war, in late 1919, but even then more than half of the bodies could not be identified. There are a lot of late-1916 graves – Durhams, Northumberlands, Londons, South Africans and New Zealanders who fought here and to the east of here in October – and also 461 Australians who held trenches in the same area during the following winter. One of the New Zealanders has a VC grave – Sergeant D. F. Brown of the 2nd Otago Battalion who won his decoration for bravery and leadership in the 15 September attack and again when the New Zealanders were in action on 1 October, the day he was killed. His grave is in Plot 3, Row F, the second plot on the left.

THE RIGHT FLANK

This large area was the scene of several important phases of the 1916 battle. Guillemont and Ginchy, in the south-west corner, required two sweltering months of slogging by many British units between 15 July and 14 September to clear. The maximum advance during those two months, at Ginchy, was only a mile and a quarter.

The Official History comments that 'several British officers with much battle experience on the Western Front have stated that the Germans never fought better than they did at Guillemont and Ginchy in 1916'.[25] Then came the 15 September attack, with the tanks, when a famous advance captured Flers, covering a mile and a quarter in less than four hours. After that it was a slow, costly, undramatic but steady progress over the last two months of the battle. Combles was captured in conjunction with the French, who also took Morval, but British units pushed further north to take Lesboeufs and Gueudecourt and it was just beyond those places that the battle finally ended quietly in rain and mud in mid-November.

Guillemont

British troops first attacked here on 30 July when the 30th Division attempted to capture the village from the west. The 2nd Royal Scots Fusiliers actually entered the village that day but were nearly all killed or taken prisoner when the Germans counter-attacked. It would be five weeks before British troops were in Guillemont again. But the 30 July attack captured the ruins of a farm marked on British and French army maps as Maltz Horn Farm. This was at the junction of the two armies and was taken by the combined efforts of the 2nd Bedfords and the French 153rd Infantry Regiment. This was another place where the map makers either made a mistake or deliberately changed the name. There is no farm now, but a beautiful cross ① stands as a memorial to 'the Farm of Maltzkorn Duclercq destroyed in desperate battles'. The notes I made here refer to 'fantastic views' on all sides, not only over the local battlefields but for a great distance to the south over the uplands beyond the Somme valley.

The important *Guillemont Road Cemetery* ② stands on ground across which many costly attacks on the village were made. I always feel that this area and this cemetery constitute the heart of the 1916 battlefield; I have many times stopped and eaten my picnic lunch on the low wall at the front of this beautiful cemetery. It is easy to spot the short, irregular rows just inside the entrance on the left where the first British troops were buried. An Advanced Dressing

---

[25] Official History 1916, Vol. II, p. 181n.

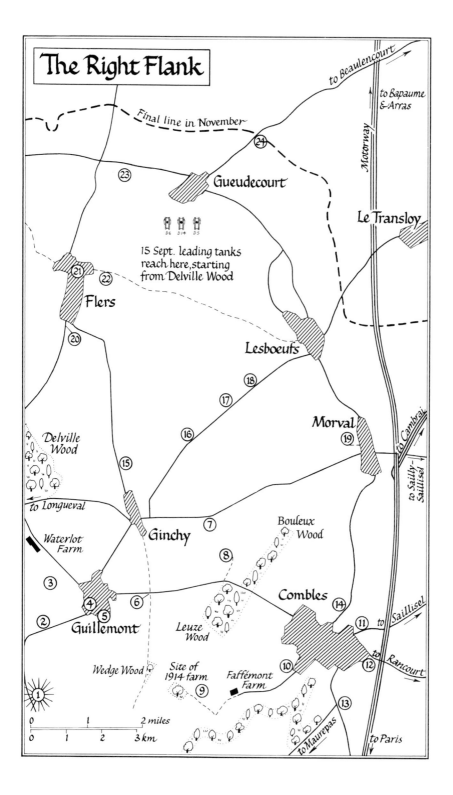

The Right Flank

to Beaulencourt

to Bapaume & Arras

Motorway

Final line in November

㉔

㉓

Gueudecourt

Le Transloy

D6 D14 D5

15 Sept. leading tanks reach here, starting from Delville Wood

㉑ ㉒

Flers

⑳

Lesboeufs

⑱

⑰

Morval

⑲

to Cambrai

Saillisel

to Sailly-

⑯

Delville Wood

⑮

to Longueval

Ginchy

⑦

Bouleux Wood

⑧

Combles

⑭

to Saillisel

Waterlot Farm

③

④

⑥

⑪ to Saillisel

②

⑤

Guillemont

Leuze Wood

⑫ to Rancourt

⑩

Faffémont Farm

Wedge Wood

Site of 1914 farm

⑨

①

⑬

to Maurepas

to Paris

0   1   2 miles
0   1   2   3 km

48 The memorial cross on the site of Maltzkorn (Maltz Horn) Farm.

Station from the 16th (Irish) Division worked here after the capture of Guillemont and men who died here and others whose bodies were brought back from the battlefield were buried in a little wartime cemetery which eventually contained 121 graves. The remainder of the plots were concentrated after the war and there are now 2,255 graves, more than two-thirds of them 'unknowns'.

One interesting aspect of this cemetery is the presence of graves of well-known families close together in the first rows of the original cemetery. The very first grave on the left is that of Second Lieutenant William Stanhope Forbes, 1st Duke of Cornwall's Light Infantry, who was killed in the fields south of the cemetery on 3 September. This young officer, an architectural student before enlisting, was the son of Stanhope Alexander Forbes, a Royal Academician and one of the founders of the Newlyn 'school of art'. The personal inscription on his headstone is: *He saw beyond the filth of battle and*

49 An Advanced Dressing Station on the Guillemont Road in 1916; one grave has already been made. The two lorries on the left carry the Shamrock sign of the 16th (Irish) Division. This scene is on or near the location of the present-day cemetery.

thought death a fair price to pay to belong to the company of these fellows. The next row contains the grave of the Prime Minister's son, Lieutenant Raymond Asquith of the 3rd Grenadier Guards, shot in the chest during the attack of 15 September between Ginchy and Lesboeufs and dying before reaching the Dressing Station. It is appropriate that the British Prime Minister's son, representing in a way the nation's sacrifice, should be buried in this part of the Somme battlefield. Further along the same row is the grave of Lieutenant Hon. Edward Wyndham Tennant, son of Baron Glenconner; Tennant was killed when his battalion, the 4th Grenadiers, was carrying out a minor attack a week later. These two men, though well separated in age (Asquith was a mature thirty-seven, Tennant only nineteen), had much in common and it is remarkable that they are buried so close together, although it is possible that Lieutenant Tennant's body was deliberately brought back from where he died

50 The Prime Minister's son's grave.

to be buried near Asquith. There are two links. The two men were related through marriage; Tennant's Aunt Margot was the second wife of Herbert Asquith and was thus Raymond Asquith's step-mother. But more than this, both men were sons in a close group of families known in society as 'the Souls'. None of these families had a military background, but the sons were almost wiped out during the First World War. One author has written: 'The sons grew up in that magic circle to share their [parents'] style of life and merge it with the dreams and rebellions that epitomized Edwardian society, and to carry a common gallantry into a war that was to destroy them and most of their contemporaries.'[26] Raymond Asquith was a barrister and a noted scholar and orator. Both men were associates of Rupert Brooke. The inscription on Raymond Asquith's grave is: *Small time but in that small most greatly lived this star of England.* Edward Tennant's is: *Killed in action in his twentieth year.*

The German trenches protecting Guillemont ran north and south across the road between the cemetery and the village. Some concrete lumps and steel girders still to be seen firmly driven into the ground on either side of the road might be parts of a former strong-point in

[26] From the Preface to *The Children of the Souls* by Jeanne Mackenzie (London: Chatto & Windus, 1986). Two more of the sons lost by 'the Souls' – the Grenfell brothers – have been referred to earlier in this book; see the entry for Boulogne Eastern Cemetery on page 36.

the German line. It was somewhere near here that Captain Noel
Chavasse, Medical Officer of the 1/10th King's Liverpool (Liverpool
Scottish), won his first Victoria Cross on 9 August, helping wounded
men on the battlefield after a failed attack. Chavasse won a second
VC in July 1917 at Ypres but died of wounds on that occasion. He
was the only double VC of the First World War.[27] The road into
Guillemont is part of the road from Combles to Albert which formed
the centre line of the westward march of two divisions of von Kluck's
First Army in August 1914 and also of the German 2nd Panzer
Division in May 1940.

In a field north of the road is a memorial ③ to a young officer
who died here but whose body was not identified. Second Lieutenant
George Marsden-Smedley was only nineteen when he died. A year
earlier he had been at Harrow where he had captained the cricket
and football teams, being described as 'probably the most outstanding sportsman of his generation' at that school. He joined his
battalion, the 3rd Rifle Brigade, in July 1916 and was killed in his
first attack, on 18 August at Guillemont, being shot by a German
officer on the parapet of the German trench. Four other subalterns
in the battalion died that day; their bodies were all identified and are
now buried in Delville Wood Cemetery; perhaps George Marsden-
Smedley's is one of the 'unknown' graves there. His father, a prominent knitwear manufacturer at Matlock, Derbyshire, was desolated
by his son's death and established four memorials of various types,
this one on the spot where he fell and three in England, one being
a new wood planted on his estate which became known as 'Mr
George's Wood'. There are three ways of reaching the memorial at
Guillemont, all on foot. If the fields are bare, it can be reached
directly from the cemetery. Another way is up the winding track
from the road nearer the village. The quickest way is from the east,
through the yard in which the grain silos now stand on the site of
what was once Guillemont Station. The local railway line once ran
past the memorial. The inscription on it ends with these words:
'Lovely and pleasant in life, in death serene and unafraid. Most
blessed in remembrance.' The memorial stone is in perfect condition
but, at the time of writing, the walled enclosure and the gateway
have deteriorated and the little garden is overgrown; negotiations

[27] Chavasse's grave, with two VCs engraved on the headstone, is in Brandhoek New British
Cemetery between Poperinge and Ypres.

are under way which will probably restore or improve the surroundings of this lovely memorial.

Next to Guillemont church is the simple *16th (Irish) Division Memorial* ④; a brigade from this division took part in the capture of the village on 3 September. One of the Irish casualties was Lieutenant Thomas Michael (Tom) Kettle of the 9th Royal Dublin Fusiliers, killed near Ginchy on 9 September 1916; he was a well-known Southern Irish politician, essayist and poet. He has no known grave.

The Germans had a particularly well-prepared set of concreted dug-outs in Guillemont, probably constructed earlier to house a divisional battle headquarters. The entrance to the dug-outs can still be seen in a small pasture on the south side of the village ⑤;

51 The cross on the Dickens 'grave'.

they all face north, indicating that the Germans were anticipating an attack from the south, but the battle developed in such a way that the attacks came from the west. The Official History mentions that Guillemont was completely ruined but that dug-outs and tunnels caused the attackers considerable difficulties.

At a crossroads to the east of the village is the tall *20th (Light) Division Memorial* ⑥, which is beginning to show signs of disrepair. This division was mainly responsible for the eventual capture of Guillemont. From that same crossroads three tanks set off across the field to the north-west in support of the 6th Division in the 15 September attack, but this was the only sector where the British effort failed that day, being held up by a particularly strong German position, called the *Quadrilateral* ⑦, the location of which can still be established, but it is littered with various dumped items, including the concrete bases of a demolished Nato radio station.

The *Dickens Cross* ⑧ is easily reached by a track and is another of those touching personal memorials which are such a delight to find, except that in this case it might also be a grave. Major Cedric Charles Dickens, grandson of the famous writer, was killed close to here on 9 September 1916 while serving with the 1/13th Londons (the Kensingtons), part of the 56th (London) Division which had fought so well at Gommecourt on 1 July and was now trying to push forward against two woods, Bouleaux Wood and Leuze Wood ('Lousy Wood' to the soldiers). His mother, Lady Dickens, was informed that he had been buried by his men at a certain spot and she purchased a strip of land there after the war. She paid for a stout and very durable timber cross for the 'grave' and planted a small avenue of typically English trees and shrubs along the approach path. She visited the spot every year until 1939 and paid the local man who cared for the site. In 1948, the War Graves Commission asked if the body could be moved to a British cemetery for more permanent care. The family agreed, but the body could not be found, so the name of Major Dickens was added to the Thiepval Memorial. The cross still remains; the timber is so sound that it will last for many years yet. On it are carved the words: 'In loving memory of our darling Ceddy.' The little garden avenue has now grown wild and appears to be a natural copse, but careful examination shows that the original trees and bushes are still there – holly, box, laburnum, cherry, rowan, dogwood, lilac, privet and syringa, although wild elderberry threatens to take over.

Combles

This large village has a different tale to tell to so many others on the Somme. It fell without a fight. On 25 September it was just ahead of the boundary between the British and French Armies and units of both sides were threatening to encircle the village, which contained a considerable number of German troops and supplies. The Germans decided to evacuate on the night of the 25th and when men of the 56th (London) Division and French troops of the 73rd and 110th Infantry Regiments entered next morning they captured 500 Germans who had not been able to get away, together with large stocks of weapons and ammunition. Combles was adopted by Portsmouth after the war.

A battlefield grave is to be found in a field at *Faffémont Farm* ⑨. (Official army maps incorrectly called this 'Falfemont Farm'. The present-day farm is not on the original site; the old farm was on a rise near the grave where a wood now stands.) In the grave are buried three members of the 1/2nd Londons. They are Captain R. (Dick) Heumann, Company Sergeant-Major B. Mills and Sergeant A. W. Torrance, all killed on 10 September when their battalion was making a minor attack just east of here. The three were buried in a shell hole and, after the war, Heumann's family, from Hampstead, bought a piece of ground from the farmer and, together with the relatives of the other two men, requested that the grave should remain undisturbed. They placed a simple stone over it. This is still there, set within a concrete border provided by the War Graves Commission and maintained by the Commission. This is an official British war grave and visitors have a right of access to it, but it would be a courtesy to ask at the farm (*'pour visiter la tombe des soldats Britanniques dans le champ'*) and to avoid damaging crops.

Closer to the village is the *Guards Cemetery* ⑩ (not to be confused with the Guards Cemetery at Lesboeufs), started in September 1916 and used throughout the following winter and again in 1918. The long rows in the main part of the cemetery then contained ninety-six graves. The fifty-six graves in the short rows on the left were brought in after the war and there are memorial headstones to thirty other men buried near Combles but whose graves were later lost. It is a quiet little cemetery in a pretty rural location. In Row D of Plot 1 is the grave of Gunner S. L. Taylor from the famous 'L' Battery, Royal Horse Artillery, which won three VCs at Néry during

52 The first Tank Corps grave.

the retreat from Mons in September 1914; Gunner Taylor had the unique service number of 111111.

At the northern end of the village is the much larger *Combles Communal Cemetery Extension* ⑪, which has a chequered history. The cemetery was started by French troops in October 1916 and was later used in turn by the British, the Germans in 1918 and the British again later in 1918. The French and German graves were moved after the war, leaving the empty space of the old Plot 1 on the left of the cemetery. There were only ninety-seven British graves at the end of the war, but a major concentration of graves brought the number up to 1,051 when the register was printed in 1927. Still more British graves were added even later when most of Row D and all of Rows E and F in Plot 3 (on the left of the cemetery) were made; many of these were 1 July 1916 graves of the 18th (Eastern) Division from the Mametz–Montauban area.

It is a handsome cemetery, despite the many changes, and there are some interesting features. In the first row on the right of the entrance is the grave of Corporal G. E. Pattinson who was killed on

15 September 1916. The register shows him to have been a member of 'C' Company, Machine Gun Corps (Heavy Branch). This was the title under which the first tanks went into action on that day; it is now the 3rd Royal Tank Regiment. Other tank men killed on 15 September have Machine Gun Corps badges on their headstones but Corporal Pattinson has the Tank Corps badge, making this the earliest dated Tank Corps headstone. The family inscription is: *He, taking death on himself, saved his comrades*; it has not been possible to find out what incident on 15 September lay behind this. Another feature is the large number of Northamptonshire Regiment graves to the left and right of the central pathway. Finally, at the very end of the cemetery, is the grave of Private J. Hollingworth, 2nd Manchesters, whose date of death was 15 August 1915. Soon after British troops took over the Carnoy–Marricourt sector from the French, this man was in a forward listening post when he was 'snatched' by a German raiding party and brought to Combles in a wounded condition. He may have been the first British soldier to have been taken prisoner on the Somme. Unfortunately he died and a Bavarian medical unit buried him in the nearby civilian cemetery. His body was later moved and his grave is now the last one in Plot 2, Row C, directly to the right of the Cross of Sacrifice.

There are two memorials to French soldiers on the side of the village where their units fought. At the side of the road to Rancourt, in what was once a quiet spot but now stands looking over the busy Paris motorway, is one of the largest private memorials ⑫ I have ever seen. It is to Sous-Lieutenant Charles Dansette from Armentières, who died here on 25 September 1916. The front face of the memorial shows a shield, a sword, the face of Christ and an inscription from Victor Hugo which translates as: 'Those who have piously died for their country have earned the right that crowds be present and pray by the side of their tomb.' This may actually be Dansette's grave. The two sides of the memorial stone quote the citations for decorations awarded to him in November 1914 and April 1915, but his regiment is not identified. At the corner of a lane south of the village is a smaller stone ⑬, surrounded by a privet hedge, to a member of the 110th Tirailleurs Regiment who 'died gloriously' on 12 September 1916. The inscription has become almost illegible, but the name appears to be Victor Hallarodittaeoez. Again, it may be the soldier's grave.

On the other side of the village, in a field behind a warehouse, is one of the few concrete bunkers ⑭ to be found on the 1916 battlefield. It was a command bunker; there are no weapons apertures, only a doorway on the side away from incoming artillery fire. An interesting feature is that the forward wall slopes steeply inward so that a shell with a normal descending trajectory would have either missed or only grazed the wall and perhaps not exploded against it.

Ginchy, Lesboeufs and Morval

Ginchy was the scene of bitter fighting, finally being captured by the 16th (Irish) Division on 9 September, but the village has no military cemeteries and the only battlefield memorial is at the north end of the village ⑮, to two French soldiers, Georges Lejoindre and Georges Pfister, and 'their comrades of the 18th Territorial Infantry Regiment' who were killed near here in September 1914. In the great attack of 15 September 1916, the Guards Division attacked out of the village in a north-easterly direction but had a tough time because the nine tanks detailed for its support suffered numerous breakdowns and were able to provide little support. The *Guards Division Memorial* ⑯ is a few yards beyond the line reached. An important German trench system known as 'the Triangle', captured by the Guards that day, was in the field immediately south of the memorial.

The Guards remained on that sector until the end of the month and were then relieved, having suffered 7,240 casualties in three weeks. One of these was Captain H. P. Meakin of the Guards Trench Mortar Battery who was killed at the spot where a personal memorial to him now stands ⑰; he has no known grave. It is a tall stone monument which has fallen into disrepair, with the rail surround broken and the lettering almost indecipherable, but it is hoped that it will be restored by the Coldstream Guards, his parent regiment, before this book is published. When the original memorial was erected, the inscription stated incorrectly that Captain Meakin was in the Guards Machine Gun Company.

Nearer to Lesboeufs is the *Guards Cemetery* ⑱. It was started when forty men, most or all from the 2nd Grenadiers killed on 25 September, were buried at the side of the road in what is now Plot 1, to the left of the entrance. The remainder of the cemetery – 3,096

graves – was a post-war concentration from the surrounding area.
It is one of the most beautiful of the concentration cemeteries. It is
situated on a high bank above a sunken road and the cemetery
architect designed a particularly attractive entrance in the bank.
There is also an unusual central pathway with the paving stones
separated to allow flowers to grow between them. In Plot 4, Row
F, the grave of Second Lieutenant T. P. A. Hervey of the 2nd King's
Royal Rifle Corps, killed in the 15 September attack, has an interesting family inscription: *In far Fiji he heard his country's call and
came and died.* He was a Hampshire vicar's son in the colonial service.
At the rear of the cemetery are three memorial headstones erected
more recently to officers of the 2nd Coldstream Guards killed on 26
September and then buried together under a private memorial on
the battlefield. Their families agreed to a proposal that the bodies
should be brought into this cemetery for permanent care but,
although the War Graves Commission exhumation party dug down
to hard chalk, the bodies could not be found at that place; the grave
marker had probably been out of position. The back of the cemetery
has good views to Flers, to Gueudecourt and all the way to Bapaume
four and a half miles away.

53 The Guards Cemetery at Lesboeufs.

The village of Lesboeufs, with nearby Morval, was adopted by Canterbury, Kent, after the war, probably because the 1st Buffs – the East Kents – of the 6th Division were involved in a successful advance on 25 September 1916 which captured both villages.

Morval is another village often overlooked by visitors. It was on the extreme right flank of the British sector and was captured by the 5th Division in a good attack on 25 September, with the 2nd King's Own Scottish Borderers reporting that the German defenders were seemingly 'demoralized and not inclined to show much fight' and with 'nearly every man in the battalion securing a trophy'.[28] The village passed into the sector occupied by French troops soon afterwards. *Morval British Cemetery* ⑲ is a tiny one on the edge of the village, prettily situated among fields with farm animals and mature trees nearby. There are only fifty-five graves, one of a German prisoner of war who died in September 1916 and fifty-four of men of the 38th (Welsh) Division which made a fighting advance through here in late August and early September 1918. It is the only British cemetery on the 1916 battlefield which does not contain a 1916 British casualty. There are only two rows of graves. The parents of Private Ernest Appleyard of the 13th Welch, buried in the front row, chose this inscription: *Be his dear face the first to greet us and bid us welcome home.* A captain and six subalterns are buried side by side in the second row.

Flers and Gueudecourt

At the southern end of Flers is a memorial ⑳ to the French 17th and 18th Infantry Regiments of the 82nd Territorial Division which fought here in September 1914. But the village is better remembered for its successful capture by infantry and tanks on 15 September 1916. Thirteen tanks of 'D' Company, Heavy Branch Machine Gun Corps (later the 4th Tank Battalion and later still the 4th Royal Tank Regiment) started out that morning from positions near Delville Wood; they were particularly lucky in having few break-downs and their crews were particularly bold and skilful in using this new weapon. Twelve tanks reached the German front line; eleven reached the German trench which ran level with the

---

[28] Official History 1916, Vol. II, p. 376; the battalion was temporarily attached to the 5th Division for this operation.

southern end of Flers; six penetrated beyond the village and three nearly reached Gueudecourt which was two and a half miles from their starting-point. One tank – D16 – actually went right through Flers village: 'firing as it went, the tank lurched up the main street followed by parties of cheering infantry . . . a scene without precedent in war'.[29] That tank was commanded by a Lieutenant Arnold who, when returning past the western side of Flers from his successful foray, left his tank to help a wounded infantryman and was himself wounded by a German machine-gun which was still in action. Gunner Glaister took command and the tank returned safely to its starting-point. Lieutenant Arnold won the Military Cross and Gunner Glaister the Military Medal, the first decorations for tank men. The records for the two tank companies in action that day are not complete, but it appears that three officers and six men were killed and ten men were listed as missing.

The enthusiastic infantry with the tanks in Flers were from the 41st Division which has its memorial at the north end of the main street ㉑. It is topped with the lovely bronze statue of a fully equipped infantryman whose head is looking back down the main street up which the infantry and tanks advanced. This division was the last to be formed from Kitchener's New Army volunteers and had only been on the Western Front since May; this was its first attack. Undoubtedly helped by the performance of the tanks in and around the village, the 41st Division's advance was the day's most successful. Flers was adopted by Portsmouth because the 15th Hampshires were in action here on that day.

Bulls Road Cemetery ㉒ was so named because it was on the road (now only a track) to Lesboeufs, which is French for 'the bullocks'. It is an attractive cemetery with 755 graves in two distinct parts. The three long rows of Plot 1, just inside the entrance and containing 154 graves, were started after Flers was captured, but most of the main cemetery, down some steps to a new level behind the Cross of Sacrifice, was concentrated from the local battlefields after the war. Among the graves are those of 120 New Zealanders who were fighting to the west of Flers in September 1916 and 148 Australians who fought north of here soon afterwards. Among several August 1918 graves is one of an officer whose register entry shows an unusual war service. He was Lieutenant F. W. Woods whose grave

[29] Official History 1916, Vol. II, p. 323.

is in Plot 3, Row L. He was a Hampshire man, a pre-war Territorial, who served in India from 1914 to 1916 and then on the Western Front with the Dorsets until November 1917, when he was sent to the United States as a musketry instructor before returning to die with the 4th Dorsets in August 1918 at the age of thirty-seven.

Gueudecourt is the last village in the British part of the 1916 battlefield to be described. It was hoped that it could be captured on 15 September. Three tanks – D5, D6 and D14 – almost reached the village and a duel with a German artillery battery took place, but the infantry never caught up and all of the tanks became casualties, although one was recovered the following day. Most of the men killed in tanks on 15 September suffered their fate at the southern entrances to Gueudecourt. The village fell on 26 September after a successful attack which included infantry, tanks, a strafing RFC aircraft and even cavalry patrols. The first men to enter the village were dismounted troopers of the 19th Lancers and the South Irish Horse, closely followed by infantry of the 6th Leicesters, 21st Division. There was little further movement on this sector during the remaining seven weeks of the battle. Australian divisions returned to the Somme and manned trenches north and to the west of the village for much of that time and during the following winter months.

The only military cemetery in the area is *AIF Burial Ground* ㉓, which was started by Australian troops in November 1916. (AIF were the initials for the Australian Imperial Force.) The original cemetery was no more than the first two rows of Plot 1, just to the left of the entrance, and contained only thirty-two graves. A large post-war concentration then took place, but in two distinct stages. Most of Plots 1 to 6 were made, including the French graves in Plot 6, and the architect designed the cemetery layout of pathways and walls on the assumption that there would be no further burials. But then the decision was made to make a further expansion. This was probably in 1927 when Thiepval was chosen for the Memorial to the Missing and the clearance of cemeteries there took place. Approximately 1,500 further bodies were transferred to this cemetery and buried in the ten plots numbered 7 to 16 which were made along what would have been the side pathways of the original cemetery, in the far corners and in an extra section on the right-hand side. (The base of the original right-hand side wall can still be seen between Plots 15 and 16 and the earlier plots.) This operation nearly doubled the size of the cemetery, altering its original shape and character and losing the spaciousness of the original plan. A large proportion of these later graves are 'unknowns', but those that are identified show dates and units involved in actions in the Thiepval area in 1916 and 1918, including many men of the 36th (Ulster) Division from 1 July 1916.

Much of this can be deduced by observation of the cemetery and a study of the plan in the register, but I am fortunate in having documentary evidence also. The only man to win the Victoria Cross from my home district was Sergeant Harold Jackson from Kirton, near Boston, Lincolnshire, who won his VC with the 7th East Yorks in the German Spring Offensive of 1918 but was later killed at Thiepval in August 1918. His family was sent a letter by the War Graves Commission, dated 23 March 1927, stating that 'in order to secure the relevant maintenance of the grave in perpetuity' his body had been removed from Thiepval to this cemetery. His grave is now in the front row of Plot 15, right up against the front wall. Two more well-decorated men are with him, CSM E. England, DCM, MM, of the 6th Dorsets and Private C. Hant, MM, of the 10th West Yorks. All three were in the 17th (Northern) Division which recaptured Thiepval in August 1918 and are typical of the decorated veterans who fought in the middle years of the war but sadly died in the closing months.

The cemetery contained 3,450 graves when completed, making it, with Warlencourt British Cemetery, the fifth largest British cemetery on the 1916 battlefield; but it is hardly known to visitors, being situated up a track in a near-forgotten corner of the battlefield. At least 400 Australians and eighty New Zealanders are buried here and there are 163 French graves. The number of 'unknowns' is 2,262, nearly two-thirds of the total. One grave was added at a much later date. Lieutenant-Colonel the Earl of Feversham, a cavalry officer, was given command of the 21st King's Royal Rifle Corps in the 41st Division but was killed on 15 September, his battalion's first day in action. He was buried on the battlefield about 200 yards south of the cemetery and remained in a private grave until after 1945 when his body was reburied in Plot 3, Row L, halfway up the cemetery and immediately left of the central pathway.

On the road from Gueudecourt to Beaulencourt is to be found the *Newfoundland Memorial* ㉔, a smaller version of the Caribou Memorial in the Newfoundland Park at Beaumont-Hamel. It is a lovely little memorial standing above a short section of preserved trench, all in a small enclosure. I always think that this is an appropriate place to end a tour of the British area of the 1916 battlefield. The Newfoundlanders fought on the first day of the battle, with terrible consequences, but they returned here in October and carried out a workmanlike, efficient attack on 12 October which captured a German position called Hilt Trench. Their memorial now stands on the very furthest limit of the British advance of 1916; that trench became the front line held during the following winter. It is also right on the boundary between the Somme and Pas-de-Calais *départements*.

I hate to be pedantic but it must be said that the trench by the memorial is not the one captured by the Newfoundlanders but is Mild Trench which was taken by the 2nd East Lancs on 23 October. It is possible that a genuine mistake was made when the Newfoundlanders came to erect their memorial after the war, or it may have been that Mild Trench was the only one remaining at that time. The memorial is on high ground, giving a good view over the fields to Bapaume, two and a half miles away, a town which the British generals hoped to have captured in the first days of the 1916 battle. The line on which the memorial was erected represents, quite by chance, the furthermost British advance in 1916, being just six miles from the German trenches in front of Montauban which were captured by the 30th Division on 1 July. The advance from there had been made at an average rate of seventy-five yards per day.

THE FRENCH SECTOR

I have to state that the above title is a slight misnomer, because this area does not contain all of the French share of the 1916 battlefield; the southern part of it – about a quarter – fits better geographically into the description of the 1918 battlefield which will come later in the book.

The original plan for the 1916 battle envisaged a joint Anglo-French offensive astride the Somme, with the two armies making equal contributions. That plan had to be amended following the

German attack at Verdun in February. The great battle which followed drew in most of the French Army and their contribution to the Somme offensive had to be reduced by about half. The British accepted that this was necessary and the operations which started on 1 July progressed in relative harmony and with co-operation 'as satisfactory as could be expected', according to the British Official History. The French attacks after 1 July were not often co-ordinated with British efforts, but the Germans were obliged to defend both sectors and it was one of the best joint Allied efforts of the war. The maximum British advance of six miles was matched by the French, although on a smaller frontage. The French suffered about 200,000 casualties. So, in effort, gains and cost, the French share was always about half that of the British, a creditable effort for a nation which had suffered so much at Verdun as well as bearing the brunt of the 1915 fighting.

There are two reasons why touring the French sector is not as rewarding as the British areas. The 1916 Somme battle was never the emotional experience for the French that it was for the British; there are no national monuments, preserved trenches or memorial parks. The second reason is the French practice of making larger but fewer military cemeteries. The places of interest are more widely scattered than in British sectors. But the French cemeteries are impressive and there are many interesting memorials. There are also five British cemeteries in this area, made either when the Germans withdrew in 1917, by which time the British had taken over part of the area from the French, or after the 1918 fighting when this was wholly a British sector.

At the side of the Péronne Road near Maricourt is a large granite memorial ① to the memory of Lieutenant Robert Brodv, a company commander of the 224th Infantry Regiment, and to his men who died here in an attack in December 1914. It is an impressive memorial, surrounded by an evergreen hedge, and the plot was entirely planted with marigolds on our visit, showing that it is still tended. It is in the middle of the No Man's Land over which troops of the French 11th Division attacked successfully and at modest cost on 1 July 1916. There are two memorials near the village of Hardecourt. A simple stone ② commemorates two soldiers of the 153rd Infantry Regiment, Marcel Boucher and his friend Romeo Lapage, who died here on 28 July 1916. Only a few yards away ③ is

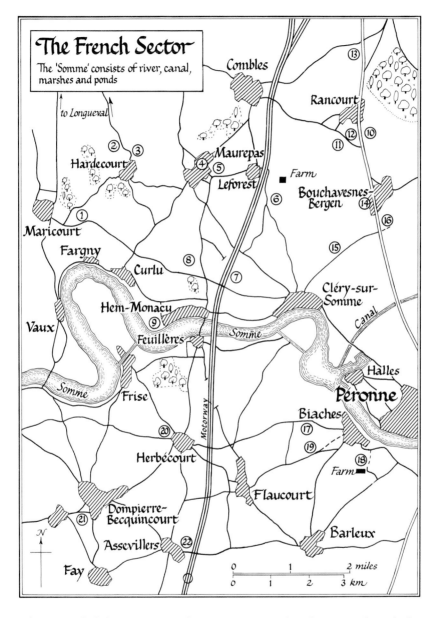

The French Sector

The 'Somme' consists of river, canal, marshes and ponds

to Longueval

Combles

Rancourt

⑬

⑫ ⑩

⑪

Hardecourt

② ③

Maurepas

④ ⑤

Leforest

⑥

Farm

Bouchavesnes-Bergen ⑭

⑯

Maricourt

①

Fargny

Curlu

⑧

⑦

⑮

Cléry-sur-Somme

Canal

Vaux

Hem-Monacu

⑨

Feuillères

Somme

Somme

Frise

Halles

Péronne

Biaches

⑰

⑲

⑱

Farm

Herbécourt

⑳

Motorway

Flaucourt

N

Dompierre-Becquincourt

㉑

Asservillers ㉒

Barleux

Fay

0   1   2 miles

0   1   2   3 km

a large and elaborate wrought-iron cross with a fantasy of symbolic items – chains of machine-gun belts, shells and a fallen soldier being borne to heaven by angels. This is in memory of Captain Augustin Cochin, killed here on 8 July 1916; 'wounded three times and arm broken, although disabled he returned to the battle for love of his

country and of his men . . . The harder the ordeal, the more necessary
to be there.' His unit, not recorded on the memorial, was the 4th
Battalion of Chasseurs.

In the centre of Maurepas, on the edge of the village green ④, is
a memorial to the men of the 1st Infantry Regiment who died
liberating the village in 1916. Outside the village is the *Maurepas
National Cemetery* ⑤, where 3,678 French soldiers, nearly all of
whom died in 1916, are buried on a pleasant open country site.
Passing under the motorway at the north end of Leforest, one comes
to the family memorial ⑥ to a French soldier. The inscription has
become worn, but the name Edouard Naudier and the year 1916
are legible, also a reference to his dying at 'a hospital'. The nearby
farm is named Ferme de l'Hôpital. By the side of the motorway is
Cléry-sur-Somme National Cemetery ⑦ with 2,332 graves. On a bank

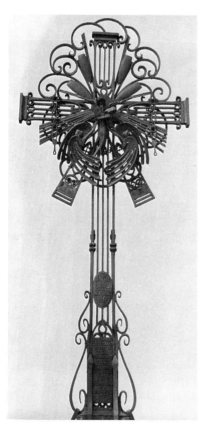

54 The elaborate cross on the memorial
to the French Captain Cochin at
Hardecourt.

above the access road to the cemetery, overlooking the motorway, is a new horizontal stone block memorial to the 363rd Infantry Regiment and 'its victorious battles on 7 August and 3 September 1916'. On the other side of the motorway, a stone memorial in the hedge ⑧ at the junction of the road from Maurepas is inscribed simply to 'H.R., 12 Août 1916'.

Just outside the village of Hem-Monacu is *Hem Farm Military Cemetery* ⑨, a little-known British cemetery in an out-of-the-way location. It is a pleasant cemetery of 597 graves on a quiet track close to the present-day Hem Farm. The back of the cemetery looks out across fields to the wooded valley of the River Somme. The ground in front of the cemetery was the scene of heavy fighting by French troops in the first week of July 1916 and the tumbled chalk of trenches and shelling can easily be seen if the land is bare. The original cemetery, in Rows E, F and G on the left of the pathway, was started in January 1917 when the British took over this sector from the French and probably used the farm as a Dressing Station; the cemetery was used again in 1918 and there were sixty-three graves at the end of the war. The remaining plots were concentrated after the war. Among particular features of the post-war additions are five rows – Rows A, B, E, F and G of Plot 2 – filled almost entirely with South African soldiers, though many not identified by name, all killed on or around 24 March 1918 when the South African Brigade was overwhelmed attempting to halt the German advance three miles away at Leforest. The last four rows of Plot 2 contain at least 138 Australians, mostly from August and September 1918.

There are two VC graves in the cemetery. Second Lieutenant G. E. Cates of the 2nd Rifle Brigade was one of the original burials, in Row G on the left. He was killed in March 1917; a grenade was uncovered while a trench was being deepened and he placed his foot on it to save the lives of the men around him. The second VC is the Australian Private R. Mactier of the 23rd (Victoria) Battalion whose grave is in the third row from the back on the right. He won his decoration in the famous Australian attack against Mont St Quentin on 1 September 1918 for single-handedly wiping out or capturing the Germans in three posts before being killed.

Moving north, to Rancourt, one comes to a place where there are three cemeteries close together near the old main road to Paris, a quieter road now that the motorway takes most of the heavy traffic. The *Rancourt French National Cemetery* ⑩ is just inside the furthermost line reached by the French in 1916. This cemetery was obviously located on the Paris road to attract visitors. It is the 'prestige' French cemetery on the Somme and, with 8,567 graves, the largest, although several of the German cemeteries contain more burials. There is a memorial chapel which is usually locked, though the key can probably be obtained from the custodian. But the chapel has a colonnade along which there are some interesting memorials and displays. Among the items to be seen is an exhibition of French uniforms and decorations, a memorial showing a complete list of French infantry, artillery and cavalry units which fought on the Somme from 1914 to 1918 and a host of individual memorial plaques. One section is devoted to British plaques. It is obvious, from the dates and places of death, that these are not just 'Somme' memorials. British families were probably encouraged by the French to make donations to the building of the chapel in return for the right to place memorials here. I made note of five of the more interesting ones and later ascertained where the men concerned are now buried, if they have a grave:

Captain Guy Drummond, 13th Canadian Battalion, died in the gas attack at Ypres on 22 April 1915, buried at Tyne Cot Cemetery.

Second Lieutenant S. L. Mansel-Carey, 8th Devons, 'mortally wounded on 24 February 1916 by the bursting of a shell in the trenches at Fricourt', buried at Corbie Communal Cemetery; Mansel Copse, where the Devonshire Cemetery is now, was probably named after this officer.

Second Lieutenant Henry Coxe, a BE2c pilot of No. 6 Squadron, 'killed in aerial fight on 1 July 1916 after bombing Cambrai', buried at Point-du-Jour Military Cemetery near Arras.

Captain Viscount P. R. H. Clive, 1st Welsh Guards (son of the Earl of Powis), died on 13 October 1916 of wounds received on the Somme, buried in Wales.

The largest of all the British memorial plaques is to a junior NCO – Corporal A. G. Leeson, 102nd Canadian Battalion, killed in an attack on Regina Trench near Courcelette on 21 October 1916, commemorated on the Vimy Memorial.

The *Rancourt German Cemetery* ⑪ is down a side lane and attracts less attention, although there are more graves – 11,422 – there than in the French cemetery. In a field between the two is the homely little British *Rancourt Military Cemetery* ⑫ with just ninety-two graves. The register states that the cemetery was started by the Guards Division in the winter of 1916–17, but there are no members of the division buried there, at least not in the identified graves. The first known deaths are two NCOs of the 2nd Worcesters who had the bad luck to die on Christmas Day 1916, but most of the graves are from the 47th (London) Division from August and September 1918. There are also the sad graves of three unidentified British airmen shown simply as 'May 1940', probably the crew of a Blenheim or a Fairey Battle. The graves of more than 20,000 soldiers are in this area, mostly killed in 1916. The French and Germans find it a useful place to have joint ceremonies in their cemeteries on 1 July each year.

Sailly-Saillisel British Cemetery ⑬ is easy to find on the main road. It is situated at the northern extremity of the ground captured by French troops in 1916 and then taken over by the British. The cemetery is on a ridge and the back looks out over the French and British battlefields of 1916. It is a post-war concentration cemetery with 763 graves from the winter of 1916–17 and from the spring and autumn of 1918. There are many Guards Division graves of the winter of 1917 and London units graves from 1918.

The village of Bouchavesnes, south of Rancourt, has a splendid statue of Marshal Foch ⑭ at the side of the main road and then two memorials to French soldiers in the countryside to the south. At the side of the road from Cléry-sur-Somme is a cross ⑮ in memory of twenty-year-old Gustave Fumery, a private soldier of the 132nd Infantry Regiment, and of his 150 comrades killed near here on 4 October 1916. This is the note I made when Mary and I found the cross: 'There is complete silence here except for the birdsong, and wild flowers and fresh spring foliage are everywhere. I am struck by the contrast and cannot visualize what it must have been like when poor Fumery and his 150 comrades were killed here.' Just across the main road, up a rough track, is a much larger stone memorial ⑯ topped by a cross, the whole standing twenty feet high among a row of small trees. This is for Aspirant Philippe Louis Calle of the 106th Infantry Regiment; a long inscription shows how he was 'recalled to God on 25 September 1916 ... with remarkable sang-froid performing a perilous mission for which he voluntarily offered himself'.

The village of Biaches, just across the River Somme from Péronne, marked the limit of the French advance in 1916. The *Biaches National Cemetery* ⑰ is one of the smaller French cemeteries, with 1,361 graves. The hamlet of La Maisonnette was the scene of particularly severe fighting in October 1916. French troops captured it early in the month, but the Germans were determined not to lose this ground which provided observation across the Somme into Péronne and they regained it later in the month. One memorial marked on French maps proved hard to find but was finally discovered almost covered in bushes in a field on the north-east side of a track running from a large house towards Biaches. It turned out to be the once fine memorial ⑱ to the 56th Battalion of Chasseurs à Pied who were in action here in July 1916, although I did not think French troops reached this point until later. Faint lettering on the front of the memorial mentioned Captain Dufour and the men of his 'Chasseurs Driant'. This refers to the famous Lieutenant-Colonel Émile Driant, the commander of the 56th and 58th Chasseurs who led those battalions in an epic stand on the first two days of the German offensive at Verdun in February 1916. Driant and most of his men were killed, but the German timetable was badly disrupted by their defence and his name obviously lived on in the memory of the rebuilt battalion which fought here later in the year. Not far away, and more easy to find, is the *Colonial Memorial* ⑲ in a small triangular enclosure; the entrance, up a bank, is well marked. It seems to be a general memorial to the 'colonials' who died here in 1916 but it is also the grave of Sous-Lieutenant Marcel Brocheriou of the 22nd Colonial Infantry Regiment who died 'facing his objective' in August. It is a ten-foot-high memorial, in good condition, although the little park once laid out carefully is now a tangle of overgrown bushes.

Herbécourt British Cemetery ⑳ is a simple little cemetery of just three and a half rows containing fifty-nine graves. There were six burials in early 1917 when the 48th (South Midland) Division took over here from the French; the remaining graves are all of late 1918, mostly Australians who were pushing the Germans back here at that time. The 55th (New South Wales) Battalion is particularly well represented.

Dompierre-Becquincourt National Cemetery ㉑ contains the bodies of 7,034 French soldiers. It lies on or near the trenches which became established in late 1914, held throughout 1915 and from where the 1 July 1916 attack took place. A rough survey of dates on the crosses shows that about three-quarters of the graves are from the 1916 battle, with most of the remainder being from 1914–15. There are six 'ossuary' mass graves at the rear containing 1,666 bodies of which only twenty-six could be identified when they were buried. A strange little memorial in the cemetery is 'to our French friends who have died for their country, from the Italian residents of Dompierre'. There was a large sugar-beet factory at Dompierre; perhaps Italian workers there made the memorial.

Asseviilers New British Cemetery ㉒, with 777 graves, is a completely post-war assembly of graves. There is a wide range of dates, a few 1915s brought down from areas to the north, more from early 1917 when the British took over this area and many from the March and August offensives of 1918. There are twenty-five memorial headstones at the back of the cemetery to men of the 2nd Middlesex known or believed to be buried among the 332 'unknown' graves; the Middlesex men were killed holding a bridge over the Somme and then making a fighting withdrawal through this area in March 1918. The cemetery is attractive and spacious and was particularly well located on a country lane next to a 'Crucifix Corner' around which the cemetery wall still bends, but the Paris motorway is now only 100 yards away and there is a large service area and modern hotel nearby.

THE SOMME VALLEY

This area consists of a winding section of the River Somme and an expanse of open upland between the Somme and Ancre valleys. In 1915 and 1916 it was the immediate rear for the French and British units holding trenches or fighting on the battlefield. The roads were always busy with troops and transport, and the town of Bray and the local villages provided billets for troops going up to the front line, often their last experience of human habitation. For the wounded it was the area where medical units were located to receive casualties from the battlefield. The armies moved on in 1917, but the northern flank of the German advance passed through here in March 1918 and Bray and the villages provided the same shelter for German

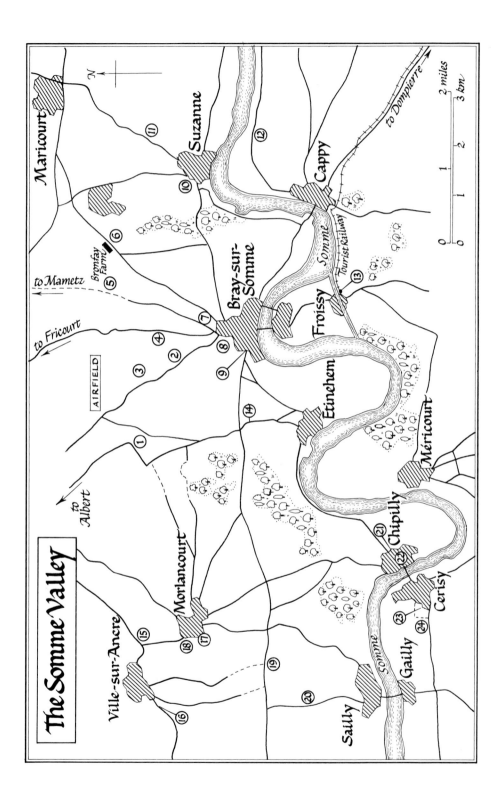

The Somme Valley

soldiers as they had earlier for French and British until the area was fought over again in August and recaptured by British troops.

I see this as a homely area. Bray and the villages survived the 1918 fighting relatively intact and the River Somme here is particularly attractive. It is in two parts, a canal and a river which is often in the form of wide ponds. There are always trees and the little cafés used by fishermen are just as hospitable to battlefield visitors. There are many cemeteries, usually of a small and intimate nature.

Five roads or tracks fanned out northwards from Bray to cross a wide, almost featureless plateau to reach the 'old front-line' trench sectors between Fricourt and Maricourt. It would have been a bleak march in bad weather, a shadeless and sweaty one under the summer sun. *Grove Town Cemetery* ① , with 1,392 graves, is alongside one of those tracks. It was made after September 1916 when a railway was constructed to this point allowing Casualty Clearing Stations to be provided closer to the fighting area. The first men to be buried died following the battle of 15 September and are buried in Row C, on the right of the entrance.

There are some interesting graves, particularly in the right-hand rows. In Row B are Lieutenant-Colonel C. J. W. Hobbs, DSO, and Major E. R. Street, DSO, the CO and Second-in-Command of the 2nd Sherwood Foresters, both mortally wounded on 15 October. In Row C is Lieutenant George Macpherson, the first tank officer to die, on 15 September; other tank officers hit on that day are recorded as dying the next day. His headstone has the Machine Gun Corps badge because tanks were still 'Heavy Branch MGC' at that time. In Row J is Sergeant Leslie Coulson, a pre-war journalist who became one of the war poets. He was wounded fighting near Lesboeufs with the 2nd Londons and died here on 8 October. His poems were widely published after his death. Further back, in Row H, the widowed mother of Private Frank Hitchin of the Machine Gun Corps chose this inscription for his headstone: *If this is Victory, then let God stop all wars – His loving mother.*

Bray Vale British Cemetery ② is a pretty little spot on a bank above the Albert–Bray road. It is on two levels. The rear section is made up of wartime and immediate post-war burials, nearly all men of the 58th (London) Division which fought here in August 1918. The lower section was added in 1923, made up of 165 bodies moved from the 1916 battlefield to make a total in the cemetery of 279.

Most of the later graves are 'unknowns', but there is sufficient identification to show that many were from the Thiepval area. One of them, Major George Gaffikin, buried to the left of the entrance, was a well-known Ulsterman of the 9th Royal Irish Rifles (West Belfast Volunteers) who went into the attack on 1 July waving an orange handkerchief and was killed that day. Just north of this cemetery is a deep curving valley which was called *Happy Valley* ③. The soldiers called several places by this name, but this was the only Happy Valley shown on army maps and used in official accounts of the war.

Bray Hill British Cemetery ④ is on another of the roads over the upland and was also made by the 58th (London) Division in August 1918 and from more bodies brought in from the surrounding area after the war. This simple little cemetery has 104 graves, at least sixty-five of them from London units.

Alongside the next track is an area known as *The Loop* ⑤. A pre-1914 narrow-gauge railway line running northwards from Bray made a distinctive 'loop' around a bowl in the ground here. British troops constructed a link to this line from the railway station on the main line at Dernancourt and this was used to bring supplies in from the main line to here. The loop became the unloading point. It was to this place that the first tanks were brought in August 1916 and they carried out a demonstration with infantry over rough ground resembling a battlefield. Sir Douglas Haig attended this on 26 August 1916. It is easy to see where the railway looped around the low ground below a small triangular wood. The military railway was later extended from here, northwards into the battlefield and east to Bronfay Farm.

Bronfay Farm still stands, at the side of the next road. Its buildings were used by medical units in 1915 and it became the XIV Corps Main Dressing Station during the 1916 battle. *Bronfay Farm Military Cemetery* ⑥ is just across the road and was made from the men who died here. The August 1918 fighting was fierce in this area and many men from that period are buried in the rear part of the cemetery. There are eleven long rows containing 524 graves. The road here was a particularly important access to the battlefield in the later months of 1916 and elaborate arrangements were made for its shared use by British and French transport. It is very quiet now.

The little town of Bray-sur-Somme is the focal point for the area and was also jointly used by British and French troops in 1916. It contains cemeteries from three armies. *Bray Military Cemetery* ⑦ served British medical units all though the 1916 fighting and on into 1917, with most of the graves being of the early months of 1917 when a Casualty Clearing Station was at Bray. There were further burials from the 1918 fighting and a small plot at the rear was made for Indian troops and for Egyptian labourers working for the British Army. Further graves were concentrated at the front of the cemetery after the war to make a total of 875. A Southern Irish soldier, Sergeant M. Healy, buried in Plot 2, Row B, deserves outstanding mention. Serving with the 2nd Royal Munster Fusiliers, this NCO earned a DCM and an MM and Bar before being mortally wounded in March 1917 when a grenade thrown by another soldier hit the parapet and fell back into the trench. Sergeant Healy dashed to retrieve the grenade and hurl it away, but it exploded before he could do so. He was awarded the Albert Medal and is one of only two such medal holders buried in Somme cemeteries. It is a pity that the medal is not engraved on the headstone as its successor, the George Cross, is.

The French *Bray-sur-Somme National Cemetery* ⑧ is best reached through the nearby civilian cemetery. The old concrete crosses were about to be replaced when we made our visit and the name-plates had been removed so that I was unable to see the years of death, but 1914 and 1916 are certain to be well represented. The cemetery will have a smart new look by the time this book is published. There are 1,045 French soldiers buried here and one solitary British soldier, an artilleryman who died in October 1916; his War Graves Commission headstone is near the flagpole.

The *Bray-sur-Somme German Cemetery* ⑨ is on a hillside on the edge of the town; with 1,122 graves it is the smallest German cemetery in the Somme *département*. It is a simple, square plot surrounded by a high hedge – a secluded place. The dates on the crosses are in date order through the spring and summer months of 1918, showing that the Germans used Bray as a medical centre. Their front line was four miles to the west at that time. An unusual feature is a newly erected tall stone column engraved with several hundred names, probably a record of the men buried in a mass grave, though the only obvious communal grave was marked as having forty-three bodies.

*

55 Suzanne Communal Cemetery and the British extension, a good example of this type of cemetery showing the contrast between the civilian and the British plots.

It is worth making the trip to Suzanne, if only to see one of the prettiest villages literally 'on the Somme'. The *Suzanne Communal Cemetery Extension* ⑩ is also a perfect example of that type of cemetery. It is in a pretty valley below the village. It was started by the 5th Division which took over trenches from the French in August 1915, but a large proportion of the graves are of Manchester and Liverpool 'Pals' of the 30th Division which held the line that winter. There was then a long gap until fourteen Australians and one London man were buried in late 1918. There are 155 graves, all identified.

Suzanne Military Cemetery No. 3 ⑪ is completely different. It is on an open upland site but is attractively laid out. There is a great range of dates and units and most of the graves were moved in after the war to replace the bodies of French soldiers taken to their own cemetery. Some of the post-war moves are 1 July 1916 deaths from as far away as Thiepval and Beaumont-Hamel. There are 138 graves, forty-two of them 'unknowns'.

Eclusier Communal Cemetery ⑫ is on the south side of the river. There are just twenty-three British graves, mostly infantry of the 48th (South Midland) Division or gunners from an anti-aircraft battery which was here in early 1917 when British troops relieved the French in this area. The five anti-aircraft men were all killed in the same incident on 6 February 1917, possibly an accidental explosion.

A four-mile-long section of old narrow-gauge railway running from a little station at Froissy ⑬ to Dompierre has been brought back into use and excursions now run on certain days between April and October. The line would certainly have been used during the First World War and one of the engines which pull the trains is an old army steam engine, the other a diesel one from the Maginot Line.

Moving to the other side of Bray, the French *Côte 80 National Cemetery* ⑭ is near Etinehem village. There are 1,004 French graves, mostly from the 1916 battle. The cemetery was started by French medical units who also buried twelve British soldiers, mostly artillerymen, in the middle of the cemetery in late 1915 and in 1916. There was fighting here in August 1918 and thirty-one Australians were then buried at the back of the cemetery. The British graves were all allowed to remain after the war. Also at the back of the cemetery, flanked on either side by the Australian graves, is the grave of and large private memorial to a French army chaplain, Abbé Thibaut, who was wounded while attached to the 1st Infantry Regiment in September 1916. The memorial, erected by the priest's brother, also pays tribute to the men of the regiment, which was formed with men from Cambrai. That little group at the back of the cemetery – the graves of the French soldiers (most with crosses, a few with Muslim tablets), the white headstones of the Australians (one of them engraved with the Star of David) and then the dominating feature of the chaplain's memorial – is very moving.

One of the best-preserved Demarcation Stones on the Somme stands at a road junction ⑮ near Ville-sur-Ancre. It has a French helmet on top, even though British troops of the 35th Division were responsible for halting the German advance here in March 1918. The base of the stone has an inscription which shows that it was paid for by the 27th (New York) National Guard Division. The *Ville-sur-Ancre Communal Cemetery and Extension* ⑯ has several groups of British graves. Near the middle of the civilian cemetery are twenty 1916 casualties, including eleven Royal Engineers killed in June 1916 when a heavy shell struck their billet in the village. Also in

the civilian cemetery are four Australian graves from 1918 and
four men killed in May 1944. In the War Graves Commission
Extension there are 106 graves, forty-five burials from August 1918
and a further sixty-one brought in after the war. Most of the latter
are unidentified, but the graves of two men of the 15th Lancashire
Fusiliers (1st Salford Pals) killed on 1 July 1916 show that this was
another cemetery used to take graves moved from Thiepval after
the war.

The village of Morlancourt spent the first part of the war comfort-
ably in the Allied rear, being used extensively as a billeting village
and by medical units; an Army Field Cashier was based there.
But the German advance of March 1918 reached this area and
Morlancourt became a front-line village just in the German lines.
There are two small cemeteries. *Morlancourt British Cemetery No. 1*
⑰ was mainly made during the 1916 battle by the burial of men
who died of wounds. Many of the seventy-six graves are of the 38th
(Welsh) Division following its battle in Mametz Wood, including one
battalion commander, Lieutenant-Colonel O. S. Flower, 13th Royal
Welch Fusiliers (1st North Wales). *Morlancourt British Cemetery No.
2* ⑱ is on or near the German front line which was attacked in
August 1918. This area was the extreme northern flank of the great
battle fought at that time. The German defence held on the first day,
the 8th, but the 12th (Eastern) Division captured the village on the
9th. The division made the cemetery soon afterwards and nearly all
of the fifty-four graves are of men killed in August 1918. Morlancourt was adopted by Folkestone after the war.

Two more cemeteries are to be found in the open country between
Morlancourt and Sailly-Laurette and, as at Morlancourt, one
belongs mainly to 1916 and one to 1918. *Beacon Cemetery* ⑲ is a
handsome cemetery with good views over the surrounding area
and a lovely cemetery shelter and a Cross of Sacrifice near a straight
road which cannot fail to catch the eyes of passing motorists.
This ground was approximately on the line from which the 18th
(Eastern) Division – back on the Somme yet again – advanced in
the 8 August 1918 attack and the division buried the dead of that
battle in what are now four close-packed rows near the centre of
the cemetery (Rows C, E, G and I of Plot 3). The large post-war
concentration which took place cleverly incorporated those rows
and the visitor will see how the next plot, Plot 4, has similar-length
rows to provide a balance. There are 768 graves, nearly all from

1918 and mostly men from London and Eastern Counties regiments and Australians who were involved in the August attack; there are 257 'unknowns'. The cemetery was named after a tall brickworks chimney which stood at that time in the field to the south-west, but it is not there now.

Dive Copse British Cemetery ⑳ brings us back to 1916 when a Main Dressing Station commanded by an officer called Dive was located nearby. The 1916 casualties – 387 'died of wounds' – were buried in the long rows of Plots 1 and 2 in the centre and right of the cemetery. I could not help but think of the suffering which took place at the Dressing Station (which was located behind the Cross of Sacrifice) and led to so many men dying before they could reach the surgical facilities and proper nursing of a Casualty Clearing Station. One grave was added in March 1918 when an American pilot, Second Lieutenant L. V. Harding, was buried at the back of Plot 1. The cemetery register shows that he was killed 'while flying over German infantry' during the March offensive; he was flying a Sopwith Dolphin of No. 79 Squadron RFC. The first three rows of Plot 3 were made after the August 1918 fighting and the remainder of that plot was concentrated after the war – again Londons, Eastern Counties men and Australians. There are 579 graves in the cemetery.

Chipilly is a pretty village on the River Somme. It was used in 1915 as the rear base for British divisions which had recently taken over trenches from the French. *Chipilly Communal Cemetery and Extension* ㉑ has 104 burials in two plots. The four rows near the chapel were made first. One of the first burials was that of Rifleman E. F. Slade of the Queen Victoria's Rifles (then attached to the 5th Division) who drowned while swimming in the Somme one Saturday in August 1915. When that little plot became full the extension was made, but there were only a few burials and the cemetery was hardly used after the opening of the 1916 battle. The green lawns made by the War Graves Commission around the British graves make a pleasant contrast with the arid, gravel-surfaced civilian cemetery, and the British graves look out over the Somme valley to Cerisy church spire just beyond the river.

In Chipilly itself is to be found a unique memorial. It is in front of the church, at the junction of several roads ㉒, and was erected by the local people to the memory of the 58th (London) Division, the Territorial division which recaptured the village on 9 August

56 The 58th
(London) Division
Memorial at Chipilly.

1918. The lovely white stone memorial shows a driver and his injured horse. The inscription, prepared by someone who had carried out careful research, states that the division 'was one of the only English divisions which, in co-operation with the French Army and the Army Corps of Australia and Canada, succeeded in penetrating the German defences between Le Quesnoy and Montdidier on 8th August 1918, resulting in the start of the German retreat which ended in the Armistice of 11th November 1918'.

The area around the bridge over the river between Chipilly and Cerisy is one of the loveliest spots on the Somme; there is a well-placed fishermen's café there. To the west of Cerisy is a complex of British and French cemeteries which have an unusual background and are well worth a visit. The largest is the *Cerisy National Cemetery* ㉓, where 990 French soldiers are buried in what, judging by the standard of care, is a 'prestige' cemetery. Attached to the French cemetery are two substantial plots of British graves which actually form an entrance to the French cemetery and are separated from it only by low hedges broken by a wide passage which does not have a gate. These British plots sit harmoniously with the large French cemetery. I may be jumping to conclusions but I feel that there is some element of symbolism here and that, when the British were looking for places to rebury dead after the war, the French suggested this plot so that the joint Allied effort on the Somme could be commemorated here. There are 393 British graves; 296 are 'unknowns', but there is sufficient identification to show where most of the bodies came from. The largest group is of 34th Division men killed near the Lochnagar Crater at La Boisselle on 1 July 1916. There are also Ulster Division men from Thiepval as well as casualties of the March 1918 offensive and Australians from September 1918. The major battles of the Somme are thus all represented in the British graves. Not only is the juxtaposition of the British and French graves interesting, but the surroundings are most attractive.

Further down the same grass pathway is the *Cerisy–Gailly Military Cemetery* ㉔, which is entirely British. It is a long, narrow cemetery with 745 graves made up of several distinct groupings. The first two rows are mostly Canadians, with a few United Kingdom heavy artillery and tank men, typical of the contents of one of the battlefield

57 British graves from La Boisselle and Thiepval alongside the French cemetery at Cerisy.

cemeteries from the Canadian sector of August 1918 and obviously moved to this cemetery after the war. It was sad to see the graves of some well-decorated veterans who failed only by three months to survive the war, particularly Captain David McAndie of the 10th (Alberta) Battalion, born in Scotland; he held the MC, DCM and MM. The remainder of that plot, Plot 2, obviously contains the entire contents of a cemetery of 260 graves which once stood at Maricourt crossroads and was probably intended to remain there, because the map in the introduction to the other Maricourt ceme- tery – Péronne Road Cemetery – published in 1928 shows it still at that village, but it then had to be moved to here. The second half of the cemetery is also in two parts. The long rows of Plot 1, on the right, are the original graves made in February 1917 to March 1918 when a British Casualty Clearing Station was located here and used again in the autumn by advancing Australian troops. Finally, Plot 3, on the left, is a post-war concentration including yet more graves of the Ulster Division and other units which were cleared from Thiepval after the war.

The war poet Wilfred Owen had a soft spot for this area. He was at the Casualty Clearing Station there in March 1917 after injuring himself in a fall, and again, suffering an illness, two months later. His evacuation to the base by river led to his poem 'Hospital Barge at Cerisy':

> *Budging the sluggard ripple of the Somme,*
> *A barge round old Cerisy slowly slewed ...*

Owen was evacuated to England, returned to France in September 1918 and was killed in action just one week before the Armistice.

ALBERT

The town of Albert, with about 12,000 inhabitants, is the third largest in the Somme *département*. Henry V passed through the town in 1415 on his way to Agincourt. It has been a pilgrimage centre since the Middle Ages when a shepherd found a 'miraculous' statue of the Virgin Mary in a field outside the town (near the Bapaume

Post Cemetery). A large basilica was completed in 1897 with a golden Virgin and Child atop its tall tower. When the war came in 1914, Albert had about 8,000 inhabitants of whom 2,000 were metal workers. A large sewing-machine factory is mentioned as a place of shelter by many wartime soldiers.

Albert became a front-line town when the trench lines were established a mile and a half away in September 1914. A shell struck the top of the basilica tower on 15 January 1915, causing the statue to start leaning over. French engineers managed to secure it the following day and it remained in a horizontal position for the next three years, another wartime memory for French and British soldiers; it was said that the war would not end until the statue fell.

The town passed into British occupation in 1915 and sheltered many troops moving up to and back from the trenches. The tower of the basilica was used by artillery observers and the body of the church was a major Dressing Station during the opening days of the 1916 battle. The town was abandoned to the Germans on 26 March 1918, the 7th Suffolks of the 12th (Eastern) Division being the last British troops to leave and take up positions on the high ground astride the Amiens Road. German marines entered the town and were ordered to advance further but could not do so because of heavy British machine-gun fire and because too many of them had discovered the British stores of food and drink in Albert after being without rations for two days. On 16 April, British guns finally destroyed the tower of the church to deny its use to German observers and the statue fell. It was not found after the war; it was probably sent to Germany for its metal value. The town was recaptured after hard fighting by the 18th (Eastern) Division on 22 August 1918, this fine unit writing one of the last pages in its long involvement with Somme battles. A plaque on the Hôtel de Ville says that at the end of the war 'there remained only the name, the glory and the ruins'.

Albert's post-war reconstruction was helped by its 'adoption' by four places – Bordeaux, an undamaged French city which became 'godmother' to this destroyed town; Birmingham, because of the Royal Warwickshires' presence at various times during the war; Tientsin in China, which had a French community; and a town in Algeria which had French settlers from Picardy. Birmingham paid for a large old folks home, which still serves that purpose, and there is still a rue de Birmingham. (The last known link with Birmingham

58 The Basilica at Albert at the time of the town's capture by the Germans in March 1918.

was in the early 1980s when exchanges took place, old soldiers coming from Birmingham and the Mayor of Albert attending an Aston Villa football match.) The basilica was rebuilt exactly as it was before the war. The town became a centre for War Graves Commission work and was often visited by battlefield pilgrims. Later, an aircraft factory was built at Méaulte which produced twin-engined Potez 630 aircraft for the French Air Force.

There were virtually no Allied troops in this part of France when two German Panzer divisions swept through from the east in May 1940. The 7th Royal West Kents, a weak Territorial battalion which was not fully trained and had no proper anti-tank weapons, found itself at Albert on 20 May and was hit that morning by 2nd Panzer which came up the Péronne Road. There was a short battle on the edge of the town and in the square in front of the Hôtel de Ville which left twenty British dead and most of the remainder surrendering. It was the biggest fight in the whole of the eastern Somme. About fifty survivors gathered at a rallying point in Aveluy Wood and eventually reached Boulogne. Among the items captured by the Germans was a fully equipped British ambulance train which was stranded at Albert because the lines on either side of the town had been bombed. Before being evacuated, British nurses had treated one patient, a young woman refugee in labour whose baby girl the nurses delivered in a room at the station; the mother told the nurses that she would call the baby Brigitte. The birth of Brigitte Thilliez on 18 May 1940 is to be found in local records and also the fact that she married in 1965.

The Germans set up their *Kommandantur* in the Hôtel de Ville and established a garrison of about fifty men which was changed regularly so that their troops would not become too friendly with local people. The aircraft factory at Méaulte was taken over and later used to accommodate machinery from a bombed BMW factory in Germany. The factory was bombed five times by the Americans by day and once by the RAF at night. It is believed that six French people were killed in these raids, together with an unknown number of Germans. Four men from Albert died in various concentration camps in Germany including one, Dereck Peckett, whose father is believed to have been a British soldier who returned to Albert after the First World War. A fifth local man was killed at Amiens Prison when it was bombed by the RAF in February 1944.

When this area was liberated in September 1944, Albert was the scene of a set-back. A battle group made up of Sherman tanks of the 2nd Grenadier Guards, a company of infantry from the 1st Grenadiers and some Royal Horse Guards armoured cars – all from the Guards Armoured Division – approached the town from Méaulte but met with unexpected resistance outside the police station. One armoured car was hit and two men killed and one of the Grenadier infantrymen was also killed, as was an over-enthusiastic Frenchman who ran out into the street. A Royal Horse Guards officer and several men were taken prisoner. But the Germans slipped away during the night, and the 50th (Northumbrian) Division completed the liberation of Albert the next day.

Albert remains an ideal centre for touring the battlefields but only for small groups; there is not enough hotel accommodation for large coach parties. It is a quiet town, except for the constant passage of traffic, but the new bypass planned to open in 1994 will be a big improvement. The aircraft factory at Méaulte is still the main employer, currently making part of the fuselage for the European Airbus, parts of wings of Mirage fighters and also parts for Exocet missiles, some of which sank British ships off the Falklands in 1982.

*

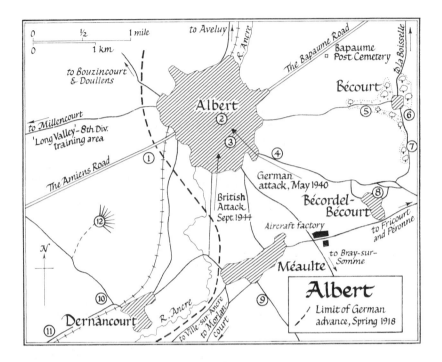

Albert has surprisingly few memorials to the wars. There is a *Demarcation Stone* ① at the side of the road to Amiens. It is accurately placed; the Germans advanced no further in 1918. The inscription on the base shows that the Somme *département* paid for the stone. The *Machine Gun Corps Memorial* ② takes the form of a plaque beside the front door of the Hôtel de Ville; it was unveiled at Easter 1939, just in time for the Second World War. But the *Albert Communal Cemetery Extension* ③ is full of interest. It is in two parts, a small raised section near the road and a much larger one behind. It is best to describe the larger section first. This was made between August 1915 and January 1917 by medical units and by units in the trenches bringing casualties back for burial. Nearly 900 men were buried during that period.

A little tour starting at the back of the cemetery will see many interesting graves. The first burial was that of Private H. Mason of the 179th Tunnelling Company who was overcome by gas and fell down a mine shaft on 31 August 1915; he is buried towards the right of the last row. On the right of the fourth row from the back (Row D) is a communal grave for thirteen men of the 10th Essex

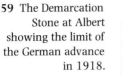

59 The Demarcation
Stone at Albert
showing the limit of
the German advance
in 1918.

killed in November 1915 when the Germans exploded a mine at
the Glory Hole at La Boisselle. On the right of Row F are the graves
of Major T. C. Richardson and Second Lieutenant A. J. Latham of
the 185th Tunnelling Company, killed with eighteen of their men
when poison gas filled mine tunnels near La Boisselle following the
explosion of a German mine in February 1916. Their men were
buried nearer the front but the two officers were brought here. The
end graves of many of the rows are occupied by officers similarly
brought back from the battlefield; for example, Brigadier-General
H. F. H. Clifford, DSO, shot by a sniper in September 1916 while
inspecting trenches near Mametz Wood while in command of a
brigade of the 50th Division, is buried at the right-hand end of Row
L. Moving across to the left side of the cemetery, near the end of
Row J, is the communal grave of eleven men of the 41st (Durham)
Siege Battery and an Army Service Corps driver, all killed one night

in July 1916 when their ammunition unloading party at Albert was hit by a heavy German shell. Finally, before coming up the steps to the upper section, there are some memorials to men known to be buried in the cemetery, including Brigadier-General R. Barnett-Barker, DSO and Bar, commander of a brigade in the 47th (London) Division, killed by a shell in Gueudecourt during the March 1918 retreat. Four men volunteered to carry his body to the rear to avoid its capture by the Germans. His brigade major, Captain E. I. J. Bell, MC and Bar, has a similar memorial stone.

The upper level of the cemetery contains graves from three periods. The 18th (Eastern) Division buried its dead after the recapture of Albert in August 1918 – sixty-nine men in four rows close to the road. Six of these men were from the 7th Royal West Kents. It was a tragic coincidence that it should be the same battalion which tried to stop the German tanks at Albert in May 1940 and some of the dead of that action were added to the same small plot. The total number of May 1940 dead is twenty, including an unidentified RAF pilot. Finally, the three men killed in the liberation of Albert in September 1944 are buried by the Cross of Sacrifice.

The *Albert National Cemetery* ④ stands in a good position on the slope of a hill by the Péronne Road. It contains the bodies of 6,292 French soldiers, including 3,011 mainly unidentified in four mass graves. It is the fourth largest French cemetery on the Somme. A rough survey of dates shows 30 per cent from 1914–15, about 60 per cent from 1916 and 10 per cent from 1918; the 1916 and 1918 bodies would have been brought a considerable distance from the east and from the south. It is a measure of the detail contained on British headstones and cemetery registers that, after the long description of the nearby British cemetery, the above is all I can find to say about this French cemetery which has more than seven times as many graves.

Just east of Albert are three lovely comrades cemeteries, only one of which was added to after the war and that in such a way that the original character of the cemetery was not affected. All three were in the immediate rear of the La Boisselle–Fricourt sector of trenches.

Bécourt Military Cemetery ⑤ is in a pretty wooded setting in a valley on the quietest of country lanes. It is necessary to go to the far end of the cemetery to find the first burials, nine Highlanders who were killed soon after the 51st Division took over this sector from the French in August 1915. The rows then proceed in date order. Among the little unit groups are sixteen Royal Engineers of the 185th Tunnelling Company killed in a mine explosion in February 1916; their officers were taken to Albert, but the men were buried in a communal grave in Row J. Another group is of ten men of the 11th Royal Warwicks, in Row U, caught by shelling in their bivouacs in Bécourt Wood in August 1916. The main burials ended in April 1917, by which time there were 432 graves. But, as so often happened in this area, there were more casualties in 1918 and the 18th (Eastern) Division buried eighty-three of their men in a separate little plot at the side of the main cemetery.

Bécourt is little more than the château and its attendant buildings, replacements of the ones used as a brigade HQ in 1915–16. The château is now used to accommodate groups visiting Albert from its various twin towns, one of which is Ulverston in Cumbria. A white-painted crucifix ⑥ at a corner is a memorial to Lieutenant Joseph de Valicourt, killed in Champagne in 1917, and to 'all the soldiers from this parish and of this sector killed, like him, for France, 1914–18'.

Norfolk Cemetery ⑦ is in a long valley where artillery batteries were located at the opening of the 1916 battle. The cemetery was named by the 1st Norfolks, 5th Division, who made the first burial when sixteen-year-old Private I. A. Laud died on 9 August 1915 and was buried in the front row near the present entrance. Three graves further on is buried Lieutenant W. R. Cloutman of the 178th Tunnelling Company who saved an injured sergeant's life by carrying him up a forty-five-foot ladder in a shaft but was then overcome by fumes and fell back to his death. Wartime burials ended here after the first week of the 1916 battle, when there were 281 graves in three long rows by the roadside. One of the last to be buried was Major S. W. Loudoun-Shand of the 10th Green Howards who won a VC on 1 July 1916 for continuing to urge his men forward despite being mortally wounded. His VC was the first of four won by New Army battalions of the Green Howards in the 1916 battle, more than awarded to any other regiment. A further 268 graves were added after the war, many of them 'unknowns'; these make up the last two rows. Many of the graves in this cemetery are of units of the 21st Division which has no cemeteries in the area of battlefield over which it advanced on 1 July 1916.

Dartmoor Cemetery ⑧ is of a similar nature and layout, also being started by the 5th Division in August 1915. The 8th and 9th Devons who came soon afterwards with the 7th Division gave 'Dartmoor' to the cemetery title. Several graves from the 1916 battle attract particular attention. They are all to be found in the long rows of Plot 1, to the right of the entrance. Buried in the front row, Row F, is Lieutenant-Colonel H. Allardice who was killed on 1 July 1916 while commanding the 13th Northumberland Fusiliers but whose headstone has the badge of an Indian Army cavalry regiment, 36th Jacob's Horse. In the second row, Row E, is buried sixty-eight-year-old Lieutenant Henry Webber, the oldest British soldier to die on the Western Front; he was hit by shell fire near Mametz Wood in July 1916 while serving as Transport Officer with the 7th South Lancs.[30] Two rows further back, in Row C, is Private J. Miller of the 7th King's Own who won a VC in September 1916 after carrying important messages, even though being severely wounded. In the back row, buried side by side, are a father and son, Sergeant G. and Corporal R. F. Lee, killed on the same day in September 1916 while serving in the same London artillery unit. There are 768 graves in this cemetery; all but six of them are identified.

Méaulte was a large village which provided accommodation for units just behind the line. Sydney Rogerson describes how this once trim place was heavily used in 1916 as 'a bottle-neck through which was fed the flood of men and ammunitions for the Somme offensive' and how it became 'muddier, lousier and more disreputable' as the months passed.[31] The small *Méaulte Military Cemetery* ⑨ is in open fields and has 291 graves, 137 from the wartime years and 154 brought in later. There was much fighting here in 1918 and about half of the graves are from that year. Row E contains the grave of an American war writer, Second Lieutenant Harry A. Butters from San Francisco who was killed in August 1916 while serving with a British artillery unit. His book, *An American Citizen*, was published in 1918. His headstone has the same words as the book title as a personal inscription.

Dernancourt was another important rear-area village during

---

[30] More details of this remarkable man are in various parts of *The First Day on the Somme*.
[31] Sydney Rogerson, *Twelve Days* (London: Arthur Barker, 1930; Norwich: Gliddon Books, 1988), p. 125.

60 Wounded – casualties awaiting treatment and evacuation at Dernancourt in September 1916.

61 Died of wounds – long rows of graves at Dernancourt.

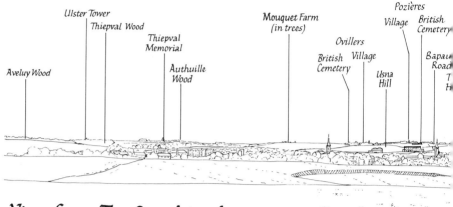

Aveluy Wood · Ulster Tower · Thiepval Wood · Thiepval Memorial · Authuille Wood · Mouquet Farm (in trees) · Ovillers · British Cemetery · Village · Usna Hill · Pozières Village · British Cemetery · Bapaume Road

View from The Grandstand

1916 because the pre-war main railway line reached as far as the village and narrow-gauge lines ran from there to the battlefield. The village became the location for medical units which could evacuate their casualties quickly by train. *Dernancourt Communal Cemetery and Extension* ⑩ is the impressive reminder of how many unfortunate men did not survive to make the train journey. A long narrow plot along the side wall of the civilian cemetery was used for the first burials, from September 1915 onwards, and for a few 1918 graves; the total here is 126. The large extension was heavily used during the 1916 battle and again during the German March 1918 offensive until the German advance came right up to Dernancourt, which became part of No Man's Land. There were 1,700 graves at the end of the war and a further 410 were made from the surrounding area later, but that addition, Plots 8 and 10 at the right of the upper level, fits in well with the original cemetery. In the back row of those concentration plots is the grave of Sergeant T. J. Harris, VC, MM, 6th Royal West Kents, 12th (Eastern) Division. In 1916 Sergeant Harris probably waited with this battalion to the west of here as part of 'Gough's Mobile Army' which was supposed to exploit a breakthrough with the cavalry at the opening of the July battle. He was back here to take part in the great August 1918 attack and to be killed winning his VC on the second day of that battle attacking a German machine-gun post at Morlancourt which is just a mile south of here.

This is an impressive, lovely cemetery made on two levels, with

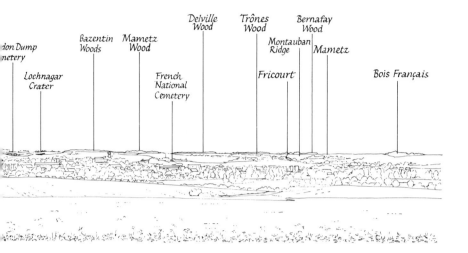

a long open front. It has become one of my favourites, the long rows representing the suffering of hundreds of seriously wounded men whose life lingered a few hours or days at this place.

A roadside memorial to the west of the village ⑪ commemorates two French soldiers, Lieutenant Garner and Sergeant Sagnes, who 'fell gloriously here' on 20 May 1940. Their unit is shown as '5 GRDI' which I think means the Reconnaissance Group of the 5th Infantry Division. Local sources cannot provide any further information. This may have been an armoured car crew or motor-cycle crew which met part of the 1st Panzer Division making its way towards Amiens that day.

Twenty years ago when preparing my first book, I read that General Rawlinson had gone to a place near Dernancourt called 'the Grandstand' to observe the opening of the battle on 1 July 1916. I believe that I have discovered that place. It is important to take the farm track about 150 yards north of a small copse. Go to the end of the metalled track ⑫ and, as far as I can estimate, you are where Rawlinson was that morning, observing an attack frontage of more than seven miles, from the 36th (Ulster) Division's sector north of Thiepval round to that of the 18th (Eastern) Division on the Montauban Ridge. The best position to be is a few yards to the left of the end of the track; that will bring into view the main road from Albert to La Boisselle and Bapaume Post Military Cemetery which are otherwise obscured by the tower of the Hôtel de Ville in Albert. Binoculars will be useful.

THE 1916 REAR AREA

The armies took control of a large area behind the battle front; the French called it the Zone of Occupation. Civilians remained but civil rights gave way to military requirements. Many British soldiers remembered that area better than their monotonous time in the trenches; their descendants often asked to be taken to villages mentioned in diaries as stopping places on the way to the front. This section will cover the large area behind the British part of the 1916 battlefield. There is much to see but it is not of great variety. There were no battles here, though the 1918 offensive came up to the edge of the area. The mobile advances of 1940 and 1944 both passed quickly through it. The chief feature today is the mass of cemeteries, nearly all associated with medical units. One of the big surprises when preparing this book was the realization of the huge numbers of men who died of wounds in the First World War.

Bertrancourt Military Cemetery ① was made in two stages. Between July 1915 and the German retirement in 1917, 218 graves were made, mostly from men who died of wounds at Dressing Stations which were here; eighty-two of those men were from 'Pals' battalions of the 31st Division which was manning the trenches on the Serre sector. Plot 2, with 198 graves, was made in 1918 when the front lines were even nearer and 117 of the men buried at that time were from the 42nd (East Lancs) Division – so it is very much a North Country cemetery.

Courcelles-au-Bois Communal Cemetery and Extension ② is behind the extreme north of the Somme battle front. There are only three September 1916 graves in the communal cemetery but the extension, which was started in October 1916, has 106 burials from medical units that autumn and winter. Many of the graves are of men from heavy artillery batteries – including the South African Heavy Battery – which would be located in the area just over two miles from the German trenches at Gommecourt. Six more men – five of them New Zealanders – were buried in 1918.

Colincamps was the last village for soldiers before going into the trenches facing Serre. I once took an old soldier of the Barnsley 'Pals' to this area and showed him the remains of the trench from

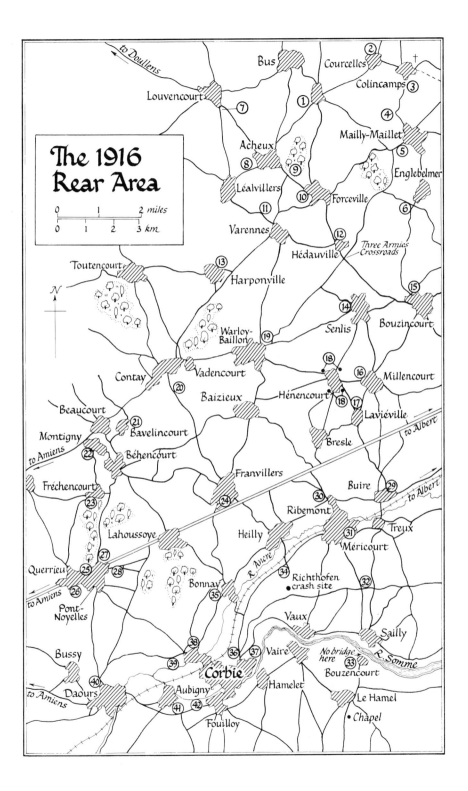

The 1916
Rear Area

0   1   2 miles
0   1   2   3 km

to Doullens

Bus
Courcelles
②
Colincamps ③
Louvencourt
⑦ ①
④
Mailly-Maillet
Acheux ⑤
⑧ Englebelmer
⑨
Léalvillers
⑩ Forceville ⑥
⑪
Varennes
⑫ Three Armies
Crossroads
Hédauville
Toutencourt ⑬
Harponville
⑮
⑭ Bouzincourt
N Warloy- Senlis
Baillon
⑲
Contay Vadencourt ⑱ ⑯ Millencourt
⑳ Baizieux Hénencourt ⑱ ⑰
Beaucourt Laviéville
Bresle to Albert
Montigny ㉑ Bavelincourt
to Amiens ㉒ Béhencourt
Franvillers Buire ㉙
Fréchencourt Ribemont to Albert
㉓ ㉔ ㉚
Lahoussoye Heilly ㉛ Treux
Méricourt
㉗ Richthofen
Querrieu ㉕ ㉘ ㉞ crash site ㉜
to Amiens ㉖ Bonnay R. Ancre
Pont- ㉟
Noyelles Vaux
Sailly
㊳ No bridge R. Somme
Bussy here ㉝
㊴ Vaire Bouzencourt
㊱ ㊲
㊵ Corbie
Daours Aubigny Hamelet Le Hamel
to Amiens ㊶ ㊷ Chapel
Fouilloy

which he went 'over the top' and was wounded on 1 July 1916, but he was far more interested in seeing Colincamps and was delighted when we found an old Frenchman there who remembered as a boy being given bully beef and cigarettes by British soldiers. The Barnsley 'Pal' also pointed out an old wayside cross past which his battalion regularly marched on their way to the trenches. The large Euston Road and Sucrerie Cemeteries between the village and the trench area have already been described. *Colincamps Communal Cemetery* ③ contains just nine New Zealand graves, all from the 1st Canterbury Regiment from April and May 1918 when the New Zealanders held the Germans in front of the village. Colincamps was adopted by Burnley after the war; a Burnley company served with the 11th East Lancs which used the village regularly in 1916 and 1917.

Mailly-Maillet is one of the largest villages in the area; the Germans found it useful for billeting troops in the Second World War. But in the earlier war it was opposite Beaumont-Hamel and suffered steadily from German shelling. There are two cemeteries. *Mailly-Maillet Communal Cemetery Extension* ④ was taken over from the French in 1915 and Second Lieutenant G. H. Wheatcroft, a heavy artillery officer whose grave is at the end of the cemetery, was the first British burial here, almost as soon as his unit arrived in August 1915. But the cemetery was not heavily used and there are only 116 graves. The larger *Mailly Wood Cemetery* ⑤ was started dramatically when thirteen men of the 2nd Seaforths, 4th Division, were buried on 25 June 1916. The preliminary British bombardment for the July offensive had started the previous day and the Germans retaliated that night by shelling the place where the Seaforths were bivouacked; fifty-one men were killed or wounded by one shell, and the dead are buried in the first row on the left. The cemetery continued to be used during the 1916 battle and its Scottish character was maintained by the 51st (Highland) Division which buried many of its men here after the November attack at Beaumont-Hamel. There are 253 Highland graves occupying nearly all of Rows C to M down the left of the cemetery. There were 600 graves at the end of the war and a further 101 were brought in later, but it remains a true comrades cemetery. Among the 1918 graves are twenty-seven New Zealanders and Sergeant H. J. Colley, VC, MM, of the 10th Lancashire Fusiliers who died of wounds in August 1918 when two platoons facing a German counter-attack were reduced to himself and three unwounded men, but they held the Germans. His grave is in the back row on the right.

Englebelmer is a village described by Edmund Blunden as 'pretty Englebelmer'; he was there several times in 1916 when his battalion was in the trenches at Hamel. The British graves in *Englebelmer Communal Cemetery and Extension* ⑥ are in two parts. The fifty-two graves in the civilian cemetery are near the entrance and the 150 in the extension are well back at the side. There is a good mixture of units from 1916 to 1918 but with sizeable contingents of Royal Naval Division graves from 1916 and 1918 and New Zealanders from 1918. The city of Winchester adopted both Mailly-Maillet and Englebelmer after the war.

The Doullens–Albert road is my favourite approach to the battle-fields. It is a direct but quiet route, passing through pleasant country-side and a succession of villages, many of which have associations, through their cemeteries, with British troops of the First World War. *Louvencourt Military Cemetery* ⑦ is of particular interest. The French had a medical centre here in 1915 and handed the cemetery, with seventy-five of their graves in it, over to the British in August of that year. British casualties were then buried until this place became too far from the front line at the end of 1916, but it was used again in 1918. The only post-war addition was of eight graves moved here from nearby Vauchelles.

The first burial was that of Captain A. G. Rollaston, 1/7th Worcesters, the first officer to be killed when British units moved to the Somme in 1915; he died of wounds on 30 July. His grave is among those of five other officers buried to the right of the entrance. The first grave of that group is where Second Lieutenant Roland Leighton of the same Worcesters battalion is buried. He died on 23 December 1915, aged only nineteen, after being hit the night before while commanding a party mending the barbed wire outside the trenches at Hébuterne. Leighton's fiancée, Vera Brittain, was so moved by his death and that of so many other young men of her generation, including her own brother who was killed in action in Italy in 1918, that she became a pacifist and wrote the famous *Testament of Youth* and *Chronicle of Youth* and also the poem 'Perhaps', the first verse of which is:

Perhaps some day the sun will shine again,
And I shall see that still the skies are blue,
And feel once more I do not live in vain,
Although bereft of You.

The family inscription on Roland Leighton's grave is: *Goodnight, though life and death take flight. Never goodbye.* Vera Brittain married later and her daughter is Shirley Williams, the former Labour cabinet minister.

At the back of the cemetery, on the right, is the grave of Brigadier-General C. B. Prowse, DSO, the most senior officer to die on 1 July 1916, hit when he went forward to find out what was happening to his brigade on the battlefield and dying at Vauchelles. Bertie Prowse, formerly of the Somerset Light Infantry, is one of my heroes, a very brave soldier. He has a farm named after him on the Ypres Salient and also a cemetery, Prowse Point Cemetery near Ploegsteert Wood, where he fought a famous action in 1914. One of the men who helped me with *The First Day on the Somme*, was CSM Percy Chappell of the Somersets who was in Prowse's company before the war. Chappell told me that, after the war, when he was a major commanding the 7th Somersets, who were still out working on the Somme, he found Prowse's grave at Vauchelles and placed on it a small metal plaque. The plaque was moved with Prowse's body to Louvencourt and is still there, inscribed 'from his old comrades'. Prowse's death in 1916 was the second loss for his family; his brother was captain of the battle-cruiser HMS *Queen Mary* which blew up in the Battle of Jutland on 31 May 1916 with the loss of all but nine members of its crew.

A further interesting point about this cemetery is that it was one of the first three trial cemeteries chosen for permanent construction by the War Graves Commission. The most obvious evidence of this is the solid block walls made from a local stone often seen in the older buildings in this area. The French also joined in the trial. Their graves were left in the cemetery and have some tall headstones of a type which I have not seen elsewhere and which are far superior to the standard crosses seen in French cemeteries. A final point of interest is the graves in one corner of the cemetery of three Royal Engineers killed in May 1940.

Acheux British Cemetery ⑧ has just five rows, containing 180 graves. The cemetery was first used by medical units in 1916 and then again in 1918; there are more graves of the later year. The cemetery register entry of one man shows that his luck eventually ran out. Private F. J. Wolfe of the 10th West Yorks, perhaps a survivor of that battalion's disaster at Fricourt on 1 July 1916, was killed in June 1918 but he had earlier been wounded twice and then torpedoed but rescued while returning sick from France with frozen feet. His grave is in the second row.

At the side of the main road ⑨ is a modern memorial to the 'Picardy Martyrs of the Resistance 1940–45'; that last year shows that French men and women were still dying in concentration camps in Germany several months after this area was liberated. The memorial gives no details of what happened here. I asked some local people and they thought that five men were shot in the nearby wood just before the Liberation but, as with many Resistance stories, they were not certain.

Forceville Communal Cemetery Extension ⑩ was another early trial cemetery, but the design of the permanent work was so successful that it can hardly be distinguished from the mature, well-proven styles used later. The extension is behind a local cemetery in which two British graves have been cleverly incorporated into the extension by a diversion of the boundary hedge. There are four plots, one for deaths up to July 1916, two for the 1916 battle and one for 1918. Among seven German graves are the crew of a two-seater plane shot down in September 1915, the only German airmen's graves I remember seeing in British cemeteries on the Somme. There are 304 British graves and the register lists the numbers of graves by regiment, the Royal Irish Rifles – mainly from the 36th (Ulster) Division – heading the list with fifty-four names; that early practice of including such lists in registers was not continued.

Varennes Military Cemetery ⑪ is on a triangular site in pleasant country surroundings. Close-packed rows contain the bodies of 1,217 men from many units, most of whom died of wounds here in 1916–17 or in 1918. There are two interesting graves just inside the entrance. One is that of Brigadier-General Philip Howell, CMG, a staff officer at II Corps HQ, killed by a shell near Authuille in October 1916. As a major in the 4th Hussars, this officer led a heroic action on 31 October 1914, a day of crisis in the First Battle of Ypres, holding a bridge and inflicting heavy casualties on attacking Germans. In the next grave is Colonel L. Fouks, a Russian cavalry officer attached to II Corps, who died on 8 October 1916, probably being wounded when Brigadier-General Howell was killed.

Hédauville Communal Cemetery Extension ⑫ is a 1918 cemetery containing 178 men who either died at a Dressing Station here or were brought in after the war and were buried in this simple, pretty little plot on the edge of the village. An unusually large number of the graves – sixty-one – are of artillerymen. This leads to a nice link with 1940. When British troops were sent to Albert to hold the German advance, a troop of four 25 pounder guns at Hédauville was their only artillery support. German tanks captured the guns on 20 May after the troop had shot off its meagre supply of ammunition. One of three 1940 graves in the cemetery is that of Sergeant A. C. Brown of that artillery troop; the date of death on his headstone is '11th May–12th June 1940' but it was almost certainly the 20th of May.

The crossroads south of Hédauville probably saw the passage of three historic military forces. Henry V's men are recorded as moving from Albert to Forceville, so they must have passed here in 1415 on the way to Agincourt. The 2nd Panzer Division certainly came the same way in May 1940, before branching off to Beauquesne and then on to Abbeville. Then, in September 1944, the Guards Armoured Division crossed the Doullens Road, coming from the left and making towards Arras.

Harponville Communal Cemetery and Extension ⑬ has thirty-four graves in the communal cemetery and 138 in the extension, all from April to August 1918 when the village was just behind the British lines. Many of the graves are from the 38th (Welsh) Division – in the communal cemetery – and the 17th (Northern) Division, in the extension.

Senlis Communal Cemetery Extension ⑭ is also a 1918 cemetery, started by the 12th (Eastern) and 38th (Welsh) Divisions when they halted the German offensive north of Albert. Forty more graves were added after the war, many of them Australian, to make a total of ninety-seven in a neat little War Graves Commission plot at the side of the civilian cemetery.

Bouzincourt Communal Cemetery and Extension ⑮ has thirty-three graves in the communal cemetery and 587 in the large extension. There are four separate little plots among the civilian graves, made

62 The 'three armies' crossroads at Hédauville. Henry V's men in 1415 and the German Panzers in 1940 crossed from right to left; the Guards Armoured Division motored towards Arras on their dash to Belgium in 1944.

by the 32nd Division in the spring of 1916 and by various units in 1918. A solitary grave at the back of the civilian cemetery is of a young Irish Catholic chaplain, Father D. V. O'Sullivan, who was killed on 5 July 1916. He was buried not with the English troops but near the cemetery crucifix among French soldiers whose graves have now been removed; it is not known whether the proximity of the cross or his common religion with the French soldiers was the reason for his burial there. The inscription on his grave simply says: *Killarney, Ireland.*

The extension was started in May 1916 and was soon needed to bury men who died in the 1916 battle; thirty-eight men died of wounds here on 1 July alone and a further ninety died in the next week. There was probably a Dressing Station here serving the units in action at Thiepval and around the Leipzig Salient three miles to the east. An interesting grave for this period is that of Major H. L. Stocks, DSO, 15th Royal Scots (1st Edinburgh City Battalion), who was killed on 1 July and was probably brought back here from the battlefield when the remnants of the 34th Division were withdrawn to Bouzincourt. The register shows that Major Stocks was a steamship owner, son of the Provost of Kirkcaldy and captain of a Boys' Brigade Company. His grave is in Plot 3, Row D.

Millencourt Communal Cemetery Extension ⑯ has 340 graves in six long rows in an attractive British plot which can be reached through the civilian cemetery, which is itself much prettier than average. The chief features of the British graves are the many 'died of wounds' from units fighting in 1916 at La Boisselle and Ovillers and a close-packed row of twenty-nine Australian graves in Row B, on the right, mainly men of the 46th Battalion killed in early April 1918. Just behind the Australian graves is that of nineteen-year-old Lieutenant G. M. Cartmel, shot down in April 1918 while flying a DH4 of No. 205 Squadron; the inscription on his grave reads: *All ye that pass this way tell England that he who lieth here rests content,* copying a formula of words first used over the Spartan dead 2,400 years earlier.

The valley between Millencourt and Albert was the training area of the 8th Division before the 1916 battle; known as 'Long Valley', its shape resembled that of Mash Valley where the division attacked on 1 July.

In *Laviéville Communal Cemetery* ⑰ are the graves of an English artilleryman of 1917, six Australians from 1918 and a corporal of the Royal Horse Guards whose armoured car was hit in the Guards Armoured Division advance on 1 September 1944.

The village of Hénencourt has four pillboxes, one at each corner of the village ⑱, and there may be two others in the village. They are of large and solid construction and were made by the Royal Engineers of the 47th (London) Division in the summer of 1918 to make Hénencourt a 'strongpoint village' in case the Germans attacked again. The sixth pillbox, on the south-west edge of the village, was left incomplete when the Allied advance commenced in August 1918.

Warloy-Baillon Communal Cemetery and Extension ⑲ is interesting but sad, because so many men died of wounds here. The forty-six graves in the civilian part of the cemetery were made up to the opening of the 1916 battle, the last burial there being that of Lieutenant-Colonel P. W. Machell, commander of the 11th Border, killed in the attack on the Leipzig Salient on 1 July 1916 and whose body was brought back here. The inscription on his headstone and an extensive entry in the register give details of his long military career and campaigns, mostly with the Egyptian Army, and his relationships with nobility, through either his mother or his German-born wife. A private memorial in the shape of a heavy bronze laurel wreath also stands on his grave.

The extension was then started when an 'Advanced Operating Centre' was located here for the 1916 battle. A total of 125 men died during the first two weeks of July. Later in the month, the body of Major-General Ingouville-Williams was brought back here after he was killed near Mametz Wood. His hearse was drawn by black horses provided by the 34th Division's artillery and his funeral was attended by many officers, the division being out of the line and billeted in this area at the time. His grave originally stood on its own but is now in a long row of fifty-five officers killed in 1916 (Plot 3, Row D). His headstone has the badge of his old regiment, the Buffs (East Kents). Only one other major-general died on the Somme, Major-General E. Feetham of the 39th Division, killed in March 1918 and buried many miles away to the west.

There were further burials here in 1918 and the extension now has 1,349 First World War graves, including seventeen Germans in a small corner plot. There are two Second World War graves near the entrance. Pilot Officer K. R. Lucas was killed in May 1940 when ten Hurricanes of No. 145 Squadron attacked a formation of German bombers escorted by fighters; seven bombers were claimed shot down for the loss of Pilot Officer Lucas. The other grave is that of Captain D. E. Pinkney, an air observation post pilot of the Royal Artillery. He was not killed in the air but was moving forward by road to find a new landing field for his unit during the September 1944 advance when his vehicle was ambushed, perhaps by one of the Hénencourt pillboxes.

Most of the villages in the valley of the little River Hallue have a British cemetery. The largest is *Contay British Cemetery* ⑳, which was opened in the middle of the 1916 battle when an additional Casualty Clearing Station came here, using the railway line which once passed between the cemetery and the village to evacuate cases to base hospitals. The first burials took place at the end of August in the left-hand corner near the road. September saw 242 burials, mostly Canadians who were fighting around Courcelette. Heavy casualties continued until the end of the 1916 battle and activities ceased in February 1917, but the cemetery was needed again in 1918 by the 38th (Welsh) Division and other units.

This is the most beautiful cemetery in this area. The graves are on two levels of a hillside facing a wood. The best feature is the use made of the area at the end of the cemetery which was not needed because the fighting moved away in 1918. The Cross of Sacrifice, two mature trees and a small walled garden with a seat make a lovely group. I made this note on our visit: 'Well done the architect. Well worth a visit.'

Bavelincourt Communal Cemetery ㉑ is not easy to find; it is part of a civilian cemetery east of the village. There are just three and a half rows of fifty-four graves, mostly of 'Londons' of the 47th and 58th Divisions from April to August 1918. A pretty little spot. *Montigny Communal Cemetery and Extension* ㉒ has a similar background, but the burials are in two parts, fifty-three in the civilian cemetery and just nineteen in the tiny War Graves Commission extension, again all set in the most peaceful of rural surroundings. The grave of Private W. T. Greenslade, in the front row of the civilian cemetery, has a private plaque on which is this touching message: *The last words of my dear boy, 19.3.1918, 'Mother, it is hard for me, but promise you will not grieve for me. It won't be long.'* His unit belonged to a Road Construction Company of the Royal Engineers and eight other men of the unit were killed on the same day in June 1918, probably by a long-range German shell.

Fréchencourt Communal Cemetery ㉓ is also difficult to find. Just before the main street in the village bends, in front of a château, a narrow gateway leads to the cemetery which is out of sight behind a farm building. The civilian cemetery is one of the smallest I have seen but it had masses of fresh flowers on the graves when we were there. The war graves are behind a tiny chapel – a really secluded spot where forty-nine men, mostly Australian artillerymen, were buried in three and a half short rows. The private inscriptions on two adjacent Australian graves caught my eye. Gunner H. C. Jacob's has mention of his brother who died at sea while being evacuated wounded from Gallipoli in May 1915, and Gunner H. T. Truman has this enigmatic inscription: *The gunner smiled as he went out west.*

The main road from Albert to Amiens runs absolutely straight, except where an aristocrat caused a diversion to be made around his château. The road reeks with history. Roman soldiers made it.

Supplies and troops used it to its maximum capacity all through the First World War, and Gough's 'Mobile Army' waited astride it in July 1916 for a breakthrough which never came. The 1st Panzer Division motored down the road after brushing the Royal West Kents aside at Albert in May 1940. The Mosquitoes which bombed Amiens Prison in February 1944 used Albert as a turning-point and then flew above the road to make their attack.

Franvillers Communal Cemetery Extension ㉔ is just off the main road. It is a simple little cemetery made in the 'quiet' months of 1918 between the spring and autumn battles. Australian units held the German advance near here in April and remained all through the summer; their 'Bursting Sun' badges on graves are particularly numerous in this area. There are 134 of them among the 248 graves in this cemetery. Later burials are English soldiers of the 12th and 18th (Eastern) Divisions which attacked to the east of here in August; in particular, there are a lot of Buffs (East Kents).

Querrieu is where the road bends round the grounds of the château ㉕ which General Rawlinson used as Fourth Army Head-quarters in 1916. It is the property of the d'Alcantara family. The Germans were here in 1940–44, using the park as an ammunition depot; some of the ordnance dumped in 1944 is still being recovered from the small lakes. Two d'Alcantara sons died in the Second World War, a pilot in the Belgian Air Force killed in 1940 and an army officer who joined the Resistance but was caught and died in a concentration camp; a third son (father of the present owner) survived a similar camp. The present Count and Countess are proud of the part played by their home in the Battle of the Somme and have a permanent photographic exhibition. They are willing to receive visitors provided there are no other commitments that day and provided visitors phone in advance – 22.401409, but check in the phone book under 'D' for d'Alcantara in case the number changes. May, June, August and September are best and afternoons are preferred. The château's stables have been converted into elegant *chambre d'hôte* (bed and breakfast) apartments; phone the same number for a booking.

Querrieu British Cemetery ㉖ was made in 1918. The 186 graves from that year include that of a gallant officer, Lieutenant-Colonel Christopher Bushell, VC, DSO, of the 7th Queen's (West Surreys) in Row E. The citation for his VC in the register describes his leadership, though badly wounded, during the spring offensive. He recovered and returned to his battalion, only to be killed in the German front line near Morlancourt in the great attack of 8 August. A Hurricane pilot shot down in May 1940 is also buried here.

There are two interesting memorials, ㉗ and ㉘, where the Battle of the Hallue was fought during the Franco-Prussian War on Christmas Eve in 1870. Much of the fighting was in the streets of Pont-Noyelles and some was in the grounds of the château. It was one of the few French successes of that war. The monument which is along a track parallel with the main road ㉗ lists the French regiments involved and their fatal casualties – seventy-two in total, thirty from the heaviest losing regiment.

The Ancre valley between Albert and the junction with the Somme contains a string of pretty villages. The main railway line here was an important means of communication in 1914–18, particularly in June to November 1916 when it fed supplies and troops into the great battle and took the wounded away to base hospitals. Buire-sur-l'Ancre was the last safe stop on the line before it was likely to be shelled and it became a major railhead. Extra sidings were built and, among other things, it was the place from where leave trains departed in quiet times. The only trace now of the British presence is six graves in *Buire-sur-l'Ancre Communal Cemetery* ㉙.

Ribemont Communal Cemetery and Extension ㉚ has four Australian graves from 1918 in the civilian cemetery and 468 graves in the extension, mostly from 1918 and including 178 Australians. It is a simple cemetery with the graves facing the village across a field.

Méricourt-l'Abbé Communal Cemetery Extension ㉛ was made by medical units close to the railway line. The first four rows on the left were made in the quiet months before the 1916 battle. Plot 2, on the right of the Cross of Sacrifice, was the result of the July 1916 fighting and includes forty-seven men who died in the first week, many of them from the 34th Division in action at La Boisselle. The cemetery then closed until 1918 when six further rows were made and, finally, the graves in the right rear of the cemetery were added after the war, including three rows made almost entirely of unidentified Australians from 1918. There are 407 graves in the cemetery, 122 of them Australian.

The *3rd Australian Division Memorial* ㉜ stands prominently on high ground at a crossroads. This division did not arrive in France until November 1916 and its battle honours start with 'Messines 1917' and then continue to include Morlancourt, Treux and Hamel in 1918, scenes of defensive actions in the spring and summer and of the successful advance in August of that year. The memorial stands at the centre of a triangle formed by those three villages. A succession of low-flying French Air Force jets swept over our heads when Mary was photographing the memorial; it is probably used as a turning-point for low-level exercises.

At the side of a lane ㉝ just south of the hamlet of Bouzencourt stands a lovely little memorial in the form of a truncated column denoting lives cut off in their prime. The inscription, in French, is to Captain Francis L. Mond and Lieutenant Edgar M. Martyn who 'fell gloriously at this spot in combat against three German aeroplanes' on 15 May 1918. On the base there has been scratched the Cross of Lorraine and a V-for-Victory sign, probably by a defiant French person in the Second World War. The two airmen were shot down in a DH4 bomber of No. 57 Squadron after attacking ammunition dumps at Bapaume. They crashed close to the British trenches at that time. Their bodies are now buried in Doullens Communal Cemetery Extension No. 2. The small enclosure around the memorial is obviously cared for by the local people. Two Mirage fighters roared directly overhead while we were there – a perfect 'fly-past'. The village of Le Hamel, just south of here, was in the middle of the sector where the Australians attacked on 8 August 1918 and they gave that action the title of 'the Battle of Hamel'. A smart, modern chapel just south of the village almost exactly marks the point where the Australian trench ran at that time and from which units of the 3rd Australian Division attacked that morning in thick fog.

We come now to the area where a group of Casualty Clearing Stations worked during the 1916 battle. A CCS was the first medical unit a wounded man could reach where surgery and nursing could be provided. The essential requirements for its location were that it had to be close enough to the front to receive casualties by ambulance from Dressing Stations but far enough back to be safe from shell fire, and it had to be near a railway so that men who could be moved could be evacuated quickly to the base hospitals on the coast to prevent overcrowding. Serious cases could be held as long as was necessary. The American MASH in Korea, as shown on television,

63 Casualty Clearing Station – stretcher cases, mostly head wounds, awaiting evacuation by the railway line at a typical CCS.

was a smaller version of a CCS but performed the same function.

When I wrote *The First Day on the Somme* I believed that the book made only two original contributions to military history – the disclosure that General Rawlinson rewrote his diaries after the war and the description of the 'ambulance train fiasco' at the opening of the 1916 battle. Two weeks before the battle, General Rawlinson personally wrote to GHQ requesting that eighteen ambulance trains per day be provided with the capacity to clear 10,000 wounded from CCSs to the base each day. He received a haughty reply from the Quartermaster-General saying that there was no cause for anxiety. But only five ambulance trains were provided on 1 July when the Fourth Army had more than 30,000 wounded men; all

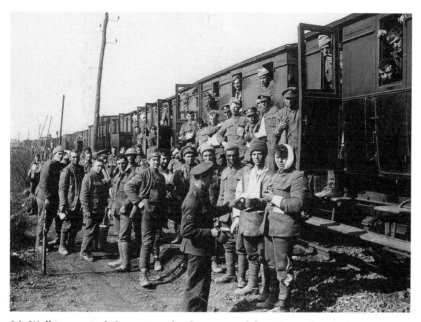

64 Walking wounded awaiting the departure of their 'sitting' ambulance train at a CCS.

but one CCS was theoretically full that evening, but more wounded continued to arrive. Barns and other buildings had to be taken over and many men were left in the open for several days. Surgeons and nurses were overwhelmed; stretchers ran out. The congestion continued for nearly a week. The situation was made worse by the geographical location of the CCSs behind the southern part of the British front. Such units would normally have been located in a 'fan' spreading north and south of the rear of the battle front, but the proximity of the boundary with the French Army – on the River Somme – and the situation of the main railway line resulted in four major groups of CCSs being located one behind the other alongside the railway line – at Heilly, Corbie, La Neuville and Daours.

Heilly Station Cemetery ㉞ served a group of three CCSs which bore the brunt of the congestion. Ambulances from the front reached that place first; ambulance trains from the rear reached it last. The cemetery bears witness to what happened. The rows of Plot 1 and part of Plot 2, at the left rear of the cemetery, show how men died in such numbers that the burial parties had to bury men on top of each other; most of the headstones show three names. Approxi-

65 Heilly Station Cemetery – badges set in a wall for those men who were buried so densely in 1916 that there was no space on headstones for their badges.

mately 260 men died in the first week of July, an appalling mortality rate. Most of those casualties came from the centre and south of the battle front, from the La Boisselle, Fricourt, Mametz and Montauban areas. A few German prisoners of war were also buried.

The congestion was eventually cleared, but the manner in which the 1916 battle developed on the southern wing of the original attack front resulted in the CCSs at Heilly being heavily used all through the battle and most of the 2,890 graves are of men who died of wounds here in 1916, among them 402 Australians and 118 New Zealanders. The most senior casualties were Brigadier-Generals Archie Buckle, commander of the 17th (Northern) Division's artillery, who died in August 1916, and D. J. Glasfurd, born in Edinburgh, but commanding an Australian brigade when he died in November, making him the seventh British general officer to die in the 1916 battle. Glasfurd's grave is the second inside the entrance and Buckle's is the right-hand grave of Plot 2, Row F.

When the cemetery came to receive its permanent construction after the war, it was found that there was no room on the headstones of the early burials for the regimental badges of the dead men, so a colonnade was built near the entrance into the wall of which 117 national and regimental badges were mounted, an inspired and unique decision which gives the poor men who had to be buried so densely the chance to have their units commemorated. One Australian soldier has a particularly unusual memorial. After Lance-Corporal J. P. O'Neill of the 13th (New South Wales) Battalion died in a grenade accident in January 1917, his friends paid a local stonemason to erect a superb marble column above his grave in defiance of regulations. This was allowed to remain after the war and is easily seen rising above the ordinary headstones of Plot 5, near the colonnade. Five graves to the right is that of Sapper David Simpson, a native of Dundee, Scotland, but serving with the Australian Engineers when he died in January 1917. His mother (who had gone to live in Brooklyn, New York) chose another of those moving inscriptions for his headstone: *In that distant land, will some kind hand lay a flower on his grave for me.*

If one drives or walks along the track which passes the cemetery and up the slope, and then turns right behind some trees, it is possible to look down on the place where Manfred von Richthofen – the Red Baron – crashed on 21 April 1918 near the buildings of an old brickworks, but the actual spot is not marked (at least not at the time of writing). On the other side of the cemetery, the little railway station and the line at which the ambulance trains stood are still there. The village itself has many interesting architectural features, including the huge boundary walls of a now disappeared château. Many of the buildings bear the marks of shell fragments from the period in 1918 when Heilly came under German fire.

Bonnay Communal Cemetery Extension ③⑤ has just four rows of 106 graves from 1918, mostly of Australian and London units. It is in a pretty rural location, giving good views along the Ancre valley.

Corbie, with about 6,000 people, is the largest town in the area and has much character. It has two small hotels. The Ancre joins the Somme nearby and the Somme Canal disappears; the river is wide enough for barge traffic from here to the sea. Corbie was very much a 'gateway' town to the 1916 battlefields. At the north end is a road junction through which thousands of British soldiers must have marched. A statue there ③⑥ has an inscription by the local people honouring their patron, Saint Colette, and remembering 'the Great War 1914–18'. The bridge over the Somme to the south of the town provided another route in another war. Helped by local

Resistance men, it was seized by armoured cars of the Royal Horse Guards on 31 August 1944 so that the Guards Armoured Division could cross the river and continue its dash from the Seine to Brussels.

Corbie Communal Cemetery and Extension ㊲ is another important Casualty Clearing Station cemetery, the first to be opened when British troops came to the Somme in July 1915. The extension was opened in 1916 and the close-packed graves reflect its heavy use in the 1916 battle. The most famous grave is that of Major W. T. (Billy) Congreve, VC, DSO, MC, son of a general who was also a VC; Billy Congreve was a staff officer killed near Longueval in July 1916 and brought back here to be buried in a separate grave which is now near the entrance. There are 249 graves in the communal cemetery and 916 in the extension. There are many interesting graves and a browse along the rows with the register can be rewarding.

There are two cemeteries at La Neuville. The *Communal Cemetery* ㊳ is just one very long row of 186 graves and was used mainly before and after the 1916 battle, with a strong emphasis on medical cases rather than battle wounds; 'sickness', 'disease' and 'gas' are common entries in the register. One of those buried here was nineteen-year-old Second Lieutenant Ian Badenoch who was killed saving the lives of others when he was in charge of men engaged in grenade-throwing practice in March 1917. He was awarded a posthumous Albert Medal and is one of only two such medal holders buried on the Somme. *La Neuville British Cemetery* ㊴ has 866 graves and is a typical 1916 Casualty Clearing Station cemetery. It started with seventy men who died of wounds received on 1 July, now buried in Plot 1, Row A, mostly 18th and 30th Division casualties from the Mametz and Montauban areas, and the graves work steadily back down the cemetery in date order during the remainder of the summer. It was used again in 1918, mostly for Australians.

Daours Communal Cemetery Extension ㊵ is another CCS cemetery which treated the wounded of the major battles of 1916 and 1918; more than two-thirds of the burials are from 1918. There are 1,224 graves, 450 of them Australians. It is a long narrow cemetery on the edge of this little town and next to the sports field of a smart modern school. Behind the Cross of Sacrifice is a small plot of Indian soldiers and Chinese labourers buried separately from the white troops; some of the Indians are from the Deccan Horse wounded in the cavalry action near High Wood on 14 July 1916.

There are two small cemeteries on the other side of the River Somme – *Aubigny British Cemetery* ④① with ninety-five graves and *Fouilloy Communal Cemetery* ④② with thirty-eight. All of the deaths are of 1918 and many were of Australians, but the very last death at Fouilloy was that of Private W. Montgomery who was in a seemingly safe Army Service Corps unit well behind the lines but who was drowned while swimming in the river in September 1918.

3·THE 1918 AREA

There is a large area of the Somme *département* to the east and south of the 1916 battlefield where two dramatic battles were fought in 1918, battles which led to the end of the First World War but which are not well known to visitors, particularly to the British whose attention is so often fixed on the 1916 battle.

In March 1917 the Germans abandoned the line they had held during the winter months and retired to a new position which they named the Siegfried Stellung and which the British called the Hindenburg Line. The German intention was to shorten their overall line and to meet any renewed Allied offensive in strong positions on well-chosen tactical ground and in trenches constructed with the benefits of the lessons learned in their defensive fighting in 1916. They systematically destroyed buildings, roads, bridges and wells in the area they evacuated, except for a few places where French civilians were collected and left for the Allies to feed. The British and French followed up, suffering casualties from German rear-guards and from booby-traps and delayed-action explosive charges.

The main battles of 1917 took place elsewhere. The Germans remained on the defensive. The French suffered badly in an attack in Champagne which temporarily demoralized their army. The British mounted two major offensives, at Arras and then at Ypres, the last battle culminating in the horror of Passchendaele. A smaller British attack then followed at Cambrai; it was an initial success due to the mass use of tanks, but the Germans recovered, counter-attacked and regained most of their lost ground. Of all those battles, only a small part of the Cambrai fighting affected the Somme *département*.

The focus of attention returned to the Somme with a vengeance in 1918. The Germans struck first. After making peace with Russia and transferring most of their forces there to the west, they were in a position of temporary superiority on the Western Front. They decided to mount a series of violent attacks, their main target – the British Army; the first effort – on the Somme; the date – 21 March 1918. Seventy-six German divisions and a large force of artillery were assembled to strike the southern part of the British-held front. This was the sector held by the Fifth Army and part of the Third where only twenty-two British divisions faced the German attack.

The British were suffering three other handicaps besides being outnumbered in divisions. Haig's offensives of 1917, bringing no strategic success, caused Lloyd George, the Prime Minister, to hold back the reinforcements needed to bring the United Kingdom divisions up to strength again. This led to the need to reduce the strength of infantry brigades on the Western Front from four battalions to three. One-quarter of the United Kingdom battalions were thus disbanded, causing considerable numbers of men to be transferred. This disruptive process was completed only seventeen days before the German attack. The second factor was that the southernmost part of the British line had only recently been taken over from the French and the defences there were weak. The final factor was that the morale of the British troops was not high. The survivors of the battles of the earlier years were war weary and most of the new men were young recruits with little enthusiasm for a three-year-old war. The Empire divisions, however, were at full strength and in better heart.

The blow fell at dawn on 21 March. The German attack was the largest military operation mounted by any army since the original German invasion of France and Belgium in August 1914. After a short but ferocious bombardment, German storm troops overwhelmed the British front line and made deep penetrations, particularly against the Fifth Army which was so thinly stretched in the south. British casualties that day are estimated at 38,512 men, of whom about 21,000 were prisoners of war. German casualties were slightly higher in number but included large numbers of wounded, many of whom would recover to fight again.[1] The British retreat which started that day lasted for two weeks. The Germans

---

[1] Casualty figures from the author's research for *The Kaiser's Battle* (London: Allen Lane, 1978; Penguin, 1983), which describes the battle of 21 March 1918 in detail.

advanced more than thirty miles and captured 1,000 square miles of territory. Allied casualties, mainly British, were about 250,000, German about 300,000, showing again that attack was costlier than defence on the Western Front. It was a time of great crisis for the Allies. The British and French armies were nearly forced apart. But no major town or ground of strategic importance was lost, the Germans ran out of steam, and the Allied defence held. The Germans carried out further attacks on other parts of the Western Front, but the Allies weathered every crisis. Then, on 8 August, at the place on the Somme in front of Amiens where the Germans had been halted in April, the Allies started a counter-offensive which proved unstoppable and which led to the end of the war. That battle will be described in more detail later.

Those two great battles of the Somme in 1918 covered about one-third of the *département*'s territory; it is an area about nine times larger than the 1916 battlefield, which was lost in two days in March 1918 but required ten days of steady effort to regain in August. The main actions took place in the extreme east, on 21 March, and in the west, in April and in August; and it is at those extremities where there is now most to see. There is less of interest in the large intervening area, although there are some French memorials of the 1916 fighting there. That extensive 1918 battlefield is mostly an area of quiet, open country, with few towns. A motorway runs from north to south across the middle of the area and a new east–west motorway is planned to link Amiens and St Quentin.

   Visiting this area cannot be as rewarding as visiting the 1916 battlefield. There were no battles of attrition concentrated in small areas, just two rapid advances separated by a summer of uneasy calm. There are no mine craters or preserved trenches. The identification of trench lines is rare; there is even little trace left of the Hindenburg Line. Field walking rarely results in interesting finds. The cemeteries are different in character to the 1916 cemeteries. Many of them are 'communals' where men were buried in civilian cemeteries. British and German graves are often found together, buried by the Germans after their March advance. Individual British graves represent the 'army of 1918', often with well-decorated veterans of earlier years among many young recruits. Headstones sometimes have details of two regiments, showing how men often

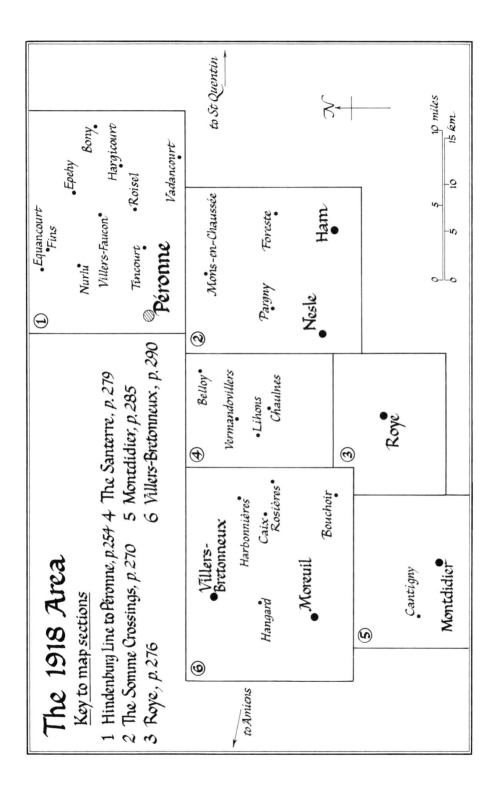

The 1918 Area

Key to map sections

1 Hindenburg Line to Péronne, p. 254
2 The Somme Crossings, p. 270
3 Roye, p. 276
4 The Santerre, p. 279
5 Montdidier, p. 285
6 Villers-Bretonneux, p. 290

to Amiens

① Equancourt
Fins
Nurlu
Villers-Faucon
Epehy
Bony
Hargicourt
Roisel
Tincourt
Péronne
Vadancourt

to St Quentin

② Mons-en-Chaussée
Paigny
Foreste
Ham
Nesle

④ Belloy
Vermandovillers
Lihons
Chaulnes

③ Roye

⑥ Villers-Bretonneux
Harbonnières
Caix
Rosières
Bouchoir
Hangard
Moreuil

⑤ Cantigny
Montdidier

N

10 miles
15 km
0 5 10
0 5 10

belonged to one regiment but were killed while 'attached to' another, the result of the mass transfers of the February reorganization or of the drafting of reinforcements from the base camps with little regard to regimental loyalty under the pressure of events of that year. This is not an area packed with interest, but there are interesting things to see and important stories to tell, and the men who fought in those momentous battles of 1918 should not be forgotten. The keen student of history will still learn much from a visit.

THE HINDENBURG LINE TO PÉRONNE

The Hindenburg Line, which British troops reached in 1917 after following up the German retirement, just touched the eastern boundary of the Somme *département* at two places; a motorway now runs almost down the same line. This was the sector where the Germans struck part of Gough's Fifth Army on 21 March 1918, the 9th (Scottish), 21st, 16th (Irish), 66th (East Lancs) and 24th Divisions being attacked on a frontage of twelve miles. Some units collapsed on the first day and there was a steady retreat thereafter. The cemeteries in this area contain the dead of four periods of war. First were those who died following up the German retirement in the spring of 1917. This was followed by a long 'line-holding' period until 20 March 1918. Next come the graves of the men killed in the March 1918 offensive; most of the 'unknown' graves in cemeteries are from this period. There are also some sad graves with dates to show how British prisoners of war were held by the Germans in the forward zone as labourers and died under British shell fire or from weakness and exposure. Finally, there are the dead of autumn 1918 when the British 'Advance to Victory' passed through here in August and September; it is not generally known that this was one of the costliest periods of the war for the British Army. There are not many memorials. In the spring of 1918 it was an area of surrenders and retreat, and the memorials for the autumn victories were mostly erected where the advance began or where it ended, not here at its mid-point.

Rocquigny–Equancourt Road British Cemetery ① is one of the few large cemeteries in this area and is also unusual in that nearly all the graves are identified. The reason for this is that it served nearby Casualty Clearing Stations for a long period in 1917 and early 1918 when British units seven miles away to the east were occupying trenches facing the Hindenburg Line. The men buried here were mostly casualties from that period of static trench warfare and also from the Battle of Cambrai which was fought ten miles away to the north-east in November and December 1917. The Germans used the cemetery after their advance in 1918, but British medical units returned in October and nearly 300 more 'died of wounds' were buried in Plots 13 and 14 on the left of the cemetery. There are 1,838 British graves, from a great variety of units, but very few Empire troops. Sixty-six German soldiers and ten French civilians are also buried here. The courageous Sergeant J. H. Rhodes, VC, DCM and Bar, of the 3rd Grenadier Guards is buried in Plot 3, Row E. He earned his VC capturing a pillbox in the Third Battle of Ypres in October 1917, but died after being wounded at Bourlon Wood in the Battle of Cambrai. The cemetery stands among fields, just above the deep alley through which the Canal du Nord is cut. The small cemetery seen to the north is *Five Points Cemetery* ②, with just 100 graves, but this is just beyond the Somme boundary.

Fins New British Cemetery ③, nearer to the front, has four distinct parts. Divisions in the line started the cemetery in July 1917 and buried 590 men in Plots 1 to 3 on the right and in the first four rows of Plot 4 on the left. The Germans then came in 1918 and buried 277 of their soldiers along the left of the original cemetery, together with some British soldiers including some whose dates of death in July and August 1918 show that they died as prisoners of war. The British advance reached here in September and a further seventy-three graves – mainly from the 33rd Division – were made, mostly behind the German graves. Finally, 591 bodies were concentrated here after the war when Plots 7 and 8 were made at the end of the cemetery. There are 1,281 British graves; eighty-seven South Africans are the only sizeable Empire group. The cemetery stands in open ground and has a pleasant open front looking out over part of Fins village and across to one of those straight, tree-lined roads which were so common in France but are disappearing because of road widening.

Heudicourt Communal Cemetery and Extension ④ was used by both

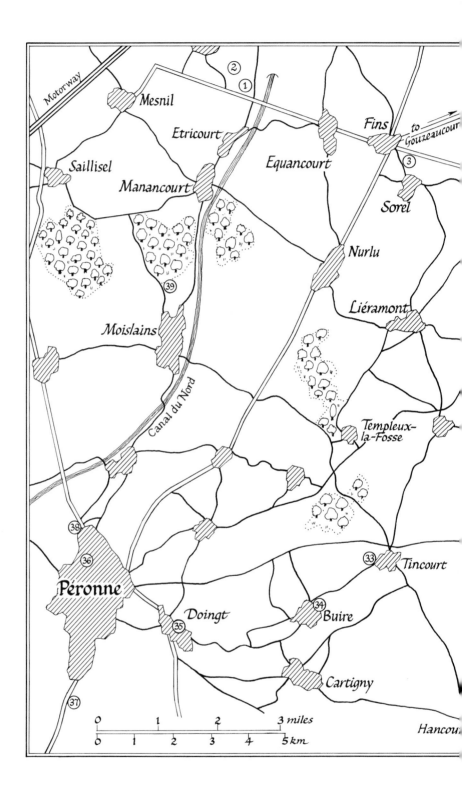

Motorway

Mesnil

Etricourt

Fins

to Gouzeaucour

②

①

③

Saillisel

Equancourt

Manancourt

Sorel

Nurlu

Liéramont

③⑨

Moislains

Canal du Nord

Templeux-la-Fosse

③③ Tincourt

③⑧

③⑥

Péronne

③④ Buire

Doingt

③⑤

③⑦

Cartigny

Hancou

0   1   2   3 miles

0   1   2   3   4   5 km

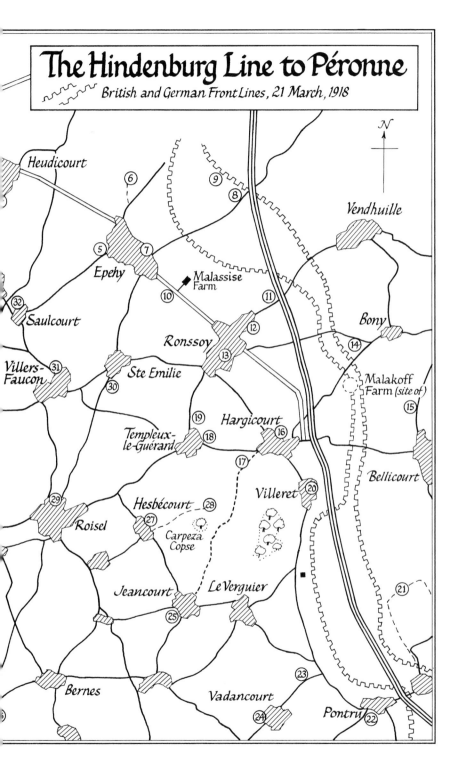

The Hindenburg Line to Péronne

British and German Front Lines, 21 March, 1918

N

Heudicourt

⑥

⑨

⑧

Vendhuille

⑤ ⑦

Epehy

Malassise Farm

⑩ ⑪

Bony

⑫

Saulcourt

㉜

Ronssoy

⑬

⑭

Villers-Faucon

㉛

Ste Emilie

㉚

Malakoff Farm (site of)

⑮

⑲ Hargicourt

Templeux-le-Guérard

⑱ ⑯

⑰

Bellicourt

Hesbécourt ㉘

Villeret

⑳

㉙

Roisel

㉗

Carpeza Copse

Jeancourt

Le Verguier

㉑

㉕

Bernes

Vadancourt

㉓

㉔

Pontru

㉒

British and German units in 1917 and 1918. There are only four British graves in the civilian cemetery. The extension at the back is reached by a path and contains eighty-five graves. It is a pretty spot, with well-spaced graves and two large trees, situated among farm buildings and small fields. The notes from our visit say 'almost the perfect small cemetery'. Two unusual graves are those of Lieutenant-Colonels E. C. Corbyn, commander of the 18th Lancers, and M. Docherty, DSO, the commander of Lord Strathcona's Horse, both killed on 1 December 1917, the first day of the German counter-offensive at Cambrai when cavalry units were in action at Gauche Wood, three miles north-west of here. The two cavalry commanders are buried side by side in Row C.

The large village of Epehy was only just behind the British front line facing the Hindenburg Line. The defending troops here on 21 March 1918 were the 6th, 7th and 8th Leicesters, who held up the German advance all that day. *Epehy Wood Farm Cemetery* ⑤ was not started until September 1918 when the 12th (Eastern) Division recaptured this area and buried 404 men in Plots 1 and 2. The remainder of the cemetery – a further 563 graves – was made after the war; most of the 234 'unknowns' among those graves were probably Leicesters or men of the 16th (Irish) Division who fought just south of Epehy on 21 March 1918.

Domino British Cemetery ⑥, up a track, is only a few yards inside the Somme boundary. The cemetery was made in September 1918 when the 33rd Division attacked here and buried fifty-one of its men in what is now a small, square battlefield cemetery. The name 'Domino' comes from the 'double three' divisional sign.

The road out of Epehy to the east – towards Honnescourt – has some interesting features. At the edge of the village is a tall concrete observation post ⑦, built by the British to look up the long valley ahead into the German lines. That peaceful and innocent looking valley – called Pigeon Ravine by the British – was the scene of three separate actions. On 1 December 1917, the German counter-attack from Cambrai reached this area and an Indian cavalry regiment – the 2nd Lancers – made a mounted charge in which its commander, Lieutenant-Colonel H. H. F. Turner, was killed, the third cavalry commander to die that day; he is buried at Tincourt New British Cemetery. On 21 March 1918, the British front line running across the valley 1,000 yards from the village was held by the 8th Leicesters, who fell back on the village. When the fog lifted later that morning, the three Leicester battalions at Epehy inflicted severe casualties on the Germans revealed in the open ground here. Finally, British troops of the 33rd Division fought here again in late September and made *Pigeon Ravine Cemetery* ⑧, which is a simple little battlefield cemetery in a field just in front of the old Hindenburg Line. There are just three rows, containing 135 graves, mostly of the 2nd Worcesters, the battalion which nearly four years earlier made an epic attack at Gheluvelt during a critical stage in the First Battle of Ypres in October 1914. One wonders whether any 'old sweats' who survived Gheluvelt are buried here; several headstones show men of sufficiently mature age.

This cemetery is the most easterly in the Somme *département*. I came to it hoping that I could discover the identity of the soldier buried in the most easterly grave. But the headstone on that grave, the first on the right inside the cemetery, shows that it is of an 'unknown' of the Worcesters killed on 29 September 1918. It is a lovely little cemetery and we were moved by our visit. The visitors book contained just two British names for the previous twelve

66 Pigeon Ravine Cemetery containing the most easterly British graves on the Somme.

months. The motorway is only a quarter of a mile away but there is no exit there. *Meath Cemetery* ⑨, across the fields but in the Nord *département*, was also made by the 33rd Division in 1918 and contains 122 graves.

Coming out of Epehy to the south-east, the *12th (Eastern) Division Memorial* ⑩ stands near the junction of a lane and a light railway track. This division fought twice on the Somme in 1916 but, after the division captured Epehy in September 1918, this site was chosen for its only memorial in the *département*. The memorial is in the form of a fine white cross topped by the 'Spade' (from the playing-card suit) divisional sign. The division's battle honours are named on the base, from 'Armentières 1915' through to 'Victory'. Not far away is Malassise Farm whose original buildings formed part of the forward line of what the British called the 'Battle Zone' in March 1918, where the main attempt to hold any German attack was to take place. The farm was held by the 2nd Royal Dublin Fusiliers on 21 March, but the violent German attack in the fog that morning quickly overran the farm.

   Unicorn Cemetery ⑪ is beyond the Somme boundary. It is situated just behind the British front line held from spring 1917 to March

67 The 12th (Eastern) Division Memorial near Epehy.

1918, but the cemetery was started in September 1918 by the 50th (Northumbrian) Division which recaptured the area; the 'Unicorn' is from its divisional badge. There are 998 graves, most of them post-war concentrations. Nearly half are unidentified and are probably from the March 1918 fighting. *Lempire Communal Cemetery* ⑫ has eleven graves from 1917 – mostly 19th Durham Light Infantry – and one British 'unknown', but this is also just outside the Somme.

The forty-five British graves in *Ronssoy Communal Cemetery* ⑬ are in three parts. Inside the entrance, on the right, are six graves of the 6th Connaught Rangers – including the Medical Officer – killed in December 1917, together with an unidentified Inniskilling Fusilier. One man of the 7th Queen's, killed in January 1917, is buried alone among some French soldiers' graves. At the bottom of the cemetery, in a War Graves Commission plot, are thirty-eight English and Australians and one German, casualties of the September 1918 fighting.

The *American Somme Cemetery* ⑭ at Bony is actually just outside the Somme boundary (and also just behind the old Hindenburg Line). There are 1,844 graves in this beautifully laid out and meticulously maintained cemetery. There is a visitors centre and a chapel; on the walls of the chapel are recorded the names of 333 Americans who have no known grave. Several American regiments fought alongside British and French troops on the Somme in the autumn 1918 advance and most of the men buried here died in that campaign. Three of the graves are of men who were members of British units – two RAF pilots and a man who served in a New Zealand infantry battalion; their graves have standard American crosses. The impressive American monument north of Bellicourt ⑮ (also outside the Somme) commemorates the achievements of the 90,000 Americans who fought alongside British units in 1917–18. A map on the back of the memorial illustrates these American operations.

The road from Bony to Hargicourt passes the ruins of Malakoff Farm, the site of which is easily seen 200 yards up a track on a small rise. This was part of the British front line on 21 March 1918 and was held by the 2/8th Lancashire Fusiliers who were quickly overwhelmed in the fog and most of them captured. The British 'Battle Zone' ran just behind Hargicourt village, through some quarries which can still be seen; men of the 2/5th and 9th Manchesters fought here on 21 March. *Hargicourt Communal Cemetery*

68 Part of the American Somme Cemetery at Bony with the Memorial Chapel.

Extension ⑯ became isolated from the civilian cemetery when a plot of German graves was removed after the war. There are seventy-three British graves, men of the 34th Division who were holding the line nearby in 1917 and also casualties of the British advance twelve months later. The larger *Hargicourt British Cemetery* ⑰ has 309 British graves. It was used by many units until the German attack in March 1918 and again in the autumn of that year. The 34th Division is again well represented. There are also twenty-two Indian cavalrymen in their own plot on the left of the cemetery. They were holding trenches at various times in 1917. They come from a variety of unusual-sounding regiments, including 'Sam Browne's Cavalry', a unit I did not know existed. It is an interesting cemetery.

Templeux-le-Guérard was held by the 6th Lancashire Fusiliers on 21 March; a stout resistance was offered, but the Germans eventually captured the village. *Templeux-le-Guérard British Cemetery* ⑱ is on a particularly attractive site outside the village, on a slope among fields and small woods, and with an old metal 'calvary' set into a corner of the cemetery boundary. The Cross of Sacrifice at the back of the cemetery is on a raised platform, neatly flanked on either side with eight 'Believed to be buried here' headstones. It is obvious that the cemetery architect devoted much care and skill to the design of the cemetery and it is well worth a visit. There are 757 graves. Like many cemeteries in this area it reflects the trench-holding period of 1917 and early 1918 and then the autumn 1918 advance. The casualties of the 21 March fighting are probably among the 188 'unknown' graves. A marked feature of the headstones of the late 1918 period is the frequency of the 'attached to' inscription where men from base camps were sent to other regiments than the ones in which they had previously served; the right-hand three rows in the cemetery – H, J and K of Plot 1 – have many of these. Most of those graves were from the 50th (Northumbrian) Division which had suffered so heavily in the March and April fighting of 1918 that the division had to be reconstituted. In October 1918 its infantry included battalions as far distant from Northumbria as Munster Fusiliers, Yorkshire Light Infantry and Wiltshires, showing that not only did individual soldiers have to transfer to strange regiments but battalions were transferred to makeshift divisions in those final months of the war. The achievements of those units in the final advance are rarely remembered, but theirs were the men who finally beat the Germans.

Templeux-le-Guérard Communal Cemetery Extension ⑲ was started by the 59th (North Midland) Division when it followed up the German retirement early in 1917. There are 130 British graves in three long rows – casualties of the 59th Division, of the 34th Division holding trenches in 1917, a row of graves at the back of the cemetery made up of March 1918 casualties buried by the Germans and, finally, from the fighting in late 1918. The front row has gaps where German and American bodies were removed after the war. There are many Lincolns – Territorials from the 59th Division and Grimsby 'Chums' from the 34th.

There are five cemeteries and a memorial which are along the old Hindenburg Line and in the March 1918 battle area which are beyond the Somme boundary but visitors may wish to know of them. *Villeret Churchyard* ⑳ has twenty British graves, including a company commander and at least nine men of the Manchesters killed in the March 1918 fighting. The *4th Australian Division Memorial* ㉑ needs to be reached by tracks running north from Pontruet or Bellenglise. It stands just beyond the old Hindenburg Line which the Australians attacked in October 1918. *Berthaucourt Communal Cemetery* ㉒ was made in the autumn 1918 advance and has seventy-one British graves from that time. *Maissemy German Cemetery* ㉓ has 15,478 graves from 1917 and 1918, including 7,814 in mass graves. *Vadancourt British Cemetery* ㉔ is alongside a large farm and has 753 graves including many cleared from the March 1918 battlefield after the war. One of these is the grave of Lieutenant-Colonel J. H. Dimmer, VC, MC, killed on 21 March 1918 leading the 2/4th Royal Berks into a counter-attack on horseback near Holnon Wood (south of here and not on the map for this section). His Victoria Cross had been won in 1914 at Ypres. *Jeancourt Communal Cemetery Extension* ㉕ has 492 British and 167 German graves. The British graves are mainly from the 59th and then the 34th Division which was holding this sector in the quiet times of 1917 and early 1918, from the 24th Division and the 66th (East Lancs) Division which was pushed back by the Germans in March 1918, and Australians from late 1918.

Hancourt British Cemetery ㉖ is a nice little battlefield cemetery containing 118 graves on the edge of the village. The second, third and fourth rows were made by Australian troops who advanced through here in September 1918. The remaining three rows of graves were added after the war and are mostly from units of the 50th (Northumbrian) Division which fought here in the March 1918 retreat; many of these graves are from the 1/4th East Yorks.

Hesbécourt Communal Cemetery ㉗ is behind the church in this tiny village. It contains fourteen British graves in various parts of the cemetery with dates between September 1916 and September 1918. The most interesting grave is that of Captain G. L. Cruikshank, DSO, MC. He was a Gordon Highlanders officer who transferred to the Royal Flying Corps and received both of his decorations in 1915, being one of the prominent British pilots of that period; his decorations were for carrying out hazardous long-range reconnaissance flights. He was killed on the morning of 15 September 1916 while flying a Sopwith $1\frac{1}{2}$-Strutter of No. 70 Squadron. This was the day of the great infantry–tank attack on the Somme and Cruikshank's mission was to observe the movement of reserves in the German rear, but he was shot down by Oswald Boelcke, one of the leading German fighter aces of that period. It was Boelcke's twenty-fifth success but he died six weeks later. Cruikshank's observer, Lieutenant R. A. Preston, MC, is buried with him.

A long track runs out of Hesbécourt to the east, towards two copses. The first is Carpeza Copse which was at the forward edge of the 'Battle Zone' held by the 66th (East Lancs) Division on 21 March. The smaller, more easterly copse was *Trinket Post* ㉘ in March 1918, a position successfully held by part of the 2/6th Manchesters that day. There is a monument among the bushes, tall and well built, but the plaque has disappeared. Enquiries made later at the village and at Manchester failed to identify whose memorial it was.

Roisel Communal Cemetery Extension ㉙ is up a lane at the north end of this large village. It was started in late 1918 when Roisel was an important Casualty Clearing Station centre and 307 British graves were made, many of them Australians. There were also many German and American burials. A further 557 graves were concentrated here after the war. The American graves were removed, but about 500 German graves still remain and the British total is 864, 106 of them Australian. It is an important 1918 cemetery, mostly from the spring and autumn of that year. It is also well laid out on a good hilltop site looking over fields outside the town; some small factory buildings nearby are in a hollow and are not intrusive. There is a 'comrades in death' character to the cemetery with so many British and Germans buried together and, just over a hedge, the *tricolore* flies above a plot of French soldiers' graves in the civilian cemetery. There is one VC grave, that of Second Lieutenant J. C. Buchan of the 1/7th Argyll and Sutherland Highlanders. He fought seven miles south of here on 21 March 1918 and led his platoon in a heroic defence for twenty-four hours, despite being wounded early in the action, and was last seen cut off but still fighting.

Ste Emilie Valley Cemetery ㉚ was started by the Germans who made three large graves of British dead after capturing this area in March 1918. The remainder of the cemetery was concentrated after the war. The original burials are easy to spot – three closely packed rows of headstones on the left of the path. They contain the bodies of men of the 16th (Irish) Division, which was pushed back more than a mile almost to this point on the first day of the German attack, and of the 39th Division which was sent into action from reserve that afternoon. There are 492 graves in the cemetery now.

Most of the identified graves are dated September 1918, but the 222 'unknowns' are probably from March. Ste Emilie is a factory village, but the cemetery is a quarter of a mile away from any buildings and the open front looks out over farmland and the local football pitch.

Villers-Faucon Communal Cemetery and Extension ③ has 227 British and ninety German graves, nearly all from 1917, in the civilian cemetery and 453 British and sixty-six German graves from 1917 and 1918 in the extension. The smaller plot, in the civilian cemetery, has some particularly interesting graves. Row A, which is mainly composed of officers' graves, has two VCs. In June 1917 the 1st (Royal) Dragoons provided dismounted parties to man the trenches. Second Lieutenant J. S. Dunville was decorated for leading a trench raid despite being severely wounded; he died of his wounds. Second Lieutenant H. F. Parsons, 14th Gloucesters, received his VC for defending a forward post during a German raid in August 1917, despite being burnt by a flame-thrower; he too died as a result of his injuries. In the back row of the plot is a group of officers all killed when the battalion headquarters of the 1/6th Gloucesters were blown up in a dug-out in April 1917 when a delayed-action or booby-trapped charge left by the Germans exploded. The CO, Second-in-Command, Adjutant, Chaplain, Medical Officer and one other officer were all killed. The CO and the Adjutant – Lieutenant-Colonel T. W. Nott, DSO, and Captain L. C. Nott, MC – were brothers; a third brother in the same battalion had been killed on the Somme almost exactly a year earlier.[2] In the same row is the grave of Brigadier-General V. A. Ormsby, CB, commander of a brigade in the 42nd (East Lancs) Division which had just arrived in France from Egypt when he was hit by a shell fragment and bled to death on 1 May 1917. His headstone has the badge of his old regiment, the 3rd Gurkhas.

The extension was made by both British and German units and was then enlarged after the war. Two of the first graves inside the entrance are of Majors F. Atkinson, DSO, and A. I. Fraser, DSO, fellow squadron commanders of 9th Hodson's Horse, both long-serving cavalry officers of the Indian Army, both killed in mounted action on 30 November 1917 while attempting to hold the German

[2] The third brother was Lieutenant H. P. Nott who is buried in Hébuterne Military Cemetery. The brothers came from Stoke Bishop, near Bristol.

counter-attack in the Battle of Cambrai at Gauche Wood which is four miles from here.

Saulcourt Churchyard Extension ㉜ is a charming, secluded little War Graves Commission plot of ninety-five British and seven German graves, all wartime burials. The access is not obvious. Go to the church, then turn right and proceed thirty yards along a lane to find a path up a steep bank leading to the war plot. The two larger rows, A and B, were British burials of 1917 or late 1918. The shorter but densely packed Rows C and D were men killed on 21 and 22 March 1918 and buried by the Germans, many being Leicesters who fought so well at Epehy at that time.

Moving further south and further to the rear of the March 1918 line, one comes to the large *Tincourt New British Cemetery* ㉝ which has 2,189 graves of various nationalities – United Kingdom, Australian, Canadian, South African, Indian, German and Chinese. There were also 136 American graves, but these were moved after the war. Most of the cemetery was made between June 1917 and March 1918, when Tincourt was a Casualty Clearing Station centre, and in the advance of late 1918, but 575 graves were brought in after the war from small local cemeteries, which explains why there are few other military cemeteries in this area.

Buire Communal Cemetery ㉞ has just eight British graves, two artillerymen of March 1918 and six Australians from September of that year.

Doingt Communal Cemetery Extension ㉟ was made in September and October 1918 when 417 British and 115 American soldiers died at a Casualty Clearing Station and were buried in three neat plots, the middle one of which was reserved for the Americans whose bodies were later removed. The British graves are mainly of United Kingdom men of various units, but there are also sixty-seven Australians.

Péronne

This is the largest town in the eastern part of the Somme. Modern war has not treated it kindly. It was heavily bombarded by the Prussians in 1870 and it was under German occupation from 1914 until the Germans retired from the area in March 1917 after having demolished most of the buildings. It was the British turn to abandon the town on 23 March 1918, when the remnants of the 66th (East Lancs) Division retreated through it, the Germans having advanced nearly twelve miles in three days. But the British returned in the autumn when troops of the 2nd Australian Division drove the Germans out on 1 September. The town was rebuilt and adopted by Blackburn, whose men were there in March 1918. Péronne escaped serious damage in the Second World War. There was no fighting when German armour swept through in May 1940 and it was liberated just as easily in September 1944. While Albert was just in the British sector of the Allied advance across France in 1944, Péronne was on the extreme left of the American sector, so it was their troops who entered the town in September 1944.

Péronne can be a useful place to stay. There are at least three hotels, and a good bypass – the rue des Australiens – leaves the main part of the town relatively clear of heavy traffic. A prestigious First World War museum, archive and study centre has been built in the grounds of the old château. The project was financed by the Somme *département* at an approximate cost of 60 million francs (about £6 million). This new centre was completed in 1992 and is now an important feature for visitors to the battlefields.

Péronne Communal Cemetery Extension ㉟ is in the northern part of the town, next to the civilian cemetery which is in the rue des Platanes near the hospital. It is surrounded by houses and allotments, but it is a quiet and discreet part of the town. From the First World War there are 1,584 British graves and ninety-seven German graves. The actual wartime burials of 177 British graves and the Germans are all on the left; the much larger plots on the right were made after the war, mostly from the August and September 1918 period of the British offensive and include more than 500 Australians. Among the original graves on the left – in Plot 2, Row C – is the grave of Corporal A. H. Buckley, 54th (New South Wales) Battalion, who won a Victoria Cross in Péronne when the Australians took the town in September 1918. He captured one German position, taking twenty-two prisoners, but was then killed rushing a footbridge across a moat, possibly near the château. Also buried on this side of the cemetery, at the far end of Plot 1, Row C, is

Brigadier-General G. A. S. Cape, CMG, the artillery commander in the 39th Division who was killed by a German shell on 18 March 1918.

There are five Second World War British graves in the cemetery, one unidentified airman and four men who died in late 1939 or early 1940. Two of those early burials are the pilot and observer of a Lysander reconnaissance aircraft of No. 13 Squadron RAF which crashed in December 1939. This was a sad repeat of a 1914 incident. In the adjacent civilian cemetery is the grave of Corporal F. J. P. Geard of No. 5 Squadron RFC who was killed in a crash when returning from a reconnaissance flight on 18 August 1914, when the BEF was moving forward from Amiens – a very early First World War casualty. Corporal Geard's grave is three-quarters of the way up the central pathway of the civilian cemetery on the left, opposite an 1870 memorial and some French soldiers' graves of 1914–18.

La Chapelette British and Indian Cemeteries �37 are really one cemetery in two parts. The British cemetery, on the right, has about 250 graves of men who died of wounds here, either in the quiet times of 1917 or in the advance of autumn 1918; included in that number are forty-nine Australians and several men described as 'Christian Indians' who were not buried with the Indians of other faiths in the much larger Indian plot on the left. The British plot is unique in that every single grave is identified. The Indian graves are mostly Labour Corps men who worked at Péronne when the town was safely behind the lines in 1917 and early 1918; there are many winter deaths of men who succumbed to the European climate. One headstone has an interesting badge. Labourer Santaik was in the Burmese Company of the Indian Labour Corps and has a very rare badge of a Burmese temple on his headstone. There are 577 graves in the combined cemeteries.

Mont St Quentin, on the other side of Péronne, is a village on a hill that was an important German position in 1918, dominating as it did the approaches to Péronne. The presence of modern buildings partly conceals its tactical importance at that time. The view of the hill approaching from the north, rather than from Péronne, is more revealing, with the wooded crest of the hill on the left (the east) of the road being the dominant feature. It was strongly held when the Australians attacked and captured it in a brilliant operation on 31

69 The 2nd Australian Division Memorial at Mont St Quentin.

August 1918. The *2nd Australian Division Memorial* ㊳ commemorates this feat and is one of the most striking memorials in
France. The original memorial had an Australian soldier with his
foot on the neck of a German eagle which he was bayoneting, but
that was destroyed by the German occupiers in 1940 and the
present Australian soldier stands in a less aggressive posture, legs
astride, rifle slung, 'digger's' hat on, gazing east in the direction of
the Australian advance. Bronze plaques on the sides of the base
show infantrymen clearing a trench, an artillery team moving its
gun and the list of the division's battle honours.

The *Moislains National Cemetery* ㊴, with only 465 graves, is the
smallest French military cemetery on the Somme. It stands on a
hillside below a large wood.

*

THE SOMME CROSSINGS

This section covers a large area in the south-east of the Somme *département* which changed hands four times in the First World War but where there was never any pitched battle. The main action was in March 1918. The River Somme – actually a meandering stream with marshy banks and a canal here – runs right across the region, for the most part in a northerly direction. It was this alignment of the river, at right angles to the German advance in March 1918, which caused it to be chosen as the line on which a serious attempt was made to stop the Germans. On the evening of 23 March, Haig ordered the Fifth Army to 'hold the line of the Somme river at all costs. There will be no withdrawal.'[3] But no major reserves were available and the tired divisions which had been attacked on the first day and had then carried out a fighting retreat of up to fourteen miles were not strong enough to hold that river line. The Germans forced a crossing, first in the south, then in the centre and north, and the retreat was in full spate again forty-eight hours after Haig's order. It is an area of only moderate importance for battlefield visitors, but every place of interest will be described and the area may draw those who have the time and wish to see everything, or those following particular units or battles, or those just passing through on a cross-country journey to Paris or other parts of France.

Ham is one of a series of small towns situated close to the southern boundary of the Somme. It is more attractive than some of the others and, with two small hotels, is a possible overnight stopping place.

When the Germans retired through this area in 1917, Ham was one of three towns spared from destruction so that more than 10,000 'useless French mouths' – old people, women and children – could be left behind for the French to feed. When the Fifth Army attempted its stand on the river in March 1918, those men of the 17th, 18th and 19th King's Liverpool of the 30th Division who had survived the retreat formed a bridgehead on the north side of the town, facing the German advance. The Somme on either side of the

[3] Official History 1918, Vol. I, p. 368.

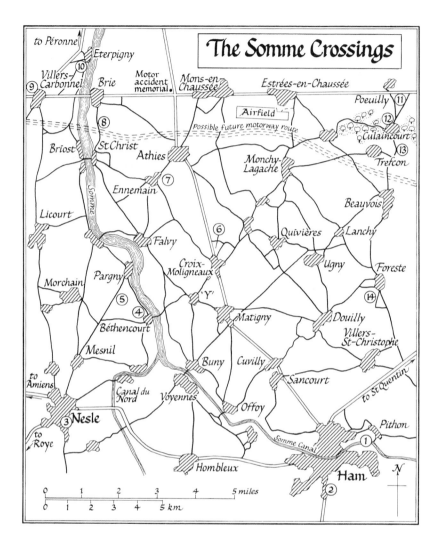

town was a formidable obstacle, particularly the marshes and ponds. The Germans discovered some stone causeways over the marshes on the east side of the town, near the village of Pithon. They crossed the small stream of the river but were then faced by the major obstacle of the canal. But, in early morning mists on 23 March, they seized a railway bridge over the canal which was only weakly defended by a unit called the 21st Entrenching Battalion. That was the first breaching of the river line. The Germans then moved on

70 The Somme Canal at Pithon showing the remains of the railway bridge over which the Germans made the first breach of the Somme river line in March 1918.

Ham and fired on the Liverpool battalions from their rear at the same time as other German units attacked frontally. Two bridges in the town were blown but were only partially destroyed. The Liverpools fought on for two more hours, but the Germans were now in possession of three bridges and across the Somme in strength.

The railway bridge at Pithon where the first crossing took place is no longer there, but the stone abutment for it stands on the northern bank ①. It can be reached by finding a path to the river from the far end of Pithon (coming from Ham); that path is on one of the stone causeways over the marshes which the German soldiers found that March morning. The remains of the bridge are 100 paces to the right after reaching the canal bank.

Ham British and German Cemeteries ② are situated side by side just south of Ham; a lane leads off from the road to Noyon to the combined site which stands in quiet fields. The German cemetery comes first, with 1,534 graves. The British cemetery was started during the war as an extension of the German cemetery, but the graves were regrouped after the war and many more added to form the present cemetery of 431 graves in neat plots surrounded by a

71 Ham British Cemetery.

particularly attractive screen of linked espalier trees. This is one of the best of the March 1918 cemeteries, both for the contents and the appearance. More than 200 of the graves are 'unknowns' but many of them have partial identifications. This was not a British sector in 1917 or in late 1918, so the graves are nearly all of the March 1918 retreat. There are only a few exceptions. Just inside the cemetery entrance is a 1914 grave, a rare find on the Somme. It is of Private T. Duffy of the 1st Royal Irish Fusiliers who died in August 1914 during the retreat from Mons. Close by are the graves of two Royal Flying Corps men who died in December 1915.

The smaller town of Nesle (pronounced 'Nell-er') was also spared by the Germans in 1917 as a place where French civilians were concentrated. The Fifth Army Headquarters were here in early 1918 but they left before the town fell to the Germans on 25 March. There is a plot of 135 British graves in three long rows in *Nesle Communal Cemetery* ③, which is on the south side of the road to Ham. The burials are from April to June 1917 when a Casualty Clearing Station was here; most are from April when British troops were in action with rearguards during the German retirement. About half of the graves are from units of the 32nd Division. Five graves with dates of April and May 1918 must have been of prisoners of war forced to work in this area by the Germans. The British plot is a lovely oasis of green lawn and white headstones, with a Cross of Sacrifice, set in a mainly grey, disordered French cemetery with its rusty memorials.

Béthencourt-sur-Somme German Cemetery ④ is a pleasant triangular-shaped cemetery almost on the banks of the Somme and containing 1,242 graves, nearly all of men who were killed in 1918. In 1415 Henry V and his army crossed to the other side of the Somme over a bridge here before turning north to make for Péronne and, eventually, Agincourt.

Pargny British Cemetery ⑤ was a treat to visit. I made this note at the time: 'How nice to see a completely British cemetery after a day spent seeing so many graves in communal cemeteries. What a pretty cemetery, at the side of a quiet country road, a tapering site running up a hillside with woods nearby.' And then the parish priest of Nesle came in to talk to us and was pleased to share a cold drink on a scorching day. The cemetery stands just behind that part of the Somme where units of the 8th Division attempted to hold the line on 24 March, but German troops had made footbridges during the night and crossed in strength to force the 2nd East Lancs and the 2nd Royal Berks back from the river bank and outflank the 2nd Rifle Brigade in Pargny village.

There are 617 graves in the cemetery, but 489 are 'unknowns', though many have enough identification to show that they came from the 8th Division and from the 20th (Light) Division which was defending the river further south. After the war, however, space was found on the ends of some of the rows for further burials. These can be seen in the fourth to the ninth rows back from the entrance. Many are unidentified, but it is obvious that this was a clearance of surplus graves from the 1 July 1916 battlefield on the Serre Road, including graves from the two Royal Warwicks Territorial battalions which fought there.

On the other side of the river is a roadside memorial ⑥ near Croix-Moligneaux which is in sharp contrast to recent visits. It is in memory of a French naval air pilot, Lieutenant Georges Feltz, and his radio operator, shot down on 20 May 1940.

Ennemain Communal Cemetery Extension ⑦ contains seventy-five graves which were assembled after the war with the full War Graves

Commission treatment in what is now a pretty plot at the end of the civilian cemetery. The graves come from various dates in 1917 and 1918. The largest identified group is of seventeen graves of the 1st Sherwood Foresters, another unit of the 8th Division which was fighting here in the March retreat, but the dates run on to 15 April 1918, showing either that badly wounded prisoners could not be evacuated or that ordinary prisoners were kept in the area and died of privation, in either case a sad end for the men concerned.

Brie British Cemetery ⑧ is a neat wartime cemetery made systematically by a Casualty Clearing Station which was here in late 1918 and buried 309 men of many units in neat rows. A further eighty-five bodies were buried after the war, more than half of them unidentified, probably victims of the March retreat.

The *Villers-Carbonnel National Cemetery* ⑨ contains the bodies of 2,297 French soldiers who all died when their offensive just reached this area at the end of the 1916 battle. Two mass graves at the rear contain 1,289 bodies, only ninety-five of which could be identified. The village placed its own 1914–18 war memorial inside the cemetery, with the names of thirteen soldiers and six civilians and these words: 'They died for France, just like all of those who lie here.'

Eterpigny Communal Cemetery Extension ⑩ is another little plot associated with the March 1918 fighting. The Germans buried twenty British soldiers and some of their own men, and then seven Australians were buried in August 1918. The German bodies were removed after the war, leaving a gap in the middle of the plot, but the British graves were left undisturbed and this was made into a permanent cemetery. I made this note: 'One marvels at the time, work, and expense involved in building a small cemetery like this and then maintaining it through the years – just for twenty-seven soldiers' graves in this out-of-the-way corner of France.' Most of the March 1918 graves are of men of the 2nd Middlesex, 8th Division. One company of the Middlesex held the bridge at the nearby village most gallantly for two days. The bridge changed hands six times before the Germans crossed the river further to the north and cut off the Middlesex men from the rear. This is the same battalion whose commander committed suicide after the heavy casualties suffered in Mash Valley near La Boisselle on the first day of the 1916 battle.

A long, straight Route Nationale runs from Brie eastwards to the Somme boundary, passing a large memorial to two French racing drivers killed in the Grand Prix de Picardy in 1933 and then an airfield at which British squadrons were based in both world wars. Then, just 150 yards short of the departmental boundary marker, at the lowest part of the road ⑪, are the memorials – and probably the graves – of a French officer and an NCO who were killed here in 1871 in a Franco-Prussian War action.

To the south of that point there are three British cemeteries which are just outside the Somme boundary. *Culaincourt Communal Cemetery* ⑫ has only nineteen graves from 1915, 1917 and March 1918. *Trefcon British Cemetery* ⑬ was made by the 6th and 32nd Divisions when they advanced here in September 1918 and the 283 graves are mostly of their units. *Foreste Communal Cemetery* ⑭ has 117 graves from the spring of 1917 and from March 1918.

ROYE

The little town of Roye was a military communications centre as long ago as Roman times, when it was a staging post on the way to Boulogne. Today the Lille–Paris motorway passes nearby and there are several hotels in the town for those who want to make an overnight stop. The French held it as a front-line town from 1914 to 1917 and it was just inside the French sector when the Germans advanced in March 1918 and were pushed back again in August. But the dead of three armies of 1914–18 are buried around the town.

Beuvraignes National Cemetery ① contains 1,856 French graves spread over the wartime years; an abbey nearby was probably a field hospital. *Roye German Cemetery* ② is closer to the town and has 6,545 graves from their costly campaigns of 1918. At the side of the road to Noyon is the attractive *Roye New British Cemetery* ③, which was made after the war by the concentration of 417 bodies from a wide area of the 1918 fighting, mostly of men who were

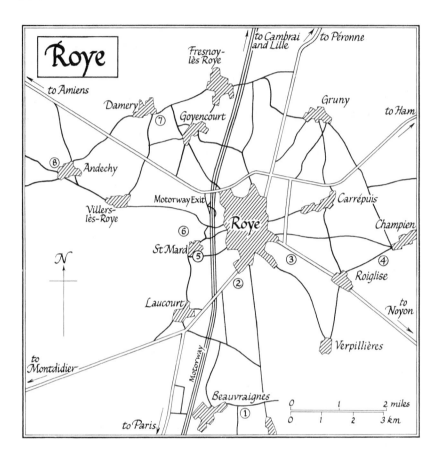

held by the Germans as prisoners of war and of August 1918 casualties when the boundary between the French and British advance was just north of Roye. Along the side walls are memorial headstones to 117 men who were buried in four other cemeteries but whose graves were later lost. Finally, the graves of forty-three Second World War RAF men are to be found on either side of the entrance and, in one case, against a side wall. Nearly all are Bomber Command men and nearly all are from the spring of 1944 when raids were being made on French railway targets in preparation for the invasion of Normandy, although one of the crews, flying a Stirling of No. 90 Squadron, was shot down dropping supplies to the French Resistance. One of the RAF dead was Wing Commander A. G. S. Cousens, DSO, DFC, commander of No. 635 (Pathfinder) Squadron, who was shot down while acting as Master Bomber in a raid on the railway yards at Laon in April 1944.

There are three Second World War memorials near Roye. A roadside monument ④ near Champien is in memory of a French officer, a cadet and five men of the 25th Tank Battalion killed here on 6 June 1940 when the Germans started to drive southwards after the Dunkirk evacuation ended and is a reminder that the Battle of France continued for a further two weeks after Dunkirk. The little memorial is in good condition and the local people plant fresh flowers and keep the hedge trimmed. There are two memorials at St Mard. To the south of the village ⑤ is a ten-foot-high brick memorial bearing the three names of the crew of a French bomber shot down here on 7 June 1940. North of the village, on the bank at the side of a lane ⑥, is a small stone the inscription on which tells how four 'Picardy soldiers of the FFI' – the Resistance Army – 'died as heroes for the liberation of this area'.

Damery Communal Cemetery ⑦ contains the graves of one British soldier killed in the March 1918 retreat and eleven killed in the August offensive, ten of them Canadians. This place was the southern limit of the British sector in both the March and August 1918 battles. The much larger *Andechy German Cemetery* ⑧ contains 2,254 graves. The main Amiens–Roye road marked the boundary between British and French forces in the August 1918 attack, so the German cemetery lies in the French sector.

THE SANTERRE

The ancient name 'Santerre' given to the northern part of this section has two possible derivations. The most likely is that it comes from the Latin *sanis terram* ('fertile land'), but it may have been *sanguis terram* ('bloody land') from battles fought here long ago. It is indeed fertile, a large, open area of agricultural land with no river valleys and few woods. Blood was certainly shed here again in the

First World War. The 'old front line' of 1914–16 ran right down this area and it was here that the southern part of the French participation in the 1916 offensive took place. When the Germans advanced through the area in March 1918, the open ground provided no natural line of defence and the British units falling back were too tired and weak to make a stand. British and French troops recovered the ground in August. Although there were two battles here in 1918, it is the French memorials and cemeteries from their 1916 offensive which provide the main interest now.

There is a memorial in the village church ① at Belloy-en-Santerre to the well-known American soldier-poet, Alan Seeger. Seeger, from New York and educated at Harvard, lived in Paris and joined the French Foreign Legion with forty fellow Americans, serving with distinction on the Western Front until killed in an attack near here on 4 July 1916 – American Independence Day. He is best remembered for his poem 'Rendezvous', which starts:

I have a rendezvous with Death
At some disputed barricade...

He has been described as 'an American Rupert Brooke'. Seeger's body was buried in a communal grave on the battlefield and was long regarded as being lost, but French records discovered in 1982 showed that the bodies in that grave had been moved after the war to the Lihons National Cemetery (see page 281) and are now in the mass grave marked Ossuaire No. 1, although Seeger's name is not recorded on the grave marker. The memorial in Belloy church consists of the simplest of metal plates, bearing only his name. Below it is a larger plaque listing the names of the local men who died in 1914–18 and also commemorating 'the volunteers from Barcelona who fell as victims of the war' – probably more men of the Foreign Legion who fell here. The village is very proud of its association with Alan Seeger; the office at the Mairie has a copy of his poem displayed in French and his name has been added to the local war memorial. Also, Seeger's family provided the bells for the church when it was rebuilt in the 1920s 'so that the voice of Alan Seeger should call out across the Somme forever'.

At the side of the main road at Estrées-Deniécourt ② is a stone memorial in the angle of the road to Fay. It is in memory of the men

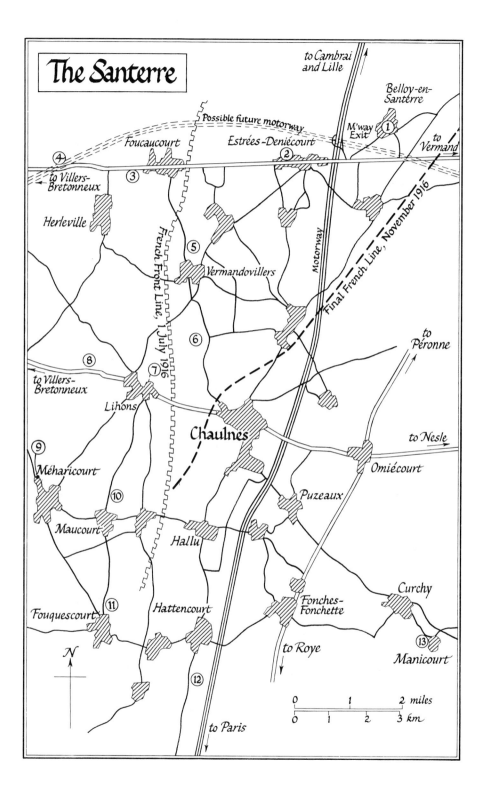

The Santerre

to Cambrai
and Lille

Belloy-en-
Santérre

Possible future motorway

M'way
Exit ①

Foucaucourt

Estrées-Deniécourt

to
Vermand

④

③

to Villers-
Bretonneux

②

Motorway

Herleville

⑤

Vermandovillers

French Front Line, 1 July 1916

Final French Line, November 1916

⑥

to
Péronne

⑧

⑦

to Villers-
Bretonneux

Lihons

Chaulnes

to Nesle

⑨

Méharicourt

Omiécourt

⑩

Puzeaux

Maucourt

Hallu

Curchy

⑪

Fouquescourt

Hattencourt

Fonches-
Fonchette

⑬

Manicourt

N

to Roye

⑫

to Paris

0	1	2 miles
0	1	2	3 km

of the French 329th Infantry Regiment who died on 4 July 1916 when they attacked 'sans peur et sans reproche avec un élan irrésistible' under Lieutenant-Colonel Puntons, who was killed together with seven of his officers. The inscription goes on to tell how an attack the following day under a new commander 'ejected the enemy from the village at the point of the bayonet'.

There are eight British graves in *Foucaucourt Communal Cemetery* ③, a Machine Gun Corps officer buried by the Germans in March 1918 and seven men who died in August and September. A little further along the main road, in a dip on a bend ④, is a small monument in memory of Colonel Rabier of the French 33rd Brigade who was killed near here in September 1914.

Vermandovillers German Cemetery ⑤ lies in the old No Man's Land of the long period of static warfare before the French attacked in 1916. It is the largest cemetery – in its numbers of burials – of any army and of either war in the whole Somme *département*. A large expanse of plots contain 9,432 graves marked by crosses which usually bear four names. Along the rear edge of the cemetery are no less than fourteen mass graves containing more than 13,000 bodies. The cemetery is still being used for the burial of newly found remains. The total number of dead at present is 22,632. The cemetery stands on completely open, flat ground – typical of the Santerre – and contains some large willow trees and just one large, black, metal cross. This is a large concentration cemetery with graves from all of the wartime years, even of 1919 when German prisoners working on the battlefields died in the influenza epidemic or from other illnesses.

The dates on two memorials to French soldiers near Lihons village show that this was the southern end of the French 1916 battle front where action was only intermittent. A substantial stone cross in a field ⑥ is where Captain Jean Delcroix of the 327th Infantry Regiment 'died gloriously for France at the head of the brave men he commanded' on 6 September 1916. A much grander memorial, which is also a grave, is to be found up a track north-east of the village ⑦; ask for the 'Monument Murat' if in difficulty. The simple, standard French soldier's cross shows that Maréchal de Logis Louis Murat of the 5th Regiment of Chasseurs, killed on 21 August 1916, is buried there. His rank is not as grand as it sounds; a Maréchal de Logis was the NCO of a unit in charge of billeting or carrying out liaison work. A large private memorial stone shows that he was the

son of Prince Murat of Pontecorvo and a grand-nephew of Napoleon.
Further research shows him to have been the grandson of Marshal
Joachim Murat, Napoleon's brother-in-law and the cavalry commander in Napoleon's later campaigns. Marshal Murat's career,
particularly his cavalry breakthrough at the Battle of Jena, is supposed to have inspired Sir Douglas Haig!

Lihons National Cemetery ⑧ contains 6,585 French soldiers'
graves in a long cemetery alongside a wood. This was just behind
the French 'old front line' and some of the graves are from as early
as August 1914 when the line was established. The communal
grave on the right at the rear is the one that contains Alan Seeger's
body. There are also six British graves from various dates in 1917
and 1918. A point of additional interest is the tall wooden gantry
of an old manual telegraph station on the nearby hill, one of a chain
of such stations whose large semaphore arms could relay important
messages faster than a man could travel on horseback – another
link with Napoleonic times.

Méharicourt Communal Cemetery ⑨ brings a big jump forward in
time. German units based at a nearby airfield in the Second World

72 The Murat grave and memorial at Lihons.

War buried the crews of RAF aircraft which crashed in the area in the civilian cemetery. The War Graves Commission plot contains forty-one graves. The grass, the white headstones and the Cross of Sacrifice make a pretty spot in this typical village cemetery. Most of the graves are of bomber crews shot down while attacking French railway targets in 1944. One of them is of the only Second World War VC in the Somme *département*. The decoration was awarded posthumously to a Canadian, Pilot Officer A. C. Mynarski who was mid-upper gunner in a Lancaster of No. 419 Squadron which was attacked by a night fighter while bombing a target at Cambrai in June 1944. The Lancaster caught fire and the crew were ordered to bale out. Mynarski was badly burnt trying to free the rear gunner trapped in his turret, and although Mynarski eventually parachuted he died soon afterwards. Among other interesting graves are those of six men of Pilot Officer G. H. Weeden's crew who were shot down in December 1943. What is of interest about this crew is that they were one of five crews loaned by No. 617 Squadron – the Dambusters – for a routine supply-dropping operation to the Resistance, an unusual operation for the Dambusters. Then there is the grave of Pilot Officer Claude Weaver, a Spitfire pilot of No. 403 (Canadian) Squadron, shot down in combat with German fighters in January 1944. What is remarkable is that Weaver, an American from Tulsa, Oklahoma, had won the DFC and the DFM and Bar and was still aged only nineteen when he was killed. The inscription at the foot of his headstone shows that his brother, aged twenty, was killed at Iwo Jima in the Pacific in 1945.

A further link with the United States is that the handsome local 1914–18 memorial in the village centre is inscribed as being the gift of 'two friends of France', Mr and Mrs Metcalf of Providence, Rhode Island. Their son, Sergeant Harry Metcalf of the 106th Infantry Regiment, was killed near here in September 1918 and is buried in the American cemetery at Bony.

Maucourt National Cemetery ⑩ contains the graves of 5,294 French soldiers and of six RAF men who were killed when their Halifax of No. 51 Squadron was shot down in April 1944.

Fouquescourt British Cemetery ⑪ is made up of 368 graves assembled after 1918, all in neat rows of ten except for the odd eight graves which are in two fours flanking the Cross of Sacrifice. It is a perfect example of a small concentration cemetery. Most of

73 The grave of Pilot Officer
Mynarski, the only Second World War
VC grave on the Somme.

the 239 identified graves are from two periods – 1917 when British forces took over trenches to the north of here from the French, and August 1918 when the British advance reached here. Among the dead from August 1918 are 137 Canadians. Somewhere in the cemetery is believed to be buried Lieutenant J. E. Tait, VC, MC, of the 78th (Manitoba) Battalion, of Scottish parentage and with an American wife. His posthumous VC was awarded for leading his men forward and capturing twenty Germans and twelve machine-guns in the August 1918 offensive. His memorial headstone, in the right corner of the cemetery, has the Victoria Cross engraving on it.

Hattencourt National Cemetery ⑫ is mistakenly marked on the French IGN map as being German. It is near the 1916 front line, but most of the 1,949 French graves are of 1917 or 1918. It is close to a railway, so there was probably a field hospital there. *Manicourt German Cemetery* ⑬ contains the bodies of 7,326 German soldiers, 4,225 in normal grave plots and 3,101 in mass graves.

MONTDIDIER

This is the most westerly of the string of little towns running across the southern reaches of the Somme *département*. It is smarter and appears to be more prosperous than Ham, Nesle and Roye, but it only has one small hotel at the time of writing. It was well in the French rear until the German advance reached here on 27 March 1918, the day on which the Germans came closest to forcing apart the British and French armies. The line then became stabilized just west of Montdidier until French troops recaptured the town in the August counter-offensive. A plaque in the Hôtel de Ville refers to Montdidier as 'an important and much disputed position, suffering total destruction but eventually being redelivered from the horror of brutal occupation and contributing with its ruins to the country's victory'.

There are more than 15,000 graves in war cemeteries at Montdidier, including an unusual British contribution. *Montdidier National Cemetery* ① once stood in open country, but new building has now reached the boundaries of this large cemetery in which 7,418 French soldiers are buried, about three-quarters of them being 1918 casualties. In the far right corner there are twenty-four British graves in four small groups where the crews or parts of crews of four RAF planes are buried. The earliest were three men of No. 418 (Canadian) Squadron who were killed when their Boston night-fighter 'Intruder' was shot down attacking Montdidier airfield in April 1942. The other three crews were all flying Lancasters of No. 8 (Pathfinder) Group when ninety-two aircraft of the group carried out a raid on the same airfield on the night of 3 May 1944. The airfield was an important German bomber base and its destruction was required before the invasion. The raid was successful but four Lancasters were shot down, three near Montdidier. On our visit there was no indication on the gateway of the cemetery that British graves were present and a visitor would need to be well inside the cemetery before spotting them; but they are well cared for in a peaceful corner, resting alongside those thousands of French soldiers from an earlier war. These are the most southerly British graves on the Somme.

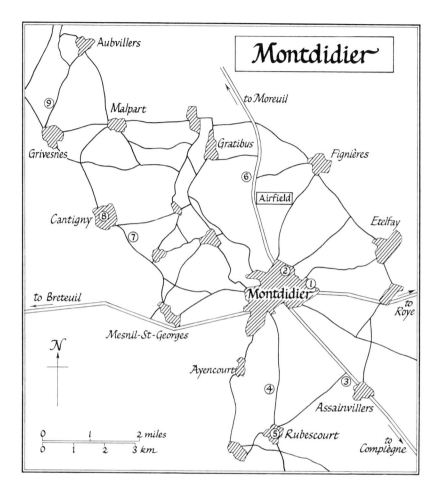

In the northern part of the town ②, beyond the upper part of the civilian cemetery, are two more military plots. The first is a large French group of 745 graves, mostly in long rows but with twenty Muslims and one Indo-Chinese buried separately. It is not classed as a 'National Cemetery', although it is maintained to the same standard as one. Just beyond this is a German cemetery with 8,051 graves reflecting the huge cost to the Germans of their 1918 offensive.

There are seven memorials around the town, all from 1918. At a road junction near Assainvillers ③ is a substantial yet simple and dignified French memorial to General Latour's 169th Infantry Division with its battle honours from 'Lorraine 1914' onwards and all the division's units listed. An inscription on the back of the memorial tells how the original, erected in 1921, was destroyed by the Germans in 1940 and how the present one was erected by local people in 1955.

Not far away ④ is a touching personal memorial 'In honor of an American boy who fell here fighting for France, 1st April 1918, H. H. Houston Woodward, Corporal Pilote, Spad, 94 Lafayette Flying Corps.' Young Woodward, from Philadelphia, came to France in 1917 to serve with an American ambulance unit but transferred to the Lafayette Squadron of the French Air Force whose pilots were mainly American volunteers. A plaque in the church at nearby Rubescourt ⑤ says that the clock and one of the church bells were given by the Woodward family in his memory. This is the most southerly war memorial in the whole Somme *département*. Corporal Woodward is buried in the Suresnes American Cemetery on the outskirts of Paris.

North of Montdidier, on a roadside site ⑥ overlooking the airfield, is another French memorial made of a large base with two big boulders on top. It commemorates the achievements of the 19th Battalion of Chasseurs à Pied in both World Wars. A plaque, probably added in 1954 on the centenary of the unit's formation, lists its battle honours from 1854 – the Alma – through the Franco-Prussian War and the First World War and on to battles in 1939–40 and in 1945. An inscription says: 'Les hommes passent; l'espirit demeure' ('Men may pass; the spirit lives on').

The road from Montdidier to Cantigny leads to the scene of the first action by a complete American division in the war, when the 1st Division made a local attack which recaptured the village of Cantigny on 28 May 1918. On a bank above a road near the village ⑦, looking across a valley at a wood, is the division's memorial in the form of a slender square column in the shape of the figure 1 of the division's number, with an eagle mounted on the top. The division suffered 199 killed and 867 wounded in that action and the names of all the dead are listed on the sides of the memorial – regiment by regiment, company by company. In the centre of Cantigny ⑧ is a much larger memorial commemorating that first

74 'In honor of an American boy ...'

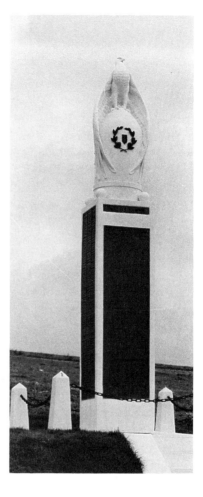

75 The 1st United States Division
Memorial near Cantigny.

American unit action in the First World War. The monument and
its surrounding enclosure occupy a large part of the village green.
The memorial was unveiled in 1930 and looks as fine now as it
did then, probably better because of the mature trees and well-
established garden around it.

Finally, at the side of the road north of Grivesnes ⑨ is a memorial
to the French 125th and 325th Infantry Regiments which halted
the German advance here in 1918. The monument is in a pretty
rural location; it has a screen of trees behind it and looks out over
a valley.

VILLERS-BRETONNEUX

This area is of particular importance in the history of the First World War. The fighting did not come here until 1918, but two major battles were fought then – one which halted the Germans' offensive in the spring and a second which started an Allied advance which justifiably became known as the 'Advance to Victory'. Unfortunately, those battles have never received the literary attention they deserve, nor has the area attracted visitors in the way that the 1916 area has. Perhaps only the Australians appreciate the true importance of Villers-Bretonneux and the surrounding ground; their men were involved here from first to last and made the greatest contribution.

The exhausted remnants of Gough's Fifth Army were pushed back to here at the end of March 1918. But the Germans were also exhausted and the fighting died down at the end of March without the Germans having been able to secure any strategic success. The British and French armies were still in touch and still forming a defence line; the vital communications centre of Amiens still remained in Allied hands. On 27 March, General Gough was ordered to relinquish his command, 'to rest' himself and the senior members of his staff. General Rawlinson took over and the Fifth Army was renumbered to become the Fourth Army on 2 April; it was the old 1916 combination again. Gough was then officially dismissed and sent back to England. The Germans tried to break through to Amiens again in early April but failed. They made a more determined effort on 24 April and captured the important town of Villers-Bretonneux, but counter-attacks by United Kingdom and Australian troops regained the village within twenty-four hours. That was a vicious engagement but it turned out to be the end of the German offensive here.

The next three months were mostly quiet. Great battles were fought further north where the Germans again tried to break the British lines, but without success. The tired divisions in front of Amiens were withdrawn to rest and to be brought up to strength again. The whole Australian Corps of five divisions gathered and took over a long sector north of Villers-Bretonneux. The Canadian Corps of four divisions, which had not been in any recent heavy action, came into the line south of the Australians in readiness for the great counter-stroke which was being planned. Meanwhile the French, further south, with some help from the Americans, made a local advance and pushed the Germans back from their furthest line as far as the River Avre which would become their jumping-off point in the south in the coming attack.

Then came 8 August 1918, a day which certainly rivals 1 July 1916 in historical importance – though not in popular memory. Rawlinson's Fourth Army attacked on a frontage of fifteen miles at 4.20 a.m. supported by a hurricane bombardment and more than 400 tanks. French troops attacked on a nine-mile front immediately to the south. It was a misty morning and there were some set-backs but, by the end of the day, the centre of the attack had advanced six and a half miles. The ground gained that day was almost as much in area as that captured by the British in the 140 days of the 1916 Somme battle. It was a brilliant success. The Germans called it their 'Black Day'. The advance continued for a further three days, by which time the Germans had suffered 75,000 casualties – including nearly 30,000 who surrendered; the Germans also lost 500 guns. Allied casualties were about 40,000. The French XXXI Corps made a major contribution in the south and have a fine memorial to commemorate this; and three British divisions – the 12th and 18th (Eastern) and the 58th (London) – attacked on the northern flank (beyond the area covered by this section of the book). But the main victory was won by the Australians and the Canadians who attacked in the centre, made the deepest advances and captured most prisoners and guns. The Australians, in particular, deserve great credit. They had helped recover Villers-Bretonneux in April, held a long line all through the summer and continued to take part in the autumn advance well into September. Approximately 12,000 Australians were killed from March to September 1918 and there is hardly a cemetery in a huge area bounded by Amiens, Albert and Péronne and beyond the Hindenburg Line which does not contain Australian graves. The Germans were being beaten soundly on the battlefield for the first time in the war. They were pushed steadily back and were suffering irreplaceable casualties. The battle which started on 8 August 1918 was the first successfully sustained offensive on the Western Front by any side in exactly four years of war. The Germans sued for peace in November and the fighting stopped

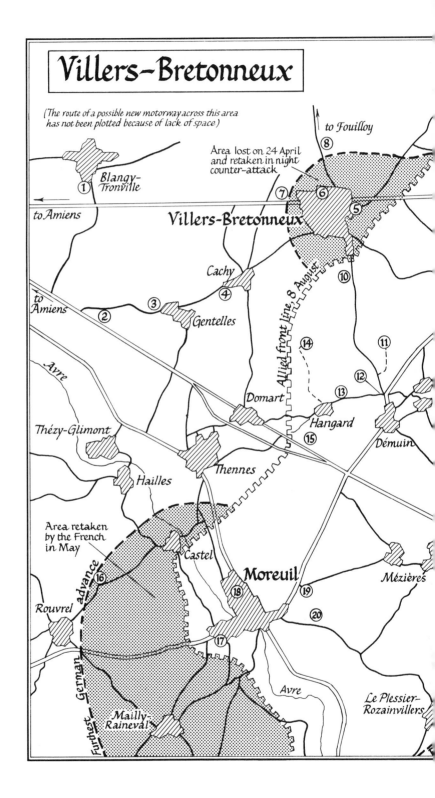

Villers-Bretonneux

(The route of a possible new motorway across this area has not been plotted because of lack of space)

to Fouilloy
(8)

Area lost on 24 April and retaken in night counter-attack

Blangy-Tronville
(1)

to Amiens

(7) (6) (5)

Villers-Bretonneux

Cachy
(4)

(10)

to Amiens

(3) (2)

Gentelles

Allied front line, 8 August

(14) (11)

(12)

(13)

Avre

Domart

Hangard

(15)

Démuin

Thézy-Glimont

Thennes

Hailles

Area retaken by the French in May

Castel

Moreuil

Mézières

German advance

(16)

Rouvrel

(18)

(19)

(20)

(17)

Furthest

Avre

Le Plessier-Rozainvillers

Mailly-Raineval

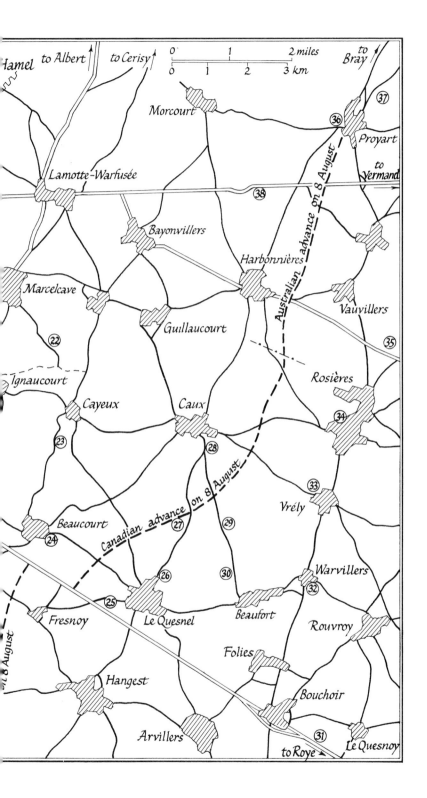

Hamel to Albert to Cerisy

0   1   2 miles
0   1   2   3 km

Morcourt

to Bray

Lamotte-Warfusée

③⑥ ③⑦

Proyart

to Vermand

③⑧

Australian advance on 8 August

Bayonvillers

Harbonnières

Vauvillers

Marcelcave

Guillaucourt

③⑤

②②

Ignaucourt

Rosières

Cayeux

Caux

③④

②③

②⑧

③③

Vrély

Canadian advance on 8 August

Beaucourt

②⑦

②⑨

②④

Warvillers

②⑥

③⓪

③②

②⑤

Fresnoy

Le Quesnel

Beaufort

Rouvroy

Folies

on 8 August

Hangest

Bouchoir

Arvillers

③①

to Roye

Le Quesnoy

on the 11th. The whole thing was over in less than 100 days, and it all started at Villers-Bretonneux.

An unusual feature about the British cemeteries in this area reflects the different policies employed in the post-war treatment of the Australian and Canadian graves of the August 1918 offensive. The dead of both countries had been buried in small cemeteries on the battlefield, but most of the cemeteries in the Australian sector were emptied after the war and the graves were gathered in a few large concentration cemeteries. These now contain plots which are almost exclusively Australian. Most of the little battlefield cemeteries in the Canadian sector, however, were left in their original positions and they are still there now. One further point about the Australian plots and the Canadian cemeteries: both the Australian and the Canadian Corps were supported by tanks, cavalry, heavy artillery and RAF squadrons manned mainly by United Kingdom men, so that the large numbers of Australian and Canadian graves nearly always contain a sprinkling of 'home country' graves from those supporting units. The Memorials to the Missing of this period are a different matter again. The Australian names are recorded here because their national memorial on the Western Front was placed at Villers-Bretonneux, but the Canadian names are forty miles away on the Vimy Memorial, north of Arras, and the missing of the United Kingdom units are nearly as far away on the Vis-en-Artois Memorial which is east of Arras.

Blangy-Tronville Communal Cemetery ① was four miles behind the fighting line of 1918 and contains the graves of forty-two casualties from the spring of that year in rows set against the walls of the little civilian cemetery. More than half of the men buried were artillery-men.

In a complete contrast, a memorial at the corner of Gentelles Wood ② records a 1944 killing. A notice-board informs the visitor that 'in August 1944, twenty-seven patriots were savagely struck down and their blood bathed this ground so that you can remain free'. A further notice says that the local Resistance unit discovered the bodies 'at this charnel house' soon after the Liberation, and a shallow cave is marked as the place where the bodies were found. A fine memorial looks over the fields towards Amiens, from where the victims were probably brought to be executed just before the Germans evacuated this area. Only nineteen names are on the memorial; the remaining bodies may have been foreigners or unrecognizable.

Gentelles Communal Cemetery ③ has twenty-three British graves, mainly in one row. All were April 1918 casualties and there is a mixture of English infantry, artillery and engineers, an Australian major and CSM, an airman, two unidentified and three men known to be buried but whose graves were destroyed by shell fire. The neat British headstones and strip of lawn maintained by the War Graves Commission are the only signs of beauty in a particularly scruffy civilian cemetery.

At the end of the civilian cemetery at Cachy ④ is a military memorial which was used no less than four times. The front face has the original inscription, to the men of the French 4th Regiment of the Line and to a cavalry officer, all killed near here in September 1870. The village then used the two sides to record the names of eight local men killed in 1914–18 or 1939–45 and, finally, the rear face became the memorial to the French 4th Colonial Division which fought here in May and June 1940. In the civilian cemetery just behind the memorial is the single white headstone of Lieutenant H. H. Thompson of the 18th (New South Wales) Battalion who died of wounds in April 1918.

The small town of Villers-Bretonneux, on the main Amiens–St Quentin road, became the focus of the historic events of this area in 1918. Fifth Army Headquarters moved back to here on the third day of the German offensive but had to retire again on 25 March when the Germans drew even closer. By the end of the month the Germans were just over two miles away, but they paused for three days to bring up fresh troops before making a determined effort to capture Villers-Bretonneux and open the way to Amiens, less than seven miles away. The 'Amiens Defence Line' ran through Villers-Bretonneux and there would be little to prevent the Germans reaching the city if this was breached. The attack came at dawn on 4 April. The British units in the line were the 14th (Light) and 18th (Eastern) Divisions, which had retreated all the way from the Hindenburg Line, and the newly arrived 9th Australian Brigade. Heavy fighting raged all day in which Brigadier-General G. N. B.

Forster, a brigade commander of the 14th Division, was killed.[4] Some ground was lost, but the Germans were held on the eastern end of the town.

They made an even more determined effort on 24 April. Four German 'stormer' divisions came up; they were supported by heavy artillery and fifteen tanks and there was a Jäger division ready for further exploitation. The British defenders were the 8th Division and a brigade of the 58th (London) Division – survivors of the retreat again. The Germans attacked with tanks on either side of the village in the fog and achieved considerable success; the defenders in the town itself were neutralized by a heavy gas bombardment. The Germans established a new line west of Villers-Bretonneux and brought up many machine-guns which were able to cover the open ground over which any counter-attack would take place.

There now took place one of the war's epic little battles. It was decided that a counter-attack should take place at night. It was entrusted to the command of Major-General W. G. C. Heneker, commander of the 8th Division. The forces available for this desperate effort included his own division and a 'scratch' brigade of the 18th Division – 7th Royal West Kents, 7th Bedfords and 9th Londons – but the main effort was provided by two strong brigades of the 5th Australian Division. The attack commenced at 10.00 p.m., with no artillery preparation. From that time onwards, units fought more or less independently of any central control. Most of the ground lost the previous day was regained and a new line was established on the edge of the village. The Germans never came any nearer to Amiens – at least, not until 1940.

Villers-Bretonneux was adopted by Melbourne after the war; the 13th Australian Brigade which had helped recapture the town came from the state of Victoria. The town school was rebuilt in 1923 with money collected by children in the state's schools. The building is no longer a school but houses a war museum which was closed on our visit, but visitors enquiring at the Mairie would probably be given a key and a guide. There are two hotels – the Victoria and the Melbourne – and the town is now twinned with Robinvale in Victoria. Many of the older buildings bear the scars of the 1918 fighting. A *Demarcation Stone* ⑤ is on the eastern edge of the town

---

[4] Brigadier-General Forster has no known grave and is commemorated on the Pozières Memorial.

but is not accurately placed because the Germans reached the other side of the town on 24 April 1918; nor does the French helmet on top give any credit to the United Kingdom and Australian troops who held the Germans here. The inscriptions on the base show that the stone was paid for by the city of Amiens. Another memorial in the centre of the town ⑥ commemorates some members of the Resistance executed and 'politicals' deported and dying in Germany in 1940–44 and also the 'Liberators' who, with the help of the Resistance, 'drove out the Nazis' on 31 August 1944.

There are four cemeteries outside Villers-Bretonneux, one at each point of the compass. *Adelaide Cemetery* ⑦ is about on the line that the Germans reached in their 24 April attack. The cemetery was not started until June but it is an important one, directly connected with the local fighting. A strangely empty space in front of the Cross of Sacrifice is probably where five Australian units and the 22nd Durham Light Infantry erected wooden memorials. Plot 1 is the original cemetery of ninety graves, with broad rows across the cemetery's width and containing mixed Australian and British graves from June 1918 onwards. A further 864 graves were brought in after the war to make two plots further up the cemetery. It is here that the policy of making all-Australian plots can be seen. Plot 3, on the left, with 428 graves, is entirely Australian except for one 'unknown' and one English grave. Plot 2, on the right, is made up entirely of United Kingdom and Canadian graves. One of the graves in Plot 2 – in Row G – is that of Lieutenant-Colonel S. G. Latham, DSO, MC and Bar, who was killed leading his battalion, the 2nd Northamptons, in the night counter-attack on 24 April.

Villers-Bretonneux Military Cemetery and the *Australian National Memorial* ⑧ stand on the crest of a broad hill and the entrance gives a superb view across open ground west to the city of Amiens and north to the valley of the Somme. There are 2,141 First World War graves, including 779 Australians, 267 Canadians and 607 'unknowns'. This is not a particularly 'Villers-Bretonneux' cemetery; it is a concentration cemetery made after the war and the graves come from a wide area and from all the months of 1918 from March onwards. The cemetery was made in two stages. Twenty plots were made in 1920, each with six spacious rows of ten graves; eleven of these plots were made up almost entirely of Australian graves. But space then had to be found for more graves and four further plots – 3A, 13A, 6A and 16A – were made on ground which had probably been intended for open spaces. These plots have close-packed rows containing twenty-three graves. Still more space was needed, so the 'AA' rows now found inside the boundaries of the central lawn were made and other graves were added at the ends of most of the original twenty plots. Those later additions contain a high proportion of 'unknowns' and come from a wide area. So the spacious cemetery originally proposed eventually held about 860 more graves than planned, making it the largest cemetery on the 1918 battlefield.

One of the later graves is that of Lieutenant John Brilliant, VC, MC, 22nd (Quebec) Battalion, who showed outstanding courage in the 8 August 1918 action, leading attacks on German machine-gun posts and a field gun until collapsing from his wounds. He was a French-Canadian and the family inscription on his grave is in French. It tells of how he 'fell gloriously on the land of his forefathers' and ends with the words: 'Bon sang ne peut mentir' ('Good blood cannot lie'). His grave is in Plot 6A, Row B, to the left of the Cross of Sacrifice. There are two Second World War graves at the front of the next plot, Plot 7, where the two New Zealand crew members of a Mosquito of No. 487 Squadron are buried. They crashed in April 1945 while taking off from the airfield at Rosières-en-Santerre. At the end of the cemetery on the right – in Plot 20, Row A – is the grave of Lieutenant E. H. D. Edgerton of the Australian 24th Battalion who won the unusual combination of DSO, MM and Bar, before being killed in the August 1918 attack.

Standing on a large lawn at the back of the cemetery is the Australian Memorial. This is both a national memorial to all the Australian dead on the Western Front in the First World War and a memorial to 10,797 named Australians who have no known grave. These are not all the Australian missing on the Western Front; a further 5,000 are listed on the Menin Gate at Ypres and 1,298 at VC Corner Cemetery at Fromelles. Most of the names at Villers-Bretonneux are of men who died on the Somme where Australian forces were so often engaged in 1916 and 1918, but other sectors in France are also represented.

The memorial takes the form of a tower and two broad arms on which are the panels of names. The 28th (Western Australia) Battalion has the greatest number of names – 365. The top of the tower gives good views of the area and has an orientation table with directions and distances to some distant places such as Gal-

76 The Australian Memorial at Villers-Bretonneux Military Cemetery.

lipoli – 1,500 miles – and Canberra, which has two arrows, south-eastwards and south-westwards, depending on which way round the world you want to go. The lawn in front of the memorial is where the crowd assembled when King George VI unveiled it in July 1938 and where a parade takes place each 25 April. That date is Anzac Day, the anniversary of the landings at Gallipoli in 1915 and also, by coincidence, the anniversary of the night in which Australians took part in the counter-attack at Villers-Bretonneux in 1918, an action which took place just a few hundred yards behind the memorial.

There was also a small action here in June 1940 when Senegalese troops installed a machine-gun and an observation post at the top of the tower. One of two German tanks attacking from the direction of Villers-Bretonneux came through the southern boundary of the cemetery (the right-hand side), crossed part of the last two plots of graves on the right (Plots 19 and 20) and opened fire on the memorial. A Messerschmitt 109 also machine-gunned the position. The worst of the damage was repaired after the war, but bullet marks on the Cross of Sacrifice, on some of the headstones and on the memorial itself – including one through the metal register holder – were left as honourable scars of war.

On the eastern side of Villers-Bretonneux, the *Marcelcave Buttes National Cemetery* ⑨ has 1,610 French graves, but most of these burials are 'died of wounds' from a field hospital which was located by the railway line near the cemetery in 1916.

Crucifix Corner Cemetery ⑩, south of Villers-Bretonneux, may not attract as much attention as other cemeteries in this area but it is an important one. It is situated in the old No Man's Land over which the 2nd Canadian Division attacked successfully at dawn on 8 August 1918. A small battlefield cemetery was then made; this now forms most of Plot 1 which is inside the cemetery on the right. The cemetery was enlarged after the war, but in a special way. Most of the left-hand side of it was allocated to French graves so that French and British graves lie side by side facing the east, almost certainly symbolizing the way the two armies halted the German advance in the spring of 1918 and then advanced from here in August. There is also a small memorial tablet, placed by local people, to 'the heroes who died in the defence of Villers-Bretonneux, 23–25 April 1918'. There are now 656 British graves, 142 French and two Russian. Although the original battlefield cemetery was mainly Canadian, the 293 Australian bodies brought in after the war now outnumber the seventy-six Canadians.

Moving into the area over which the Canadians advanced in August 1918, *Toronto Cemetery* ⑪ is a battlefield cemetery set in open country, up a rough track. The gateway has a Maple Leaf badge to show its 'Canadian' status. It is a small cemetery of the simplest kind, containing just four short rows of graves, a Cross of Sacrifice and two bushes. The first three rows and the start of the fourth are all Canadian casualties of 8 August, mainly from Ontario and Quebec battalions. Twenty-eight more graves were added later; nearly all are unidentified but they were probably from the March retreat. *Démuin British Cemetery* ⑫ is even smaller – with forty-two graves in two rows – and is even more truly representative of the Canadian attack on 8 August. All the dead are Canadians, except for an English tank officer and one completely 'unknown', and all are of 8 August except for a Canadian engineer officer killed later in the month. Most of the graves are of the 16th (Manitoba) Battalion.

Hangard village was the scene of fierce fighting when the German offensive was halted here in April and much of the village lay in No Man's Land until the August attack. When the Canadians advanced here, they made a small cemetery of thirty-two graves from bodies which had lain out in the open since April; these can be seen in the left corner near the road of the present *Hangard Communal Cemetery Extension* ⑬. A post-war concentration of 515 further graves took place, mostly from the April fighting, but the graves in a row in the far right corner are surprisingly dated 1915 and were brought fourteen miles from near Bray-sur-Somme. It is an attractive cemetery, surrounded on three sides by farmland and cut off from the civilian cemetery by a screen of trees.

We found *Hangard Wood British Cemetery* ⑭ particularly interesting. The access track from Hangard village runs right up the No Man's Land over which the 1st Canadian Division advanced on 8 August. The cemetery is in a narrow neck of land between two woods, a peaceful spot now but it was just about on the German front line which was attacked by the 13th (Quebec) Battalion supported by the 4th Tank Battalion in the mist that morning. The 141 graves are of great interest, reflecting both the local fighting in 1918 and the way small groups of graves had to be moved long distances after the war. The Canadians made two rows and two half-rows of their men immediately after the August battle. These now form part of Plot 1 in the left half of the cemetery. In the back row is the grave of Private J. B. Croak who was born in Newfoundland (not then in Canada) but lived in Nova Scotia and won a Victoria Cross here. His headstone has this lovely family inscription: *Do you wish to show your gratitude? Kneel down and pray for my soul.* The Canadians also buried bodies which had been out on the battlefields since April, identifying some of them as men of the 18th (Eastern) Division and twenty as French soldiers. These are buried in Plot 2, on the right. This plot was filled up after the war to balance Plot 1 by the addition of seven unidentified Australians from Villers-Bretonneux (in the back row) and a row of fifteen bodies brought all the way from the area of the Butte of Warlencourt on the Bapaume Road, twenty miles away. Identification of two bodies in that row shows that they were from the 9th (Scottish) Division and were killed in October 1916.

Hourges Orchard Cemetery ⑮ is a simple cemetery of 130 graves in two incomplete rows at the side of the Amiens–Roye road which was on the extreme right flank of the Canadian attack on 8 August.

The left row and the first part of the right one are the original burials – mostly Canadians of the 43rd (Manitoba) and 116th Battalions, but with one English tank officer. These men were buried so close together that there are two names on most of the headstones. The remainder of the right row are graves of April 1918 men, including an officer of the 3rd Hussars, and four Australian graves from August 1918 which have different coloured headstones showing that they were brought here more recently.

Moving across the River Avre, one comes to a French roadside memorial ⑯ which is at a useful place for describing part of the 1918 fighting. The memorial, in an enclosure at the corner of a wood, is to the 'Anciens' (the 'old chaps') of the 12th Cuirassiers à Pied and the 'Light Group' of the 7th Colonial Division. The Germans reached this point in early April 1918; it was the extreme western limit of their advance. The French eliminated most of the German salient over the River Avre in a series of local attacks in May, enabling their part in the 8 August offensive to start from the Avre and not from as far back as this point.

Morisel German Cemetery ⑰ is close to the Avre and contains the graves of 2,640 Germans, nearly all of whom died in the closing stages of the German offensive in March and early April 1918. The Germans retained a small bridgehead over the river here after the subsequent French advance and the French attack of 8 August started from behind and on either side of the place where the cemetery now stands.

The town of Moreuil formed the boundary between the British and French forces at the end of the March offensive and 182 British bodies – more than half unidentified – were buried in the *Moreuil Communal Cemetery Allied Extension* ⑱ after the war. The cemetery is no longer 'Allied', nor is it any longer an extension of the civilian cemetery, because over 1,000 French graves were removed after the war, leaving what is now a paddock between the British plot and the civilian cemetery. For this reason, the British graves cannot be reached from the civilian cemetery but must be approached along a street below the Amiens–Montdidier road, from the north-east. The graves are from many units, representing the way any troops available were thrown into action at that desperate stage of the March retreat. There are some unusual examples of cavalry regiment badges on headstones and the cemetery register has some

77 The French XXXI Corps Memorial near Moreuil.

interesting entries. Lieutenant A. V. S. Nordheimer of the Royal Canadian Dragoons is recorded as voluntarily dropping two ranks in order to leave Canada; his grave is in the front row on the right. On the extreme right of the third row is the grave of Captain C. T. A. Pollock, 1/4th East Yorks, son of Baron Hanworth, who was killed while attempting to carry his wounded batman to safety. His headstone has the very rare badge of the Inns of Court Officers' Training Corps.

The French units which carried out the August attack on this sector were in XXXI Corps which has an imposing memorial east of the town ⑲. The inscription tells how the corps broke through here and pursued the enemy until 7 November when 'German plenipotentiaries seeking armistice terms presented themselves to the advance positions of the corps'. A separate inscription tells how the monument was destroyed by the Germans in 1940 and rebuilt in 1955.

I came to a monument marked on the map just south of here expecting to find another 1918 memorial, but it was a small stone at the corner of a wood ⑳ where Captain Aubry, a French *chasseur* officer who became a pilot 'fell gloriously' in May 1915. It is possible that he crashed at a landing ground here; this place was eight miles behind the lines at that time.

Moving back to the right flank of the Canadian advance in August, *Mézières Communal Cemetery Extension* ㉑ has twenty-six graves made immediately after the battle and 107 more which were gathered from nearby after the war. There are lots of Canadian and English infantry, some artillerymen and a few cavalry and tank men – all true March retreat and August advance casualties of 1918.

Wood Cemetery ㉒ is another of those delightful little battlefield cemeteries in the middle of a field on the scene of the Canadian advance of 8 August. There are forty-nine graves in two rows and one isolated grave. Forty-one of the dead are Canadians, mostly from New Brunswick, Quebec and Central Ontario battalions.

Cayeux Military Cemetery ㉓ is completely different from other cemeteries in this area, having no link with the 1918 battles. It is a pretty cemetery but with a tricky access; a car can just negotiate a nearby track, then a footpath through a wood has to be taken. The cemetery was started in 1917 when a British Casualty Clearing Station was located here and seventy-five casualties were buried in the first five rows of Plot 1. These British graves were well outnumbered at the end of the war by French and German graves but these were later removed. Some of the empty spaces were then filled with 140 British bodies. Most of these are 'unknowns', but there is sufficient identification to show that they were mostly casualties from the first day of the 1916 battle – Ulstermen from Thiepval, and Tynesiders and other 34th Division men from La Boisselle – another example of the extreme pressure the burial authorities encountered on the 1916 battlefield.

Beaucourt British Cemetery ㉔ is one of the loveliest small cemeteries I have seen. It is perched on a bank above a lane outside Beaucourt-en-Santerre. The little plot of eighty-four graves appears at the top of some steps, with trees at the sides and with farmland rising on the hillside behind. Two of the three short rows are close-packed mass graves of men killed on 8 and 9 August 1918 – Canadian infantry, mostly Central Ontario battalions, and six Englishmen of the 1st Tank Battalion. There is a fine château in the village with a strange-looking pinnacled tower in the grounds. The lady owner told us that the tower is all that remains of one wing of the original château which was burnt by the Germans in 1918. The post-war rebuilding was on a smaller scale, so that tower was left as a feature in the garden and as a reminder of the older building.

The nearby main road marked the boundary between the Canadian and the French advance in August 1918. The *Canadian Memorial* ㉕ at Le Quesnel is in a park on the 'Canadian' side. The road is now a dual carriageway; if you are travelling from the east you will be able to park easily, but if coming from the Amiens direction it is better to take the side road towards Le Quesnel village and enter the park at the rear. The large stone memorial has inscriptions in English and French which tell how, on 8 August 1918, 'The Canadian Corps, 100,000 strong ... drove the enemy eastward for eight miles.' The memorial is a few yards beyond the line reached by the Canadians that day. The scale of the entrance and the layout of the park are larger than those of other Canadian memorials of this kind and reflect the importance of the Canadian achievement in that advance.

Le Quesnel Communal Cemetery Extension ㉖ is a simple little walled plot of graves on the other side of the village, another of those Canadian battlefield cemeteries allowed to remain after the war. The majority of the seventy-two burials are in a mass grave, mostly of men killed on 9 August 1918 when the village was captured by the 78th (Manitoba) Battalion. The very first grave is that of the gallant Lieutenant D. Gibson, MC, MM and Bar, of the 5th (Saskatchewan) Battalion, whose luck ran out here. Other graves include three English tank men, three Lancashire men killed in an accident in February 1918 when a Trench Mortar School was here and seven RAF men who died in accidents in 1939 and early 1940 when their squadrons were based near here.

Hillside Cemetery ㉗ is another Canadian battlefield cemetery of 101 graves, mostly from the 78th (Manitoba) Battalion and including a high proportion of officers – two majors, two captains and eight lieutenants. (There do not seem to have been any Canadian second lieutenants.) Seven United Kingdom graves represent the units supporting the Canadians in the August advance – four heavy artillerymen, two RAF pilots (flying Bristol Fighters of No. 48 Squadron) and a cavalryman (North Somerset Yeomanry).

The notes I made when we came to Caix village and its cemeteries ㉘ say 'graves all over the place'. The civilian cemetery has the carefully tended grave of a British officer who died in April 1918 when this place was in German hands, and then three rows containing 140 French graves, men who died of wounds in 1916. Next comes *Caix German Cemetery* containing 1,264 graves from April and May 1918 in a triangular plot at the angle of two lanes, a place made gloomy by black metal crosses and heavy trees. A hundred yards further on is *Caix British Cemetery*, refreshingly open, light and airy, a good example of a small post-war concentration cemetery, probably made from some of the battlefield plots which it was found impracticable to maintain. There are 360 graves, 218 of them Canadian, all in neat rows of ten graves. There are some interesting graves – Lieutenant-Colonel A. J. A. Menzies, DSO, the English-born commander of a Canadian medical unit, killed in an air raid on 9 August 1918 (Plot 1, Row E); Trumpeter J. Moylan, DCM, 11th Hussars, killed with the Canadians on the same day (Plot 2, Row E); Captain T. B. Tatham, MC, 3rd Rifle Brigade, a reminder that the March retreat passed this way and his headstone informing us that he was a Fellow and Junior Bursar of Trinity College, Cambridge (Plot 2, Row G); Private W. H. Eagles, 7th Dragoon Guards, killed on 9 August, whose wife later placed a little stone tablet on his grave (Plot 1, Row I).

Manitoba Cemetery ㉙ is a perfect example of the small Canadian cemeteries on this battlefield – five rows of graves and two single graves. All but two of the 119 men buried here were Canadians and most were from the 8th (Manitoba) Battalion which fought here on the second day of the August offensive and gave the cemetery its name. The CO, Lieutenant-Colonel T. H. Raddall, DSO, is buried with eight of his officers in Row A. There are just two English graves, a man of the 1st Tank Battalion and one from the 17th Lancers, the skull and crossbones of whose 'Death or Glory' badge is in stark contrast to the gentle Maple Leaf badges on the Canadian headstones. The little square cemetery has four maple trees, two old ones and two new ones, probably to ensure that the cemetery is never without such trees. There is a Canadian plaque on the gate and one of their bilingual visitors books.

We then came on one of those unexpected places at the side of the road ㉚ where there was a memorial which was not marked on the map. But it was a sad memorial, of an atrocity, for the inscription states that 'on this very spot, on 7th June 1940, thirty-one disarmed French soldiers of the 41st Infantry Regiment and

78 Manitoba Cemetery, typical of the small cemeteries preserved on the Canadian sector of the 1918 battlefield.

the 10th Artillery Regiment, from Rennes, were massacred by the Germans. Remember them.' Twenty-two years after Canadian soldiers died clearing the Germans out of this area!

Bouchoir New British Cemetery ㉛ has a complicated access because of the dual carriageway road, but it is well signposted. It is a post-war concentration cemetery with the graves coming from the two major battles of 1918. Most of the 257 'unknowns' are from the March retreat and most of the 527 identified graves are from the August advance. There are 216 Canadian graves from August, but this was the area where United Kingdom units took over the advance from the Canadians and the 32nd Division was put into the battle, to meet stiffening German resistance and suffer nearly 2,000 casualties on 10 and 11 August. The many graves of Royal Scots, Lancashire Fusiliers, Dorsets, King's Own Yorkshire Light Infantry and Argyll and Sutherland Highlanders are all from that division. A sad memorial stone just inside the gateway commemorates Lieutenant W. C. Cutmore, an eighteen-year-old naval pilot of No.

206 Squadron, shot down in his DH9 Bomber in June 1918 and whose grave in a German cemetery was later lost.

Warvillers Churchyard Extension ㉜ is behind a very old village church, through an unmarked door in the far right corner of the civilian cemetery. The little extension looks out over the fields where the Canadians advanced in August. There are just two rows of graves containing thirty-five Canadians and twelve United Kingdom tank and cavalry men, most of whom were killed on 9 August. *Vrély Communal Cemetery Extension* ㉝ is also tucked out of sight behind the high wall of the civilian cemetery. Its forty-three graves in two rows are of Canadians and tank and cavalry men from August 1918. Many of the men buried here were French-Canadians of the 22nd (Quebec) Battalion.

Rosières Communal Cemetery and Extension ㉞ has ten early 1917 graves in the civilian cemetery and 434 graves in the extension. The extension started as a Canadian plot of ninety-seven graves in 1918; these can now be seen in the far right corner of the cemetery. The remaining graves were added after the war, mostly from August 1918 but some of March 1918 and a few of 1917. The sixty-six Australian graves here show that this place is nearly on the boundary between the Canadian and the Australian advance in August 1918. *Rosières British Cemetery* ㉟ is just one long row of fifty-nine British graves of men who died in the March retreat. Most of the graves are identified and the presence of many artillery and rear unit graves and of 'died of wounds' infantrymen indicates that the burials took place before the Germans reached here. The cemetery is on an open site, its two small trees permanently leaning away from the prevailing wind, for we are back on the open ground of the Santerre.

Village war memorials to local Frenchmen killed in the wars have not been included in this book, but the one at Proyart ㊱ is an exception. It is a superb miniature replica of the Arc de Triomphe standing in a park opposite to the local château, with a tiny cannon in front of it and with a flower bed in the shape of a Croix de Guerre. A statue in the centre is of a French soldier, his right foot defiantly placed on a German helmet above the words, 'On les a' ('We have them') and a dedication 'To the Glory of the brave defenders of the Somme, French and Allied.' Two lovely side panels show a group of a soldier and his family – 'the departure' – and then a symbolic

79 The village war memorial at Proyart.

female 'France' mourning the soldier after his death. The memorial bears the names of twenty-six local soldiers and six civilians who died in 1914–18 and one soldier from the Second World War. The memorial was paid for by a local couple, but their family name does not appear among the list of casualties. *Proyart German Cemetery* ㊲ is just outside the village and has 4,643 graves, nearly all of men killed in this area in 1918.

Heath Cemetery ㊳ could not be in a more appropriate place to end this description of the 1918 battlefield. It is a completely post-war concentration cemetery of 1,862 graves and is the second largest cemetery in this area. It is situated right in the middle of the ground over which the Australian Corps advanced on 8 August 1918. The attack here was helped by armoured cars of the Tank Corps driving along the main road and firing into all the places where German troops might be sheltering in the mist. The little wood in the valley on the Amiens side was known as Buchanan Wood; it marks the western end of the Santerre plateau. The 8th Brigade, of the 5th Australian Division, captured hundreds of German reserves in the wood that morning.

It was mentioned earlier that none of the Australian battlefield cemeteries now remain. This was the place where the Australian dead from many of the battlefield cemeteries from August 1918 were gathered after the war, not to be buried indiscriminately with other casualties but in large plots which are now made up of rows and rows of headstones with the Australian 'Bursting Sun' badge on them, with occasional graves among them where cavalry, tank and air force men and heavy artillerymen from the 'home country' units supporting the Australians were buried. Two Australian VCs from the August attack are buried here. Lieutenant A. E. Gaby, 28th (Western Australia) Battalion, led his men in gallant attacks on 8 August and again on the 11th when he was killed; his grave is in Plot 5, Row E, near the road. There is a small mystery about the second VC, Private R. W. Beatham of the 8th (Victoria) Battalion, whose grave is at the back of the cemetery, to the left of the stone shelter. The citation for his VC describes his capture of four machine-gun posts on 9 August and then being 'riddled with bullets and killed' later in the day, but he is shown in the register and on his headstone as dying on the 11th.

The other plots in the cemetery are made up of United Kingdom and 'unknown' graves, mostly from the March retreat when the remnants of the 8th, 39th, 50th (Northumbrian) and 66th (East Lancs) Divisions were all fighting in this area. So some of the plots in the cemetery represent the exhausted units which faced the German offensive in March 1918 and other plots are full of the mainly Australian units which helped to turn the tide at Villers-Bretonneux and then, with the Canadians in their smaller cemeteries to the south, carried out that magnificent attack in August which led to complete victory for the Allies in November.

4·DOULLENS

The town of Doullens was situated behind the northern part of the Somme front all through the First World War and was an important communications centre and forward base. There are three small hotels, but it is not a central location for touring the battlefields. It does, however, lie on one of the approach roads and I always think of Doullens as being the gateway to the battlefields.

The *Hôtel de Ville* ① – the Town Hall – was the scene of an important meeting on 26 March 1918 between British and French commanders and politicians. It was a time of crisis. Both British and French forces were falling back under the German offensive and

80 The March 1918 Conference Room in the Hôtel de Ville at Doullens.

there was a danger that the two armies might become separated due to the lack of unified command. The main problem was the shortage of reserves in front of Amiens. Sir Douglas Haig said that he was willing to place British forces under the control of General Foch, the French Chief of the General Staff. The French responded by taking over part of the British line at Amiens and bringing in more reserves. The result was that there was unified command on the Western Front for the first time in the war and Amiens was saved. Doullens took great pride in the town being the scene of this important event and preserved the room in which it took place, keeping the same table and chairs and adding a stained-glass window and a painting of the meeting. It makes an interesting visit. Just go to the Hôtel de Ville and ask to see the *Salle de Conférence*. The English-language leaflet provided, however, is not impressive. References to 'despair' and the possibility of surrender at the time of the meeting may have entered French minds, but that was not the British mood; and, in references to the subsequent counter-offensive and the final advance to victory, there is no mention of the dominant role played by British forces, but only to that of the French.

Doullens Communal Cemetery ② has 1,729 British graves in two areas of the cemetery. The men who are buried here were mostly those who died of wounds at military hospitals based in the town. Most of the graves are from 1918 when the German offensive reached the British-held sectors east of Doullens. The British plots are beautifully laid out and maintained by the War Graves Commission, but the men buried came from a large variety of units and there are no particularly notable graves.

In May 1940, Doullens was first bombed by the Luftwaffe and then attacked by the 6th Panzer Division. The town was defended by the 6th Royal West Kents, sister battalion to the unit fighting at Albert. The defence lasted two and a half hours and twenty-four British soldiers were killed and are now buried with the First World War casualties in the civilian cemetery. The Vauban fort – *La Citadelle* ③ – became a major collecting point for British prisoners of war; the same place had been used as a British hospital in the First World War. The massive ramparts are still there and can be reached from the road to Amiens. The gates to the fort are normally locked but should be open in the afternoons at weekends and on

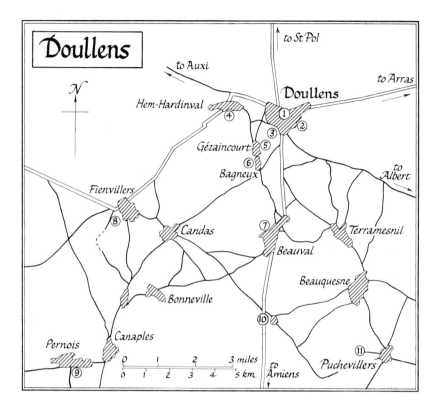

public holidays, although most of the buildings inside, which were used as a military hospital in the First World War, have been demolished.

Hem Communal Cemetery ④ was used in 1916–17 by a Casualty Clearing Station which dealt with infectious medical cases. Thirty-two graves were made.

The villages of Gézaincourt and Bagneux, just outside Doullens, were on a railway line and were heavily used by Casualty Clearing Stations during the First World War. *Gézaincourt Communal Cemetery and Extension* ⑤ has nine early graves in the civilian cemetery, but a large extension was needed for the 590 British soldiers and seventy-five Germans who died here, mainly from the battles of 1916 and 1918. There are some interesting graves. Row D of Plot

2 has fourteen graves of men who died in an accident involving their leave train at the local station in November 1916; one of them, Major S. G. Traill of the 1st Cameron Highlanders, had been wounded in 1914 and again in 1915, only to meet this unexpected fate. Another veteran was Second Lieutenant H. W. Wellings, DCM, a cavalryman who was commissioned for his bravery at Messines in 1914; he died of wounds serving in the Machine Gun Corps in June 1918 and is buried in Plot 1, Row M. By contrast, Plot 2, Row L, has the grave of a nineteen-year-old vicar's son, Second Lieutenant B. W. St John Mildmay, a Sopwith Camel pilot of No. 70 Squadron who crashed and died in April 1918. The cemetery register describes him as 'Count of the Holy Roman Empire by inheritance, last of the line of Hazelgrove Mildmays'. The cemetery was used again in the Second World War to bury six British servicemen who died of illness or accidents in the early months of the war and, finally, to bury one German soldier who was killed when this area was liberated in September 1944. The cemetery is in a pretty country location, on a hill overlooking a little valley.

Bagneux British Cemetery ⑥ occupies a similar site, on a hillside outside Bagneux village. The cemetery was the last to open in this area. When the German offensive was halted in April 1918, medical units which had been operating further forward had to retire to the Doullens area and this new burial place was needed. There are 1,373 graves in the neat, regular plots which are often the hallmark of 1918 cemeteries when plans were being made for their permanent construction after the war. The graves are all of 1918 and at least half of them are the result of just nine days of fighting – 21–29 August – when the British Third Army carried out a major attack north of Albert, taking over the offensive from the Fourth Army which had been advancing in front of Amiens. All but one of the divisions involved in that attack were made up of United Kingdom troops, half of them 'boy recruits' recently arrived from England. The only Empire unit involved in this little-known battle was the New Zealand Division; 181 of their men are buried in the cemetery.

In Plot 3, Row A, are buried twenty-two soldiers and three Canadian nurses killed on 30 May 1918 when a German plane bombed a Canadian hospital in the Citadelle at Doullens; the graves of two officers killed in the bombing were lost and they have memorial headstones at the back of the cemetery. A casualty of September 1918 was Brigadier-General L. O. W. Jones, DSO, a brigade com-

mander in the 5th Division who died of pneumonia. He had started
the war as a captain in the 2nd Essex and had taken part in nearly
every battle on the Western Front; he was the last of twelve British
general officers to die on the Somme. His grave is in Plot 5, Row F.

The British graves in *Beauval Communal Cemetery* ⑦ are in the
prettiest French civilian cemetery I have seen; it is unusually extensive and elegant, full of fine architecture and obviously the burial
ground of wealthy families. The British plot is near the far right
corner and the War Graves Commission architect used much
imagination in making it. The Cross of Sacrifice looks out over a
sunken garden and then over seven simple rows containing 248
graves. A Casualty Clearing Station was located near here from
1915 to the end of 1916 but it was never overwhelmed with
casualties. The only small rush was when thirty-two men died in
the first week in July 1916, mostly 29th Division casualties wounded
at Beaumont-Hamel. The last row is an all-officer row, some being
RFC pilots from squadrons based near here.

On a bank on the left of the plot are two separate graves. The first
is of Private Paul Chant, an Army Service Corps man who died on
26 July 1915, only the third fatality when British forces were taking
over this area from the French. Alongside him is the grave of Flying
Officer M. I. Fraleigh, a pilot of No. 181 Squadron shot down in his
Typhoon in an air battle near here on 19 August 1943. So the first
and last burials in this war plot, separated by twenty-eight years,
are together on that bank. A further coincidence is that both Chant
and Fraleigh came from Ontario, though neither was serving in a
Canadian unit. The presence of the Typhoon pilot's grave has a link
with the stone memorial plaque now resting at the foot of the Cross
of Sacrifice which says, in French, 'From a group of young people,
19.8.43', but was originally intended for the Typhoon pilot's grave.

Fienvillers British Cemetery ⑧ is another place to which medical
units came in 1918. It is a simple little cemetery on the side of a
lane outside the village, with just four rows containing 124 graves.
The majority of the men who died here were wounded at the end
of August and in early September 1918, when British forces were
attacking around the River Ancre on the old 1916 battlefield. Many
of the graves are from the 17th (Northern) and 38th (Welsh)
Divisions.

Pernois British Cemetery ⑨ is also a 1918 Casualty Clearing

Station cemetery, but being further south, its 403 burials were from the spring fighting north of Villers-Bretonneux and the 8 August attack. There are 133 graves from London units and sixty-three Australians, also seventeen German graves behind the Stone of Remembrance. The grave of Private Albert Jones, 2/4th Londons, a nineteen-year-old boy recruit who was gassed in August, has a photograph of himself in uniform attached to the headstone on his grave which is in Plot 3, Row C.

Vert Galand Farm ⑩ was a well-known First World War airfield used by British squadrons. The farm was used as the Officers' Mess and fields on both sides of the main road were used as landing grounds. Captain Albert Ball flew from here on his last flight, in his SE5 of No. 56 Squadron in May 1917, dying before his twenty-first birthday having won the VC, the DSO three times and the MC. The farm is still almost in its original condition and the family welcomes visitors. They have wartime photographs showing that the workshops and administrative buildings were in the corners of the crossroads and the hangars were on both sides of the main road south of the farm.

Puchevillers British Cemetery ⑪ is probably the most important and most interesting cemetery in this area. If it proves difficult to find, make for the local water tower and then take the lane to the right.

Two Casualty Clearing Stations came here for the opening of the 1916 battle. When the battle started in July, men were dying at the rate of twenty a day, casualties from the 36th (Ulster), 32nd and 34th Divisions on the front from Thiepval to La Boisselle. During the first few days of that time, Sir Douglas Haig was at a forward headquarters at Beauquesne, only a mile and a half away, trying to control a battle that was not going according to plan. His diary tells of a visit to 'two Casualty Clearing Stations at Montigny' on 2 July, a day on which most medical units were under severe strain due to unexpectedly high casualties and failures in the ambulance-train system. Haig wrote of 'everything seeming to go well' and of the wounded being 'in wonderful spirits'.[1] His medical staff must have steered him away from the worst scenes; there were no major medical units at Montigny.

---

[1] *The Private Papers of Douglas Haig, 1914–1919*, ed. Robert Blake (London: Eyre & Spottiswoode, 1952), p. 154.

The men who died here during the 1916 battle were buried shoulder to shoulder in long rows of densely packed graves. I found the grave of Captain Marcus Goodall, Siegfried Sassoon's friend. They were both Marlborough College men – though Sassoon was eight or nine years the senior – and they had been together for a month before the battle at the Fourth Army School for junior officers. Goodall was a company commander in the 1/5th York and Lancasters, 49th (West Riding) Division. The battalion War Diary[2] describes how he was wounded. Two nights after the disastrous Ulster Division attack at Thiepval, Captain Goodall took out a patrol of twenty volunteers 'to assess the strength of the Bosch line', but the patrol was fired on as it tried to cut through the German wire. Goodall and one other man were hit. He took eleven days to die. He was twenty-one, a vicar's son – how many vicars' sons died in that war? The news of his death reached Sassoon who was then ill in hospital; it severely depressed Sassoon and led to a poem – 'Elegy: For Marcus Goodall' – and it was probably one of the steps along the road which led to Sassoon's anti-war protest in 1917. Captain Goodall is buried in a group of officers' graves near the end of Row B, Plot 1; the family inscription is: *Tell England that we who died serving here rest here content.*

Approximately 1,688 men from the 1916 battle are buried here. The fighting around Pozières and Courcelette is strongly reflected in the 416 Australian and 214 Canadian graves. Seventy-four Germans who died as prisoners have their own rows at the side of the cemetery. A further seventy-five men died in 1917 and 1918; they are buried in a separate plot through an archway at the back of the cemetery. In October 1919, the wife and brother of an Australian officer, Second Lieutenant H. W. Crowle of the 10th (South Australia) Battalion, came here from Adelaide. They engaged a local mason to erect a private cross over his grave, either in ignorance of or in defiance of regulations for the war cemeteries. The cross remains, recording that Crowle was a veteran of Gallipoli and was wounded at Mouquet Farm five days before he died here in August 1916. A plaque leaning against the Cross of Sacrifice is a memorial from local people honouring 'Our Glorious Allies' and was placed there on the fiftieth anniversary of the opening of the 1916 battle.

[2] Public Record Office WO 95/2805.

5 · AMIENS

Amiens is the capital, not only of the Somme *département*, but of a wider region. It has over 130,000 inhabitants, nearly a quarter of the entire Somme population. It is a centre both of commerce and of tourism, with twenty-nine hotels at the latest count, and is a very busy place, particularly in the late afternoon rush hour. It will be an even more important place if it becomes the centre of a proposed new network of motorways. The city escaped serious damage in the two world wars. For most of 1914–18 it was a safe rear area, much visited by officers. The famous Godbert's restaurant is mentioned in many diaries; I was fortunate in dining there just before it closed in the 1970s. On 20 May 1940 another of those weak British Territorial battalions – the 7th Royal Sussex – had the misfortune to be attacked by the 1st Panzer Division which had earlier that day dealt with similarly ill-prepared battalions at Albert and Doullens. There are some interesting war memorials and cemeteries, and the city would be a suitable place to spend a day looking at some of these, combined with shopping or sightseeing; the cathedral and the Musée de Picardie should not be missed. The country area north of Amiens will also be included in this section.

The thirteenth-century *Cathedral of Notre Dame* ① is the largest in France. After the First World War many organizations and individuals asked to place memorials there. There are eleven of these, all located on the walls or pillars nearest to the south door. One is a War Graves Commission plaque honouring the 600,000 dead 'from the armies of Great Britain and Ireland who fell in France and Belgium'; similar plaques are in other major churches in France and Belgium. Other British memorials are to the Australian Imperial Force, the New Zealand Division and the Royal Canadian Dragoons – for their parts in halting the German advance in 1918 – to the South Africans, to the Newfoundlanders 'who fell in the First Battle

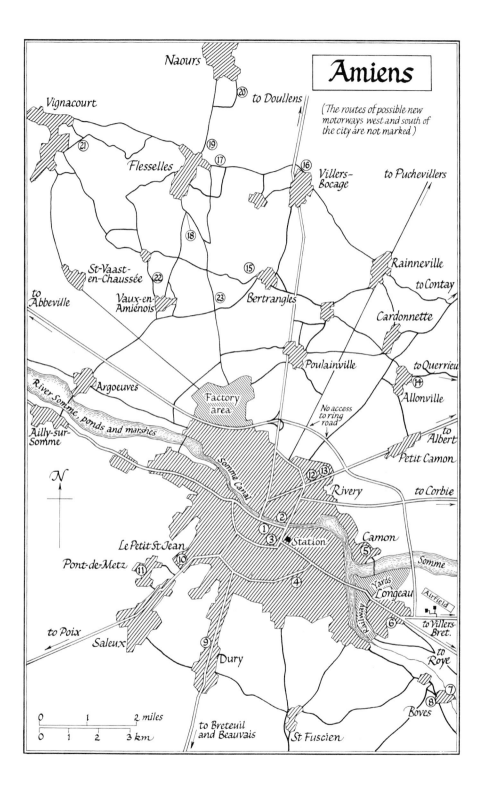

Amiens

(The routes of possible new motorways west and south of the city are not marked)

Naours

⑳ to Doullens

Vignacourt

⑲

to Puchevillers

㉑

⑰

Flesselles

⑯ Villers-Bocage

Rainneville

to Contay

⑱

St-Vaast-en-Chaussée ㉒

⑮

Cardonnette

Vaux-en-Amiénois

to Abbeville

㉓

Bertrangles

to Querrieu

Poulainville

⑭

Allonville

River Somme, ponds and marshes

Argoeuves

Factory area

No access to ring road

Ailly-sur-Somme

Somme Canal

to Albert

Petit Camon

⑫⑬

Rivery

to Corbie

N

②

①

③ ■ Station

Camon

⑤

Somme

Le Petit St Jean

⑩

Pont-de-Metz ⑪

④

Longeau

Yards

Airfield

Railway

⑥

to Villers-Bret.

to Poix

Saleux

⑨

Dury

to Roye

⑦

⑧ Boves

to Breteuil and Beauvais

St Fuscien

0   1   2 miles
0   1   2   3 km

of the Somme' and to Raymond Asquith. French memorials commemorate Marshal Foch, the Allied Supreme Commander in 1918,
and General Debeney, who commanded the French forces in front
of Amiens in 1918, and there is a memorial to the French colonial
troops. One American unit – the 6th Engineer Regiment – has a
memorial; 500 railway engineers of this unit formed part of Carey's
Force, a makeshift British force which held part of the line in front
of Amiens in the last days of March 1918. Then, after the Second
World War, a further memorial was added for General Leclerc,
the famous Free French commander who was a native of the
Somme.

The best car parking is near the cathedral, not far away from the
old port of Amiens on the River Somme which has been preserved
as a tourist area. At the eastern end of the port area is a bridge ②
on which a small memorial records that 'on 31st August 1944, the
patriots of Amiens, in heroically defending this bridge, permitted
the rapid advance of Allied troops and so avoided the Battle of
Amiens'. South of the cathedral, down the rue Victor Hugo, is the
Place René Goblet ③ in the centre of which is a small park whose
two ends were used for Second World War memorials. One is a fine
modern statue to General Leclerc and the other is the Picardy
Martyrs Memorial to the men and women who died for the Resistance. Those who wish to visit the excellent Musée de Picardie, with
its art and geological treasures – and no mention of war – should
proceed west from here along the rue des Jacobins and then south
on the rue de la République.

The original British Expeditionary Force paused briefly at Amiens
in August 1914 on its way from Le Havre to its first battle at Mons.
A link with that brief stay can be found at the *St Acheul National
Cemetery* ④, which is an extension of a large civilian cemetery in
the south-eastern part of the city. Just inside the south-west gateway
is a small but interesting plot of British graves. The first two burials
were of Second Lieutenant E. W. C. Perry, an RFC pilot, and Air
Mechanic H. E. Parfitt. These two were the crew of a BE8 of No. 3
Squadron which crashed at Amiens airfield and caught fire on 16
August 1914, just four days after the first British forces reached
France. They were the first casualties of the BEF on active service
in the war and the first ever on active service of the RFC. The
inscription on Perry's grave is: *First on the Role of Honour; all glory*

81 Amiens memorials – General Leclerc's memorial in the city centre and 'grieving French womanhood' in the St Acheul Military Cemetery.

to his name. (Lieutenant-General Sir James Grierson, commander of II Corps, died the following day when he collapsed on a train at or near Amiens, but his body was taken home for burial at Glasgow.) The plot contains ten other British graves, also twelve Belgian, one French and one Russian grave of the First World War and two unidentified French soldiers of 1939–45.

Greatly exceeding the size of this little plot is the nearby French military cemetery with 2,774 graves, approximately three-quarters of them being of men who died of wounds at Amiens in 1914–15. A beautiful feature of the French cemetery is the elegant memorial in the form of a figure representing grieving French womanhood.

Camon Communal Cemetery ⑤ contains eighteen graves from 1918 in a small group on the left of the civilian cemetery. Among the dead are an Anglo-French artillery officer, six Australian Ordnance Corps men killed on the same day in May, presumably by long-range shelling or in an air raid, and an Australian machine-gunner drowned while swimming in the nearby River Somme.

Just across the river, Longeau's railway yards formed a major link in the British supply organization throughout the various battles of the Somme. In the crisis of spring 1918 when the Germans threatened Amiens, trains bringing reinforcements stopped here and the men then marched up to the battle front only six miles away. The Germans bombed and shelled it at that time and the RAF bombed it again in 1944 to prevent the Germans sending their reinforcements in the opposite direction to Normandy. *Longeau British Cemetery* ⑥ was in the country when it was made in 1918, but housing has now reached it. This small, tidy cemetery has 202 graves, made up of almost equal numbers of United Kingdom, Australian and Canadian troops who died of wounds received at the nearby front in 1918 or were killed in air raids. Only a mile away, at Amiens-Glisy Airfield, the local flying club erected a small statue of Baron von Richthofen near their clubhouse, but the statue was stolen in the 1970s and there is nothing there now – unless someone decides to replace it.

The village of Boves is situated astride the River Avre. Henry V's army crossed here in 1415 to continue its eastward march along the south bank of the Somme. One of his soldiers went into the village church and stole the pyx, the small container of gold or silver in which the Blessed Sacrament is kept. Henry V ordered him to be hanged. British soldiers returned in 1918 when Casualty Clearing Stations were located here and twelve men were buried in *Boves East Communal Cemetery* ⑦, close to the grave of a Prussian officer who was buried here in 1870. Most of the 1918 burials, however, were in *Boves West Communal Cemetery and Extension* ⑧. Forty-five graves were made in the civilian cemetery and ninety-one more in the extension, which is just a long, narrow strip on the edge of the civilian cemetery, but it has a Cross of Sacrifice and is a proper War Graves Commission plot. Most of the men buried were either Canadians or heavy artillerymen. An unidentified Second World War airman is also buried here.

The village of Dury – now much developed – was the final resting place of Gough's Fifth Army Headquarters at the end of the March 1918 retreat and the important conference held at Doullens nearly took place at Dury. There is an interesting memorial ⑨ at the side of the main road, just on the Amiens side of a modern water tower and a television mast. There, set in a clump of trees, is what is really three memorials in one. The original tall, centre column commemorates the Battle of Dury in November 1870. Stone monuments on either side are memorials to the men of the French 56th Infantry Regiment and of the 7th Colonial Infantry Division who fought here in June 1940.

A stone block ⑩ at Le Petit St Jean has this inscription, in French: 'To the memory of the members of the 7th Bn, The Royal Sussex Regiment, who resisted the German offensive from the 18th to the 20th of May 1940.' I believe that this is the only memorial on the Somme to a British unit which fought there in the 1940 campaign. Unfortunately it has no enclosure and stands on an unattractive site beside a busy main road. *Pont-de-Metz Churchyard* ⑪ contains the graves of thirty-three British soldiers who were killed in that fighting, many of them being from the 7th Royal Sussex.

On the other side of Amiens, in the suburb of Rivery, there are two places on the main road to Albert which are of interest. *Amiens Prison* ⑫ was the target of a famous RAF bombing raid on 18 February 1944. The Resistance in Northern France was under great pressure at this time because of the imminence of the Allied invasion. Confessions under torture and some treachery had resulted in about 180 Resistance members and other political prisoners being held at the prison. The French asked for a raid to breach the outer walls and the prison blocks to allow a mass escape; casualties would be accepted because many of the French people concerned would be executed or sent to concentration camps anyway.

It was a snowy day when the raid took place. Fourteen Mosquitoes of Nos. 21, 464 and 487 Squadrons flew to Albert, turned and flew above the main road towards Amiens. There were no houses opposite the prison at that time and the final approach was from that direction. The raid was successful and approximately eighty Resistance and political prisoners were among those who escaped, although ninety-four people were killed. The raid was led by Group Captain P. C. Pickard, a veteran of many wartime operations. His was the only aircraft shot down near the target, although another Mosquito crashed near the coast. Pickard and his navigator and the navigator of the second lost Mosquito were killed. The prison walls clearly show the rebuilt brickwork where the breaches were made and there is a memorial by the prison gateway referring to 'the French patriots killed in this prison where the barbarian Nazis were

82 Plaque at Amiens Prison commemorating the RAF raid which breached the walls.

martyring them' – a judicious choice of words which avoided the mention of RAF bombs.

Only a few yards away is *St Pierre Cemetery* ⑬, a large civilian cemetery which contains many war graves. The largest plot is of 1,372 French soldiers from the First World War, more than half of whom died of wounds in 1916. The British plot has 676 First World War graves from a variety of units and dates from September 1915 until 1919. Seventy-three British airmen who died in the Second World War and nine soldiers who were killed when this area was liberated in 1944 were buried between the pathways of the earlier graves. Among them were Group Captain Pickard and his navigator, Flight Lieutenant J. A. Broadley; the seven decorations for bravery marked on their headstones are testimony to their long and courageous wartime service before the prison raid.

Moving out into the country, *Allonville Communal Cemetery* ⑭ was used to bury fifty men who died at a Casualty Clearing Station in 1916, mostly from illnesses, and then Australian units buried twenty-eight of their men in 1918. A British soldier who died in May 1940 is also buried there.

Bertangles Communal Cemetery ⑮ was where Baron von Richthofen was buried on 22 April 1918, the day after his death. A photograph taken at the time shows the grassy area near the cemetery gate where he was buried. His body was moved to Fricourt German Cemetery after the war, then to Berlin in 1925 and more recently to his home town of Wiesbaden. That part of the cemetery is quite unchanged; there is still just a grassy area with no sign that Germany's most famous airman was once buried there. But the grave of another pilot is close by, that of Second Lieutenant J. A. Miller of No. 24 Squadron, killed when his SE5A crashed a few weeks before Richthofen died. Miller was an American, born in Hawaii; the family inscription on the War Graves Commission headstone is: *And bright with many an angel and all the martyr throng.* His is the only military grave now in the cemetery.

Villers-Bocage Communal Cemetery Extension ⑯ was used by British units from 1915 to 1917, often for men who died of accidents or illnesses. There are eighty First World War graves and two from the Second World War – a soldier who died in March 1940 and a Spitfire pilot of No. 129 Squadron shot down in July 1943.

On 1 September 1944, the large village of Flesselles lay in the path of the British 8th Armoured Brigade which was advancing as part of the dash to the north which was taking place all across the Somme on that day. The brigade's War Diary[1] describes how a small German battle group of tanks, anti-tank guns and infantry at Flesselles was bypassed 'by a great cross-country gallop' which took most of the brigade on to Doullens, which was liberated later in the day. But three British soldiers were killed at Flesselles and the village later erected two memorials at the places where they died. By the road from Villers-Bocage ⑰ is the memorial to Rifleman H. Ruffell, a lorried infantryman of the 12th King's Royal Rifle Corps. The second memorial is at the south end of the village ⑱, on a grassy plot near a garage and a railway crossing. It is for Sergeant L. Cribben, MM, and Trooper J. A. Sharpe, tank crewman of the Nottinghamshire Yeomanry. Both memorials carry the inscription: 'From the Commune of Flesselles to its Liberators.' Both were freshly painted on our visit and a man in the local café told us how the village continues to care for the memorials. The three soldiers are buried together in a carefully tended plot in a corner of the local cemetery ⑲. All three headstones have touching family inscriptions.

Another reminder of the Second World War is to be found on a bank at the side of a lane ⑳ near Naours. A small white painted monument, again obviously well cared for by local people, is to the memory of 'Prochnicki, André, Lt, Pilote de la RAF, tombé au

---

[1] Public Record Office WO 171/613.

combat le 19 Août 1943'. Later research showed this to be the grave of Flight Lieutenant Andrej Prochnicki, a Polish pilot of No. 316 Squadron, whose Spitfire crashed here. (The nearby town of Naours has a complete underground 'town' where the inhabitants took refuge 'in barbarian invasions' of ancient times; it contained two kilometres of passageways, 300 rooms, three chapels, stables and a bakery. It is sometimes open to visitors.)

Vignacourt British Cemetery ㉑ was started when the Germans nearly reached Amiens in April 1918; two Casualty Clearing Stations moved here and used this cemetery until August. The railway line for the ambulance trains is still nearby. This is an important cemetery, very much reflecting the defence of Amiens and then the successful British offensive in August. The burials start inside the gateway and progress in date order in neat and regular rows and plots, ready to be made into a permanent cemetery after the war. There are 423 Australian graves, nearly three-quarters of the 584 in the cemetery. Another feature is the presence of twenty-three RAF graves, mostly in pairs where two-men crews were buried. Among these is Lieutenant R. J. Fitzgerald, MC, of No. 35 Squadron, whose grave is in Plot 2, Row E, and whose entry in the register shows that he had earlier escaped from a German prisoner-of-war camp to return to duty. The bodies of six men who were earlier buried in the local civilian cemetery were brought in after the war and buried at the far end of the cemetery, where there is also a small plot of forty-four graves of German prisoners who died here. Finally, two soldiers killed in May 1940 are buried near the cemetery entrance.

There is one more interesting feature, a unique one. Halfway down the cemetery, near a side wall, is a lovely statue of a French soldier looking out over the British graves. The inscription translates as: 'Brothers in arms of the British Army, fallen on the field of honour, sleep in peace; we are watching over you.' The statue was erected by local people whose village had been spared the ravages of fighting and occupation by the efforts of the units whose mortally wounded were buried here. It is the only example I know of such a memorial in a British war cemetery.

Accidents at a trench-mortar school provided most of the fifteen British graves in *Vaux-en-Amiénois Communal Cemetery* ㉒; three officers and five men, mostly Northumberland Fusiliers, were killed

83 The unique French statue overlooking the graves in Vignacourt British Cemetery.

in one day in December 1916. At the side of the road not far away ㉓ is a memorial recording a different kind of violence. It is another 'Picardy Martyrs' memorial near a small wood. It seems to have been the German practice to take men marked for execution out into the country and shoot them on the edge of woods. There are no details on the memorial, but a private plaque from the wife and child of André Foucart, a sergeant in the FTPF, tells how he and his comrades were 'assassinated by the Germans in August 1944'. The FTPF was the military wing of one of the resistance movements and took its name from the 'Franc-Tireurs et Partisans' who opposed the Prussian occupation in 1870.

6 · THE WESTERN SOMME

There is almost as much of the Somme *département* remaining between Amiens and the sea as there is in the areas described so far in this book. The great battles of 1914–18 did not reach this far, but there are still interesting things to see. The Battle of Crécy was fought here in 1346. Some small war cemeteries are reminders of the presence of British medical units and other establishments in the First World War. The largest battle in the Somme of the 1940 campaign was fought here and the years of occupation have also left their marks in the form of memorials to members of the Resistance and the graves of RAF men killed in air raids and of various servicemen washed up along the coast. There is also a large German cemetery where the bodies of all their Second World War dead from an area much larger than the Somme *département* were gathered and buried. It is not an area of major importance for battlefield tourers, unless they are studying Crécy or the 1940 campaign, but visitors using Dieppe, Le Havre or the Normandy ports to cross from England may find themselves in the area. The countryside is pleasant and the roads are mostly quiet, although new motorways are planned for the Channel Tunnel era.

THE 1940 RIVER LINE

The twenty-five-mile stretch of the Somme between Amiens and Abbeville was the scene of major fighting in 1940. After their armoured thrust across France to the coast, the Germans secured a bridgehead over the river at Abbeville but left the remainder of the River Somme as their left flank while they concentrated their

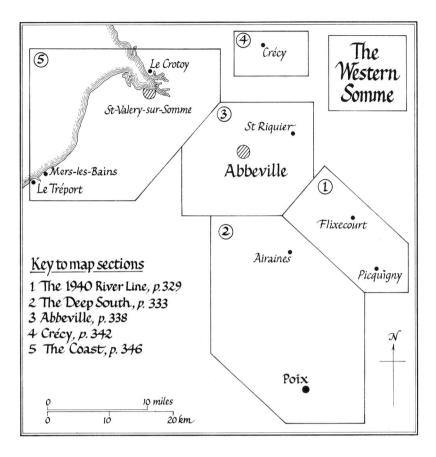

The Western Somme

⑤ Le Crotoy

St-Valery-sur-Somme

Mers-les-Bains
Le Tréport

④ Crécy

③ St Riquier

Abbeville

① Flixecourt

② Airaines

Picquigny

Poix

Key to map sections

1 The 1940 River Line, p. 329
2 The Deep South, p. 333
3 Abbeville, p. 338
4 Crécy, p. 342
5 The Coast, p. 346

𝒩

0 _____ 10 miles
0 ___ 10 ___ 20 km

attentions against the British and French units falling back in the north towards Dunkirk. The river has no canal here, only a wide main waterway surrounded by marshes and ponds; it was a difficult obstacle. After Dunkirk, the Germans turned, lined their divisions up on the Somme and then recommenced their offensive on 5 June, driving south towards Rouen and Paris. A considerable battle developed which eventually led to the fall of France by the end of the month.

The first memorial to this fighting is near the village of Breilly, on the old main road from Amiens to Abbeville. It is up some steps at the side of the road ① and is to the memory of the French 13th Infantry Division 'which fought heroically in this area from 27 May to 6 June 1940'. All the units in the division are listed on the sides of the memorial. It looks out over the road on to one of the large ponds at the side of the Somme.

Picquigny British Cemetery ② shows how this area alternates between 1918 and 1940 interest. Two Casualty Clearing Stations came here in April 1918 and 124 British soldiers and one French soldier were buried during that month. The British casualties included several senior officers – a lieutenant-colonel and four majors. Six further First World War bodies were later transferred from smaller cemeteries. One of these was Major-General E. Feetham, CB, CMG, commander of the 39th Division, who was killed by a shell when he went up to the front during heavy fighting on 29 March 1918, the second divisional commander to die on the Somme in the First World War. Seven soldiers of the Second World War are also buried here. The cemetery is at the side of the road rising out of Picquigny towards Soues.

Crouy British Cemetery ③ was also where medical units came in April 1918, but these stayed until August and produced the largest British cemetery in this area, with 740 British, forty-four German and six French graves. The cemetery is outside the village, in a pleasant location on a hillside, with woods across nearby fields. Although it is a wartime cemetery, the graves were made in carefully prepared plots ready for post-war permanent construction.

The main feature of the cemetery is the large number of Australian and Canadian graves. The 275 Australians are mostly buried in the early plots, on the left of the cemetery, and are from the defence of Amiens in May to July 1918, while the 179 Canadians were wounded in the August offensive and are mostly on the right. The 281 United Kingdom graves, however, are still the largest group and are to be found throughout the cemetery. Two of the English graves caught my eye. In Plot 1, Row C, is buried Sergeant Band-master C. F. G. Coles of Queen Victoria's Rifles, a professional musician and composer who enlisted in London in 1914 and died of wounds received while acting as a stretcher-bearer in April 1918. In Plot 4, Row B, is the grave of Captain A. K. Shenton, MC, son of a vicar in the East End of London, who died in August 1918 while serving with a Royal Engineers Signal Company. The inscription on his headstone lists the battles in which he took part from Loos 1915 onwards, and a private tablet placed at the grave refers simply and touchingly to 'Austin, loyal heart and true'.

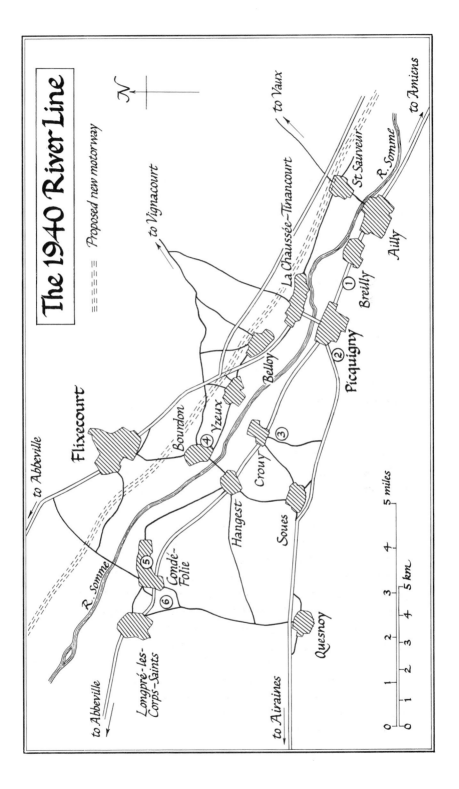

The 1940 River Line

≡≡≡≡ Proposed new motorway

N

to Abbeville

Flixecourt

to Vignacourt

to Vaux

to Amiens

R. Somme

St Sauveur

Ailly

Breilly

①

Picquigny

②

La Chaussée–Tirancourt

Bourdon

Belloy

Yzeux

④

③

Crouy

Soues

Hangest

Condé-Folie

⑤

⑥

Longpré-les-Corps-Saints

R. Somme

to Abbeville

Quesnoy

to Airaines

R. Somme

5 miles
0   1   2   3   4

5 km
0   1   2   3   4   5

It is necessary to cross the Somme to reach *Bourdon German Cemetery* ④, which at the latest count has 22,213 graves of German soldiers killed in the Second World War. But this huge number of men did not all die on the Somme; there are no other German Second World War cemeteries between here and the Belgian border, so most of the casualties from the fighting at the Channel ports and from the *départements* of Pas-de-Calais and Nord are buried here. It is not quite the largest military cemetery on the Somme in its number of graves; the German First World War cemetery at Vermandovillers has slightly more.

The cemetery is well situated, on a hill looking out over the Somme valley from the northern side of the river where the German units lined up before opening their attack in June 1940. There is a visitors centre and a resident custodian, the only German cemetery on the Somme to have those features. To enter the cemetery it is necessary to pass through a strange and sombre chamber which contains a towering statue of grieving German womanhood. The cemetery is then found to be on three levels, containing forty-four plots of graves. It must have become more heavily used than originally anticipated, because the last five numbered plots are all along what was obviously intended to be a central parkway. It is

84 The Second World War graves in Bourdon German Cemetery.

difficult to appreciate that so many men are buried here because the trees and the different levels of the cemetery break up the overall area and because the squat stone grave markers mostly bear six names. I made as careful a survey as possible of the years of death, with this result:

1940, approximately 60 per cent – 13,328 deaths.
1941–3, approximately 15 per cent – 3,332 deaths.
1944, approximately 25 per cent – approximately 5,553 deaths.

The large proportion of 1940 deaths shows that the conquest of France was not achieved without considerable loss to the Germans. The 1941–3 casualties would mostly have been from air raids, Resistance activity, accidents and illnesses. Most of the 1944 deaths were probably from the area of the Channel ports; the liberation of the inland areas was achieved without serious fighting.

The French chose to have their main Second World War cemetery at Condé-Folie ⑤, on the side of the river they were defending in 1940. There are actually two cemeteries, one on either side of the road close to the church in the old part of the village near the river. The total number of identified graves is 2,436, split almost exactly between homeland French and colonial units. The burials are in various plots according to nationality and religion. There are two plots on the south side of the road, one with approximately 1,200 French graves, the other with 800 colonial graves which all have Muslim headstones. On the north side of the road, in the more attractive part of the cemetery which runs up to the edge of the river, is a plot of 440 further colonial graves, but most with Christian crosses. Then at the back of that part of the cemetery and right up against the edge of the river, is a mass grave of approximately 1,000 unidentified men of mixed races, units and religions.

The location of *Longpré-les-Corps-Saints British Cemetery* ⑥ can be confusing because the Michelin maps show the 'Brit.' abbreviation to be nearer to Condé-Folie, but the cemetery is easily found at the side of the road leading out from Longpré towards Quesnoy. The original cemetery was made in April 1918 by British medical units and thirty-five men were buried in two rows. The graves from another small 1918 cemetery were moved here after the war, as well as two isolated 1916 graves, to make a total of seventy-eight, twenty-eight of which are from London units and twenty are Australians. It is a delightful miniature cemetery, situated in farmland looking out over the nearby Somme valley, with the Cross of Sacrifice 'looking great' (my visit notes say) 'against a little copse on the other side of the lane'.

THE DEEP SOUTH

A main road runs almost due south from Abbeville, through thirty miles of Somme countryside, then on to Beauvais and eventually to Paris. There are eight memorials or cemeteries on or near that road, mostly from the Second World War. It is a particularly pretty area, with rolling countryside, woods and charming villages, and with more grass fields than other parts of the Somme.

In the middle of the small town of Airaines is a fine, tall memorial ① 'to the glorious dead of the 53rd Infantry Regiment, Colonial Mixed Senegalese, who were in action at the Crossing of the Somme held by the 5th Colonial Infantry Division on June 5th–7th 1940'. The images of two soldiers' heads are near the top of the memorial stone, one with European features, the other with African. *Airaines Communal Cemetery* ② is just east of the town, where the road to Quesnoy reaches the top of a hill. In it are buried seven British soldiers, all killed in one incident on 1 September 1944. The 4th Armoured Brigade was pushing forward fast at that time and one of its reconnaissance groups was ambushed. The dead consisted of Lieutenant-Colonel R. B. Littledale, DSO, commander of the 2nd King's Royal Rifle Corps, an artillery battery commander, their RASC driver and four riflemen escorts.

On the east side of the main road at Tailly ③ is a memorial erected by the local people to honour 'General Leclerc de Hautecloque at the place where he chose to live and where the villagers got to know and love him'. This was the General Leclerc who brought French troops in the Chad over to the Free French side and then commanded the French 2nd Armoured Division in the liberation of France in 1944. The personal tank on which he entered Paris had TAILLY painted on its side. He is the Somme's most famous son of modern times. The château on the opposite side of the road was his residence. Leclerc was born at Belloy-St-Leonard where two of the windows

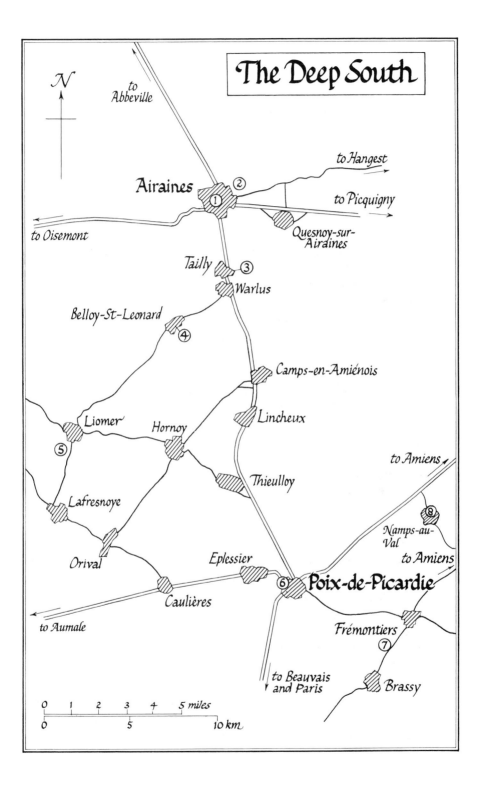

The Deep South

N

to
Abbeville

to Hangest

to Picquigny

Airaines ②
①

to Oisemont

Quesnoy-sur-
Airaines

Tailly ③
Warlus

Belloy-St-Leonard

④

Camps-en-Amiénois

Liomer

Lincheux

Hornoy

⑤

Thieulloy

to Amiens

Lafresnoye

⑧

Namps-au-
Val

Orival

Eplessier

to Amiens

Poix-de-Picardie

⑥

Caulières

Frémontiers

to Aumale

⑦

to Beauvais
and Paris

Brassy

0   1   2   3   4   5 miles

0   5   10 km

85 The beautiful Alpine Chasseurs Memorial near Liomer.

in the pretty little church ④ have been made into memorials facing the roadway. One is to seven local men who died in the two world wars, including Count de Hautecloque, killed in 1914, and who was probably an uncle of General Leclerc. On the ground in front is a rusty old wheeled mortar. The second window honours General Leclerc, lists his nine battle honours, ending with 'Hanoi', and then tells how he 'died for France'; he was only forty-seven when he perished in a plane crash in Morocco in 1947.

One of the most striking Second World War memorials I have seen is near the attractive old village of Liomer ⑤, on the road to Lafresnoye. It is to the men of the 13th Battalion of Alpine Chasseurs from Chambéry, a town in the Savoy Alps, and of the 5th Demi-Brigade who fought here in June 1940. It is a modern memorial, standing on a semi-circular site on the edge of a wood and made of boulders which were doubtless brought from Chambéry, and it is topped by a superb metal head wearing the distinctive floppy Chasseur beret. A private plaque is for Captain Montjean and the men of No. 2 Company. Our visit was on the first day of the shooting season and the present-day *chasseurs* were very active in the nearby fields.

There was a wartime airfield near the town of Poix-de-Picardie.

The Luftwaffe used *Poix Churchyard* ⑥ as the burial place for 148 British airmen and one Polish airman shot down over a wide area during the middle war years. The airmen's graves are in a pretty grassed plot – a peaceful spot right next to the west door of the lovely old church. There are four and a half rows of graves, most of them being in groups of up to seven, where bomber crews were given communal burials. Most of the men were from Bomber Command, many shot down while attacking railway targets in France in support of the invasion in 1944, but a solo grave is that of Flight Lieutenant R. W. Sampson, the New Zealand navigator in one of the Mosquitoes shot down in the raid on Amiens Prison in February 1944.

Poix lies on the River Selle, on the line of which the French attempted a stand in June 1940 after the Germans had crossed the Somme. On a hillside above the village of Frémontiers is a small memorial ⑦ in an enclosure commemorating 'the heroic defence of Frémontiers by the 3rd Battalion of the 21st Infantry Regiment, 7th June 1940'.

Namps-au-Val British Cemetery ⑧ is in the northern part of the village of the same name, close to a railway line where three Casualty Clearing Stations were located during the closing stages of the German offensive in 1918. It is a simple cemetery in an attractive setting and is the resting place for 403 British soldiers who died here in just three weeks. The grave of Captain G. M. Flowerdew, VC, is at the left end of Row H of Plot 1. He was wounded leading a squadron of Lord Strathcona's Horse in mounted action the day before his death on 31 March 1918.

ABBEVILLE

Abbeville is the second largest town in the Somme *département*. It was a major hospital and communications centre for French and British forces throughout the First World War, but its interest is that it was the scene of important events in the German invasion of France in 1940. After taking part in Guderian's breakthrough in the Ardennes and then sweeping across France in six days, the 2nd Panzer Division reached Abbeville on the evening of 20 May. The town was packed with refugees and had been bombed all day by the Luftwaffe; numerous buildings were on fire and hundreds of civilians were killed. The French authorities also panicked and fired on a group of refugees trying to cross one of the Somme bridges, believing them to be Fifth Columnists, and killed twenty-four of them, mostly Belgians. No one was ever able to count the exact number of people who died in Abbeville that day; some estimates are as high as 5,000 but the true figure is probably less than that. The German tanks passed through a gap between French and British troops – three Territorial battalions of the Queen's were there – entered Abbeville and established a substantial bridgehead south of the River Somme. They thus secured the last bridge before the sea capable of bearing tanks and completed the encirclement of the Allied forces in Northern France and Belgium – perhaps the most dramatic moment of the 1940 campaign.

It was not the German plan to proceed further here, so 2nd Panzer handed over to a motorized division two days later and turned north towards Dunkirk. The French tried to eliminate the bridgehead and restore the defence line on the river. British forces taking part in these actions were the 51st (Highland) Division, made up of Regular and Territorial Highland battalions, and part of the 1st Armoured Division which was only equipped with light tanks. Several attacks were made between 27 May and 4 June; one of the most successful French divisional commanders was Charles de Gaulle. It was the largest Allied counter-offensive of the 1940 campaign, with up to 500 French and British tanks taking part. The Germans were pushed back most of the way to the river but managed to retain a bridge-head, and German anti-tank guns caused heavy casualties among both French and British tanks; it was the first occasion in which the Germans used 88 mm anti-aircraft guns against tanks and found that they unwittingly had a devastating anti-tank weapon. The Germans then launched a general offensive all along the Somme line on 5 June and the Allies were pushed back. The Highland Division fought further actions but finished up stranded at St Valery-en-Caux (outside the Somme *département*) and most of the division was taken prisoner.

The years of occupation passed. The airfield north of the town became a major Luftwaffe fighter base, the home of what Allied airmen called the 'Abbeville Boys', and was often bombed. Liberation came on 4 September 1944 when the 1st Polish Armoured Division entered the town. Abbeville was rebuilt. Much of its old character has gone but some charming corners remain. There are eight hotels but it is a busy place. The *Château de Bagatelle* ①, in the south part of the town, contains a good museum of the 1940 fighting in which the part played by the Highland Division is given due credit.

Abbeville Communal Cemetery and Extension ② is the large local cemetery, well signposted at the northern end of the town; it is known locally as the 'Cimetière de Menchecourt'. It is an important cemetery containing many burials of the First and Second World Wars. Because of the widespread location of the various war plots and because the British plots have a confusing system of numbering, visitors may wish to take the following suggested route.

The best entrance is through the gate at the end of the lane which runs along the left side of the cemetery. Two plots of mainly French First World War graves will be found across the cemetery from that gateway. The first of those plots contains just six scattered British graves of 'Old Contemptibles' who were wounded at Ypres in November 1914 and died at Abbeville. The second French plot contains a further eighty-five early British graves dating from December 1914 to October 1915. One unusual headstone here is over the grave of Private M. T. Barker, a member of the British Red Cross attached to the Friends' Ambulance Unit; it is at the right-hand end of the fourth British row.

A major new area was allocated for British graves when British units took over the Somme front in 1915. To reach this, it is necessary to walk some distance up the cemetery, that is, away from the town end. Two more groups of war graves can be seen before reaching the new British plots. An old board in front of a section of French soldiers' graves proclaims: 'They shed their blood for their country; you who pass pray for them.' They were probably local men whose families made private graves in 1914–18, and there are a few graves of Resistance men from the 1940s. Those men all deserve better than the forlorn, untidy collection of rusty crosses and memorials which mark their graves. Near the left wall of the cemetery are several rows of civilian victims of the May 1940 bombing. There are 107 graves also with rusty crosses; some are marked as 'unknowns' and were probably refugees.

The main area of British graves, at the upper end of the cemetery, is a pleasant contrast, with its Cross of Sacrifice, rows of regular white headstones, grassed areas and high standard of maintenance. The numbering of the plots can be confusing if you are looking for

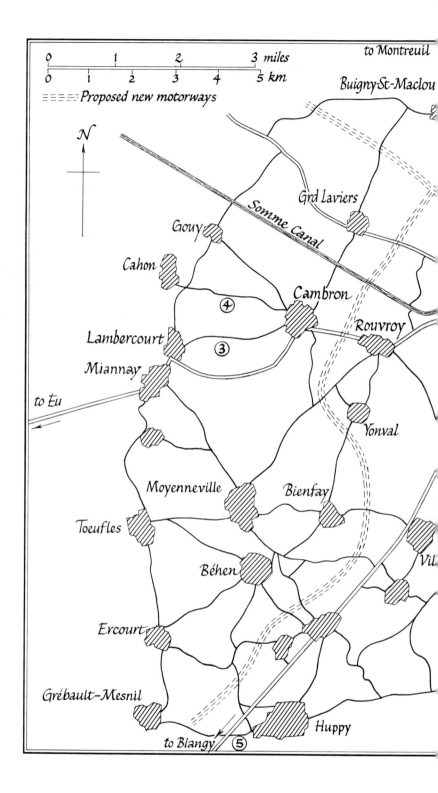

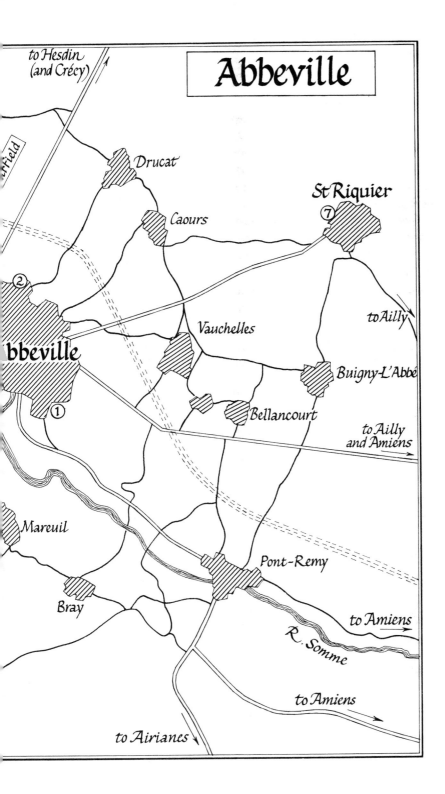

Abbeville

to Hesdin
(and Crécy)

...field

Drucat

Caours

②

bbeville

①

Mareuil

Bray

Vauchelles

Bellancourt

St Riquier

⑦

Buigny-L'Abbé

to Ailly

to Ailly
and Amiens

Pont-Remy

to Amiens

R. Somme

to Amiens

to Airianes

a particular grave. The first four plots are Nos. 3 to 6 of the Abbeville Communal Cemetery. (Plots 1 and 2 are the mainly French graves seen earlier.) The grassy bank behind the four plots marks the boundary of the civilian cemetery; the plots above the bank form the extension and the plots there start with No. 1 again. There are 1,755 First World War graves. The Somme battles of 1916 and 1918 are represented by the graves of many men who died of wounds at Abbeville. Plot 4, Row C, on the right of the extension, has a sad group of nine girls or women with the humble rank of 'Worker' in the Auxiliary Army Corps who were killed in an air raid in May 1918. Nine men died on Armistice Day 1918 and about 100 more in the immediate post-war period. The last was CSM T. F. Murphy of the Royal Inniskilling Fusiliers who died in March 1920; his grave is just to the left of the long platform on which the Cross of Sacrifice stands.

No doubt, all concerned thought that would see the end of war victims here, but just two yards on in the same row is the grave of Sapper T. Lucas who died on 16 May 1940, the first of nearly 400 Second World War men buried here. Their graves filled up the last row of the last First World War plot and then required four more plots across the back of the cemetery as well as additions at the end of many of the rows in other First World War plots. There are 201 soldiers' graves, nearly all from 1940; the greatest number are from the 7th Royal Sussex which was in action with a Panzer division at Amiens. The 170 airmen come from all of the war years and include a senior officer, Group Captain W. V. L. Spendlove, DSO, Station Commander of Swanton Morley, shot down by flak in a Ventura bomber of No. 21 Squadron in June 1943; his grave is in Plot 6, Row B.

There are 2,911 British graves in the various plots of this cemetery – 2,529 of the First World War and 382 of the Second World War. It is the largest group of British Second World War graves on the Somme.

There are two Second World War memorials in the countryside west of Abbeville. By the side of the country lane from Cambron to Lambercourt (not the main road) is a small, dignified monument ③ to three French soldiers of the 10th Light Cavalry Regiment killed here on 29 May 1940. This was probably a tank crew killed in one of the series of attacks against the German bridgehead.

A sign on the roadside near the Cambron end of a small wood on the Cahon–Cambron road marks the entrance to a short pathway in the trees – the 'Allée des Martyrs' – at the end of which is a memorial ④ to three Resistance men. The inscription says: 'Never forget this place where, after hours of suffering, our finest comrades were assassinated by the barbarians of Hitler's Germany, 31st July 1944.' A small private plaque says: 'Cher Papa, at the place where you suffered so much, Mother and I will never forget you. Jacques.'

A new monument just outside Huppy ⑤ reveals a more forgiving spirit. It is at the place where an Anglo-French attack on the bridgehead commenced on 28 May 1940 and made an advance of five miles in four days. The memorial, built in 1990, has the shapes of French, British and German steel helmets on top and the main inscription is: 'To all the soldiers killed on the soil of Picardy.' Other inscriptions include: 'Reconciliation'; 'France 1940 – Europe 1990'; and quotations from de Gaulle and Adenauer.

Moving north-eastwards from here, one comes to the Monts de Caubert, the high ground above the Somme which formed the heart of the bridgehead seized here by the Germans in May 1940. On the southern flank of the high ground is the village of Mareuil in the communal cemetery ⑥ of which are buried 122 British and thirty-five French soldiers who died in those actions. It was near here that the 4th Cameron Highlanders participated in French attacks in the early days of June 1940. When, in turn, the Germans resumed their offensive on 5 June, the Camerons were still here and sustained further casualties; the 4th Seaforth Highlanders were also in action. The bodies of the Highlanders who died and of some British tank crews were brought here to be buried after the war. The cemetery is in an attractive country location and the war plot, up some steps from the civilian cemetery, has received the full War Graves Commission treatment. It is a nice touch that the French soldiers who died here were buried with the British. Unfortunately, eighty-two of the British graves are unidentified, although many of them are known to be Highlanders. Five members of a Lancaster bomber crew of No. 467 (Australian) Squadron shot down in June 1944 are also buried here.

On the other side of the River Somme, *St Riquier British Cemetery* ⑦ was started in 1918 by a Casualty Clearing Station which was using a local seminary. The cemetery contains eighty-three First World War graves, including thirty-eight Indian soldiers, eleven

Australians and eleven RAF pilots from local airfields. Twenty graves were added during the Second World War – seventeen soldiers from 1940 and three airmen from 1944.

CRÉCY

Crécy and the 1346 battlefield lie close to the largest and oldest forest in the Somme *département*. Opposite a shooting lodge at a junction on the forest road from Abbeville is a small memorial ① to two foresters who were killed while serving as soldiers in the First World War, one an officer killed at the front in 1914, the other killed at Abbeville Station, possibly while on leave, in an air raid in May 1918; presumably this was the same raid which killed the nine British women auxiliaries who are buried at Abbeville.

The little town of Crécy-en-Ponthieu is full of historical interest.

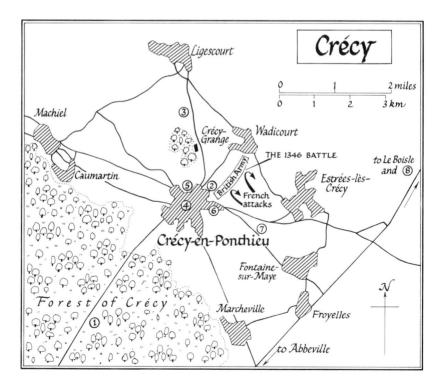

86 Crécy – the observation tower on the site of the windmill from which Edward III directed the English army in the 1346 battle.

The famous battle of 26 August 1346 was fought just outside the town, to the north and east, when an English (and Welsh) army defeated a French force three times as strong to maintain control of Aquitaine. King Edward III controlled his forces from the vantage-point of a windmill on high ground north of the town. A wooden observation tower ② has recently been built on the same site so that visitors can have the same view of the battlefield. The English troops were led by his son, the Prince of Wales – the Black Prince – and were mainly deployed in an arc to the east of the windmill. The French, led by King Philippe, were on the lower ground and had to attack uphill. A map at the visitors centre near the tower shows the dispositions and describes the progress of the battle. A notice in the tower itself, when translated, gives an interesting summary:

England's longbowmen won the battle, destroying France's nobility which lacked a sense of organization and discipline. Casualties were rather light on the English side but heavy on the French. Among the dead were Jean of Luxembourg, King of Bohemia and also Philippe's own brother, together with many members of France's oldest families. Without doubt this battle marked an end to the supremacy of feudal chivalry on battle-fields and marked the new power of infantry.

I would have thought that the longbowmen of 1346 were the equivalent of field artillery or machine-gunners rather than of infantry. The battle was virtually won on the first day. Edward III is reputed to have filled the windmill with timber and set it alight that night to illuminate any further French approach. There was little fighting the next day and the French then withdrew, leaving 1,500 dead.

Moving north from Crécy, the large farm of Crécy-Grange marked the corner of the British perimeter. A little further on the same road is the surprising contrast of a large Second World War bunker ③, the aperture of which is large enough to have allowed a field gun to cover the open ground to the south-west. A local lady explained that the Germans had an airfield on that ground and the bunker was part of its defences.

The town is charming and smart, with two hotels if one fancies an overnight stop here. Just outside the Hôtel de Ville ④ is a monument to Jean of Luxembourg, King of Bohemia, 'and his brave companions in arms who died for France at Crécy'. This nobleman was almost blind but had insisted on going into battle; he did so, on horseback, with a knight on either side holding the reins of his horse. All three men and their horses died.

There are three other reminders of war in the town – but of three other wars. In the local cemetery ⑤ are the graves of a Royal Horse Artillery driver and an RASC man who died here in the First World War. In the centre of the town, not far from the Jean of Luxembourg monument, is the *Lanterne de Mort*, a memorial erected in 1189 by Queen Eleanor, the French wife of the English King Henry II, to commemorate her sons, Richard the Lionheart and John, whom she believed to have died on the Crusades. In fact, they were still alive and returned home safely. This is the earliest known war memorial in the *département* of the Somme. On the eastern outskirts of the town, opposite some warehouses, is a memorial ⑥ to six Resistance men, 'victims of the barbarous Germans, shot on 3rd September 1944'. That must have been just as the last Germans were evacuating the area before Allied troops arrived, and that killing must have been one of the last acts of wartime violence in the Somme. So here at Crécy, known for its battle of 1346, are actually the first and last war memorials on the Somme, situated less than a mile apart.

The last memorial in the area brings us back to 1346. The *Cross of the King of Bohemia* ⑦ is where Jean of Luxembourg died after being carried wounded from the battlefield. The Prince of Wales found the body and took the plume of ostrich feathers from Jean's helmet as a spoil of war, adopting both the feathers and Jean's motto – 'Ich dien' or 'Ich dene' ('I serve') – as his own. They have been the emblem and the motto of the Prince of Wales ever since and the badges of most Welsh regiments incorporate those features. The cross where Jean died now has a modern base. The inscription is in Old French, not easy to translate, but refers to Jean's 'vigorously expressed request' to be led towards the enemy and how, 'fighting most bravely', he struck with his sword three or four times.

On the country lane between Le Boisle and Boufflers (just off our map and only a few yards inside the Somme boundary) is a small memorial ⑧ to seven local people who were killed in June 1944 when a V-1 flying bomb came down and exploded soon after being launched.

THE COAST

The coastline of the Somme *département* is only about twenty-five miles long. It is not a particularly attractive area. The countryside is plain and there are no fashionable resorts, although there are some interesting little fishing ports, one of which, St Valery-sur-Somme, has an unusual historical background. There were some small military hospitals along the coast in 1914–18 and some cemeteries contain the graves of the bodies washed up on the coast from various Second World War actions.

We visited Le Crotoy because I wanted to see the grave of a British officer who was executed here in January 1917 and who was buried in *Le Crotoy Communal Cemetery* ①. The officer was Sub-Lieutenant E. L. A. Dyett of the Nelson Battalion, Royal Naval Division, who was accused of failing to make his way up to the fighting line from the reserve as ordered during the attack on the Ancre in November 1916; it was his first action. His trial and execution became public

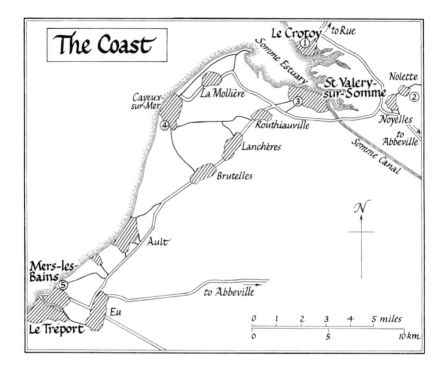

knowledge and there were doubts over whether he had been fairly treated. Dyett was one of only two British officers executed for desertion on the Western Front. He was a wartime volunteer who hated trench warfare and had several times requested to be transferred to sea duty. The cemetery is in the western part of the village. I had hoped to find Dyett's grave overlooking the sea, but this was not the case. He is buried in a plot of First World War graves, mostly of French soldiers. There were only four British graves; by coincidence Dyett's is flanked by the graves of two seamen of the Royal Naval Division who died when their units were resting here. One of the 'French' graves was that of an American, Lieutenant Roger Dix, who died in 1918. The Second World War graves include three British sailors, an unknown Polish airman, a Russian, four 'unknowns' washed up by the sea and four Arab 'Démineurs' – men who died while clearing mines from the German beach defences in 1945.

A routine visit to *Noyelles-sur-Mer Chinese Cemetery* ② proved to be a pleasant surprise because of its attractive setting and appear-

87 The gateway of
Noyelles-sur-Mer
Chinese Cemetery.

ance. It is approached along a well-signposted track from the hamlet
of Nolette. The cemetery is in open country, among grass fields and
near a stream running through a shallow valley. The base camp
for the Chinese Labour Corps was at Noyelles-sur-Mer and there
was a hospital for the labourers. Nearly 90,000 Chinese labourers
were recruited for work with the BEF, of whom nearly 2,000 died.
The 847 men buried here were mostly victims of disease in the last
months of the war and in the post-war battlefield clearance period.
This is their largest cemetery. The permanent construction work
was done with much care and feeling. An elegant arched entrance
has Chinese inscriptions which, according to the introduction in
the cemetery register, 'are to the honour of the dead and monograms
which bear the meaning of Eternity'. There are twelve well-spaced
rows of graves among which grow some cedar trees which manage

to give an oriental appearance to the cemetery. A set of wall panels carrying the names of forty-six Chinese whose graves were lost is a reflection of the diligence with which the records of these labourers were maintained.

The old port of *St Valery-sur-Somme* ③ has two links with the Norman conquest of Britain in 1066. Harold Earl of Wessex, as he was then, was driven ashore here in 1064 and imprisoned by the Count of Ponthieu in a castle, the stone foundations of which can still be seen on the beach. Two years later, William of Normandy had to wait in the harbour with his invasion fleet for two weeks before finding a fair wind to take him to England and to defeat Harold, now King of England, at Hastings and change for ever England's way of life. In 1430 Joan of Arc passed through here as prisoner of the English on the way to her death at Rouen. In 1940 part of the 51st (Highland) Division fought here, but this is not the 'St Valery' where most of the division was captured; that was St Valery-en-Caux, fifty miles further down the coast to the south-west. There are four hotels in the town and, as it is now bypassed by heavy traffic, it is a useful place for an overnight stop. The communal cemetery, on the road out to Lanchères, contains the graves of six British soldiers who died here in 1916–17 and, in the newer part of the cemetery, ten Second World War British graves.

As at Le Crotoy, we came to *Cayeux-sur-Mer Old Churchyard* ④ to see a particular grave – that of Private J. Land of the 2/4th King's Own Yorkshire Light Infantry who died at a hospital here in September 1917. His is the most westerly British First World War grave on the Somme. The cemetery is at the south end of the village, behind the local war memorial and actually inside the ruins of a large old church destroyed in some way in the thirteenth century – a unique and interesting setting. Private Land is buried with a group of eight French soldiers in a perfectly maintained plot. The crosses on the French graves and the solitary British headstone are painted pure white, the effect of which on the standard British headstone is unusual but pleasing. Behind the graves is a memorial to the nine soldiers on which Private Land's name is given pride of place. In other parts of the cemetery are two groups containing thirty-two mixed British Second World War graves; they include two soldiers from 1940, several airmen, a Danish soldier and many bodies washed ashore of whom two were identified as a Commando and a Canadian soldier from the Dieppe Raid in August 1942.

We come now to the end of this tour of the Somme. The little town of Mers-les-Bains is in the extreme western corner of the Somme *département*, at the mouth of the River Bresle along the line of which the Highland Division made another stand in their 1940 retreat. Across the river is the larger town of Le Tréport which is in the *département* of Seine-Maritime. Le Tréport British Cemetery has 445 First World War graves and was actually the first permanent cemetery to be made by the War Graves Commission after the war. But that was not the object of our travelling to this area. I knew that there are eleven British Second World War graves in *Mers-les-Bains Communal Cemetery* ⑤ and was curious to know which of those graves was the most westerly 'on the Somme', hoping that it might be on a site overlooking the sea. The last wish was not fulfilled. The cemetery is pleasant enough but is situated in low ground behind the coastal cliffs, just off the road to Ault. The British graves are in two groups, on well-cared-for grassy plots against a wall. One of the graves was an unidentified sailor; the other ten were all Canadians though only three were identified. The dates on the eleven graves indicate that they were all washed ashore after the Dieppe Raid of August 1942. The right-hand grave – the most westerly one – was marked as belonging to an unknown Canadian soldier and was dated 18th September 1942, that probably being the date on which his body was found. So, separated by eighty miles and nearly a quarter of a century from the unknown Worcestershire Regiment man's grave at Pigeon Ravine Cemetery at the eastern end of the Somme, lies this unknown Canadian, one of 807 Canadians who were killed in that costly operation at Dieppe.

Appendix: Cemeteries, Graves and 'Lost' Bodies

The decision of the War Graves Commission to commemorate the name of every British soldier who died, either by name on the headstone above his grave or on one of the various types of memorial to those whose bodies were never identified, together with the publication of registers for the cemeteries and the memorials, presents a unique opportunity to produce several useful sets of statistics and conclusions. The name of every dead British soldier, with his unit and date of death, is recorded somewhere. The coverage is as near perfect as possible; duplications and omissions have mostly been corrected. A few men recorded as missing may have deserted and successfully changed their identities, but the number cannot be sufficient to alter the overall statistics by more than a small fraction. Some statistics for French, German and American deaths will be added later, but these will not be based upon such precise evidence as the British figures. (The figures quoted for British cemeteries and casualties refer to all British Empire and Commonwealth burials and missing in the *département* of the Somme from 1914 to 1918 and the immediate post-war period and from 1939 to 1945. The figures include men buried or lost just beyond the Somme boundary in the Gommecourt, Serre and Martinpuich–Warlencourt areas during the 1916 battle. Communal cemeteries with less than ten British graves have not been included, but the graves in those small cemeteries are counted in the overall statistics; communal cemeteries with extensions are counted as one cemetery.)

British Cemeteries and Graves, 1914–18

There are 243 First World War British cemeteries on the Somme containing 153,443 British graves, of which 100,034 are identified, leaving 53,409 graves of unidentified bodies. It is possible to

88 A soldier in a Scottish battalion and a German soldier killed in the March 1918 fighting.

allocate the location of the cemeteries roughly to the following areas. The cemeteries made by medical units immediately behind the battlefields are included in appropriate years; those deep in the rear are under 'Bases'.

Area	Cemeteries	Graves	Identified (%)	Unidentified (%)
1915–16	135	110,752	65,245 (58·9)	45,507 (41·1)
1917–18	102	36,304	28,422 (78·3)	7,882 (21·7)
Bases	6	6,387	6,367 (99·7)	20 (0·3)
Totals	243	153,443	100,034 (65·2)	53,409 (34·8)

The largest cemeteries are all in the 1916 area; fourteen cemeteries there contain more graves than the largest 1918 cemetery which is Villers-Bretonneux Military Cemetery with 2,143 graves. The cemeteries contain the graves of twenty-four men who won the Victoria Cross, sixteen of them from 1916.

British Missing, 1914–18

Approximately 106,973 British soldiers died on the Somme and have no known grave. That figure is reached by taking the number of names on the Thiepval Memorial and the New Zealand Memorial at Caterpillar Valley Cemetery, which are all Somme deaths, then adding estimated proportions from seven other memorials which are devoted to Empire countries or to the 1918 campaigns, none of which is confined to the Somme. A figure of 1,000 has also been estimated for the memorial headstones in cemeteries commemorating men whose graves in nearby cemeteries were later destroyed by shell fire, etc. It is accepted that the figure of 106,973 is not entirely accurate, but the reliable figure of 73,279 from the Thiepval and Caterpillar Valley Memorials gives it a sound start.

That missing figure, taken with the number of identified graves in cemeteries and using the dates of death recorded in registers, opens the way to three further interesting calculations: the total number of British dead on the Somme in 1914–18; the allocation of that number between various battles and 'quiet' periods; and the number of 'lost' bodies on the Somme, that is, men whose bodies were never found, even as unidentifiable.

British Dead, 1914–18

The total number of dead is easy to establish; the addition of identified graves in cemeteries and the names of the missing produces a figure of 207,007. It is a reflection of how much the Somme dominated British actions in the First World War that the number of men who died there was 39 per cent of the 530,879 killed in all parts of France and was nearly 30 per cent of all British casualties on the whole of the Western Front. The numbers who died as a result of the fighting on the Somme must have been even greater, because none of the main base hospitals were in the Somme *département*. The Somme 'died of wounds' at base hospitals and at hospitals in the United Kingdom may well have numbered a further 15,000 to 20,000. But the Somme deaths do not quite come up to the numbers who died around Ypres, where approximately 250,000 British died, though over a nine-month-longer period of the war.

British Dead by Periods, 1914–18

The allocation of the Somme deaths to different periods of the war has been achieved by sampling pages from every cemetery and memorial register and studying the dates of death. Again, it is accepted that the results cannot be perfect but they should be sufficiently accurate to provide reasonable conclusions. An estimated 500 of the men buried on the Somme died before British troops took over trenches on the Somme in 1915 or after fighting ended there in 1918. That leaves 206,507 deaths in 1,168 days from 20 July 1915 to 29 September 1918, the day on which the last Germans were driven out of the Somme; the average number of deaths was 177 per day during that time. The period can be split up into six phases.

Period	Deaths	Deaths per day	Identified (%)		Missing (%)	
Trench holding, 20.7.15–30.6.16	5,314	15	5,026	(94·6)	288	(5·4)
The 1916 battle, 1.7.16–20.11.16	127,751	893	49,220	(38·5)	78,531	(61·5)
Winter, German retirement and trench holding, 21.11.16–20.3.18	16,766	35	11,176	(66·7)	5,590	(33·3)
The German offensive, 21.3.18–30.4.18	25,104	612	11,404	(45·4)	13,700	(54·6)
Trench holding and minor operations, 1.5.18–7.8.18	6,532	66	4,308	(66·0)	2,224	(34·0)
The Allied offensive, 8.8.18–29.9.18	25,040	472	18,400	(73·5)	6,640	(26·5)
Totals	206,507	177	99,534		106,973	

89 A post-war British search team. The soldier on the right has a VC medal ribbon and it is believed the young officer next to him is also a VC holder. It is possible that this may be a special party recovering one of the bodies from which the Unknown Soldier in Westminster Abbey was chosen.

The high proportion of missing in the 1916 battle was a result of the pulverized nature of the battlefield in that year, and the high proportion for the German offensive in 1918 reflects the way an advancing army disposes of the bodies of the enemy without taking too much care over identification.

Lost British Bodies, 1914–18

The known figures of identified and unidentified bodies buried in graves in British cemeteries, together with the names of men recorded as being missing, lead to the calculation of how many of the missing lie in 'unknown soldier' graves and how many bodies were never recovered, either because they were shattered or because they were buried so deep in unmarked graves that they have never been found. The figures show that almost exactly half of the 'missing' do have graves in war cemeteries but that half are still lost.

53,409 – Buried in 'unknown soldier' graves
53,564 – Lost bodies

In simple terms, the bodies of more than a quarter of the British soldiers who died on the Somme still lie under those fields, either shattered or deep buried or lost in other ways.

Other Nationalities, 1914–18

The numbers of men buried in French and German cemeteries on the Somme, whether in identified or unidentified graves, are known, so some comparisons can be made with the British figures. If the numbers of lost bodies are in the same proportion as the British, then the following combined figures can be given:

	British	French	German
Graves	153,443	66,828	88,705
Lost bodies	53,564	23,330	30,967
Total dead	207,007	90,158	119,672

These figures are less accurate than earlier ones because of the assumption made that French and German lost bodies were in the same proportion to British figures. The German total of lost bodies is probably underestimated; they had been on the retreating side in two of the three main battles and they were forced to rely on the victorious Allies in the post-war search for bodies. But the figures still show two things – how costly the Somme was for the British Empire and how expensive the offensive battles waged by the British and French were compared to the mainly defensive actions fought by the Germans.

Of other nationalities, the American cemetery at Bony has 1,844 graves and a memorial to 333 missing. Although the cemetery is just beyond the Somme boundary, most of these American bodies had been transferred from Somme cemeteries. There are also thirty-five Belgian soldiers' graves on the Somme and those of a handful of Russians who were fighting on the Allied side.

90 A War Graves Commission mason re-engraving a headstone; the Commission's charter charges it to maintain the cemeteries in perpetuity.

The Second World War

The figures for the men of various nationalities buried in the Somme are known but for various reasons they do not accurately reflect the different campaigns as well as the First World War figures do. The French and British burials are local ones, but many of the German dead in their one cemetery at Bourdon came from the Pas-de-Calais and Nord *départements*, and all American Second World War bodies on the Somme were reburied elsewhere. With these major reservations, the following figures can be given:

22,213 – German graves
2,482 – French graves
1,494 – British graves

No assumptions are made about lost bodies; the numbers are unlikely to be high. Most of the German and French dead were from the 1940 campaign. The Somme authorities were unable to give details of French deaths from Resistance activities or from bombing or deportation to Germany; the combined numbers may perhaps have been an additional 1,000 French deaths. The British dead can be subdivided as follows:

1939–40 – 650 soldiers, 70 airmen.
1941–4 – 662 airmen.
Liberation, August and September 1944 – 88 soldiers.
Washed ashore from naval actions and the Dieppe Raid – 16 sailors, 8 soldiers.

Total Somme Dead

It is possible now to give the estimated total dead – whether buried in cemeteries or lost bodies – of the two world wars on the Somme. (The French figures include an estimated 1,000 civilian deaths in each war and the total for 'Others' includes the Americans buried or recorded as missing at Bony Cemetery.)

	1914–18	1939–45	Total (%)	
British	207,007	1,494	208,501	(46·7)
German	119,672	22,213	141,885	(31·8)
French	90,158	3,482	93,640	(21·0)
Others	2,200	100	2,300	(0·5)
Totals	419,037	27,289	446,326	(100·0)

With the German lost bodies of the First World War probably having been underestimated here, this means that nearly half a million human beings were killed or died of wounds, gassing, illness or privation during the two world wars in that one *département* of France which is only as large as my home county of Lincolnshire, and that the British were the greatest sufferers.

Acknowledgements

As usual, the generous and willing help of many people and organizations has helped produce this book and we would like to express our heartfelt thanks to all of them. Pride of place must go to Chris Everitt of Eton Wick, Windsor, a friend and colleague of many years, who has carried out more than 100 researches at the Public Record Office. Close behind come the Wall family from Harpenden – George, June and Steve – who produced some of the cemetery visiting reports and Trevor Tasker of Swansea for generously allowing the use of some of his aerial photographs. The following all helped in lesser but significant ways; naming them in alphabetical order allows us to thank them all equally: Tony Batten, Richard Bone, Phil Brooks, Margaret Brough, Frank Bryan, Danny and Mark Connelly, Ted Coote, Terry Cork, K. Dunn, H. H. Fovargue, Norman Franks, Peter Gilhooley, Geoff Goodyear, David Haller, Anne Hardy, Trevor Harvey, John Hayward, Jimmy Hill, Mike Hodgson, David Holland, Brian Huggett, Colin Kilgour, Rosalie McFerran, Patrick Mahoney, Christopher Marsden-Smedley, Malcolm Penny, Fred Perrin, Cliff Pettit, Jonathon Raper, Paul Reed, Ernie Shillock, Alan Stansfield, Ray Sturtivant, R. F. Suffield, John Tamplin, Emma Tennant, Major-General David Tyacke and Stephen Watson.

The staff of the Commonwealth War Graves Commission could not have been more helpful, lending cemetery registers and providing answers to 120 research questions; so, many thanks to Roger Dalley, Bernard McGee, Andrew Turnbull, Peter Staff and all others who helped. Members of other organizations to whom we are very grateful are Anne Bell (our daughter) of the Fleet Air Arm Museum, Mrs P. A. Bozdan of the House of Commons Public Information Office, Wendy Chandley of Tameside Archive Service, Gordon Davidson of the Western Front Association, J. M. Hamill, Freemasons' Librarian and Curator, Tom Hodgson, Collections Assistant of Canterbury City Council, Eric Munday of the Air Historical Branch

(MOD), Helen Pugh of the British Red Cross Archives Section, B. Stephenson of Bedford Central Library, Tony Woodhouse, Historian of the Yorkshire County Cricket Club, and the staff of Boston Library.

We are also fortunate in having been able to draw upon the records held by various regimental historians and would like to thank the following: Border Regiment, Duke of Cornwall's Light Infantry, King's Regiment, Queen's Regiment, Royal Army Medical Corps, Royal Artillery, Royal Engineers, Royal Highland Fusiliers, Royal Irish Rangers, Royal Tank Regiment, Staffordshire Regiment, West Yorkshire Regiment, Worcestershire and Sherwood Foresters Regiment.

We have made some good friends in France during our research tours. Our base was the Hôtel de la Basilique at Albert where not only did Claude and Danielle Petit look after us consistently well but Claude wrote letters to any *commune* in France for which we had questions. Also deserving of mention is the chef, Jean-Marie Serpette, not only for his personal attention to our meals but, as an old soldier, for his explanations of the meanings of rank and unit abbreviations on French military memorials. Other helpful people in France were René Cretel of Albert, Jean-Michel Declerc of Ligny-Thilloy, Tom and Janet Fairgrieve of Delville Wood, Arthur Leach of Hamel, Yves and Yola – Count and Countess – d'Alcantara of Querrieu, Mark Weightman of Villers-Bretonneux and, further afield, Henri de Wailly of Paris who is an expert on the 1940 campaigns around Abbeville. We also wish to thank for their help Anne-Marie Goales of the Comité Départmental du Tourisme de la Somme at Amiens, Jacques R. Adelée of the French office of the American Battle Monuments Commission – as well as Colonel Bill Ryan, an old friend at the Commission's headquarters in Washington – and the staffs of the Directorate of History of the Canadian National Defence Headquarters in Ottawa and the Australian National Memorial at Canberra.

The verse from Vera Brittain's poem 'Perhaps' on page 232 is included with the permission of Paul Berry, her literary executor.

Finally, we would like to thank and congratulate our new typist, Margaret Gardner, for producing two drafts of the typescript with much diligence and skill.

Bibliography

BATTLE OF CRÉCY

Barber, Richard, *Edward Prince of Wales and Aquitaine* (London: Allen Lane, 1978).

FIRST WORLD WAR

Official Histories of the War: *Military Operations, France and Belgium*, particularly Vols. I and II of 1916 and I, II and IV of 1918, ed. Brigadier-General Sir J. E. Edmonds (London: HMSO, 1922–48).

The Private Papers of Douglas Haig, 1914–1919, ed. Robert Blake (London: Eyre & Spottiswoode, 1952).

Siegfried Sassoon's Diaries, 1915–1918, ed. Rupert Hart-Davis (London: Faber, 1983).

Blunden, Edmond, *Undertones of War* (London: Cobden-Sanderson, 1928; Four Square Books, 1962).

Chapman, Guy, *A Passionate Prodigality* (London: Nicholson & Watson, 1933; Buchan & Enright, 1985).

Eberle, V. F., *My Sapper Venture* (London: Pitman, 1973).

Gladden, Norman, *The Somme 1916* (London: Kimber, 1974).

Graves, Robert, *Goodbye to All That* (London: Cape, 1929; Harmondsworth: Penguin, 1960).

Hughes, Colin, *Mametz: Lloyd George's 'Welsh Army' at the Battle of the Somme* (Gerrards Cross: Orion Press, 1979).

Mackenzie, Jeanne, *The Children of the Souls* (London: Chatto & Windus, 1986).

Middlebrook, Martin, *The First Day on the Somme* (London: Allen Lane, 1971: Penguin, 1984).

Middlebrook, Martin, *The Kaiser's Battle* (London: Allen Lane, 1978; Penguin, 1983).

Norman, Terry, *The Hell They Called High Wood* (London: Kimber, 1984).

Oldfield, Paul, and Gibson, Ralph, *Sheffield City Battalion* (Barnsley: Wharncliffe, 1988).

Putkowski, Julian, and Sykes, Julian, *Shot at Dawn* (Barnsley: Wharncliffe, 1989).

Rogerson, Sidney, *Twelve Days* (London: Arthur Barker, 1930; Norwich: Gliddon Books, 1988).

SECOND WORLD WAR

Histories of the Second World War: *The War in France and Flanders 1939–1940* Vol. I, and *Victory in the West*, Vol. II, ed. Major L. F. Ellis (London: HMSO, 1953 and 1968).

Coillot, André, *Quatre Longues Années d'Occupation* (Arras: published privately, 1985).

Fishman, Jack, *And the Walls Came Tumbling Down* (London: Souvenir, 1982); an account of the Amiens Prison Raid.

Middlebrook, Martin, and Everitt, Chris, *The Bomber Command War Diaries* (London: Viking, 1985; Penguin, 1990).

Several editions of *After the Battle* magazine, for details of V-weapon and gun-battery sites in the Pas-de-Calais.

WAR GRAVES

Gibson, T. A. Edwin, and Ward, G. Kingsley, *Courage Remembered* (London: HMSO, 1989).

Longworth, Philip, *The Unending Vigil* (London: Constable, 1967; Leo Cooper, 1985).

Organized Battlefield Tours

Martin Middlebrook runs a small organization that takes parties of visitors to the First World War battlefields, different tours covering the whole length of the Western Front from the Belgian Coast to Verdun. Every two or three years a tour also visits Normandy to cover the 1944 invasion beaches.

The tour parties are kept small – between 20 and 30 people only – in order not to become unwieldy and to allow a more personal service to be provided. Travel is by a small Mercedes coach starting from Boston, Lincolnshire, which allows people from the north to stay overnight in Boston at reasonable expense; there are other pick-up points on the way to the Channel ports. Tours last from four to six days and are 'non-smoking' (people are expected not to smoke while in the company of other members of the group).

Further details can be obtained from:

> Middlebrook-Hodgson Battlefield Tours
> Lancaster Farm
> Tumby Woodside
> Lincoln
> PE22 7SP

Hotel Lists for Private Travellers

Lists of all the hotels in the Somme Département may be obtained from:

> Comité Départemental Du Tourisme,
> 21 rue E. Cauvin,
> 8000 Amiens,
> France.

Index

PART 1 – GENERAL

Adenauer, Konrad   341
'Advance to Victory', the   6, 252, 288
Aiken, Alex   171
Albert Medal graves   18, 209, 246
American cemeteries
  policy on   20–21
  Normandy American Cem.   21
  Somme American Cem.   4, 20, 259–60, 282, 356–7
  Suresnes American Cem.   286
American National Memorials
  Bellicourt   259
  Cantigny   286
Amiens Prison Raid   219, 239, 321–2, 335
Armistice, the   22, 64, 216
Arras, Battle of   1, 46, 248
Asquith, Herbert   183–4
Australian memorials   128–9, 261, 267, 295–7, 316

Belgian graves   30, 319, 356
Black Watch, 1st Bn   170; 1st/6th Bn
Bohemia, King of, (Jean de Luxembourg)   343–5
Bonaparte, Napoleon   33, 35, 281
British cemeteries, policy on and types of   8–18, 53
British Red Cross   30, 337
Brittain, Vera   231–2

Cambrai, Battle of   248, 253, 256, 265
Cameron Highlanders, 1st Bn   170, 312
'Canadian' cemeteries   9, 10, 14, 32, 292, 298, 304

Canadian memorials   46, 175, 303
Casualties   52–3, 59, 69, 76, 81, 118, 128, 133, 155, 160, 165, 175, 350–58
Channel gun batteries   31
Channel Tunnel   4, 31, 326
Churchill, Winston   8
Commonwealth War Graves Commission
  maps   4
  early policy and work   8–21, 87, 92, 127, 218, 232, 313, 349
  French H.Q.   47
  gardeners   25, 53, 80, 121
  its memorials   112, 316
  private graves, treatment of   135, 187–8, 192
  records   319
  subsequent work   95, 358
Crusades memorial   344
Czechoslovak graves   32

Danish graves   348
Demarcation stones   22–3, 67, 211, 220–21, 294
Derby, Lord   149
Dickens, Charles   187
Dieppe Raid   31, 348–9, 357
Dover Patrol   31
Dunning, Richard   124

Edward III   30, 343–4

Fouchat, Christianne and Yves   129–30
Franco–Prussian War   5, 240, 265, 267, 275, 286, 293, 320–21

French military cemeteries, policy on 18–19

Gallipoli Campaign 68, 81, 88, 96, 129, 238, 297, 315
George VI 297
George Cross graves 15, 17–18, 33, 209
German cemeteries, policy on 19–20
German memorial 79
Godbert's restaurant 316

Harold II and Battle of Hastings 348
Henry V 39, 53, 216, 234, 273, 320
Hindenburg Line 6, 52, 248, 250–51, 253, 257, 259, 262, 289
Hugo, Victor 190

Imperial War Graves Commission, see Commonwealth War Graves Commission

Jewish graves 14, 17, 21, 141, 211
Joan of Arc 138, 348
Julius Caesar 4, 167
Jutland, Battle of 232

Kilner, Roy 77
Kipling, Rudyard 13, 15
Kitchener, Lord 7, 159
Kitchener's New Army 1, 93, 102, 194

Lauder, Sir Harry 121
Leach, Ben 80
Le Cateau, Battle of 37, 48
Liberation 1944 4, 7, 22, 53, 233, 266, 292, 295, 311, 323, 336, 357
Lloyd George, David 159, 249
'Lost' bodies 355
Lutyens, Sir Edwin 112

Maginot Line 211
Maps, advice on 4–5
Marne, Battle of 48
Memorials to the Missing, policy on 21–2

Mons, Battle of and retreat from 1, 272, 318
Murat, Marshal J. 281
Musée de Picardie 318

Neuve Chapelle, Battle of 42
New Zealand graves policy 14
New Zealand memorials 166–9, 316, 352

Observation posts 63, 92, 96

Philippe, King of France (1346) 343
Polish forces 7, 336, 346
  airman 323–4
  graves 32
Portuguese graves 34, 36

Resistance 1940–45 7, 24, 39–40, 47, 53, 62, 117, 233, 277, 282, 292, 295, 318, 321, 325–6, 331, 337, 341, 344, 356
Rodin, Auguste 30
Russian graves 234, 298, 319, 346, 356

'Souls' families 36, 184
South African Memorial 167–8

Tallboy bombs 41–2, 44

Unknown Soldiers 43–4, 353

V-weapons 32, 41–2, 44–5, 345
Victoria Cross graves, policy on and totals of 15, 17–18, 223, 351, 353; individual references are too numerous to index

Wales, Henry, Prince of (1346) 343–5
Western Front Association 179
William the Conqueror 348
Williams, Shirley 232

Ypres, Battle of 202, 234, 248, 253, 257

PART 2 – PLACE NAMES

FRANCE

Note: If a place has multiple entries, its main one will be in **bold lettering**. If a cemetery has the same name as the local town or village then the cemetery may not have a separate index entry; if the full title of a cemetery cannot be found, look under the local place name. Abbreviations used are: British – Brit.; Cemetery – Cem.; Communal – Com.; Extension – Extn; French National – Fr. Nat.; German – Ger.; Military – Mil.

Abbeville   7, 27, 33, 52–3, 171, 326–7, 332, **335–40**
Acheux   229, 232–3
Achiet-le-Petit   61
Adanac Mil. Cem.   13, 176–8
Adelaide Cem.   295
Agincourt   29, **39**, 53, 134, 216, 234, 273
AIF Burial Ground   179, 195–6
Airaines   332–3
Aire Com. Cem.   29, 42
Aisne, *département*   5, 43
Albert   48, 52–3, 55, 93, 96, 105, 118, 134, 143, **216–22**, 234, 266, 289, 312, 316, 321
Albert Com. Cem. Extn   220–22
Albert Fr. Nat. Cem.   222
Allonville   317, 322
Amiens   7, 24, 27, 33, 48, 52, 171, 227, 250, 288–9, 312, **316–22**, 326–7, 340
Ancre Brit. Cem.   88
Ancre, River and Valley   11, 55, 68, 70, 88, 96, 99, **101**, 103, 240, 245, 345
Andechy Ger. Cem.   276–7
Ardres   28, 41

Armentières   190, 258
Arras   1, 27, 29, 39, 42–3, **46–7**, 53, 61, 80, 132, 202, 234
Artois   5
Assainvillers   285–6
Assevillers   199, 205
Aubigny   229, 247
Auchonvillers   71, 82, 95–6
Authuille   98, 101–3
Authuille Wood   105, 153, 226
Aveluy   98, 103–5
Aveluy Wood   100–103, 105, 143, 153, 218, 226
Azincourt, *see* Agincourt

Bagneux   311–12
Bailleulmont   47
Bapaume   27, 46, 192, 197
Bapaume Post Mil. Cem.   119, 216–17, 227
Bapaume Road, the   118–32, 134, 173, 175, 178, 226
Bavelincourt   229, 238
Bazentins, the villages and woods   144, 153–4, 157, 161–2, **163–4**, 227
Beacon Cem.   212
Beaucourt   68, 71, 88–9
Beaucourt-en-Santerre   291, 302–3
Beaufort-en-Santerre   291
Beaumont-Hamel   48, 68–9, 71, 80, **81–5**, 89, 91, 173, 196, 210, 230, 313
Beaumont-Hamel Brit. Cem.   82
Beauquesne   234, 311, 314
Beauraines   47
Beauval Com. Cem.   311, 313
Bécourt   48, 143, 220, 222–3
Bécourt Mil. Cem.   164
Bellicourt   255, 259
Belloy-en-Santerre   278–9

Belloy-St-Leonard 332–4
Bernafay Wood 137, **154–8**, 165, 227
Bertangles 317, 322–3
Berthaucourt 262
Bertrancourt 228
Béthencourt-sur-Somme Ger. Cem. 273
Béthune 29, 42
Beuvraignes Fr. Nat. Cem. 275–6
Biaches 199, 203–4
Blangy-Tronville 290, 292
Blériot-Plage 30
Blighty Valley Cem. 102–3, 120
Bois Français 142–4, 227
Bonnay 229, 245
Bony 255, 259–60, 356, 358
Bordeaux 217
Bouchavesnes 199, 203
Bouchoir 291, 305
Boufflers 345
Boulogne 4, 28, 32, **33–7**, 121, 218, 275
Boulogne Eastern Cem. 33, 36–7
Bourdon Ger. Cem. 329–31, 357
Bourlon Wood 253
Bouzencourt 229, 241
Bouzincourt 229, 234–6
Bouzincourt Ridge Cem. 104–5
Boves 317, 320
Bray Hill Brit. Cem. 208
Bray-sur-Somme 205–9, 299
Bray Vale Brit. Cem. 207
Breilly 327–9
Brie 270, 274
Bronfay Farm 206, 208
Buire 254, 265
Buire-sur-l'Ancre 229, 240
Bull's Road Cem. 194–5
Butte of Warlencourt 178, 299

Cachy 290, 293
Caffet (Caftet) Wood 136, 150
Cahon 338, 341
Caix 291, 303
Calais 4, **26–31**, 33, 37, 39, 41
Calais Canadian War Cem. 32

Calais Southern and Northern Cems. 30
Cambrai 202, 211
Cambron 338, 341
Camon 317, 319
Canal du Nord 253
Cantigny 285–6
Cap-Blanc-Nez 31
Cap-Griz-Nez 31
Carnoy 50, 137, 150–51
Carpeza Copse 255, 263
Casino Point 137, 150
Caterpillar Valley 157, 161
Caterpillar Valley Cem. 13, 155, 164–6, 353
Cayeux Mil. Cem. 291, 302
Cayeux-sur-Mer 348
Cerisy-Gailly 151, 206, 214–16
Cerisy-Gailly Fr. Nat. Cem. 9, 214–15
Chambéry 334
Champien 276–7
Chipilly 206, 213–14
Citadel New Cem. 143, 145
Cléry-sur-Somme 199–201, 203
Colincamps 92–3, 228–9
Combles 52, 173, 180–81, **188–90**, 199
Condé-Folie Fr. Nat. Cem. 329, 331
Connaught Cem. 109
Contalmaison 119, 125–7
Contay 229, 237
Corbie 53, 229, 243, 245–6
Corbie Com. Cem. and Extn 145n, 202, 246
Côte 80 Fr. Nat. Cem. 211
Courcelette 125, 127, **175–6**, 202, 237, 315
Courcelles-au-Bois 228–9
Crécy 326, 342–5
Croix-Moligneaux 270, 273
Crucifix Corner (Authuille) 103
Cruxifix Corner (Bazentin) 164, 170
Crucifix Corner Cem. (Villers-Bretonneux) 9, 298
Crouy 328–9
Culaincourt 270, 275

Damery   276–7
Dantzig Alley Cem.   144, 149
Daours   229, 243, 246
Dartmoor Cem.   224
'Death Valley'   161
Delville Wood   4, 144, 154–5, 157, **166–8**, 181, 194, 227
Delville Wood Cem.   12, 167
Démuin   290, 298
Dernancourt   208, 220, 224–7
Devonshire Cem.   145–8, 202
Dieppe   326, *see also* Dieppe Raid
Dive Copse Brit. Cem.   213
Doingt   254, 265
Domino Brit. Cem.   256
Dompierre-Becquincourt   199, 204, 211
Douai   53, 80
Doullens   43, 96, 241, **309–12**, 316
Dunkirk   7, 32–3, 327
Dury   317, 320–21

Eclusier Com. Cem.   210–11
Englebelmer   229, 231
Ennemain   270, 273–4
Epehy   255–8, 265
Eperlecques Bunker   41
Escalles   31
Estrées-Deniécourt   278–9
Étaples   28, 37–8
Eterpigny   270, 274
Etinehem   206, 211
Euston Road Cem.   92, 230

Faffémont (Falfemont) Farm   181, 188
Fargny   50, 199
Faubourg d'Amiens Brit. Cem.   47
Field of the Cloth of Gold   40–41
Fienvillers   311–13
Fillièvres   39
Fins   253–4
Five Points Cem.   253
Flatiron Copse Cem.   161–3
Flers   129, 169, 177, 179–81, **192–4**
Flesselles   317, 323

Foncquevillers   48, 55, **58–61**
Forceville   9, 229, 233–4
Foreste   270, 275
Foucaucourt   279–81
Fouilloy   229, 247
Fouquescourt   279, 282
Framzelle   31
Frankfurt Trench Brit. Cem.   90
Franvillers   229, 239
Fréchencourt   229, 238
Frémontiers   333, 335
Frévent   29, 44
Fricourt   11, 48–50, 52, 125, **134–44**, 153, 161, 173, 207, 227, 233, 244, 322
Fricourt Brit. Cem. (Bray Road)   134–5
Fricourt Ger. Cem.   141–2
Fricourt New Cem.   139–40, 142
Froissy   206, 211
Fromelles   296
Fruges   28, 39, 41

Gauche Wood   256, 265
Gavrelle   89n
Gentelles   290, 292–3
Gézaincourt   311
Ginchy   155, 179–81, 186, **191–2**
Givenchy   24, 36
Glory Hole, the   122, 221
Gommecourt   4, **58–67** *passim*, 74, 187, 228, 351
Gommecourt Brit. Cem. No. 2   65
Gommecourt Wood New Cem.   61–2
Gordon Cem.   148–9
Gordon Dump Cem.   125, 227
Grandcourt   96, 108, 116–17
Grandcourt Road Cem.   115–16
Grandstand, the   226–7
Grivesnes   285, 287
Grove Town Cem.   207
Guards Cem. (Combles)   188
Guards Cem. (Lesboeufs)   191–2
Gueudecourt   180–81, 192, **194–6**, 222
Guillemont   24, 48, 52, 155, 162, **179–87**

Guillemont Road Cem.   180–84
Guines   28, 41

Ham   269–72, 287
Hamel   71, 87, **97–100**, 106
Hancourt   254, 262
Hangard   290, 298–9
Hangard Wood Brit. Cem.   299
Happy Valley (official)   208
   (unofficial)   161
Harbonnières   291
Hardecourt   189–200
Hargicourt   255, 259–60
Harponville   229, 234
Hattencourt Fr. Nat. Cem.   279, 283
Hawthorn Ridge   81–2, 87
Heath Cem.   307
Hébuterne   50, **58–67** *passim*, 92,
   231, 264n
Hédauville   229, 234–5
Heilly   229, 243–5
Hem Com. Cem.   311
Hem-Monacu   199, 201
Hénencourt   229, 236
Herbécourt   199, 204
Hesbécourt   255, 262–3
Hesdin   38
Heudicourt   253, 255
High Wood   10, 97, 144, 154–5, 157,
   164–5, **169–72**, 175, 179, 246
Hillside Cem.   303
Holnon Wood   262
Hourges Orchard Cem.   299
Huby-St Leu Brit. Cem.   39
Hunter's Cem.   87
Hupy   338, 341

Jacob's Ladder   106
Jeancourt   255, 262

Kern Redoubt   62
Knightsbridge Cem.   96

La Boisselle   23, 48, 51, 118–20, **122–
   5**, 153, 173, 178, 215, 221, 227,
   236, 240, 244, 274, 302, 314

La Chapelette Brit. and Indian
   Cems.   267
Lambercourt   338, 340
La Neuville   243
Laon   277
Laviéville   229, 236
Le Boisle   345
Le Crotoy   345–6
Leforest   199–201
Le Hamel   229, 241, 291
Le Havre   326
Leipzig Salient   107, 113–15, 235–6
Lempire Com. Cem.   259
Le Petit St Jean   317, 321
Le Quesnel   291, 303
Le Quesnoy   214
Le Sars   173–4, 177–8
Les Barraques Mil. Cem.   30–31
Lesboeufs   180–81, 188, 191–4
Le Transloy   181
Le Tréport   346, 349
Leuze Wood   181, 187
Lihons   278–81
Lillers   29, 42
Liomer   333–4
Lochnagar Crater   5, 123–5, 215, 227
London Cem. and Extn   9, 171–2
Longeau   317, 320
Longpré-les-Corps-Saints   329, 331–2
Longuenesse Souvenir Cem.   41–2
Longueval and the Ridge   144, 149,
   154–7, 165, **166–9**, 246
Lonsdale Cem.   114–15
Loop, the   208
Loos   43
Louvencourt   9, 229, 231–2
Luke Copse Brit. Cem.   10, 72, 74

Mailly-Maillet   229–31
Maissemy Ger. Cem.   262
Malakoff Farm   255, 259
Malassise Farm   255, 258
Maltzkorn (Maltzhorn) Farm   180, 182
Mametz   11, 48–9, 52, 136, **144–9**,
   189, 227, 244, 246
Mametz Wood   144, 149, 153–4,
   157, **159–63**, 212, 221, 227

Manicourt Ger. Cem. 279, 283
Manitoba Cem. 304–5
Mansel Copse 145, 202
Marcelcave Buttes Fr. Nat. Cem. 291, 298
Mareuil 339, 341
Maricourt 52, 137, **151**, 198–9, 206–7, 216
Martinpuich 4, **173–5**, 177, 179, 351
Martinsart 50, 98, 105–6
Marquise 28, 33
Mash Valley 119–21, 123, 128, 236, 274
Maucourt Fr. Nat. Cem. 279, 282
Maurepas 199–201
Méaulte 143–4, 218–20, 224
Meath Cem. 258
Meerut Mil. Cem. 36
Méharicourt 279, 281–2
Mers-les-Bains 349
Mesnil 96, 98, 106–7
Mesnil Ridge Cem. 96
Mézières 290, 302
Millencourt 229, 236
Mill Road Cem. 109, 111
Mimoyecques V-3 site 32–3
Minden Post 136, 150
Miraument 77
Moislains New Cem. 254, 268
Montauban and the Ridge 48, 52, 137, 144, 149, **152–3**, 156–8, 165, 189, 197, 227, 244, 246
Montdidier 214, 284–7
Montigny 229, 238, 314
Montreuil 28, 37–8
Monts de Caubert 341
Mont St Quentin 201, 267
Moreuil 290, 300–301
Morisel 300
Morlancourt 206, **212**, 226, 240–41
Morval 4, 173, 180–81, **193**
Mouquet Farm 102, 107–8, **115**, 128, 176, 226, 315

Nab Valley 119–20
Namps-au-Val 335

Naours 317, 323–4
Néry 43, 188
Nesle 270, 272–3, 287
Neuville St Vaast Ger. Cem. 47
Newfoundland Park 82–5, 96–7, 196
New Munich Trench Brit. Cem. 90
Noeux-lès-Auxi 40
Nord *département* 258, 330, 356
Norfolk Cem. 223
Normandy 10, 39, 44, 53, 276, 320, 326
Notre Dame de Lorette Fr. Nat. Cem. 46
Noyelles-sur-Mer Chinese Cem. 346–8

Oise *département* 5
Omaha Beach 21
Ovillers 35, 103, **119–23**, 128, 153, 226, 236
Owl Trench Cem. 66

Pargny 270, 273
Paris 44, 48, 269, 327
Pas-de-Calais 4, 27, 32, 38, 55, 197, 330, 356
Peake Wood Cem. 119, 127
Pernes 29, 43
Pernois 311, 313–14
Péronne 52, 134, 199, 203, 254, **265–7**, 273, 289
Péronne Road, the **134–53**, 198, 218, 222
Péronne Road Cem. 151, 216
Picardy 5, 39, 217
Picquigny 328–9
Pigeon Ravine Cem. 256–7, 349
Pihen-les-Guines 32
Pithon 270–71
Point-du-Jour Mil. Cem. 202
Point 110 Old and New Mil. Cems 144
Poix-de-Picardie 333–5
Pont-de-Metz 317, 321
Pont-Noyelles 229, 240
Pontru 255
Pozières 115, 119, 125, **128–33**, 176, 226, 315
Pozières Memorial 130–33, 294n

Proyart   291, 306–307
Puchevillers   311, 314–15
Puisieux   25, 67, 92

Quarry Cem.   154, 156
Queen's Cem.   74
Querrieu   229, 239

Railway Hollow Cem.   75
Rancourt   190, 199, 201–3
Redan Ridge   76, 80
Regina Trench Cem.   176–7
Rennes   305
Ribemont   229, 240
Rivery   317, 321
Rocquigny-Equancourt   Road   Brit.
   Cem.   253
Roisel   255, 263
Ronssoy   255, 259
Rosières-en-Santerre   291, 296, 306
Rossignol Wood   65–6
Rouen   138, 227
Roye   275–7, 284
Rubescourt   285–6

Sailly-Saillisel   203
St   Acheul   Fr.   Nat.   Cem.,   Amiens
   318–19
St Charles-de-Percy Mil. Cem.   10
Ste Emilie Valley Cem.   255, 263–4
St Étienne-au-Mont   37
St Hilaire Cem. and Extn   44
St Mard   276–7
St Nicolas   38
St Omer   29, 38, 41–2
St Pierre Cem., Amiens   322
St Pierre Division   108
St Pol   29, 42–4
St Quentin   107, 132
St Riquier   339, 341
St Valery-en-Caux   336, 348
St Valery-sur-Somme   345–6, 348
Santerre, the   277–87, 306
Saulcourt   255, 265
Sausage Valley   124
Schwaben   Redoubt   88, 96, 107–9,
   111

2nd Canadian Cem.   127
Seine Maritime *département*   349
Senlies   229, 234
Serre   4, 10, 48, 68–71, **76,** 79, 91,
   351
Serre   Road,   the   22, 53, 70, **75–80,**
   165, 273
Serre Road Cem. No. 1   76
Serre Road Cem. No. 2   9, 75, **79–80,**
   126, 171
Serre Road Cem. No. 3   75
Sheffield Memorial Park   70–74
Siracourt V-1 site   44–5
Stump Road Cem.   116–17
Sucrerie Mil. Cem.   93–5, 230
Sunken Road Cem.   127
Suzanne   206, 210

Tailly   332–4
Tambour, the   138–9, 143
Tank Memorial   129
Tara Hill and Redoubt   105, 120, 124,
   226
Templeux-le-Guérard   255, 260–61
Ten Tree Alley Cem.   91–2
Terlincthun   10, 33–5, 121
Thiepval   6, 48, 102, **107–14,** 117,
   153, 165, 196, 208, 210, 212,
   215–16, 227, 235, 302, 314–15
Thiepval   Anglo-French   Cem.   9, 18,
   113
Thiepval   Memorial   9, 18, 51, 74,
   105, **111–14,** 143, 187, 195, 226,
   353
Thistle Dump Cem.   164
Tincourt   254, 256, 265
Toronto Cem.   298
Touvent Farm   70, 74, 77, 92
Trefcon   270, 275
Treux   229, 241
Triangle Point   152–6
Trinket Post   263
Trônes Wood   154–7, 165, 227
Tyneside   Scottish   and   Irish   Mem-
   orial   122

Ulster Tower   107–10, 226

Usna Hill and Redoubt 105, 120, 124, 226

Vadancourt 255, 262
Varennes 229, 233
Vauchelles 231–2
Vaux-en-Amiénois 317, 324–5
VC Corner Cem. 296
Verdun 1, 44, 51, 170, 198, 204
Vermandovillers Ger. Cem. 279–80, 330
Vert Galand Farm 314
Vignacourt 317, 324
Villeret 255, 261
Villers-Bocage 317, 323
Villers-Bretonneux 9, 11, **288–99**, 308, 314, 352
Villers-Bretonneux Mil. Cem. and Australian Memorial 18, 295–8
Villers-Carbonnel Fr. Nat. Cem. 270, 274
Villers-Faucon 255, 264
Ville-sur-Ancre 206, 211
Vimy Ridge 44, 202, 292
Vis-en-Artois Memorial 292
Vrély 291, 306

Waggon Road Cem. 91
Warlencourt 12, **178–9**, 196, 351
Warloy-Baillon 229, 236
Warvillers 291, 306
Waterlot Farm 155, 165–6, 168
Watten V-2 site 28, 41
Wavans 39–40
Willow Stream 161
Wimereux 28, 33–4
Wizernes V-2 site 29, 42
Wood Cem. 302

'Y' Ravine Cem. 86
'Y' Sap 119, 121, 124, 174

AUSTRALIA

Adelaide 315

Canberra 128, 297

Melbourne 294

New South Wales 204, 245, 266, 293

Robinvale 294

South Australia 315

Victoria 43, 201, 294, 308

Western Australia 296, 308

BELGIUM

Adegem Canadian Cem. 10

Brandhoek New Brit. Cem. 185n
Brussels 53, 246

Cement House Cem. 10

Essex Farm Cem. 33

Gheluvelt 257

Hill 60 162

Langemarck 10

Menin Gate 83, 296
Messines 123, 312

Plugsteert Wood 232
Poperinge 1, 185n
Prowse Point Cem. 232

Sanctuary Wood 1

Tyne Cot Cem. 202

Ypres and the Salient 1, 36–7, 43, 55, 83, 185, 202, 232, 233, 296, 337, 353
Ypres Reservoir Cem. 140

CANADA

Alberta 216

Manitoba 178, 283, 298, 300, 304

New Brunswick 302–3
Newfoundland 299, *see also* Newfoundland Park

Nova Scotia   299

Ontario   176, 298, 302, 313

Quebec   296, 298–9, 302, 306

Saskatchewan   303

Toronto   82

GERMANY

Berlin   322

Hamburg   39

Kassel   19n

Neuengamme   39

Wiesbaden   322

UNITED KINGDOM

Accrington   70, 74–5

Banbury   49
Barnsley   71, 228–9
Battle   135
Belfast   106, 108, 113, 116, 208
Biggin Hill   32
Birmingham   76, 217–18
Blackburn   266
Boston   196
Bradford   66, 71, 75, 77, 93
Bristol   167, 264

Cambridge   123, 304
Cardiff   162
Carmarthen   162
Carnarvon   149
Chorley   75
Culloden   171

Derby   60
Down   105
Dudley   49
Dundee   245
Durham   71, 179

Ealing   162

Edinburgh   167, 235, 244
Evesham   64

Folkestone   212

Glasgow   90, 114–15, 167
Grimsby   123, 261

Hampstead   188

Kensington   187
Kirkcaldy   236
Kirton   196

Leeds   71, 75–7, 92
Liverpool   149, 151–2
London   32, 167, 328

Maidstone   152
Manchester   1, 131, 151–2, 263
Matlock   185

Newcastle   113

Portsmouth   188, 194

Salford   90, 110–11, 212
Sheffield   71, 74–6, 93–4
Southend   96
Stoke Bishop   264
Swansea   150
Swanton Morley   340

Ulverston   223

Winchester   81, 145, 231
Wolverhampton   62

UNITED STATES

Brooklyn   245

Harvard   278
Hawaii   323

New York   278

Providence, RI   282

San Francisco   224
South Carolina   177

Tulsa   282

PART 3 – MILITARY UNITS

AUSTRALIAN (1914–18)

General references 103, 115, 119, 125, 128–30, 164–5, 176, 194–6, 201, 211–15 *passim*, 234–47 *passim*, 259–74 *passim*, 288–308 *passim*, 315, 324, 328, 331, 342
Australian Corps 214, 288, 292, 307

DIVISIONS
1st, 128, 131; 2nd, 128, 266–8; 3rd, 240–41; 4th, 128, 261; 5th, 294, 307

BRIGADES
8th, 307; 9th, 293; 13th, 294

BATTALIONS
8th, 308; 10th, 315; 13th, 245; 18th, 293; 23rd, 201; 24th, 296; 28th, 296, 308; 46th, 236; 54th, 266; 55th, 204; 58th, 43
Engineers 245
Machine Gun Corps 130
Ordnance Corps 319

BRITISH (1914–18)

British Expeditionary Force and GHQ 6, 31, 38, 41, 151, 318, 347

ARMIES
Third 47–8, 50–51, 58, 113, 131–2, 249, 252, 312
Fourth 50, 69, 113, 151, 239, 242, 288–9, 312
Fifth 69, 131–3, 249, 272, 288, 293, 320

Reserve (Gough's Mobile) 51, 226, 239

CORPS
II 233–4, 319
V 70, 76–90 *passim*
VIII 68–9
X 97, 102
XIV 208

DIVISIONS
Guards 145, 191, 203
Royal Naval, *see* 63rd
2nd 80, 167
3rd 156–7, 164, 167
4th 48, 67, 76, 80–81, 96, 230
5th 48–50, 166–7, 193, 210, 213, 223–4, 313
6th 187, 193
7th 143, 145, 148–9, 157, 162, 169, 224
8th 102, 118, 120, 122, 128, 236, 273–4, 294, 308
9th (Scottish) 156–7, 164, 166–7, 252, 299
11th (Northern) 115
12th (Eastern) 104, 120, 122, 212, 217, 226, 234, 239, 256, 258, 289
14th (Light) 132, 167, 293–4
15th (Scottish) 173–4
16th (Irish) 182, 186, 191, 252, 256, 263
17th (Northern) 135, 138, 167, 196, 234, 244, 313
18th (Eastern) 49–50, 104, 107–17 *passim*, 149, 152, 157–8, 189, 212, 217, 222–3, 227, 239, 246, 289, 293–4, 299
19th (Western) 116, 122–3
20th (Light) 187, 273

21st 125, 138, 140–3, 157, 162, 195, 223, 252
23rd 126, 178
24th 145, 252, 262
25th 114–15, 120
29th 68, 81, 83, 95, 313
30th 149, 151–2, 156, 158, 180, 197, 210, 246, 269
31st 68, 70, 74, 76, 92, 228
32nd 89, 91, 97, 107, 114, 235, 273, 305, 314
33rd 170–71, 253, 256–8
34th 23, 118–19, 123, 125, 160, 236–7, 240, 260–62, 302, 314
35th 211
36th (Ulster) 88, 96–7, 100, 106–11, 115–16, 196, 215–16, 227, 233, 302, 314–15
37th 160
38th (Welsh) 100, 104, 159–60, 162, 165, 193, 212, 234, 238, 313
39th 88, 97, 111, 237, 263, 267, 308, 328
41st 174, 194, 196
42nd (E. Lancs) 63, 95, 228, 264
46th (N. Midland) 58–60, 62, 65, 113
47th (London) 170–71, 174–5, 178, 203, 222, 236, 238
48th (S. Midland) 48, 58, 64, 68, 76, 92, 120, 178, 204, 210
49th (W. Riding) 97, 100, 107, 111, 315
50th (Northumbrian) 174, 178, 221, 261–2, 308
51st (Highland) 48–50, 69, 81, 85–6, 89–90, 123, 223, 230
56th (London) 58–9, 64–5, 113, 187–8
58th (London) 207–8, 213–14, 238, 289, 294
59th (N. Midland) 261–2
62nd (W. Riding) 92
63rd (R. Naval) 69, 86, 88–9, 99–100, 106, 231, 345–6
66th (E. Lancs) 252, 262–3, 266, 308

BRIGADES
11th 95
70th 102, 120
97th 90
102nd (Tyneside Scottish) 119
103rd (Tyneside Irish) 120, 124, 126

CAVALRY
1st Dragoons 36, 264
7th Dragoon Guards 169, 304
3rd Hussars 300
4th Hussars 233
11th Hussars 304
17th Lancers 304
18th Lancers 256
N. Somerset Yeomanry 303

INFANTRY
Argyll and Sutherland Highlanders 305; 1/7th Bn, 263; 8th Bn, 48, 82, 121
Bedfords 1st Bn, 48; 2nd Bn, 180; 4th Bn, 105; 7th Bn, 294
Black Watch 1/6th Bn, 86; 8th Bn, 167
Border 1st Bn, 87, 96; 2nd Bn, 162; 5th Bn, 150; 11th Bn, 90–92, 114, 236
Buffs (E. Kents) 132n, 237, 239; 1st Bn, 193; 6th Bn, 43; 7th Bn, 116
Cameron Highlanders 1st Bn, 312; 5th Bn, 166
Cheshires 9th Bn, 123; 10th Bn, 115; 13th Bn, 97
Coldstream Guards 1st Bn, 145; 2nd Bn, 192
Devons 8th Bn, 146–8, 162, 202, 224; 9th Bn, 145n, 146–8, 224
Dorsets 305; 1st Bn, 102, 174; 4th Bn, 195; 5th Bn, 115; 6th Bn, 196
Duke of Cornwall's Light Inf. 61; 1st Bn, 144, 182
Durham Light Inf. 76, 132, 179; 22nd Bn, 295
E. Lancs 2nd Bn, 197, 273; 11th Bn, 74, 230
E. Surreys 1st Bn, 162; 8th Bn, 150

E. Yorks   1, 150; 1/4th Bn, 262, 301; 6th Bn, 115; 7th Bn, 139, 196

Essex   76, 122; 1st Bn, 96; 2nd Bn, 48, 313; 10th Bn, 220

Gloucesters   1, 163; 1/5th Bn, 48, 50; 1/6th Bn, 264; 8th Bn, 122; 12th Bn, 166; 14th Bn, 264

Gordon Highlanders   262; 2nd Bn, 148; 1/7th Bn, 86

Green Howards   125; 7th Bn, 135; 8th Bn, 126; 9th Bn, 125–6; 10th Bn, 223

Grenadier Guards   191; 2nd Bn, 145, 191; 3rd Bn, 183, 191; 4th Bn, 183

Hampshires   1st Bn, 81, 95, 99; 15th Bn, 194

Highland Light Inf.   61; 1/9th Bn, 171; 12th Bn, 151; 16th Bn, 89–90; 17th Bn, 89–90, 114–15

Honourable Artillery Company   100

Inns of Court OTC   301

King's Liverpool   113, 149, 210; 1st Bn, 131; 1/8th Bn, 39; 1/10th Bn, 185; 12th Bn, 150; 17th Bn, 151, 269–71; 18th & 19th Bns, 269–71

King's Own Royal Lancasters   76; 1st Bn, 48; 7th Bn, 224

King's Own Scottish Borderers   2nd Bn, 193

King's Own Yorkshire Light Inf.   66, 261, 305; 2nd Bn, 50, 89, 92; 2/4th Bn, 348; 8th Bn, 102

King's Royal Rifle Corps   128; 1st Bn, 168; 2nd Bn, 192; 21st Bn, 196

Lancashire Fusiliers   305; 1st Bn, 82; 6th Bn, 260; 2/8th Bn, 259; 10th Bn, 230; 15th Bn, 110–11, 212; 16th Bn, 90–91, 111

Leicesters   265; 1/4th Bn, 61; 6th Bn, 195, 256; 7th & 8th Bns, 256

Lincolns   1; 8th Bn, 66; 10th Bn, 123, 261

Londons   113, 179, 203, 238, 245, 331; 1/2nd Bn, 188, 207; 2/4th Bn, 314; 9th Bn, 294; 1/13th Bn, 187

Loyal N. Lancs   163

Manchesters   1, 61, 113, 132, 156,

210, 261; 2nd Bn, 91, 190; 2/5th Bn, 259; 2/6th Bn, 263; 9th Bn, 259; 11th Bn, 115; 12th Bn, 127; 17th Bn, 152; 18th Bn, 47; 20th Bn, 143–4; 21st Bn, 144; 22nd Bn, 149; 24th Bn, 144

Middlesex   1st Bn, 162; 2nd Bn, 121, 205, 274; 1/8th Bn, 162; 16th Bn, 82, 87, 96

Naval Bns   Anson 100; Hood 89, 106; Nelson 100, 345

Norfolks   1st Bn, 48, 61, 223; 8th Bn, 150

Northamptons   190; 1st Bn, 164; 2nd Bn, 295; 6th Bn, 150

Northumberland Fusiliers   113, 140, 178n, 179, 324; 12th Bn, 162; 13th Bn, 224; 16th Bn, 113; 21st & 22nd Bns, 123

N. Staffords   62; 1/5th Bn, 62, 66; 1/6th Bn, 66

Notts and Derbys, see Sherwood Foresters

Oxford and Bucks Light Inf.   1/4th Bn, 48–50, 62

Queen's (Royal West Surreys)   132n; 2nd Bn, 149, 169; 7th Bn, 239

Queen Victoria's Rifles   65, 213, 328

Rifle Brigade   76, 132; 1st Bn, 96; 2nd Bn, 42, 201, 273; 3rd Bn, 185, 304; 8th Bn, 36

Royal Berks   122; 2nd Bn, 273; 2/4th Bn, 262; 6th Bn, 150

Royal Dublin Fusiliers   1st Bn, 87; 2nd Bn, 258; 9th Bn, 186

Royal Fusiliers   31, 113, 122; 2nd Bn, 87; 20th Bn, 170; 22nd Bn, 77, 91; 24th Bn, 95–6

Royal Iniskilling Fusiliers   340

Royal Irish Fusiliers   1st Bn, 272

Royal Irish Rifles   233; 8th Bn, 116; 9th Bn, 208; 10th Bn, 106; 13th Bn, 105; 14th Bn, 113

Royal Munster Fusiliers   261; 2nd Bn, 209

Royal Scots   132, 305; 12th Bn, 165; 15th Bn, 235

Royal Scots Fusiliers 2nd Bn, 180

Royal Sussex 122; 8th Bn, 104; 11th Bn, 95, 97

Royal Warwicks 64, 76, 93, 113, 217, 273; 1st Bn, 94; 11th Bn, 223

Royal Welch Fusiliers 149; 1st Bn, 143; 13th Bn, 212; 14th Bn, 149

Royal West Kents 6th Bn, 226; 7th Bn, 117, 152, 222, 294

Scottish Rifles (Cameronians) 9th Bn, 165

Seaforth Highlanders 2nd Bn, 94, 230; 1/6th Bn, 48

Sherwood Foresters 62; 1st Bn, 274; 2nd Bn, 207; 1/5th Bn, 61; 11th Bn, 102

Somerset Light Inf. 232; 1st Bn, 79, 95; 7th Bn, 232

S. Lancs 140; 7th Bn, 224

S. Staffords, 62; 1st Bn, 169; 8th Bn, 135

S. Wales Borderers 2nd Bn, 96

Suffolks 2nd Bn, 74; 7th Bn, 217; 11th Bn, 123

Welch 13th Bn, 193; 15th & 16th Bns, 162

Welsh Guards 1st Bn, 202

West Yorks 75-6, 122; 1/5th Bn, 110; 10th Bn, 138-40, 142, 196, 233; 15th Bn, 77;16th Bn, 66

Wiltshires 261; 1st Bn, 114

Worcesters 349; 2nd Bn, 203, 257; 3rd Bn, 114; 1/7th Bn, 49, 231; 1/8th Bn, 48

York and Lancasters 1/5th Bn, 315; 8th & 9th Bns, 102-103; 12th Bn, 70, 74-6, 93-4

Yorkshires, see Green Howards

Machine Gun Corps 91, 93, 100, 132, 177, 190-91, 207, 220, 280, 312; Heavy Branch see Tank Corps

Royal Army Medical Corps 93

Royal Army Service Corps 61, 221, 247, 313, 344

Royal Engineers 63, 103, 164, 211, 238, 328; 82nd Field Coy, 164; Tunnelling Coys, 68, 220-21, 223

Royal Field Artillery 224

Royal Flying Corps, Royal Naval Air Service and (from April 1918) RAF Squadrons 2 Sdn, 44; 3 Sdn, 318; 5 Sdn, 267; 6 Sdn, 202; 24 Sdn, 323; 35 Sdn, 324; 48 Sdn, 177, 303; 56 Sdn, 311; 57 Sdn, 241; 60 Sdn, 40; 70 Sdn, 262, 312; 79 Sdn, 213; 98 Sdn, 173; 201 Sdn, 40, 46; 205 Sdn, 236; 206 Sdn, 305-306

Royal Garrison Artillery 221, 230

Royal Horse Artillery 344; 'L' Battery, 43, 188

Tank Corps 111, 129; 1st Bn, 302, 304; 3rd Bn, 129, 190; 4th Bn, 193, 299; Armoured cars, 307

OTHER UNITS

Army Graves Service 8

Chinese Labour Corps 30, 37, 42, 265, 347-8

Carey's Force 318

Egyptian Labour Corps 36, 209

Friends' Ambulance Unit 337

Labour Corps 61, 100

Shanghai Light Horse 156

21st Entrenching Bn 270

West India Regt 112

Women's Auxiliary Army Corps 340

BRITISH (1939-45)

XXX Corps 53

DIVISIONS

Guards Armoured 53, 80, 219, 234, 246

1st Armoured 336

50th (Northumbrian) 219

51st (Highland) 336, 348-9

BRIGADES
4th Armoured   332
8th Armoured   323

INFANTRY
4th Cameron Highlanders   341
1st & 2nd Grenadier Guards   219
2nd Irish Guards   33
King's Royal Rifle Corps   2nd Bn, 30,
    31, 332; 12th Bn, 323
Queen's battalions   336
Queen Victoria's Rifles   30
7th R. Sussex   321, 340
Royal West Kents 6th Bn, 310; 7th Bn,
    218, 222, 239
1st Rifle Brigade   30
4th Seaforth Highlanders   341
2nd Welsh Guards   33

Commandos   31, 348
Notts Yeomanry   323
Royal Artillery   234, 237
Royal Engineers   232
Royal Horse Guards   219

RAF
Bomber Command   43, 276
No. 8 (Pathfinder Force) Group   284
Squadrons   13 Sdn, 267; 21 Sdn, 321,
    340; 26 Sdn, 31; 51 Sdn, 282; 90
    Sdn, 276; 129 Sdn, 323; 145 Sdn,
    237; 181 Sdn, 313; 316 Sdn, 324;
    403 Sdn, 282; 418 Sdn, 284; 419
    Sdn, 282; 427 Sdn, 61; 464 Sdn,
    321; 467 Sdn, 341; 487 Sdn, 296,
    321; 617 Sdn, 41–2, 44, 282; 635
    Sdn, 277

CANADIAN (1914–18)

General   references   119,   125–30
    passim, 175–8, 215, 265, 277,
    283, 288–308 *passim*, 315, 328,
    348–9
Canadian Corps   11, 46, 175, 214,
    288, 292, 303

DIVISIONS
1st, 299; 2nd, 129, 174–5, 298; 3rd,
    175

BATTALIONS
Princess   Patricia's   Canadian   Light
    Inf. 175; Royal Canadian Regt,
    176; 5th, 303; 8th, 304; 10th,
    216; 13th, 202, 299; 16th, 178,
    298; 18th, 176; 22nd, 296, 306;
    43rd, 300; 78th, 283, 303

CAVALRY
Lord   Strathcona's   Horse,   256,   335;
    Royal Canadian Dragoons, 301,
    316

CANADIAN (1944–5)

First Canadian Army   32
Highland Light Infantry of Canada   32

FRENCH (1914–18)

Sixth Army   151
XXXI Corps   289, 301

DIVISIONS
7th Colonial   300; 11th, 198; 82nd,
    193; 169th, 286
33rd Brigade   280

REGIMENTS
1st   200, 211; 17th, 193; 18th, 191,
    193; 19th, 121; 22nd Colonial,
    204; 26th, 143; 69th, 152; 73rd,
    188; 106th, 203; 125th, 287;
    132nd, 203; 153rd, 180, 198;
    156th, 138; 224th, 198; 233rd,
    78; 243rd, 78; 325th, 287;
    327th, 78, 280; 329th, 280;
    363rd, 201

Chasseurs   4th, 200; 5th, 280; 19th,
    286; 56th & 58th, 204
12th Cuirassiers   300

110th Tirailleurs   190
Foreign Legion   278
Lafayette Air Squadron   286

FRENCH (1939–45)

DIVISIONS
2nd Armoured   332
4th Colonial   293
5th Colonial   332
7th Colonial   321
13th Infantry   327
5th Demi-Brigade   334

REGIMENTS
10th Artillery   304
10th Light Cavalry   340
21st Infantry   335
41st Infantry   304
53rd Infantry   332
56th Infantry   321

Chasseurs   13th, 334; 19th, 286
5th Divisional Recce Group   227
Senegalese troops   297

GERMAN (1914–18)

First Army   48, 185
IV Reserve Corps   48
Guard Fusilier Regt   120
Lehr Regt   159
Württembergers   76, 81, 113

GERMAN (1939–45)

XIX Panzer Corps   52
1st Panzer Division   52, 142, 227, 239, 316
2nd Panzer Division   52, 185, 218, 234–6
6th Panzer Division   310

INDIAN (1914–18)

General references   43, 102, 265, 341
Deccan Horse   169
9th Hodson's Horse   264
2nd Lancers   256
36th Jacob's Horse   224
Labour Corps   267

NEWFOUNDLAND (1914–18)

Newfoundland Regt   83, 87–8, 97, 197, 316

NEW ZEALAND (1914–18)

General references   62–7 passim, 93, 95, 165–6, 169, 179, 194, 196, 230–31, 244
New Zealand Division   60, 166, 174, 312, 316
Canterbury Regt   230
New Zealand Rifle Brigade   166
Otago Regt   166, 179
Engineers   177
Airmen   296, 395

SOUTH AFRICANS (1914–18)

General references   112, 132, 166, 179, 201, 253, 265, 316
S. African Infantry Brigade   167–8, 201
Heavy Artillery Battery   102, 228
Labour Corps   37

UNITED STATES (1917–18)

General references   259, 289, 356
1st Division   286–7
27th National Guard Division   211
106th Infantry Regt   282
6th Engineer Regt   318
1941–5 Troops and airmen   7, 41

PART 4 – SOLDIERS AND AIRMEN

BRITISH

Allardice, Lt-Col H.   224
Anderson, Lt-Col W. H., VC   151
Appleyard, Pte E.   193
Arnold, Lt   194
Asquith, Lt R.   183–4, 318
Atkinson, Maj. F.   264
Ayre, Capt. B. P.   150
Ayre, Capt. E. S.   88
Ayre, 2/Lt W. D.   97

Badenoch, 2/Lt I.   246
Ball, Capt. A., VC   314
Baring, Lt-Col Hon. G. V.   145
Barker, Lt C. N.   39
Barker, Pte M.T.   337
Barnett-Barker, Brig.-Gen. R.   222
Barwell, Gp/Capt P. R.   32
Bassett, Rfmn H.E. & P. J.   65
Baxter, Lt E. F., VC   39
Bayly, 2/Lt V. T.   102
Beatham, Pte R. W., VC   308
Bell, 2/Lt D. S, VC   125
Bell, Capt. E. I. J.   222
Bernard, Col H. C.   106
Blakeway, 2/Lt N. C.   174
Blunden, Edmund   95, 97, 99, 105–6, 231
Boon, Pte J. C.   91
Boote, Lt-Col C. E.   62
Booth, Lt M. W.   77
Boyle, Lt-Col E. C. P.   100
Braithwaite, 2/Lt V. A   79
Brilliant, Lt J., VC   296
Broadley, F/Lt J. A.   322
Brooke, Rupert   88, 106, 184
Brown, Sgt A. C.   234
Brown, Sgt D. F., VC   179
Buchan, 2/Lt J. C., VC   17, 263
Buckle, Brig.-Gen. A.   244

Buckley, Cpl A. H., VC   266
Bull, Pte A. E.   75
Burg, Lt-Col N. O.   100
Bushell, Lt-Col C., VC   239

Callow, Marine A. J.   31
Campbell, Capt. F. W., VC   36
Campbell, Ldg Aircraftwoman M.   32
Cape, Brig.-Gen. G. A. S.   267
Cartmel, Lt G. M.   236
Carton de Wiart, Lt-Col A., VC   122
Castleton, Sgt C. C., VC   130
Cates, 2/Lt G. E., VC   201
Chant, Pte P.   313
Chapman, Guy   160
Chappell, CSM P.   232
Chase, Maj. A. A.   104
Chavasse, Capt. N., VC & Bar   185
Christy, Ptes J. W. & R.   131
Clifford, Brig.-Gen. H. F. H.   221
Clint, Sgt D.   94
Clive, Capt. Viscount P. R. H.   202
Close, Sdn/Ldr G. C. N.   17, 36–7
Cloutman, Lt W. R.   223
Coles, Sgt C. F. G.   328
Colley, Sgt H. J., VC   230
Collings-Wells, Lt-Col J. S., VC   105
Congreve, Maj. W. T., VC   246
Corbyn, Lt-Col E. C.   256
Cornish, Ptes J. A. & T.   95
Cornwell, Pte G. C.   95
Cotter, Cpl W. R., VC   43
Coulson, Sgt L.   207
Cousens, Wg/Cdr A. G. S.   277
Coxe, 2/Lt H.   202
Cribben, Sgt L.   323
Croak, Pte J. B.   299
Crowle, 2/Lt H. W.   315
Cruikshank, Capt. G. L.   262–3
Cuninghame, Capt. A. K. S.   145
Cutmore, Lt W.C.   305

Dean, 2/Lt R. F. M.   93
De Silva, Pte P. R.   82
Destrubé, L/Cpl C. G. & Pte P. J.   77
Dickens, Maj. C. C.   187
Dickson, Lt-Col A.   140
Dimmer, Lt-Col J. H., VC.   262
Docherty, Lt-Col M.   256
Dodgson, Capt. F.   126
Drummond, Capt. G.   202
Duffy, Pte T.   272
Dunville, 2/Lt J. S., VC   264
Dwyer, Cpl E., VC   162
Dyett, Sub-Lt E. L. A.   345–6

Eagles, Pte W. H.   304
Eames, Pte E.   99
Edgerton, Lt E. H. D.   296
Edwards, Pte A.   177
Ellis, Pte S.   82
Ellisson, Spr C. D.   164
England, CSM E.   196

Feetham, Maj.-Gen. E.   237, 328
Fellows, L/Cpl H.   162–3
Feversham, Lt-Col, Earl of   196
Fitzgerald, Lt R. J.   324
Flower, Lt-Col O. S.   212
Flowerdew, Capt. G. M., VC   335
Footman, Pte F.   144
Forbes, 2/Lt W. S.   182
Forster, Brig.-Gen. G. N. B.   293–4
Forsyth, Sgt S., VC   177
Fraleigh, F/O M. I.   313
Fraser, Maj. A. I.   264
Fraser, 2/LT A. W.   87
Freyberg, Lt-Col B. C., VC   89

Gaby, Lt A. E., VC   308
Gaffikin, Maj. G.   208
Geard, Cpl F. J. P.   267
Gibson, Lt D.   303
Gill, Sgt A., VC   168
Glaister, Gnr   194
Glasfurd, Brig.-Gen. D. J.   244
Goodall, Capt. M.   315
Goodwin, Lt H. D.   82

Gough, Gen. Sir H.   51, 69, 89, 239, 288, 320
Graves, Robert   143–4
Green, Capt. J. L., VC   61
Greenslade, Pte W. T.   238
Grenfell brothers   36
Grierson, Lt-Gen. Sir J.   319
Gunstone, L/Cpl F. & Pte W. W.   74

Haig, Field-Marshal Sir D.   38, 172, 208, 249, 281, 310, 314
Hant, Pte C.   196
Hardy, Chaplain T. B., VC   66–7
Hardwidge, L/Cpl H. & Cpl T.   162
Harman, Sgt A. G.   31
Harmsworth, Lt Hon. V.   88–9
Harris, Sgt T. J., VC   226
Hawes, Pte W.   99
Healy, Sgt M.   209
Heaton, 2/Lt E. R.   82
Henderson, Lt-Col H. M.   104
Heneker, Maj.-Gen., W. G. C.   294
Herbert, A. P.   89
Hervey, 2/Lt T. P. A.   192
Heumann, Capt. R.   188
Higgins, Spr J.   164
Higginson, Lt G. N.   90
Hitchcock, Lt H. W.   111
Hitchen, Pte F.   207
Hobbs, Lt-Col, C. J. W.   207
Hodgson, Noel   146
Hollingworth, Pte J.   190
Horrocks, Lt-Gen. Sir B.   53
Hosking, Cpl H. N.   82
Howe, Lt P.   139n
Howell, Brig.-Gen. P.   233–4
Humphries, Lt-Col C. F. G.   61
Hunter-Weston, Lt-Gen. Sir A.   68–9

Ingham, Pte A.   47
Ingouville-Williams, Maj.-Gen. E. C.   16, 157, 160, 237
Iredale, CSM E. E.   110

Jackson, Sgt H., VC   196
Jacob, Gnr H. C.   238
Jones, Pte A.   314
Jones, Brig.-Gen., L. O. W.   312

Kelly, Lt-Cdr F. S.   106
Kennedy, Majs. P. & D.   32
Kettle, Tom   186
Knott, Maj. J. L.   140

Land, Pte J.   348
Latham, 2/Lt A. J.   221
Latham, Lt-Col S. G.   295
Laud, Pte I. A.   223
Lauder, Capt. J. C.   121
Lee, Sgt G. & Cpl R. F.   224
Leeson, Cpl A. G.   202
Leighton, 2/Lt R. A.   231–2
Little, Flt Cdr R. A.   40
Littledale, Lt-Col R. B.   332
Loudoun-Shand, Maj. S. W., VC   223
Lovett, Pte R. D.   96
Lucas, Lt F. L.   117
Lucas, P/O K. R.   237
Lucas, Spr T.   340
Lyle, Lt-Col W.   119

Machell, Lt-Col P. W.   236
Macpherson, Lt G.   207
McAndie, Capt. D.   216
McCrae, Lt-Col J.   34
McCudden, Maj. J. T. B., VC   40
McIntyre, Pte A.   95
Maddison, Lt-Col B. L.   103
Mactier, Pte R., VC   201
Mansel-Carey, 2/Lt S. L. M.   145n, 202
Marsden-Smedley, 2/Lt G. F.   185
Martin, Capt. D. L.   146–8
Martyn, Lt E. M.   241
Mason, Pte H.   220
Maxse, Maj.-Gen. F. I.   117
Meakin, Capt. H. P.   191
Menzies, Lt-Col A. J. A.   304
Mildmay, 2/Lt B. W. St J.   312
Miller, Pte J., VC   224
Mills, CSM B.   188
Mitchell, Sgt S. J.   44
Mond, Capt. F. L.   241
Montgomery, Pte W.   247
Mossop, Sgt M. H.   76
Moylan, Trumpeter J.   304
Munro, H. H. ('Saki')   91

Murphy, CSM T. F.   340
Mynarski, P/O A. C., VC   282

Nelson, Maj. D., VC   43
Nevill, Capt. W. P.   137, 150
Newburn, Lt J. C.   176
Noble, Cpl C. R., VC   42
Nordheimer, Lt A. V. S.   301
Nott, Lt H. P., Capt. L. C. & Lt-Col T. W.   264

O'Brien, Cpl R.   143
O'Neill, L/Cpl J. P.   245
Ormsby, Brig.-Gen., V. A.   264
O'Sullivan, Chaplain D. V.   235
Owen, Wilfred   91, 216

Palk, Lt-Col Hon. L. C. W.   95
Palmer, Pte T.   61
Parfitt, Air Mech. H. E.   318
Parry, Gnr A. B.   64
Parsons, 2/Lt H. F., VC   264
Pattinson, Cpl G. E.   189–90
Perry, 2/Lt E. W. C.   318
Philby, Ptes E. & H.   162
Phillpotts, Brig.-Gen. L. M.   145
Pickard, Gp Capt. P. C.   321
Pinkney, Capt. D. E.   237
Pollock, Capt. C. T. A.   301
Preston, Lt R. A.   263
Pritchard, 2/Lt D.   144
Prowse, Brig.-Gen. C. B.   232

Raddall, Lt-Col T. H.   304
Ralphs, Capt. W. J.   156
Raper, Maj. R. G.   135, 143
Rawlinson, Gen. Sir H.   50–51, 69, 152, 227, 239, 242, 288–9
Reynolds, Maj. D., VC   37
Rhodes, Sgt J. H., VC   253
Richardson, Piper J. C., VC   178
Richardson, Capt. M.   144
Richardson, Maj. T. C.   221
Ritchie, Pte G.   176
Ritchie, Rfmn J.   113
Rogerson, Sydney   145, 224
Rollaston, Capt. A. G.   49, 231

Rosevear, Capt. S. W.　46
Ruffell, Rfmn H.　323

Sampson, Flt/Lt R. W.　335
Sandys, Lt-Col E. T. F.　121
Sassoon, Siegfried　136, 142–4, 315
Saunders, Lt-Col F. J.　99
Seddon, Capt. R. J. S.　64
Sellar, 2/Lt W. R.　173
Shann, Capt. J. W.　140
Sharpe, Tpr J. A.　323
Shenton, Capt. A. K.　328
Short, Pte W. H., VC　126
Sillery, Lt-Col C. C. A.　119
Simpson, Spr D.　245
Slade, Rfmn E. F.　213
Smith, Pte S. G.　158
Smith, Sgt T. W.　177
Spendlove, Gp Capt. W. V. L.　340
Stocks, Maj. H. L.　235–6
Street, Maj. E. R.　207
Streets, Sgt W.　93
Swainstone, Pte W. E.　94

Tait, Lt J. E., VC　283
Tarver, Pte W.　94
Tatham, Capt. T. B.　304
Taylor, Gnr S. L.　188–9
Tennant, Lt Hon. E. W.　183–4
Thicknesse, Lt-Col J. A.　95
Thomas, 2/Lt D.　144
Thompson, Lt H. H.　293
Torrance, Sgt A. W.　188
Trail, Maj. S. G.　312
Tregaskis, Lts A. & L.　162
Trevor, Chaplain, E. W.　110
Truman, Gnr H. T.　238
Turnbull, Sgt J. Y., VC　115
Turner, Lt-Col H. H. F.　256
Tyler, Capt. G. C.　61

Verner, Ptes A. & R. H.　74

Walker, Surgeon G. A.　100
Ward, Rfmn C. E.　92
Wardill, 2/Lt C. H. & Pte S. G.　74

Webber, Lt H.　224
Weeden, P/O G. H.　282
Wellings, 2/Lt H. W.　312
Wheatcroft, 2/Lt G. H.　230
Whitaker, Pte W.　93
Whitlock, Pte E.　49, 62
Williamson, Henry　91, 100
Wolfe, Pte F.　233
Woods, Lt W.　194–5

FRENCH

Aubry, Capt.　301
Boucher, M.　198
Brocheriou, S/Lt M.　204
Brody, Lt R.　198
Calle, Aspirant P. L.　203
Cochin, Capt. A.　199–200
D'Alcantara family　239
Dansette, S/Lt C.　190
Debeney, Gen.　318
De Chabot-Tramecourt family　39
De Gaulle, Gen. C.　336, 341
Delcroix, Capt. G.　280
De Monclin, Capt. H. T.　152
De Valicourt, Lt J.　223
Driant, Lt-Col É.　204
Dufour, Capt.　204
Feltz, Lt G.　273
Foch, Marshal F.　203, 310
Foucart, A.　325
Fumery, G.　203
Garner, Lt　227
Hallarodittaeoez, V.　190
Lapage, R.　198
Latour, Gen.　286
Leclerc, Gen. J. P.　318–19, 332, 334
Lejoindre, G.　191
Montjean, Capt.　334
Murat, Maréchal de Logis L.　280–81
　Naudier, E.　200
Peckett, D.　219
Pfister, G.　191
Puntons, Lt-Col　280
Rabier, Col.　280
Sagnes, Sgt　227

Thibaut, Abbé   211
Tomasin, H.   143

GERMAN

Boelcke, Hauptmann O.   262–3
Guderian, Gen. H.   52–3, 134
Von Kluck, Gen.   48, 118, 185
Von Richthofen, Baron M.   245, 320,
    322–3

UNITED STATES

Butters, 2/Lt H. A.   224
Dix, Lt R.   346
Harding, 2/Lt L. V.   213
Metcalf, Sgt H.   282
Miller, 2/Lt J. A.   323
Seeger, Alan   278, 281
Shaw, Flt/Lt E.   177
Weaver, P/O C.   282
Woodward, Cpl H. H. H.   286–7